First World War
and Army of Occupation
War Diary
France, Belgium and Germany

35 DIVISION
Headquarters, Branches and Services
General Staff
1 July 1918 - 31 March 1919

WO95/2470/1

The Naval & Military Press Ltd
www.nmarchive.com
Published in association with The National Archives

Published by

The Naval & Military Press Ltd

Unit 10 Ridgewood Industrial Park,

Uckfield, East Sussex,

TN22 5QE England

Tel: +44 (0) 1825 749494

www.naval-military-press.com

www.nmarchive.com

This diary has been reprinted in facsimile from the original. Any imperfections are inevitably reproduced and the quality may fall short of modern type and cartographic standards.

© Crown Copyright
Images reproduced by permission of The National Archives, London, England, 2015.

Contents

Document type	Place/Title	Date From	Date To
Heading	WO95/2470/1 35 Div HQ Gen Staff 1918 July-1919 Mar (Not In Box) Line Register Of Messages.		
Heading	35th Division General Staff 1918 Jly-1919 Mar.		
Heading	HQ GS 35 D Vol.31 July.		
Miscellaneous	Officer i/c War Diaries A.G's Office Base.	02/08/1918	02/08/1918
War Diary	Wizernes.	01/07/1918	01/07/1918
War Diary	Oudezeele.	02/07/1918	04/07/1918
War Diary	Le Mort Homme.	05/07/1918	25/07/1918
War Diary	Terdeghem.	26/07/1918	31/07/1918
Miscellaneous	Report On Raid On Right Company Front On June 30th/1917	30/06/1917	30/06/1917
Heading	35th Division No. G. 2230 18th July 1918. 35th Division Provisional Defence Scheme Locre Sector July 1918		
Miscellaneous	Cover for Documents. Nature of Enclosures		
Miscellaneous	35th Division No. G.2230	18/07/1918	18/07/1918
Miscellaneous	35th Division. Provisional Defence Scheme. Locre Sector.	18/07/1918	18/07/1918
Miscellaneous	35th Division.	02/07/1917	02/07/1917
Miscellaneous			
Miscellaneous	III Corps.	01/07/1917	01/07/1917
Miscellaneous	Report On Raid On Right Company Front On June 30th 1917	30/06/1917	30/06/1917
Miscellaneous	35th Division. Daily Intelligence Summary No. 78. From 6 a.m. 30th July to 6 a.m. 31st July 1918	31/07/1918	31/07/1918
Miscellaneous	35th Division Daily Intelligence Summary No. 77. From 6 a.m. 29th July to 6 a.m. 30th July 1918	30/07/1918	30/07/1918
Miscellaneous	35th Division. Daily Intelligence Summary No. 76. From 6 a.m. 28th July to 6 a.m. 29th July 1918	29/07/1918	29/07/1918
Miscellaneous	35th Division. Daily Intelligence Summary No. 75. From 6 a.m. 27 July to 6 a.m. 28 July 1918	28/07/1918	28/07/1918
Miscellaneous	Interrogation of Two Prisoners of 3rd and 10th Coys.103rd R.I.R., 58th Division, captured about 11.30 p.m. 27th. July 1918, at M.30.a.1.9. (Sheet 28).	27/07/1918	27/07/1918
Miscellaneous	35th Division. Daily Intelligence Summary No. 74. From 6 am. 26 July to 6 am. 27 July 1918	26/07/1918	26/07/1918
Miscellaneous	35th Division. Daily Intelligence Summary No. 73	26/07/1918	26/07/1918
Miscellaneous	35th Division. Daily Intelligence Summary No. 72. From 6 a.m. 24th July to 6 a.m. 25th July 1918	24/07/1918	24/07/1918
Miscellaneous	35th Division. Daily Intelligence Summary No. 71. From 6 a.m. 23rd July to 6 a.m. 24th July 1918	23/07/1918	23/07/1918
Miscellaneous	35th Division. Daily Intelligence Summary No. 70. From 6 a.m. 22nd July to 6 a.m. 23rd July 1918	22/07/1918	22/07/1918
Miscellaneous	35th Division. Daily Intelligence Summary No. 69. From 6 a.m. 21st July to 6 a.m. 22nd July 1918	21/07/1918	21/07/1918
Miscellaneous	35th Division. Daily Intelligence Summary No. 68. From 6 a.m. 20th July to 6 a.m. 21st July 1918	20/07/1918	20/07/1918
Miscellaneous	35th Division. Daily Intelligence Summary No. 67. From 6 a.m. 19th July to 6 a.m. 20th July 1918	19/07/1918	19/07/1918

Miscellaneous	35th Division. Daily Intelligence Summary No. 66. From 6 a.m. 18th July to 6 a.m. 19th July 1918	18/07/1918	18/07/1918
Miscellaneous	35th Division. Daily Intelligence Summary No. 65. From 6 a.m. 17th July to 6 a.m. 18th July 1918	17/07/1918	17/07/1918
Miscellaneous	35th Division. Daily Intelligence Summary No. 64. From 6 a.m. 16th July to 6 a.m. 17th July 1918	16/07/1918	16/07/1918
Miscellaneous	35th Division. Daily Intelligence Summary No. 63. From 6 a.m. 15th July to 6 a.m. July 1918	15/07/1918	15/07/1918
Miscellaneous	Annexe to 35th Division Intelligence Summary No. 63 dated 16th July.	16/07/1918	16/07/1918
Miscellaneous	35th Division. Daily Intelligence Summary No. 62. From 6 a.m. 14th July to 6 a.m. 15th July 1918	14/07/1918	14/07/1918
Miscellaneous	35th Division. Daily Intelligence Summary No. 61. From 6 a.m. 13th July to 6 a.m. 14th July 1918	13/07/1918	13/07/1918
Miscellaneous	35th Division. Daily Intelligence Summary No. 60. From 6 a.m. 12th July to 6 a.m. 13th July 1918	12/07/1918	12/07/1918
Miscellaneous	35th Division. Daily Intelligence Summary No. 50. From 6 a.m. 11th July to 6 a.m. 12th July 1918	12/07/1918	12/07/1918
Miscellaneous	35th Division. Daily Intelligence Summary No. 58. From 6 a.m. 10th July to 6 a.m. 11th July 1918	10/07/1918	10/07/1918
Miscellaneous	35th Division. Daily Intelligence Summary No. 57. From 6 a.m. 9th July to 6 a.m. 10th July 1918	09/07/1918	09/07/1918
Miscellaneous	35th Division. Daily Intelligence Summary No. 56. From 6 a.m. 8th July to 6 a.m. 9th July 1918	08/07/1918	08/07/1918
Miscellaneous	35th Division. Daily Intelligence Summary No. 55. From 6 a.m. 7th July to 6 a.m. 8th July 1918	07/07/1918	07/07/1918
Miscellaneous	35th Division. Daily Intelligence Summary No. 54. From 6 a.m. 6th July to 6 a.m. 7th July 1918	06/07/1918	06/07/1918
Miscellaneous	35th Division. Daily Intelligence Summary No. 53. From 6 a.m. 5th July to 6 a.m. 6th July 1918	05/07/1918	05/07/1918
Heading	HQ G.S. 35 D Vol. 32. August 18		
Heading	The Officer in Charge, D.A.G's. Office at the Base. G. 3027		
War Diary	La Montagne.	01/08/1918	06/08/1918
War Diary	Terdeghem.	07/08/1918	09/08/1918
War Diary	Cassel.	10/08/1918	31/08/1918
Miscellaneous	35th Division. Daily Intelligence Summary No. 79. From 6 a.m. 31st July to 6 a.m. 1st August 1918	31/07/1918	31/07/1918
Miscellaneous	35th Division. Daily Intelligence Summary No. 80. From 6 a.m. 1st August to 6 a.m. 2nd August 1918	01/08/1918	01/08/1918
Miscellaneous	35th Division. Daily Intelligence Summary No. 81. From 6 a.m. 2nd August to 6 a.m. 3rd August 1918	02/08/1918	02/08/1918
Miscellaneous	35th Division. Daily Intelligence Summary No. 82. From 6 a.m. 3rd August to 6 a.m. 4th August 1918	03/08/1918	03/08/1918
Miscellaneous	35th Division. Daily Intelligence Summary No. 83. From 6 a.m. 4th August to 6 a.m. 5th August 1918	04/08/1918	04/08/1918
Miscellaneous	35th Division. Daily Intelligence Summary No. 84. From 6 a.m. 5th August to 6 a.m. 6th August 1918	05/08/1918	05/08/1918
Miscellaneous	35th Division. Daily Intelligence Summary No. 85. From 6 a.m. 6th August to 6 a.m. 7th August 1918	06/08/1918	06/08/1918
Miscellaneous	35th Division. Daily Intelligence Summary No. 86. From 6 a.m. 7th to 6 a.m. 8th August 1918	07/08/1918	07/08/1918
Miscellaneous	35th Division. Daily Intelligence Summary No. 87. From 6 a.m. 8th August to 6 a.m. August 1918	08/08/1918	08/08/1918
Heading	G.S. 35th Division September 1918		
War Diary	Cassel.	01/09/1918	01/09/1918

Type	Description	From	To
War Diary	Herzeele.	02/09/1918	04/09/1918
War Diary	Vogeltje.	04/09/1918	16/09/1918
War Diary	Waratah Camp.	17/09/1918	28/09/1918
War Diary	Woodcote House.	29/09/1918	30/09/1918
Miscellaneous	35 Division 'G' Register of Messages.		
Miscellaneous	35 Division 'G' Register of Messages.	21/10/1918	21/10/1918
Miscellaneous	35th Division. Daily Intelligence Summary No. 88. From 6 a.m. 4th September to 6 a.m. 5th September 1918	04/09/1918	04/09/1918
Miscellaneous	35th Division. Daily Intelligence Summary No. 89. From 6 a.m. 5th September to 6 a.m. 6th September 1918	05/09/1918	05/09/1918
Miscellaneous	Preliminary interrogation of six prisoners of 11th Company 458 I.R. 236th Division captured about noon 6th September 1918 about I.28.a.0.4		
Miscellaneous	35th Division. Daily Intelligence Summary No. 90. From 6 a.m. 6th September to 6 a.m. 7th September 1918	06/09/1918	06/09/1918
Miscellaneous	35th Division. Daily Intelligence Summary No. 91. From 6 a.m. 7th September to 6 a.m. 8th September.	07/09/1918	07/09/1918
Miscellaneous	35th British Division. Daily Intelligence Summary No. 92. From 6 a.m. 8th September to 6 a.m. 9th September 1918	08/09/1918	08/09/1918
Miscellaneous	35th British Division. Daily Intelligence Summary No. 93. From 6 a.m. 9th September to 6 a.m. 10th September 1918	09/09/1918	09/09/1918
Miscellaneous	35th British Division. Daily Intelligence Summary No. 94. From 6 a.m. 10th September 1918 to 6 a.m. 11th September 1918	10/09/1918	10/09/1918
Miscellaneous	35th British Division. Daily Intelligence Summary No. 95. From 6 a.m. 11th September to 6 a.m. 12th September.	11/09/1918	11/09/1918
Miscellaneous	35th British Division. Daily Intelligence Summary No. 96. From 6 a.m. 12th September 1918 to 6 a.m. 13th September 1918	12/09/1918	12/09/1918
Miscellaneous	35th British Division. Daily Intelligence Summary No. 97. From 6 a.m. 13th September to 6 a.m. 14th September.	13/09/1918	13/09/1918
Miscellaneous	Further Interrogation of five Prisoners of 11th Coy. 104th I.R., 40th (Saxon) Division captured about 6 a.m. 13th September, about I.27.a.3.1	13/09/1918	13/09/1918
Miscellaneous	35th British Division. Daily Intelligence Summary No. 98. From 6 a.m. 14th September to 6 a.m. 15th September.	14/09/1918	14/09/1918
Miscellaneous	35th British Division. Daily Intelligence Summary No. 99. From 6 a.m. 15th September to 6 a.m. 16th September 1918	15/09/1918	15/09/1918
Miscellaneous	Interrogation of 41 Prisoners (38 unwounded and 3 wounded) of 2nd Battalion 104th I.R. 40th (Saxon) Division, captured about 10.30. p.m. 15th September 1918, between Zillebeke Lake and the Ypres-Comines Canal.	15/09/1918	15/09/1918
Miscellaneous	Interrogation of two prisoners of 6th Coy. 181 I.R. 40th (Saxon) Division captured about 10-30 p.m. 15th September 1918 at I.33.a.6.0. (Spoil Bank).	15/09/1918	15/09/1918

Type	Description	Start	End
Miscellaneous	35th British Division. Daily Intelligence Summary No. 100. From 6 a.m. 16th Septr. to 6 a.m. 17th Septr. 1918	16/09/1918	16/09/1918
Miscellaneous	Interrogation of eight prisoners of 7th and 8th Coys. 104th.I.R. 40th (Saxon) Division, captured on 16th September 1918	16/09/1918	16/09/1918
Miscellaneous	35th British Division. Daily Intelligence Summary No. 101. From 6 a.m. 17th Septr. to 6 a.m. 18th Septr.	17/09/1918	17/09/1918
Miscellaneous	Annexe to 35th Division Intelligence Summary No. 101.- 18.9.18	18/09/1918	18/09/1918
Miscellaneous	35th British Division. Daily Intelligence Summary No. 102. From 6 a.m. 18th Septr. to 6 a.m. 19th Septr.	18/09/1918	18/09/1918
Miscellaneous	35th British Division. Daily Intelligence Summary No. 104. From 6 a.m. 20th Septr. to 6 a.m. 21st Septr.	20/09/1918	20/09/1918
Miscellaneous	35th British Division. Daily Intelligence Summary No. 105. From 6 a.m. 22nd Septr. to 6 a.m. 23rd Septr.	21/09/1918	21/09/1918
Miscellaneous	35th British Division. Daily Intelligence Summary No. 106. From 6 a.m. 22nd Septr. to 6 a.m. 23rd Septr.	22/09/1918	22/09/1918
Miscellaneous	35th British Division. Daily Intelligence Summary No. 107. From 6 a.m. 23rd Septr. to 6 a.m. 24th Septr.	23/09/1918	23/09/1918
Miscellaneous	35th British Division. Daily Intelligence Summary No. 108. From 6 a.m. 24th Septr. to 6 a.m. 25th Septr.	24/09/1918	24/09/1918
Miscellaneous	35th British Division. Daily Intelligence Summary No. 109. From 6 a.m. 25th Septr. to 6 am. 26th Septr. 1918	25/09/1918	25/09/1918
Miscellaneous	35th British Division. Daily Intelligence Summary No. 110. From 6 a.m. 26th Septr. to 6 am. 27th Septr.	26/09/1918	26/09/1918
Miscellaneous	35th Division. Narrative of Operations from 28th September to end of October, 1918	28/09/1918	28/09/1918
Miscellaneous	Summary of Lys Operations.		
Miscellaneous	Our casualties were as follows:- By dates.	28/12/1918	28/12/1918
Map	Dispositions of Troops at 'H'. Map A		
Map	Field Survey Battn. R.E. (9412) 26.7.18		
Diagram etc	Diagram 'A'. 18 Pdr. Barrage Map.		
Diagram etc	Diagram 'B'. 4.5 how. Barrage Map & Smoke Barrages.		
Heading	War Diary.		
Diagram etc	Diagram 'A' (Amended) 18 Pr. Barrage Map.		
Map	Poperinghe.		
Heading	War Diary.		
Map	Belgium and Part of France. Map B. 35th Division Operations 28th Sept To 2nd Oct 1918		
Map	Enemy Disposition Map.		
Map	Belgium		
Heading	Artillery 25th Sept. War Diary.		
Map	Ypres		
Heading	War Diary.		
Map	Ypres.		
Heading	War Diary		
Heading	War Diary G.S. 35th Divn: October 1918		
War Diary	Woodcote House.	01/10/1918	11/10/1918
War Diary	Jackdaw Camp.	12/10/1918	16/10/1918
War Diary	Terhand.	17/10/1918	17/10/1918
War Diary	Herthoek.	18/10/1918	20/10/1918
War Diary	Macke.	21/10/1918	23/10/1918
War Diary	Courtrai.	24/10/1918	26/10/1918
War Diary	Sweveghem.	27/10/1918	31/10/1918
Miscellaneous	35th Division 'G'.	14/10/1918	14/10/1918
Miscellaneous	Register of Messages.		

Miscellaneous	35th Division "G". Register Of Messages.	14/10/1918	14/10/1918
Miscellaneous	Short Summary of Operation.	14/10/1918	14/10/1918
Miscellaneous	35th Division "G".		
Miscellaneous	Register Of Messages.		
Miscellaneous	35th Division "G". Register Of Messages.	14/10/1918	14/10/1918
Miscellaneous	35th Division "G".		
Miscellaneous	Register of Messages.		
Miscellaneous	35th Division "G". Register of Messages.	14/10/1918	14/10/1918
Miscellaneous	35th Division "G".	14/10/1918	14/10/1918
Miscellaneous	Register of Messages.		
Miscellaneous	35th Division "G". Register Of Messages.	14/10/1918	14/10/1918
Miscellaneous	35th Division "G".	14/10/1918	14/10/1918
Miscellaneous	Register of Messages.		
Miscellaneous	35th Division "G". Register of Messages.	14/10/1918	14/10/1918
Miscellaneous	35th Division "G".	14/10/1918	14/10/1918
Miscellaneous	Register of Messages.		
Miscellaneous	35th Division "G". Register of Messages.	14/10/1918	14/10/1918
Miscellaneous	35th Division "G".	14/10/1918	14/10/1918
Miscellaneous	Register of Messages.		
Miscellaneous	35th Division "G". Register of Messages.	14/10/1918	14/10/1918
Miscellaneous	35th Division "G".	14/10/1918	14/10/1918
Miscellaneous	Register of Messages.		
Miscellaneous	35th Division "G". Register of Messages.	14/10/1918	14/10/1918
Miscellaneous			
Miscellaneous	Register of Messages.		
Miscellaneous	35th Division "G".	14/10/1918	14/10/1918
Miscellaneous	35th Division "G". Register of Messages.	14/10/1918	14/10/1918
Miscellaneous			
Miscellaneous	35th Division.	14/10/1918	14/10/1918
Miscellaneous	Register of Messages.		
Miscellaneous	35th Division "G". Register of Messages.	14/10/1918	14/10/1918
Miscellaneous			
Miscellaneous	35th Division "G".	14/10/1918	14/10/1918
Miscellaneous	Register of Messages.		
Miscellaneous	35th Division "G". Register of Messages.	14/10/1918	14/10/1918
Miscellaneous			
Miscellaneous	35th Division "G".		
Miscellaneous	Register of Messages.		
Miscellaneous	35th Division "G". Register of Messages.	14/10/1918	14/10/1918
Miscellaneous			
Miscellaneous	35th Division "G".		
Miscellaneous	Register of Messages.		
Miscellaneous	35th Division "G". Register of Messages.	14/10/1918	14/10/1918
Miscellaneous			
Miscellaneous	35 Division "G".	14/10/1918	14/10/1918
Miscellaneous	Register of Messages.		
Miscellaneous	35th Division "G". Register of Messages.	14/10/1918	14/10/1918
Miscellaneous			
Miscellaneous	35th Division "G".	14/10/1918	14/10/1918
Miscellaneous	Register of Messages.		
Miscellaneous	35th Division "G". Register of Messages.	14/10/1918	14/10/1918
Miscellaneous	Operations of 35th Division from September 28th to November 11th 1918	28/11/1918	28/11/1918
Miscellaneous	Our casualties were as follows:- By dates.		
Miscellaneous		29/12/1918	29/12/1918
Miscellaneous	35th Division No. G.3709	03/10/1918	03/10/1918

Map	Belgium and Part of France.		
Miscellaneous	Belgium and Part of France.		
Map	Belgium and Part of France.		
Miscellaneous	Belgium and Part of France.		
Heading	35th Div. Narrative of Opns 28/9-to end Oct 18		
Miscellaneous	35th Division. Narrative of Operations from 28th September to end of October, 1918	28/09/1918	28/09/1918
Miscellaneous	Summary of Lys Operations.		
Miscellaneous	Our casualties were as follows:- By dates.	28/12/1918	28/12/1918
Map	Dispositions of Troops at 'H'. Map A		
Map	Field Survey Batt. R.E. (9412) 26.7.18		
Map	Belgium and Part of France. 'Map B'. 35th Division Operations 28th Sept to 2nd Oct. 1918		
Heading	Narrative of Operations 31st October 1918 by 35th British Division. To accompany War Diary, Headquarters 35th Division General Staff, October 1918		
Heading	35th Division No. G.122/2. War Diary. Headquarters 35th Division General Staff. November 1918. Contents. War Diary (Army From C.2118. Sheet 1 to 5.) Volume of Narrative of Operations by 35th British Division covering period 2nd to 11th November 1918.		
Heading	35th Division No. G.122/2. War Diary. Headquarters 35th Division General Staff. November 1918. Contents. War Diary (Army From C.2118. Sheet 1 to 5.). Volume 4 of Narrative of Operations by 35th British Division covering period 9th to 11th November 1918.		
War Diary	Sweveghem.	01/11/1918	06/11/1918
War Diary	St Louis.	07/11/1918	10/11/1918
War Diary	Chateau W.4.c.0.0	11/11/1918	20/11/1918
War Diary	Harlebeke.	21/11/1918	27/11/1918
War Diary	Vogeltje.	28/11/1918	30/11/1918
Operation(al) Order(s)	35th Division Order No. 208	01/11/1918	01/11/1918
Miscellaneous	XIX Corps Special Instructions.	02/11/1918	02/11/1918
Miscellaneous	Warning Order.	03/11/1918	03/11/1918
Miscellaneous	Preliminary Instructions.	03/11/1918	03/11/1918
Diagram etc	Diagram to Accompany Preliminary Instructions for Bridging.		
Operation(al) Order(s)	35th Division Order No. 209	04/11/1918	04/11/1918
Miscellaneous	Copy of Telegram from 19 Corps dated 1125 4th November 1918	04/11/1918	04/11/1918
Miscellaneous	Copy of Telegram from XIX Corps dated 1125 4th November 1918	04/11/1918	04/11/1918
Operation(al) Order(s)	35th Division Order No. 210	06/11/1918	06/11/1918
Miscellaneous	35th Division No. 211	08/11/1918	08/11/1918
Miscellaneous	Table of Moves, 9.11.18. To accompany 35th Division Order No. 211 dated 8th November 1918	09/11/1918	09/11/1918
Operation(al) Order(s)	35th Division Order No. 212	09/11/1918	09/11/1918
Miscellaneous	Urgent Operations Priority.		
Operation(al) Order(s)	35th Division Order No. 213	16/11/1918	16/11/1918
Miscellaneous	March Table to accompany 35th Division Order No. 213 dated 16th November 1918	16/11/1918	16/11/1918
Operation(al) Order(s)	35th Division Order No. 214	26/11/1918	26/11/1918
Miscellaneous	March Table to accompany 35th Division Order No. 214 dated 26th November 1918	26/11/1918	26/11/1918
Miscellaneous	35th Division. Narrative of Operations-November 9th to 11th 1918	09/11/1918	09/11/1918

Miscellaneous	A Form. Messages And Signals.		
War Diary	Eperlecques.	01/12/1918	31/01/1919
Miscellaneous	A Form. Messages And Signals.		
Miscellaneous	Calais Operations.	28/01/1919	28/01/1919
Miscellaneous	Summary from Advanced Divisional Headquarters at 105 Inf. Bde.		
Miscellaneous	A Form. Messages And Signals.		
Miscellaneous	G.O.C. 35th Division.	29/01/1919	29/01/1919
Miscellaneous	35th Division No. G.A.615		
Miscellaneous	35th Division No. G.A.617	31/01/1919	31/01/1919
War Diary	Eperlecques.	01/02/1919	28/02/1919
Operation(al) Order(s)	35th Division Order No. 1	01/02/1919	01/02/1919
War Diary	Eperlecques.	01/03/1919	31/03/1919

WO 95 2470/1

35 Div
HQ
Gen Staff

1918 JUL ~~SEP~~ – 1919 MAR
(~~JUL AUG~~ NOT IN BOX)

(inc Register of messages

35TH DIVISION

GENERAL STAFF

~~JAN 1918 - MAR 1919~~

1918 JLY — 1919 MAR

On His Majesty's Service.

Officer i/c
War Diaries
O.C's Office
Base

1345
2.8.18

Original Copy

Sheet No.1.
Headquarters, 35th Division,
GENERAL STAFF,
JULY 1918.

Army Form C. 2118

Original copy.

WAR DIARY
~~INTELLIGENCE SUMMARY~~
(Erase heading not required.)

Instructions regarding War Diaries and Intelligence Summaries are contained in F.S. Regs., Part II. and the Staff Manual respectively. Title Pages will be prepared in manuscript.

Place	Date	Hour	Summary of Events and Information	Remarks and references to Appendices
WIZERNES	1		104th Infantry Brigade Group began detraining ST. OMER 2.0 a.m. and marched to TATTINGHEM Area. 105th Infantry Brigade Group began detraining WIZERNES 3.0 a.m. and marched to BRODEGHEM and WIZERNES. 106th Infantry Brigade Group began detraining at ARQUES about 4.0 a.m. and marched to RENNESCURE Area. 35th Division transferred to XIX Corps. 35th Division H.Q. opened at WIZERNES at 9.0 a.m. Major-General proceeded with a G Staff Officer to a conference at Second Army Ad. H.Q. CASSEL, meeting G.Os.C. XIX Corps and 7th French Division. Major-General then proceeded to XIX Corps H.Q. and arranged details of move of 35th Division to XIX Corps Reserve Area. Major-General visited 7th French Division H.Q. during afternoon. 35th Division Order No.181 issued. Artillery 35th Division started entraining at DOULLENS and CANDAS about 9-30 p.m.	O.O.181.
OUDEZEELE	2		Detrainment of Infantry Brigade Groups complete by 4.0 a.m. Artillery began detraining at ST. OMER about 5.0 a.m. and marched direct to OUDEZEELE Artillery Area. 35th Division H.Q. closed at WIZERNES at 9.0 a.m. and opened at OUDEZEELE at the same hour. Major-General visited Second Army at CASSEL, XIX Corps and XVI French Corps. Major-General, G.S.O.1 and A.A.&Q.M.G. attended Conference at XIX Corps H.Q. during afternoon, Major-General subsequently visiting 71st French Division. Infantry Brigade Groups moved during the day as follows:- 104th Infantry Brigade by bus to RATTEKOT Area, 3 battalions relieving 3 battalions of 7th French Division in neighbourhood of ABEELE in E. POPERINGHE Line defences. Transport moved to RENNESCURE Area. 105th Infantry Brigade remained BRODEGHEM and WIZERNES except Transport which moved to ARQUES Area. 106th Infantry Brigade by bus to ZERMEZEELE Area, Transport by march route.	O.O.182.
	3		Infantry Brigade Groups moved as follows:- 104th Infantry Brigade stationary except transport which moved to ABEELE Area. 105th Infantry Brigade by bus to ZERMEZEELE Area, one battalion to ABEELE, transport by march route to ZERMEZEELE. 106th Infantry Brigade by march route to WINNEZEELE Area. 35th Division Artillery moved up to relief of 7th French D.A. covering E. POPERINGHE line.	
	4		Major-General and G.S.O.1 visited LOCRE front during early morning. 105th Infantry Brigade moved from ZERMEZEELE Area to ABEELE Area during afternoon, taking over responsibility for defence/	

Wt. W.593/826 1,000,000 4/15 I.B.C. & A. A.D.S.S./Forms/C. 2118.

WAR DIARY

Army Form C. 2118
Sheet No. 2.

Headquarters, 35th Division,
GENERAL STAFF.
JULY 1918.

Instructions regarding War Diaries and Intelligence Summaries are contained in F.S. Regs., Part II. and the Staff Manual respectively. Title Pages will be prepared in manuscript.

(Erase heading not required.)

Place	Date	Hour	Summary of Events and Information	Remarks and references to Appendices
OUDEZEELE	4		defence of E. POPERINGHE Line from 104th Infantry Brigade. 19th N.F. (Pioneers) moved during afternoon to GOEDERSWAESWELDE. 2 battalions 104th Infantry Brigade and 2 battalions 106th Infantry Brigade relieved front and Reserve battalions of left and right French Regiments respectively. 1 battalion 105th Infantry Brigade relieved Support battalion of Centre French Infantry Regiment. Half 35th D.A. came into action covering LOCRE front.	
LE MORT HOMME.	5		Remainder of relief of 71st French Division completed.	
	6		G.O.C. 35th Division took over command of LOCRE Sector at 8.0 a.m. 35th Division now under tactical command of XVI French Corps, though still administered by XIX British Corps. 41st British Division, XIX British Corps, holds Sector to the N. 41st French Division, XVI French Corps holds sector to the S and is in process of relief by 36th British Division. A raid attempted by the enemy on 104th Infantry Brigade repulsed.	
	7		Quiet day.	
	8		Quiet day.	
	9		Some rain and thunder. Quiet day. Five O.R. casualties caused at H.Q. by a shell on G Office during evening.	
	10		Rain and thunder storms. Fair intervals. Quiet day.	
	11		Heavy rain. Quiet day. G.O.C. and G.S.O.1 attended conference at X Corps Headquarters ZUYDPEENE at 10.0 a.m. 11th.	
	12		Heavy rain all morning. Fine intervals during afternoon. Quiet day.	
	13		Bright fine day. An attempted enemy raid during the night on the left Brigade front was repulsed. As the result of a patrol encounter on the Centre Brigade front we lost three men missing. Hostile Artillery more active than usual during the night, chiefly in support of enemy raid.	

14th/

Sheet No. 3.

Headquarters, 35th Division
GENERAL STAFF.
JULY 1918.

WAR DIARY

~~INTELLIGENCE SUMMARY~~

(Erase heading not required.)

Instructions regarding War Diaries and Intelligence Summaries are contained in F.S. Regs., Part II. and the Staff Manual respectively. Title Pages will be prepared in manuscript.

Army Form C. 2118

Place	Date	Hour	Summary of Events and Information	Remarks and references to Appendices
LE MORT HOMME.	14		H.Q. FRANCES DAY. Heavy rain most of day. 35th Division/remain at LE MORT HOMME (Sheet 27 Square R.15.a.1.7.) one mile North-east of MONT DES CATS. Rear Headquarters 35th Division at TERDEGHEM. The 36th Division are in line (ST. JEAN CAPPEL Sector) on right of 35th Division who hold the LOCRE Sector. The 41st Division (XIX Corps) are on left (North-east) of 35th Division. The X Corps consists of three Divisions viz:- 36th and 35th in the line and 30th in Reserve. The General Staff 35th Division now consists of:- Major-General A.H.MARINDIN.D.S.O.,p.s.c., Black Watch, Commanding; Lieutenant-Colonel H.W.B.THORP.D.S.O.,p.s.c., K.O.Y.L.I.; Major R.C.J.CHICHESTER-CONSTABLE, D.S.O., Rifle Brigade; Captain G.W.HODGKINSON, General List. Lieutenant A.I.CHESNEY, Intelligence Officer. At 6-0 a.m. 14th July the XIX Corps on our left carried out a successful attack East of DICKEBUSCH LAKE. G.S.O.2 and G.S.O.3 visited 35th Division Reception Camp at Sheet 27 Square H.30.d.7.9 near OCHTEZEELE three miles W.N.W. of CASSEL. At 11-45 p.m. 14th the 104th Infantry Brigade (Left Subsector) carried out small raid on German trenches at M.24.d.0.3 but found enemy gone.	
	15		Rain and thunder at intervals and during night 15/16th. Party of Machine Gunners of United States Army were attached to 35th Bn. M.G.C. Major R.C.J. CHICHESTER-CONSTABLE.D.S.O. Rifle Brigade, G.S.O.2, 35th Division, appointed G.S.O.2 under Inspector General of Training G.H.Q. and departed for CRECY. As all three Infantry Brigades are in the line there are no Inter-Brigade reliefs to publish. The Brigades relieve their front line battalions as follows:- 104 (Left Subsector) and 105 (Centre Subsector) every four days; 106 (Right Subsector) every six days.	
	16		Thunder and rain at intervals. Conference at 35th Division H.Q. LE MORT HOMME 10.0 a.m. three Infantry Brigade Commanders.	
	17		Rain. Corps Commander X Corps called. We carried out Heavy Counter-preparation and harassing fire night 17/18th July.	
	18		Rain.	
	19		Fine. G.O.C. visited the front and all Brigades.	

20th/

Instructions regarding War Diaries and Intelligence
Summaries are contained in F. S. Regs., Part II.
and the Staff Manual respectively. Title pages
will be prepared in manuscript.

WAR DIARY
or
INTELLIGENCE SUMMARY.

(Erase heading not required.)

Sheet No. 4.

Headquarters, 35th Division, Army Form C. 2118.
GENERAL STAFF,
JULY 1918.

Place	Date	Hour	Summary of Events and Information	Remarks and references to Appendices
LE MORT HOMME.	20th		G.O.C. met Army Commander at TERDEGHEM 2-0 p.m.	
	21st		Sunday.	
	22nd		Fine morn. Rain evening. Conference at 35th Division H.Q. LE MORT HOMME. B.G.C. 106th Infantry Brigade, C.R.A., O.C. 35th Bn. M.G.C. attended. B.G.C. 90th Infantry Brigade 30th Division called with reference to attachment of 90th Infantry Brigade to 35th Division in Right Subsector in relief of 106th Infantry Brigade from 26th July.	
	23rd		Heavy rain. G.O.C. took Corps Commander round the line Centre and Left Subsectors. Major Sir E.P.D. PAUNCEFORT-DUNCOMBE, Bart., D.S.O., Buckinghamshire Yeomanry from Brigade Major 165th Infantry Brigade 56th Division joined as officiating G.S.O. 2, 35th Division, vice Major R.C.J. CHICHESTER-CONSTABLE.D.S.O.	
	24th		Fine with a few showers. Captain G.W. HODGKINSON, G.S.O. 3, takes over appointment of Brigade Major 105th Infantry Brigade. Lieutenant HARRISON (A.D.C.) takes over appointment of G.S.O. 3, 35th Division. Corps Commander called.	O.O.183
	25th		Fine day. Two battalions 90th Infantry Brigade (30th Division) relieve two battalions 106th Infantry Brigade in Right Subsector. G.O.C. visited 104th and 105th Infantry Brigades in afternoon.	
TERDEGHEM.	26th		Wet morning, fine afternoon. C.R.A. and Division H.Q. moved to Rear H.Q. at TERDEGHEM by order of the Army Commander. C.R.E. remain at LE MORT HOMME. One battalion 90th Infantry Brigade relieves one battalion 106th Infantry Brigade in Right Subsector.	
	27th		Heavy showers throughout the day. 106th Infantry Brigade at ST. SYLVESTRE CAPPEL visited by G.O.C. 90th Infantry Brigade (30th Division) take over command of Right Subsector. At/	

Army Form C. 2118.

WAR DIARY

~~INTELLIGENCE~~ SUMMARY.

(Erase heading not required.)

Instructions regarding War Diaries and Intelligence Summaries are contained in F. S. Regs., Part II. and the Staff Manual respectively. Title pages will be prepared in manuscript.

Sheet No. 5.
Headquarters, 35th Division,
GENERAL STAFF,
JULY 1918.

Place	Date	Hour	Summary of Events and Information	Remarks and references to Appendices
TERDEGHEM	27th Continued:-		At 11-30 p.m. a party of 60 men, 19th D.L.I., 104th Infantry Brigade, raided the enemy's line and after a stiff fight, captured seven men of the 58th Division and one machine gun. Five of the prisoners were killed on the way back by shell fire.	
	28th		Fine. A Conference was held at 35th Division H.Q. by the Major-General. Present:- B.G.C. and Brigade Major 106th Infantry Brigade, B.G., X Corps Heavy Artillery, Os.C. 35th, 30th and 36th M.G. Battalions and C.R.A. 35th Division. The plans for an attack by 106th Infantry Brigade were discussed.	
	29th		Fine and hot. The G.O.C. visited the 35th Division Reception Camp in the morning and again in the afternoon with the Corps Commander to witness Sports and Shooting. The G.O.C. and G.S.O. 1 attended a Conference at X Corps H.Q. at 5.0 p.m. 27th Canadian Battalion, 2nd Canadian Division, attached to 35th Division from 7-30 p.m. 29th July.	
	30th		Fine and hot. 35th Division Operation Order 184 issued. Army Commander (Second Army) inspected 106th Infantry Brigade at ST. SYLVESTRE. G.O.C. attended practice attack by 106th Infantry Brigade at 11-30 p.m.	O.O.184
	31st		Fine and hot. 27th Battalion, 2nd Canadian Division relieved the Reserve Battalion 104th Infantry Brigade in the Left Subsector. X Corps Commander and G.O.C. 30th Division visited 35th Division H.Q. at 5-30 p.m.	

H.Q. 35th Division,
31st July 1918.

[signature]
Major-General,
Commanding 35th Division.

REPORT ON RAID ON RIGHT COMPANY FRONT ON JUNE 30th/1917.

At 6 a.m. enemy opened an intense bombardment on Company front, especially at junction of FAWCUS AVENUE and front line, under cover of which enemy crept up to front line between CANNON GATE and LEITH WALK, a heavy mist was hanging over front line at that time. Owing to recent shelling of this part of the front, I issued orders that in case of shelling the men were to move over to the right near CANNON GATE, which was carried out. Enemy evidently entered front line near LEITH WALK as wire has been cut and trampled down there, and moved along front line towards CANNON GATE. In one shelter they found Sergt. DYSON, whom they took prisoner. On leaving the trench they were fired on with Lewis Guns and rifles, one being badly wounded fell in our wire and was captured. There is reason to believe that several others were hit. The raiding party was estimated at between 20 and 30, and were armed with stick bombs and automatic revolvers.

The bombardment lasted about 15 minutes, and consisted of 5.9, 4.2 and aerial torpedoes, also field guns. The trenches are badly damaged. Sergt. DYSON only joined the Company last night.

30/6/17.

(Sd) A. MACKENZIE, Capt.,
O.C. "X" Coy., 23rd Manch. Regt.

2.

To Headquarters,
104th Inf. Brigade.

I forward herewith report from O.C. Company whose front was raided by a strong enemy patrol this morning.

Acting in accordance with instructions in case of heavy bombardment during daylight, the posts in the bombarded area were withdrawn to the flank.

The enemy patrol came under Lewis Gun and rifle fire from the flanks on returning. One wounded man was captured. He has since died.

It is thought more have been hit, and endeavour will be made to verify this to-night.

The front line trenches have been badly knocked about, and also the top of FAWCUS AVENUE. They are being repaired.

June 30th 1917.

(Sd) L.M. STEVENS, Lt.Col.,
Commanding 23rd Manchester Regt.

SECRET 35th Division No G 2230
18th July 1918

35th Division
PROVISIONAL
DEFENCE SCHEME
LOCRE SECTOR
July 1918

Copy No. 18

(6339) Wt. W160/M3016 1,500,000 10/17 McA & W Ltd (E 1898) Forms W3091.   Army Form W.3091.

Cover for Documents.

Nature of Enclosures.

Notes, or Letters written.

SECRET.　　　　　　　　　　　　　35th Division No.G.2230.

18th July 1918.

Copy No. 18

To **War Diary**

1. Herewith one Copy of 35th DIVISION PROVISIONAL DEFENCE SCHEME for the LOCRE Sector; Number G.2230 dated 18th July 1918.

2. The Maps referred to in the Scheme, i.e. map shewing S.O.S. lines of Artillery and Machine Guns and map shewing Machine Gun direct lines of fire, have already been issued to 35th Divisional units with 35th Division Letter No.G.2125 dated 15th July 1918.
Copies of the maps are now forwarded only to those recipients of Copies of the Defence Scheme whose formations are marked with an asterisk thus ∅ on the distribution list set forth below.

3. All Defence Instructions for the LOCRE Sector and amendments thereto are hereby Cancelled; all copies should be destroyed.

4. Please ACKNOWLEDGE receipt.

H.Q.35th Division,　　　　　　　　　　Lieutenant-Colonel,
18th July 1918.　　　　　　　　　　General Staff 35th Division.

Copy No.1.	G.O.C.35th Division.	12.	35th Bn. M.G.C.
∅ 2.	X Corps.	13.	35th Div. Signal Co. R.E.
∅ 3.	30th Division.	14.	A.D.M.S.
∅ 4.	36th Division.	15.	A.A.& Q.M.G.
∅ 5.	41st Division.	∅ 16.	General Staff.
6.	C.R.A.35th Division.	17.	File.
7.	C.R.E.35th Division.	18.	War Diary.
8.	104th Infantry Brigade.	19.	War Diary.
9.	105th Infantry Brigade.	20.	Spare.
10.	106th Infantry Brigade.	21.	Spare.
11.	19th N.F.(Pioneers).		

SECRET.   35th Division No. G.2230.

18th July 1918.

Copy No. 18

35th DIVISION.

PROVISIONAL DEFENCE SCHEME.
LOCRE SECTOR.

Map 1/40,000 Sheets 27 and 28.

1. SECTOR - boundaries of.

   (a) The LOCRE Sector extends approximately from S.4.b.2.2 - M.28.d. Central - M.24.c.9.4. i.e. a frontage of about 3,800 yards.
   (b) The Right or South-western boundary runs roughly S.4.b.2.2 - M.20.d.2.0 - R.10.c.1.0 - EECKE Q.20.d.
   The Left or North-eastern boundary runs roughly M.24.c.9.4 - M.17.b.2.2 - M.10.c.1.9 - M.8.c.8.9 - M.1.b.1.6 - R.6.a.9.6 - R.10.b.6.8 - R.2.d.9.6 - Q.4.c.5.9 - Westwards along road inclusive to 35th Division - Q.2.d.9.7.
   (c) The boundaries between Sub-sectors are roughly as follows:-
   Between RIGHT and CENTRE. North-east edge of LOCRE CHATEAU grounds - Road Junction at M.21.d.9.3 - Cross roads at M.21.a.7.6.
   Between CENTRE and LEFT. Building at M.23.d.4.1 - Huts at M.23.d.0.7 - CH. DE NOTRE DAME DE LOURDES M.22.b.2.7 - M.22.b.6.6.

2. HEADQUARTERS AND COMMAND.

   (a) The 35th Division Headquarters are at LE MORT HOMME (R.15.a.1.7) with rear headquarters at TERDEGHEM.
   (b) The 35th Division holds the LOCRE or Left Sector of the X Corps (BERTHEN Area) front.

3. SUBSECTORS.

   The 35th Division holds the LOCRE Sector as a three Brigade front sub-divided as follows:-

	Headquarters(approximate).
RIGHT Sub-sector 106th Infantry Brigade ...	M.20.d.3.3.
CENTRE Sub-sector 105th Infantry Brigade ...	M.22.a.0.1.
LEFT Sub-sector 104th Infantry Brigade ...	M.16.b.2.9.

4. FLANKS.

   The 36th Division (H.Q. TERDEGHEM, advanced H.Q. MONT DES CATS) of X Corps are on Right of 35th Division holding the ST JANS CAPEL Sector.
   The 41st Division (H.Q. K.24.c.2.3 near ABEELE) of XIX Corps are on Left of 35th Division holding the SCHERPENBERG Sector.

   5. ARTILLERY

(Page 2.)

5. **ARTILLERY** - allotment of.

(a) The LOCRE Sector is covered by three Brigades of Field Artillery viz:-
RIGHT Sub-sector ... 38th Army Field Artillery Brigade.
CENTRE ,, ... 159th Field Artillery Brigade. 35th D.A.
LEFT ,, ... 157th Field Artillery Brigade. 35th D.A.

(b) The 2nd Brigade R.G.A. Headquarters Q.6.c.5.6 (Lieut-Colonel BARTON) is the Heavy Artillery Brigade affiliated to 35th Division.

6. **MACHINE GUNS.**

The Machine Gun Defence of the LOCRE Sector is arranged by the O.C. 35th Battalion Machine Gun Corps under instructions from Divisional Headquarters.

Three companies cover the front, approximately one covering each Sub-sector, while the fourth Machine Gun Company is held in divisional reserve at R.11.c.8.5 near M.G. Battalion H.Q.

7. **R.E. and PIONEERS.**

(a) Two Sections of a Field Company R.E. are attached to each Infantry Brigade viz:-
104th Infantry Brigade (LEFT Sub-sector) 2 sections 203rd Field Company.
105th Infantry Brigade (CENTRE Sub-sector) 2 sections 203rd Field Company.
106th Infantry Brigade (RIGHT Sub-sector) 2 sections 204th Field Company.

(b) The remainder of the Field Companies R.E. also the whole of the 19th N.F. Pioneers (H.Q. R.12.a.3.2.) work under the direct orders of 35th Division Headquarters.

8. **AIR SERVICE.**

No. 53 Squadron R.A.F. (H.Q. CLAIRMARAIS) work with X Corps.

9. **MEDICAL.**

(a) The 35th Division Main Dressing Station is at HALTE WAGENBRUGE P.12.d.2.3 and evacuates to the Casualty Clearing Station at ESQUELBECQ, (ultimately ARNEKE).

(b) Advanced Dressing Station is North of WESTOUTRE at M.9.c.3.8.

10. **RESERVES** - location of.

The third or Reserve Battalions of Infantry Brigades are stationed roughly as follows:-
RIGHT Sub-sector - Squares R.8 and R.9 (parts of) West of BOESCHEPE.
CENTRE Sub-sector - Squares R.4.a and L.34.c and d. North of BOESCHEPE.
LEFT Sub-sector - Squares R.11.a, R.5.c, R.4.d. North-east of BOESCHEPE.

The above are in Divisional Reserve.

11. **ORGANIZATION OF DEFENCE.**

11. ORGANIZATION OF DEFENCE.

The defensive system in the LOCRE SECTOR is organized as follows:-

(a) **FRONT OR BLUE SYSTEM.**

Front Line. Running roughly from S.4.b.3.0 - M.29.c.0.8 - M.24.c.9.4 - Continuous defensive line.

Supporting Points. Machine Gun Positions. Lewis Gun Positions sited to suit the ground between the front line and BLUE Line.

BLUE Line. M.27.c.3.4 - M.28.a.4.5 - M.23.a.0.3. to the left (not yet settled). This line was previously Called the Line of Strong Points or REDOUBT LINE.

(b) **INTERMEDIATE OR RED SYSTEM.**

Main Line. In front of Crest of hills. Wired and defensive line to Cover preparation for Counter-attacks.

Support Line. On reverse side of Crest of hills, intended as a jumping off place for Counter-attacks.

(c) **ARMY LINE.** Formerly known as BERTHEN Line between WESTEN MOLEN and VLENVICKHOVEN (M.1.d.5.5 - M.13.d.5.8).

There are other lines in rear but the Division holding the LOCRE Sector is only concerned with the BLUE SYSTEM and RED SYSTEM, while the Supporting Division is concerned with the ARMY LINE and with helping the Divisions in the line to maintain intact the two front systems.

12. PRINCIPLES OF DEFENCE.

(a) The following is an extract from instructions from the Army Commander:-

"The guiding principle of the defence must be the concluding paragraph of the memorandum issued on 6th June 1918 by the Field Marshal Commanding-in-Chief, which runs as follows:-

'It remains as true as ever that for all troops actually allotted to the defence of a position, there is, subject to any orders which they may receive from superior authority, only one degree of resistance, and that is to the last round and to the last man'".

(b) The 35th Division is responsible for holding to the last the BLUE SYSTEM (FRONT) and the RED SYSTEM (INTERMEDIATE). No retirement or withdrawal of any troops or machine guns is to take place whether the flanks of the 35th Division or of individual units are exposed or not.

If the enemy penetrate any portion of the line they will be dealt with from the flanks and killed, captured or squeezed out.

No unit has anything to do with positions in rear. Each unit is responsible for holding its own line or providing troops for Counter-attack or reinforcement of lines in front.

(c)

(c) The battalions in the Front or BLUE SYSTEM will hold the front lines in sufficient strength to check hostile reconnaissances, raids or minor local attacks and to give warning of and break up more serious attacks. Should there be definite indications of a heavy bombardment being imminent these garrisons of the front line will be reduced to a minimum but those which are posted there are to fight in the positions allotted to them.

At least half of each front line battalion will be told off to find fixed/garrisons for strong points in the BLUE LINE and to find mobile troops which will be told off for local and immediate counter-attacks. These mobile troops, with the aid of machine guns, will help the garrisons of the various forward positions and break up the enemy's attack.

(d) The Supporting Battalions will find -
  (i) Fixed garrisons to hold at all costs the main line of the INTERMEDIATE or RED SYSTEM which will cover the assembly of Reserves and the preparation of counter-attacks.
  (ii) Mobile troops which will be utilized as Brigade Reserves to help the front battalions to maintain the BLUE LINE and parts in front of it either by counter-attack or reinforcing as the situation may require.

(e) The Reserve Battalions will be employed either to reinforce or counter-attack in order to maintain or regain the BLUE SYSTEM. The whole of the resources of the Division will be used in fighting for the BLUE LINE and if possible for the whole of the BLUE SYSTEM. Behind the Division are the Corps Reserves which will be used for the same purpose.

(f) In case of any indication of an impending attack:-
  (i) The Reserve Battalions will be moved forward on the initiative of Infantry Brigade Commanders to selected assembly positions close up to the crest line of the hills.
  These three battalions form the Divisional Reserve and will normally be employed under orders from the Divisional Commander for prepared counter-attack or for relief or reinforcement of the troops in front. The prepared counter-attack may need the combination of two or more battalions in one sub-sector. Should communication with Divisional Headquarters fail, the senior Brigadier on the spot will take such action as may be necessary.
  In case, however, of a break through of the BLUE LINE or RED LINE, Brigadiers will use the Reserve Battalions in their sub-sectors as required by the situation, informing 35th Division H.Q. as soon as possible.

  (ii) The Reserve Company of 35th Battalion Machine Gun Corps will move forward under Divisional orders and will occupy positions which have already been selected in the

RED SYSTEM

(Page 5.)

RED SYSTEM, viz, eight pairs of guns at -
M.26.b.75.65.
M.26.b.88.85.
M.22.c.37.95.
M.22.c.88.88.
M.22.b.10.30.
M.22.b.30.36.
M.17.d.20.38.
M.17.d.43.43.

    (iii) The 19th N.F.(Pioneers) and those Sections Field Companies R.E. not attached to Infantry Brigades will stand to in their billets and await orders from 35th Division Headquarters. If working forward they will come under the orders of the Brigadier in whose sub-sector they are working.
    (iv) Tunnellers and attached Infantry will (except those who have definite stations allotted to them) stand to at their shelters.

(g) Summary of Counter-attacks.
    (i) By the garrisons of strong points in each line of defence.
        In each line small local counter-attacks will be made by any available men to maintain the line or to help neighbouring portions. These counter-attacks are immediate.
    (ii) By the mobile troops at the disposal of Battalion Commanders which will be used according to the situation -
        (a) In case of a local attack or raid they will be made to restore the situation in the front lines of the BLUE SYSTEM and will be immediate.
        (b) In the case of a general attack on a large scale these counter-attacks will only be made if they do not risk compromising the line for which the unit is responsible, i.e. the BLUE LINE. In such a case it is useless throwing in small counter-attacks but every line and locality forward must hold its ground resolutely and assist the Infantry of other lines or localities by fire.
    (iii) By the Brigade Reserve, composed of mobile troops of the Support Battalion, to assist in holding the BLUE LINE, or restoring the situation in the forward parts of the BLUE SYSTEM.
    (iv) By the Divisional Reserve - the three reserve battalions - which may either be used for a great counter-attack under Divisional arrangements, or in case of certain emergencies laid down in paragraph 12(f)(i), may be used at once by Brigadiers to restore the situation in the BLUE SYSTEM.
    (v) By the Reserve Division under Corps arrangements.

13. ARTILLERY.

    (a) Each sub-sector is covered by one Brigade Field Artillery as detailed in paragraph 5.
    The S.O.S. barrage is also supplemented by three sections of 18-prs. which are in action in Reserve, covering the ARMY LINE

An Artillery

An Artillery Liaison Officer will live at each Infantry Brigade Headquarters.

Machine guns co-operate in the S.O.S. barrage.

(b) The fire of all these Brigades of Field Artillery can be concentrated on any one sub-sector on the Code Words "CONCENTRATE RIGHT", "CONCENTRATE CENTRE", "CONCENTRATE LEFT", being sent.

In addition Mutual Support with neighbouring divisions has been arranged.

Normally, concentration will only be carried out on orders from 35th Division Headquarters, but, should communication with 35th Division Headquarters be cut off and an attack be obviously only coming on one sub-sector, concentration can be ordered by the senior Brigadier in the forward area through his Artillery Liaison Officer.

DAILY OFFENSIVE FIRE.

(c) Harassing fire will be carried out by day and by night on sensitive points and tracks. Infantry Brigade Commanders will be consulted as to useful points and roads on their front and as to the hours at which fire should take place.

(d) Concentrations of fire or "shell storms" will be put on hostile targets under arrangements made by C.R.A. A list of these targets has been issued.

DEFENSIVE FIRE.

(e) In case of any portion of our line being harassed by enemy shell fire, counter-battery work will be asked for by the Brigadier Commanding the sub-sector.

(f) In case of serious bombardment the counter-preparation scheme by all Field Artillery will be at once ordered by the Divisional Commander and application will be made to the Army Corps for the complete scheme of counter-preparation to be put in force.

(g) Enemy concentrations will on the request of the Infantry Brigadier, or, if it appears desirable, on the immediate initiative of the F.O.O., be countered by similar concentrations on sensitive points.

(h) On the S.O.S. signal being made the Divisional Artillery will open fire on their S.O.S. targets (supplemented by machine guns) along the whole of the Divisional Front for fifteen minutes; fire will then cease unless the S.O.S. signal is repeated or further information is received.

This fire will be concentrated as in paragraph 13(b) when it is discovered which sub-sector is affected.

The S.O.S. signal will only be made when it is certain that hostile Infantry are attacking. It will not be made as a signal for retaliation or counter-battery work in case of bombardment.

Map No.1 shows combined Artillery and Machine Gun S.O.S. barrage lines.

(i) In the event of an enemy attack penetrating into our front system the Artillery barrage will remain on its S.O.S. line, but F.O.Os have orders to engage with observed fire any parties or formations of the enemy which they can see within range.

Certain batteries or sections will be detailed which can come off the barrage line to fire with direct observation.

The Artillery

(Page 7.)

The Artillery barrage as such will only be brought back from its normal S.O.S. line by order of the Divisional Commander after reference, if possible, to Corps. If this is done it will come on to a second barrage line along the front of the BLUE LINE.

(j) In case of a Counter-attack special arrangements will be made for Artillery covering fire.

NOTE. Details of the above barrages are given in the Appendices to the Artillery Defence Scheme.

14. MACHINE GUNS.

(a) Machine guns will daily fire harassing fire on roads, tracks or other sensitive points. Machine Gun Group Commanders will keep in touch with Infantry Brigade Commanders and arrange suitable targets and times.

In addition the O.C. 35th Battalion Machine Gun Corps will keep in touch with C.R.A. 35th Division so that the machine gun fire may fit in with the Artillery concentrations.

(b) All machine guns are sited for direct fire on probable lines of attack of the enemy. In addition barrage lines arranged in conjunction with the Artillery are laid down.

The barrage lines are shewn in Map No. 1.
The bands of direct fire are shewn in Map No. 2.

(c) In case of S.O.S., machine guns will fire on their barrage lines in conjunction with the Field Artillery.

Should, however, the enemy break through anywhere, or should there be any bodies of the enemy within range giving targets under direct fire, any machine gun that can be brought to bear will deal with the target with direct fire, returning immediately afterwards to its S.O.S. line.

In doing this it must be remembered that gaps will be caused in the barrage line and the targets must be such as to warrant switching off fire from the barrage line.

O.C. 35th Battalion Machine Gun Corps will issue detailed instructions on this.

(d) Machine Gunners in advanced positions will stick to their guns and fight to the last. There must be no withdrawal.

==================

File Copy

> III CORPS
> GENERAL STAFF,
> "O."
>
> No. G.O. 4402
> Date 2/7/17.

35th Division.
****

Reference your No.G 27/17 of 1/7/17, will you please convey to the 23rd Manchesters the Corps Commander's appreciation of the way in which this raid was repulsed.

          C. Bonham Carter
          Brigadier-General,
          General Staff,
          III Corps.

H.Q., III Corps.
2nd July, 1917.

Very satisfactory
the 23rd Manchesters
should be
complimented
on the way they
repulsed their
raid

3S Div

Will you please
convey to the 23rd
Manchesters the
Corps Commander's
appreciation of the
way in which this
raid was repulsed.

SECRET

H.Q. 35TH DIVISION (GENERAL STAFF).
No. G 27/17.

GO 4402

III Corps.

    I forward herewith a report on raid carried out by the Germans against A1. trench on the morning of 30th June.

H.Q. 35th Division.
1st July 1917.

Major General,
Commanding 35th Division.

REPORT ON RAID ON RIGHT COMPANY FRONT ON JUNE 30th 1917.

At 6 a.m. enemy opened an intense bombardment on company front, especially at junction of FAWCUS AVENUE and front line, under cover of which enemy crept up to front line between CANNON GATE and LEITH WALK, a heavy mist was hanging over front line at that time. Owing to recent shelling of this part of the front, I issued orders that in case of shelling the men were to move over to the right near CANNON GATE, which was carried out. Enemy evidently entered front line near LEITH WALK as wire has been cut and trampled down there, and moved along front line towards CANNON GATE. In one shelter they found Sergt.DYSON, whom they took prisoner. On leaving the trench they were fired on with Lewis Guns and rifles, one being badly wounded fell in our wire and was captured. There is reason to believe that several others were hit. The raiding party was estimated at between 20 and 30, and were armed with stick bombs and automatic revolvers.

The bombardment lasted about 15 minutes, and consisted of 5.9, 4.2. and aerial torpedoes, also Field guns. The trenches are badly damged. Sergt.DYSON only joined the company last night.

30/6/17

(Sd) A.MACKENZIE, Capt.,
O.C. "X" Coy., 23rd.Manch.Regt.

2.

To Headquarters
104th Infantry Brigade.

I forward herewith report from O.C. Company whose front was raided by a strong enemy patrol this morning.

Acting in accordance with instructions in case of heavy bombardment during daylight, the posts in the bombarded area were withdrawn to the flank.

The enemy patrol came under Lewis Gun and rifle fire from the flanks on returning. One wounded man was captured. He has since died.

It is thought more have been hit, and endeavour will be made to verify this to-night.

The front line trenches have been badly knocked about, and also the top of FAWCUS AVENUE. They are being repaired.

June 30th 1917.

(Sd) L.M.STEVENS, Lt.Col.,
Commdg., 23rd.Manchester Regt.

War Diary

35th DIVISION.
DAILY INTELLIGENCE SUMMARY No. 78.
From 6 a.m. 30th July to 6 a.m. 31st July 1918.

1. OPERATIONS (BRITISH).

   (a) Infantry. A strong Officers patrol (2 Officers and 21 O.Rs) left our line at M.29.b.50.75 and proceeded up the ditch towards enemy's line. On reaching the enemy's line patrol was divided into two parties each under an Officer. One party proceeded along enemy wire to the left. Just as the second party was leaving the ditch to proceed to the right an enemy M.G. at M.29.b.8.4, which enfilades the ditch, opened fire causing three casualties. This was followed by a volley of rifle fire and hand grenades which caused three more casualties. All casualties were brought back to our line.

   (b) Artillery. At 2-45 p.m. fired concentration on NEUVE EGLISE in conjunction with Heavy Artillery. Between 2 a.m. and 3 a.m. punishment fire and trench mortar counter preparation fire in reply to the Heavy enemy shelling.

2. OPERATIONS (GERMAN).

   (a) Infantry. Nil.

   (b) Artillery. The crest, rear and forward slopes of MONT ROUGE was persistently shelled with 10.5 cm and 15 cm howitzers during the period. LOCRE and CANADA CORNER received some attention. From 9-30 p.m. onwards enemy harassed the C.T. in M.22.b, and the track leading to front line in Centre Brigade area. At 2 a.m. the enemy put down a heavy barrage on the right Brigade front at the same time the forward areas of the left and Centre Brigade were heavily shelled with shells of all calibres. The shelling increased in intensity along the whole Divisional front at 2-30 a.m. and continued till 3 a.m. when it gradually decreased.
      Trench mortars were active on the front line of Right and Left Brigades between 2 a.m. and 3 a.m.

3. AVIATION.

   At 7-40 p.m. one of our aeroplanes was brought down in M.22.c. as a result of a fight with several E.A.
   One E.A. was flying low over WESTOUTRE at 8-10 p.m. It was forced back over its own lines by anti-aircraft fire from Lewis Guns, rifles and Stokes Mortars.

   HOSTILE DEFENCES.

   (A) Machine Guns. There is a M.G. at M.29.b.8.4.

   (b) Trench Mortars. Active on Left and Right Brigade fronts between 2 a.m. and 3 a.m.

   (c) Wire. Enemy wire astride the ditch in M.29.b. is strong.

5. MOVEMENT.

   Below normal. Visibility low.

6. MISCELLANEOU

6. MISCELLANEOUS.

(i) During the bombardment this morning enemy sent up many double and single RED and GREEN lights.

(ii) Enemy dumps at T.1.b.2.5 and behind the DRANOUTRE RIDGE were seen to be on fire at 6-50 p.m. and 10.50p.m. respectively.

R.P. Harrison
Capt

H.Q. 35th Division,
31st July 1918.

Lieutenant-Colonel,
General Staff, 35th Division.

SUMMER TIME.

Date	SUN Rises	Sets	MOON Rises	Sets
Aug. 1st	5-16 a.m.	8-32 p.m.	12-43 a.m.	4-22 p.m. (2nd Aug).
2nd	5-17 a.m.	8-30 p.m.	12-43 a.m.	5-23 p.m.

35th DIVISION
DAILY INTELLIGENCE SUMMARY No. 77.
From 6 a.m. 29th July to 6 a.m. 30th July 1918.

Ref. Sheet 28 S.W.

1. OPERATIONS (BRITISH).

(a) Infantry. Patrols were out all along the Divisional front. No Germans were encountered.

(b) Artillery. Concentrations were fired on selected targets during the night. At 12.45 p.m. a concentration was fired on hostile batteries at WEUVE EGLISE in conjunction with the Heavy Artillery. 18-prs engaged a suspected dump at N.25.d.22.52.
    A dump in the wood in S.12.b was exploded at about 12.45 p.m.

2. OPERATIONS (GERMAN).

(a) Infantry. Nil.

(b) Artillery. Intermittent shelling of MONT ROUGE and M.28.a and b during the day by 10.5 cm. hows. A few 10.5 cm. shells fell in WESTOUTRE between 1.40 a.m. and 3.30 a.m., and about 40 rounds of various calibres in M.21.d. between the same hours. There were a few shrapnel bursts on the road junction at M.33.a.8.9. These are reported to have resembled the bursts of our 18-pr shrapnel.

3. AVIATION.

    Two E.A. patrolled our line about 9.0 a.m. and were driven off by M.G. fire. One E.A. was over our lines at 5.20 p.m. An E.A. dropped two small bombs on our front line in M.34.

4. HOSTILE DEFENCES.

(a) Machine Guns. Enemy M.Gs fired bursts on our front and support lines and on the wood in M.33.b. during the night.
    An M.G. post was located at S.4.b.75.15.
    An M.G. is reported to have been firing from M.29.b.8.5.

(b) Posts. An enemy listening post was located at M.29.b.5.4 by one of our patrols. Another patrol found unoccupied enemy posts at M.29.b.48.30, M.29.c.20.75 and M.28.d.9.5. This patrol was fired on by M.Gs from strong point at M.28.d.95.45; bombs were also thrown at it from the same place.

(c) Wire. A patrol found a belt of concertina wire between M.29.b.35.10 and M.29.b.60.25 with gaps in several places.
    A belt of barbed concertina wire runs S.W. across the road in M.28.d. from M.29.c.0.5.

5. MOVEMENT. Below normal. Visibility was low.

6. MISCELLANEOUS. Dugouts are suspected between N.25.b.7.1 and N.25.b.7.2.

H.Q. 35th Division,
30th July 1918.

Lieutenant-Colonel,
General Staff 35th Division.

SUMMER TIME.

Date.	SUN. Rises.	Sets.	MOON. Rises.	Sets.
Aug. 1st.	5.16 a.m.	8.32 p.m.	12.43 p.m.	4.22 a.m. 2nd Aug.
Aug. 2nd.	5.17 a.m.	8.30 p.m.	12.43 a.m.	5.23 p.m.

War Diary

35th DIVISION.
DAILY INTELLIGENCE SUMMARY No. 76.
From 6 a.m. 28th July to 6 a.m. 29th July 1918.

Ref. Sheet 28 S.W. 1/20,000

1. OPERATIONS (British)
   (a) **Infantry.** The northern end of LONG WOOD (N.29. .) was patrolled. An unoccupied piece of trench was discovered at N.29.a.25.15., connected by a track to an empty post on the edge of the wood at N.29.c.3.8. There were no signs of recent enemy occupation.
   (b) **Artillery.** The enemy's communications were vigorously harassed with a view to impeding the suspected relief of the 58th (Saxon) Division.
   (c) **Machine Guns.** Our machine guns fired 3,000 rounds on selected targets in M.35.b. and d.
   (d) **Trench Mortars.** Our T.M's fired against hostile M.G's.

2. OPERATIONS (German)
   (a) **Infantry.** Nil.
   (b) **Artillery.** MONT ROUGE again received considerable attention mainly from 10.5 cm. and 15 cm. Hows. During the evening bursts were fired onto the roads in M.16.a. and c, M.3.b. and d., M.13. and 14. The SCHERPENBERG was shelled at 9.55 a.m. and from 11.30 am to 12.30 pm.
   (c) **Machine Guns.** Active, from the direction of MONT KEMMEL. A M.G. at M.29.b.6.4. was silenced by Lewis Gun fire.

3. AERIAL ACTIVITY. At 4 a.m. 3 E.A. flew over our front line at 1,500 feet and dropped some small bombs, but did no damage. They were driven off by Lewis Gun fire.

4. ENEMY DEFENCES.
   (a) **Machine Guns.** One firing from M.29.b.6.4.
   (b) **Posts.** Unoccupied posts at N.29.a.25.15. and N.29.c.3.8.

5. MOVEMENT. Considerable movement of small parties at the farm at T.2.c.4.7.

for A.S. Cherry
Lieut.

H.Q. 35th Division,   Lieutenant-Colonel,
29th July 1918.   General Staff, 35th British Division.

FRENCH FRONT SITUATION from G.H.Q. 4 p.m. 22nd British Corps report capture of MONTAGNE DE BLIGNY after considerable hostile resistance. A few prisoners taken. Approximate line from BLIGNY runs JONQUERY - CHAMPVOISY and along South bank of OURCQ to old line. Enemy is offering strong resistance along line of the OURCQ. Captures of Fifth French Army (S.W. of REIMS) since 20th inst. 1750 prisoners 17 guns. In addition 71 French Guns have been recovered.

LATER. 10 p.m. 28th. The Line runs between LE PLESSIER HULEU and GRAND ROXOY-HILL 120 - WAILIE - GIVRAY - Station and locality of FERE EN TARDENOIS - MEUROY - SERGY - ROUCHERES - N. of CHAMPVOISON - N.W. and N. of ST. GEMME - between VILLERS AGON and BERTHENAY - HILL 250 - N.E. of OLIZY - S. edge of VILLE EN TARDENOIS and of CHAMBERGY - BLIGNY.

Summer Time.

	SUN.		MOON	
Date.	Rises.	Sets.	Rises.	Sets.
				1.55 am. (31st)
July 30.	5.13 am.	8.35 pm.	11.18 pm.	
July 31.	5.14 am.	8.33 pm.	11.56 pm.	3.12 am. (1st Aug)

35th DIVISION.
DAILY INTELLIGENCE SUMMARY No. 75.
From 6 a.m. 27 July to 6 a.m. 28 July 1918.

Ref. Sheet 28 S.W. 1/20,000.

1. **OPERATIONS (British)**
   (a) *Infantry.* A successful raid on enemy trenches at M.24.c.1.6. and M.29.b.95.95. was carried out at 11.30 p.m. 27th July by the left Brigade under cover of artillery, Machine Gun and Stokes Mortar barrage.

   The raid was made by two parties (totalling 4 Officers and 60 O.Rs.). Both parties entered the enemy's trench, which was held in strength, without difficulty and killed many of the occupants.

   Two wounded prisoners and one Machine Gun were brought back to our lines.

   Prisoners belonged to 103 R.I.R., 53th Division, --Normal-- (see Annexe).

   Our casualties were light.

   (b) *Artillery.* Destructive shoots on enemy post at M.29.c.25.35. were carried out by 4.5" Hows. on the 27th.

   Shell storms were directed on to selected targets.

   There was barrage and diversion fire in support of raid by Left Brigade.

   All batteries fired C.P. annihilating fire for 3 minutes at 3.30 a.m.

2. **OPERATIONS (German)**
   (a) *Infantry* Nil.
   (b) *Artillery.* Intermittent shelling of LOCRE, MONT ROUGE, M.21.d. and M.27.d.

   In connection with the raid the enemy put down a barrage behind the front line of Left Brigade at 11.35 p.m., consisting of 10.5 cm., 7.7 cm., and a few medium Light T.M's.

   At the same time there was slight retaliation on Centre Brigade front and the whole front of Right Brigade was shelled.

3. **AVIATION.** At 4.45 a.m. 1 E.A. flying low dropped 3 small bombs in M.23.b. Between 4.0 a.m. and 4.30 a.m. two E.A. flew over our line and returned in a S.E. direction. Two bombs were dropped in M.27.a.

4. **HOSTILE DEFENCES.**
   (a) *Trench Mortars.* A medium T.M. fired 12 rounds into valley at M.24.c.3.7. at 10 p.m. It appeared to be firing from about M.24.d.3.3.
   (b) *Posts.* An enemy post which appeared to have been recently occupied was found at M.28.d.90.25. by one of our patrols on night 26/27th July.

   A post with a sentry visible was located at the end of enemy track at M.24.c.65.00. Several direct hits were obtained by our 4.5" Hows. on this post.
   (c) *Wire.* A belt of wire consisting of a fence and barbed concertina was discovered running from M.28.d.8.3. to M.28.d.85.40.

5. **MOVEMENT.** At 5.30 a.m. 28th July, five men were seen at T.8.a.3.7. going S.E.

   Smoke of eight trains leaving and entering ARMENTIERES was seen during the day.

6. **MISCELLANEOUS.** When our barrage opened at 11.30 p.m. the enemy put up several white and orange lights followed by green and red lights which burst into two stars.

P. P. Harrison
Capt
for
Lieutenant-Colonel,
General Staff, 35th British Division.

H.Q. 35th Division,
28th July 1918.

TURN OVER/

INTERROGATION of TWO PRISONERS of 3rd and 10th Coys.
103rd R.I.R., 58th Division, captured about 11.30 p.m. 27th.
July 1918, at M.30.a.1.9. (Sheet 28).

ORDER OF BATTLE. Prisoners give the Order of Battle of 58th Division from North to South as 106th I.R., 103rd R.I.R. The 107th I.R. is in reserve in WERVICQ. The 11th Reserve Division is still in line South of the 58th Division.

INTENTIONS. Prisoners state that an offensive was planned for the 18th July but no reason has been given for its postponement; it is unlikely that a German offensive in this Sector will now take place for some time as they have heard that some of the crack divisions which were to be engaged have left this front.

DISPOSITIONS The 103rd R.I.R. has its first Battalion holding the line, the 3rd Battalion being in support, and the 2nd Battalion in reserve. The reserve Battalion is forward of NEUVE EGLISE; the position of the support Battalion could not be accurately described.

CONDITION of TRENCHES. The trench in M.30.a. is deep and protected by one belt of concertina wire; prisoners could not say whether the trench was continuous in a N.E. direction.

STRENGTH. Companies now average a trench strength of sixty, and each Company has six Light Machine Guns.

Casualties since the 58th Division have been in this Sector have been pretty severe, especially among the Artillery and are mainly attributable to our shrapnel. Last night (27/28th) prisoners saw no other Germans left alive after our raid. About the 25th June the 107th I.R. lost twelve men in one night in WERVICQ from our night bombing.

RELIEFS The 58th Division is expecting relief any day now, and talk was heard of the 238 R.I.R., 239 R.I.R. and 240 R.I.R. (52nd Res.Div.) being about to relieve them. The 11th Res.Division expects relief shortly afterwards.

The 1st Battalion R.I.R. came into line 23/24th July; date of relief uncertain.

ALARM. At 10 p.m. (British Time) 25th July, the 3rd Battn. 103rd R.I.R. was ordered to stand to as a British attack was said to be imminent.

Summer Time.

Date.	SUN Rises.	Sets.	MOON Rises.	Sets.
29 July.	5.12 am.	8.36 pm.	10.45 p.m.	1.55 am.(30th)
30 July.	5.13 am.	8.35 pm.	11.18 pm.	3.12 am.(31st)

FRENCH FRONT SITUATION. S.W. of RHEIMS 22nd British Corps assisted by French Tanks attacked on a front of 2½ k.m. and gained all objectives. Line now runs CHAUMUZY (German) - LA NEUVILLE AU LARIS(German) CUCHERY (French) - CUISLES (French) - LA MUQUERETTE (French)(N.E. of CUISLES) - PASSY GRIGNY - CHAMPVOISY - FERME VILLARDELLE (S.W. of CHAMPVOISY) - THE OURCQ between COURMANT and RONCHERES up to the MUNLIN - MONARD between CUGNY and NANTEUIL NOTRE DAME. French Cavalry reported in front of BLIGNY CHAUMERSY South of the VILLE EN TARDENOIS Road and VILLERS ARGON - ST.GEMME.

35th DIVISION.
DAILY INTELLIGENCE SUMMARY No.74.
Ref.Sheet 28 S.W.1/20,000: From 6 am.26 July to 6 am.27 July 1918.

1. OPERATIONS (British)
   (a) Infantry. 'No Man's Land' was actively reconnoitred by British patrols; no Germans were met with.
   (b) Artillery. A destructive shoot by 18-pdrs.was carried out on enemy posts at M.28.d.9.5., M.28.d.9.3., and M.29.c.05.20. Several direct hits were registered. A German battery at T.2.b.10.35. was also engaged with good results.
   (c) Machine Guns. Our M.G's. fired 1,000 rounds harassing fire on enemy tracks in M.30.d. Other targets were selected in M.29.d. and M.35.a. and harassed.

2. OPERATIONS (German)
   (a) Infantry.   Nil.
   (b) Artillery.   Quiet, with the exception of a considerable amount of activity against our battery positions. During the morning 10.5cm. Hows.registered on R.17.b., M.19.d., and M.20.a. and during the afternoon about 300 rounds 10.5 c.m. and 15 c.m. were fired on these areas.

   Between 9 a.m. and 10 a.m. the road from M.16.d.7.0. to M.16.d.2.7. was shelled by a 10.5 c.m.How.battery which was located by our observers at T.2.d.15.15. Our artillery were informed.

   The night was on the whole quiet. 10 rounds of gas shell fell on MONT ROUGE at 1.30 a.m.

3. AIRCRAFT.   E.A. inactive.
4. ENEMY DEFENCES.
   (a) Machine Guns.   A nest of three M.G's. is suspected at M.24.d.55.10.
   (b) Posts.   The barn at M.29.c.0.3 is strongly held. The wire has been recently strengthened and is now about 8 feet thick.
5. MOVEMENT.   Visibility was poor and little movement could be observed. In the early afternoon individual movement was seen on the CRUCIFIX CORNER - NEUVE EGLISE Road in T.13.d.

   Five trains were seen between LILLE and ARMENTIÈRES and one in ARMENTIÈRES.

H.Q. 35th Division,
27th July 1918.

A.J. Chesney Lieut.
for Lieutenant-Colonel,
General Staff, 35th British Division.

Summer Time.

Date	SUN Rises.	Sets.	MOON Rises.	Sets.
July 28.	5.10 am.	8.38 pm.	10.20 pm.	11.15 a.m.
" 29.	5.12 am.	8.36 pm.	10.45 pm.	12.35 p.m.

35th DIVISION.
DAILY INTELLIGENCE SUMMARY No. 73.

Ref. Sheet 28 S.W. 1/20,000.

1. **OPERATIONS (British)**
   (a) *Infantry.* A working party of 20 Germans was discovered in front of our left Subsector engaged in wiring. A small British patrol opened fire on them and hit two, dispersing the remainder and effectually stopping work. Later on in the night the enemy attempted to resume work but one of our listening posts opened fire and scattered them.
   (b) *Artillery.* Concentrations were fired at 10.12 p.m., 12.10 a.m., 2.23 a.m. and 3.4 a.m. on occupied areas in T.1.a.

2. **OPERATIONS (German)**
   (a) *Infantry* Nil.
   (b) *Artillery.* Active, mainly against our battery positions. M.22 received a good deal of attention.
   In the early evening the Germans registered with air bursts on M.13.b. and M.14.b. and at 9.15 p.m. opened a heavy destructive shoot on our Batteries in that area; 700 rounds 15 c.m. were expended. Some of the shells (10.5 c.m. and 15 c.m.) gave off a large cloud of white smoke which hung about for some seconds.
   At 3.35 a.m. a salvo of gas shells fell near the Intermediate Line in M.22.b.
   (c) *Trench Mortars.* At 1 p.m. three rifle grenades fell about S.4.b.4.2.

3. **AVIATION.** One E.A. succeeded in crossing our lines (low) and fired M.G. bursts into our trenches in M.24.c.

4. **ENEMY DEFENCES.**
   (a) *Machine Guns.* M.G's. fired from M.24.c.20.05., M.29.b.95.50 and M.30.a.75.40.
   (b) *Posts.* A post was located by one of our patrols at S.4.b.55.40.
   (c) *Work.* Sounds of digging were heard coming from approximately S.4.b.9.4.

5. **MOVEMENT.** At 11 p.m. five men were seen baling water from a trench at M.24.c.4.1. They were engaged by Lewis Guns.
   During the day three trains arrived in ARMENTIERES and six left it.

6. **MISCELLANEOUS.** At 10.45 p.m. numerous white and green flares were sent up from the direction of NEUVE EGLISE.
   Thick volumes of smoke were observed at T.1.d.7.3 (3.30pm)

for A.J. Chesney Lieut.
Lieutenant-Colonel,
General Staff, 35th British Division.

H.Q. 35th Division,
26th July 1918.

Summer Time.

Date	SUN Rises.	Sets.	MOON Rises.	Sets.
July 27.	5.9 am.	8.39 pm.	9.55 pm.	11.15 am. (28th)
July 28	5.10 am.	8.38 pm.	10.20 pm.	12.36 pm. (29th)

FRENCH FRONT SITUATION at 8 p.m. 25th. N. of the OURCQ the French have taken OULCHY LA VILLE - OULCHY LE CHATEAU and CUGNY (1 kilometre E. of the latter). Between OURCQ and the MARNE Front runs NANTEUIL N. DAME - W. of BRUYERES - S. edge of Wood E. of COINCY - BEUVARDES - LE CHARMEL - 1 kilometre S. of VINCELLES. REIMS Sector violent hostile attacks against our troops trying to recapture the old front line. No appreciable change in the position.

35th DIVISION.
DAILY INTELLIGENCE SUMMARY No. 72.
From 6 a.m. 24th July to 6 a.m. 25th July 1918.

Ref. Map 28 S.W. 1/20,000.

1. **OPERATIONS (British)**
   (a) **Infantry.** One of our patrols saw a party of 30 Germans crawling towards our lines on hands and knees in Indian file. The party occupied two posts at M.28.d.69.14. and M.28.d.9.5.
   Another patrol approached the German post at M.28.d.9.3. which was held by about 30 enemy and a sharp encounter ensued, one German being shot at 15 yards range. Our patrol (12 strong) had two men wounded and were forced to withdraw and the enemy then attempted to cut them off. The patrol leader remained behind with the two wounded men and these three are still missing.
   (b) **Artillery.** Our Artillery fired concentrations onto the woods in M.29.c. and M.35.a. 18-pdrs. fired 50 rounds on an ammunition dump at S.6.d.7.2. and caused a fire and explosion.
   (c) **Machine Guns.** Our M.G's carried out night firing on M.36.c. and d. and M.35.a & b.

2. **OPERATIONS (German)**
   Artillery. Quiet by night as well as by day. The SCHERPENBERG was intermittently shelled. German Heavy Artillery devoted some attention to MONT ROUGE.

3. **AVIATION.** E.A. rather more active than usual. In one case a formation of seven was seen.

4. **ENEMY DEFENCES.**
   (a) **Machine Guns.** One fired from M.29.c.30.85.
   (b) **Posts.** German posts are situated at M.28.d.69.14, M.28.d.9.5, and M.28.d.9.3.

5. **MOVEMENT.** Three parties, each of six men were seen at T.2.d.2.5. and another party of twelve men in T.1.d.
   The undermentioned trains were observed:-
   6.45 a.m. One in ARMENTIERES.
   9.25 a.m. ARMENTIERES to LILLE.
   6.45 a.m. ⎫
   7.20 a.m. ⎪
   8.30 a.m. ⎬ Northwards from STEENWERCK.
   1.10 p.m. ⎪
   5.50 p.m. ⎭

   5.30 p.m. ⎫
   7.10 p.m. ⎬ NIEPPE to STEENWERCK.
   8.10 p.m. ⎭

   10.20 a.m. NIEPPE towards ARMENTIERES.

6. **MISCELLANEOUS.** Fires were seen in the direction of ARMENTIERES at 11 p.m. and near NEUVE EGLISE at 2.15 a.m.

A. J. Cheney Lieut.
for Lieutenant-Colonel,
General Staff, 35th Division.

H.Q. 35th Division,
25th July 1918.

Summer Time.

	SUN.		MOON.	
Date.	Rises.	Sets.	Rises.	Sets.
July 25th.	5.6 a.m.	8.42 p.m.	9.11 p.m.	8.33 a.m. (26th)
" 26th.	5.8 a.m.	8.40 p.m.	9.34 p.m.	9.54 a.m. (27th)
" 27th.	5.9 a.m.	8.39 p.m.	9.56 p.m.	11.15 a.m. (28th)

35th DIVISION.
DAILY INTELLIGENCE SUMMARY No.71.
From 6 a.m. 23rd July to 6 a.m. 24th July 1918.

Reference Sheet 28 S.W. 1/20,000.

1. **OPERATIONS (British)**
   (a) <u>Infantry</u>. Our front was actively patrolled during the night, particular attention being paid to the area South of LOCRE in M.28.d., M.29.c., M.34.b., and M.35.a. The Cabaret at M.34.d.9.2. was reconnoitred and found to be occupied, and a German patrol, which was encountered at M.29.b.9.8., was fired on, one man being hit, No identification was obtained.
   (b) <u>Artillery</u>. Concentrations were fired during the night on Woods in M.29.c. and M.35.a. by our Field Artillery.
   Vigorous harassing fire was carried out on the enemy's roads and tracks throughout the period under review.
   At 1.50 a.m. our Field Artillery fired on their "barrage lines" in response to the S.O.S. Signal which was sent up on our Centre Subsector.

2. **OPERATIONS (German)**
   (a) <u>Infantry</u>. One hostile patrol was encountered by us at M.29.b.9.8. With the exception of this no operations have been undertaken by the German Infantry.
   (b) <u>Artillery</u>. Hostile Artillery displayed little activity during the day, but the shelling at night was both heavy and continuous.
   Between 9.45 p.m. and 11 p.m. the forward slopes of the hills from MT.NOIR to MT.ROUGE (inclusive) were very persistently shelled by guns of all calibres up to 15 c.m., a proportion of Mustard Gas shells being used. The greater part of this shelling was directed against MT.VIDAIGNE and the col between the latter hill and MT.NOIR.
   The area in M.14 was continuously bombarded from 3.30 p.m. to 7 p.m.
   At 1.35 a.m. the enemy's artillery put down a barrage on our forward trenches, extending from the southern outskirts of LOCRE to BRULOOZE CROSS ROAD M.24.a.8.3; fire eventually ceased at about 2.15 a.m.

3. **AVIATION.** Very slight activity in the air was displayed by the enemy.

4. **HOSTILE DEFENCES**
   (a) <u>Machine Guns</u>.were located at S.4.b.6.2.(suspected), M.29.b.55.15., M.30.a.00.85. and M.30.a.1.9.
   (b) <u>Trench Mortars</u>. A mortar is suspected at N.25.b.8.2. but its exact location has not yet been ascertained.
   (c) <u>Posts</u>. The cabaret at M.34.d.9.2. and a barn at M.29.c.05.20. are both reported by patrols to be occupied by the enemy, the latter being well defended by wire. An occupied post at M.29.d.05.83 and two unoccupied snipers posts at M.29.d.10.98. and M.29.d.15.90. were discovered. The second of these posts appears to have been recently used.
   (d) <u>Wire</u>. The barn at M.29.c.05.20.is surrounded by a strong belt of wire.
   There appear to be several old wire netting compounds in the S.W. corner of the area in M.29.c.

5. **MOVEMENT.** No unusual movement of troops, transport or trains has been observed.

6. **MISCELLANEOUS.**
   (a) The body of the man reported missing in para.1(a) of 35th Division Intelligence Summary No.64 dated 17th July 1918 was discovered in 'No Man's Land' by a patrol.
   (b) In addition to the Mustard Gas which was used by the enemy at 9.45 p.m., another type of Gas was also noticed on MT.VIDAIGNE. The smell of this gas was sweet, pleasant and not unlike ether. The eyes of men in the area subjected to the gas were immediately affected.

H.Q. 35th Division,
24th July 1918.

R.P.Harrison Capt

Lieutenant-Colonel,
General Staff, 35th British Division.

35th DIVISION.
DAILY INTELLIGENCE SUMMARY No.70.
From 5 a.m. 22nd July to 6 a.m. 23rd July 1918.

Reference Sheet 28 S.W. 1/20,000

1. OPERATIONS (British).
   (a) Infantry.   At 1.55 a.m. 23rd July, under cover of our 18-pdr. barrage, we raided the German post at M.29.d.1.9. Our party successfully passed through a belt of double concertina wire but found that the Germans had evacuated the post, leaving no identification. Throughout the operation there was no interference by the enemy.
   A patrol attempted to surprise the German post at M.24.c.3.1. but the garrison was alarmed by the barrage which came down in support of the raid in M.29.d. and fled before our men could reach them. They were pursued and fired on.
   (b) Artillery.   Our Artillery put down a barrage at 1.55 a.m. in support of the raid carried out in M.29.d.
   Vigorous harassing fire was continued all night and new work and suspected dumps were bombarded.
   (c) Trench Mortars. One of our Stokes Mortars opened fire on and drove off a German aeroplane.
2. OPERATIONS (German).
   (a) Infantry.   Nil.
   (b) Artillery.   Below normal, especially during the day. From 4 p.m. to 5 p.m. 15 c.m. Hows. fired 150 rounds onto M.14.d. H.V. guns were fairly active on our back areas.
   (c) Trench Mortars.

   At 12.45 a.m., a barrage consisting chiefly of Light Trench Mortar bombs was put down on our front line in response to two red lights.
3. AIRCRAFT   Nil.
4. ENEMY DEFENCES.
   (a) Machine Guns.   An M.G.(A.A.) is suspected at S.15.d.70.85.
   (b) Posts.   The post at M.24.c.3.1. is strongly held. An enemy Machine Gun crew occupy the post at M.34.b.35.70.
   (c) Condition of Ground. The valley in M.34.d. and M.35.c. is marshy and wet; progress is almost impossible.
   (d) At 10.30 a.m. flashes from a hostile battery were located at T.8.b. 60.60. and later on another one was fixed at T.2.d.20.40. In each case our H.A. were informed and took successful action.
5. MOVEMENT.   Slight movement was seen on the road in T.13.d.
   Trains were seen -
   Five going S.S.E. from NEUVE EGLISE.
   One approaching STEENWERCK from the direction of ARMENTIERES.

H.Q. 35th Division,   A.J. Chesney Lieut.
23rd July 1918.   for Lieutenant-Colonel,
   General Staff, 35th Division.

SUMMER TIME

Date.	Sun Rises.	Sets.	Moon Rises.	Sets.
24 July.	5.5 a.m.	8.43 p.m.	8.45 p.m.	5.52 a.m.(25th)
25 July.	5.6 a.m.	8.42 p.m.	9.11 p.m.	7.12 a.m.(26th)

NOTE: The farms at M.24.d.95.50. and M.34.b.2.9. are both referred to as BURGRAVE FARM on French Maps which have been taken over by 35th Division.   In future, the farm at M.34.b.2.9. only will be known as BURGRAVE FARM, the one at M.24.d.95.50. being referred to by its map reference until a name has been allotted.

FRENCH FRONT SITUATION.   As result of local operation between MOREUIL and MONTDIDIER 1st French Army captured MAILLY, SAUVILLERS, AUBVILLERS, and Hill to the South of it with some prisoners. Between the AISNE and the MARNE we have progressed S.E. of BRENY.

35th DIVISION.
DAILY INTELLIGENCE SUMMARY No. 50.
From 5 a.m. 21st July to 5 a.m. 22nd July 1918.

Reference Sheet 28 S.W. 1/20,000.

1. **OPERATIONS (British)**
   (a) <u>Infantry</u>. In addition to the usual patrolling, the positions of several German posts were reconnoitred.
   (b) <u>Artillery</u>. The enemy's forward communications and occupied areas were vigorously harassed throughout the night.
   Subsequent to a bombardment of the railway siding at N.32.c.0.0. by the Heavy Artillery during the afternoon of the 21st July, our Field Artillery directed bursts of fire onto the same target with the object of inflicting casualties and retarding the work of repair which might be in progress.

2. **OPERATIONS (German)**
   (a) <u>Infantry</u>. NIL.
   (b) <u>Artillery</u>. No unusual shelling is reported with the exception of a heavy barrage which was put down at 12.33 a.m. on our lines in M.29.a. and gradually worked southwards to M.28.central. No Infantry action developed. Our Field Artillery opened fire on their "barrage lines" at the request of the Infantry and hostile fire eventually ceased about 1.30 a.m.
   At 10.5 p.m. about 100 rounds (30% Mustard Gas) were fired onto the area in M.6. .& d. by 10.5 .m. Howitzers.
   (c) <u>Machine Guns</u>. In conjunction with the Artillery operations mentioned in para.2(b) (above) the enemy's machine guns put down a barrage about 150 yards behind our front line in M.29.a.

3. **AVIATION.** Out of a total of 12 German aeroplanes which attempted to cross the British lines during the day, eleven were driven off by machine guns, Lewis Gun and A.A.Gun fire, and forced to return to their own lines.

4. **HOSTILE DEFENCES.**
   (a) <u>Machine Guns</u>. The gun at M.24.c.85.25. was particularly active but was eventually silenced by rifle Grenade fire.
   (b) <u>Trench Mortars</u>. One active mortar was located at N.25.b.3.3.
   (c) <u>Posts</u>. were located by patrols at the undermentioned points:-
      M.24.c.3.1.
      M.34.d.75.20.(No signs of very recent occupation.)
   (d) <u>Wire</u>. The wire around the Wood in M.29.c. was reconnoitred and found to be strong on the Northern side but not so formidable on the Western side.

5. **MOVEMENT.** Considerable individual movement was observed during the day around the farm at T.2.c.4.7. and the siding at N.32.c.0.0.
   The former was engaged by 60-pdr.guns and direct hits obtained.
   The number of trains passing between LILLE and ARMENTIERES has not been abnormal.

6. **MISCELLANEOUS.** The German light signal for "barrage fire" would appear to be a series of orange flares.
   On the appearance of two red flares, the enemy's barrage perceptibly decreased in intensity and finally ceased.

G.W. Hodgkinson Capt.
Lieutenant-Colonel,
General Staff, 35th Division.

H.Q. 35th Division,
22nd July 1918.

FRENCH FRONT SITUATION at 6 p.m. 21st July. East of the SUIPPE we have recaptured our old front line. Further West we have advanced in places. Between RHEIMS and the MARNE heavy fighting continues. The line runs MARFAUX (German) - Western edge of COURTON WOOD - N. of BELVAL - REUIL. the enemy holds North bank of MARNE but the French have crossed at COURCELLES (S.W. of TEELOUP). Further West our advance continues. The line runs HARTEVES - MONT ST.PERE - EPIEDS - Western edge of WOOD S.E. of ROCOURT - . ROCOURT LA ROIX - BRENY North of the OURCQ heavy fighting. We hold MONT GRU - LE PLESSIER - HULUE - TIGNY - on outskirts of BUZANCY - COURCELLES - MERCIN - PERNANT. Violent hostile counter attacks S. of RHEIMS and N. of the OURCQ.

35th DIVISION
DAILY INTELLIGENCE SUMMARY No. 28.
From 6 a.m. 20th July to 6 a.m. 21st July 1918.

Ref. Sheet 28 S.W. 1/20,000.

1. **OPERATIONS (British)**
   (a) *Infantry.* During the night our line North of BURGRAVES FARM (M.34.b.2.9.) was slightly advanced, without opposition from the enemy.
   The outpost line in this neighbourhood now runs from North to South as follows:- M.28.d.70.70.- M.28.d.35.35.- M.28.d.28.28.- M.28.d.3.1.- M.34.b.2.8.- M.34.b.15.65 - M.34.b.20.15.(BURGRAVE FARM inclusive to us.)
   The Divisional front was actively patrolled throughout the night, but the enemy was not encountered in the open.
   (b) *Artillery.* Harassing fire has been vigorously carried out during the period under review and shell storms have been directed on occupied areas by our Field Artillery.
   An occupied hut at S.5.d.9.7. and an active trench mortar at N.25.c.3.8. were engaged by 4.5" Howitzers; the mortar was silenced.
   The railway siding at N.32.c.0.0. was shelled at intervals throughout the night.

2. **OPERATIONS (German)**
   (a) *Infantry.* Nil.
   (b) *Artillery* The activity displayed by hostile Artillery was slight during the day but increased at dusk, shelling being chiefly directed against our roads and tracks. MT. ROUGE was persistently shelled throughout the afternoon and evening by 10.5 c.m. and 15 c.m. Howitzers.
   LOCRE was subjected to heavy bursts of fire at intervals during the early part of the night.

3. **AVIATION.** Very slight activity has been displayed by the enemy. Single German Machines have been observed at intervals either crossing or patrolling our lines.

4. **HOSTILE DEFENCES.**
   (a) *Machine Guns* Nil.
   (b) *Trench Mortars* were located at the undermentioned points:-
       N.25.b. (Not exactly located) - Active.
       N.25.c.3.8. - Active.
   (c) *Posts.* One post located by patrol at S.4.b.8.3.
   (d) *Guns.* At 10.45 a.m. flashes of 10.5 c.m. Howitzers were observed at T.8.b.6.6. and a battery of Howitzers of the same calibre was located by flash at T.2.d.4.1.

5. **MOVEMENT** Considerable movement has been observed throughout the day in the vicinity of the farm at T.2.c.4.7.
   The following movement of trains was seen:-
   5.30 a.m. one train ARMENTIERES - LILLE
   5.30 p.m. "   "   STEENWERCK - NEUVE EGLISE.
   5.10 p.m. "   "   ARMENTIERES - LILLE.
   7 p.m.   "   "   Shunting in ARMENTIERES.
   7.30 p.m. "   "   NIEPPE - NEUVE EGLISE.

6. **MISCELLANEOUS.**
   (a) A lighthouse (similar to one used at sea) was observed operating from a point on a T.B. of 138° from M.22.d.03.80. about 5 miles East of NEUVE EGLISE.
   (b) A signalling lamp was seen flashing from a high position - possibly STEENWERCK CHURCH.
   (c) At 1.20 a.m. gas (possibly Blue Cross) was detected drifting across M.20.d. from a S.E. direction. There was no gas bombardment of this area at the time.

for C.W. Hodgkinson
Capt

H.Q. 35th Division,
21st July 1918.
Lieutenant-Colonel,
General Staff, 35th Division.

French Front Situation at 6 p.m. yesterday. MERCIN - VAUX 1 k.m.S.of BERZY - LE SEC 1 k.m.S.of VILLEMONTOIRE - PARCY TIGNY - MERGIER HULEUE - FOSET ST.ALBIN - BOIS DE LATILLY - SOMMELANS - MONTHIERS - 1 k.m. E. of BOURESCHES - RIVER MARNE - E.edge of TROUL - BELVAR - W.edge of BOIS DE COURTON - E.edge of MARFAUX - E.edge of BOUILLY - ST.EUPHRAISE. Over 20,000 prisoners and 400 guns.

35th DIVISION.
DAILY INTELLIGENCE SUMMARY No. 67.
From 6 a.m. 19th July to 6 a.m. 20th July 1918.

Reference Sheet 28 S.W. 1/20,000.

1. **OPERATIONS (British)**
   (a) **Infantry.** One of our patrols reconnoitred an enemy post at M.24.d.0.3. and finding it to be held by about twelve of the enemy, they attacked it and succeeded in forcing an entrance. A sharp fight ensued during which several casualties were inflicted on the enemy and three of our men were wounded, but owing to the strength of the hostile garrison, no identification was obtained.
   Another patrol went and lay in wait for the enemy to come and occupy the German post at M.28.d.5.3., but none appeared.
   (b) **Artillery.** Our 18-pdrs. engaged a suspected T.M. at M.29.b.8.2. and several suspected ammunition dumps.
   During the night shell storms were fired onto selected targets. The following fires were caused by our guns:-
           4.25 p.m.   S.12.b.
           5.40 p.m.   S.17.d.
           6.20 p.m.   M.35.a.2.8.

2. **OPERATIONS (German)**
   (a) **Infantry.** Nil.
   (b) **Artillery.** The activity of the German Artillery was below normal during the day. At night the enemy devoted a lot of attention to the roads and tracks in our Right Subsector and to the communication trench in M.20.d.
   Between 10 a.m. and 12 noon 19th July, 100 rounds were fired onto M.23.b.7.9. by 15 c.m. Howitzers.

3. **AIRCRAFT**   Activity normal. Several E.A. were driven off by our A.A. Lewis Gun fire.

4. **ENEMY DEFENCES.**
   (a) **Machine Guns.** M.G's. are reported to have fired from M.24.c.7.2, M.24.d.05.30. and S.4.b.8.2.
   (b) **Posts.** Post at M.24.d.05.30. was occupied by about 12 Germans. Post at M.28.d.5.3 was not occupied. This post, however, was found to contain several traps which consisted of German equipment, boots, etc, connected by wires to sacks of explosive concealed in a shellhole.
   (c) **Wire.** The post at M.24.d.05.30. is covered by two strong belts of concertina wire, one on the northern side and one on the western.
   (d) **Condition of Ground.** Some old trenches in front of our line in M.34.b. which had been for some time abandoned, were explored by a patrol. The trenches were found to be deep and very wet in parts. About 50 yards South of the trench is a row of weak concertina wire over grown by crops.

5. **MOVEMENT.** Small parties of Germans were several times observed to enter the Farm at T.2.c.4.6.

6. **MISCELLANEOUS.** At 8 p.m. a hostile kite balloon was seen adrift.

   Addendum to para.1 (a)   Our line at BURGRAVE FARM (M.34.b.2.9.) was slightly advanced during the night. Posts have been established at M.28.d.28.28, M.28.d.3.1., M.34.b.2.8., M.34.b.15.65.

                                              A.J. Chesney Lieut
H.Q. 35th Division,   for   Lieutenant-Colonel,
20th July 1918.   General Staff, 35th Division.

                                                    TURN OVER/

SUMMER TIME.

	SUN		MOON	
Date.	Rises.	Sets.	Rises.	Sets.
21st July.	5.1 am.	8.46 pm.	6.59 pm.	3.22 am.(22nd)
22nd July.	5.2 am.	8.45 pm.	7.42 pm.	4.34 am.(23rd)

NEWS.
    Wire from X Corps, timed 12.32 p.m. 20th July, reads:-

    French Front. Situation this morning between AISNE and MARNE. MONTAGNE DE PARIS (CREST N. of VAUXBUIN) almost entirely to French - Ridge South of VAUXBUIN - BERZY - SACONIN - advance posts at VILLEMONT - OIRE - RIDGE W. of HARTENNES - N. of PLESSIER - HULUE - DILLY - ROZET - VICHEL - NANTEUIL - WOOD N.W. of LATILLY - SOMMELANS - W. of MONTHIERS - BELLEAU. South of the MARNE we advanced about 1½ kilometres on the approximate front STAGNAN to FESRIGNY. The line runs along South edge of WOOD N. of COMBLIZY and North of Wood N.W. of FESRIGNY.

5th DIVISION.

DAILY INTELLIGENCE SUMMARY No. 66.
From 6 a.m. 18th July to 6 a.m. 19th July 1918.

Reference Sheet 28 S.W. 1/20,000.

1. **OPERATIONS (British).**

    (a) <u>Infantry</u>. Our patrols were out in front of various points along the divisional front but did not encounter any enemy.

    (b) <u>Artillery</u>. Our guns were particularly active last night against the enemy's communications; particular attention was paid to the area between 1,000 and 2,000 yards behind the front line.
    A shoot was carried out on the camouflaged objects at S.6.d.8.4.

    (c) <u>Trench Mortars</u>. At 8.30 p.m. one of our Stokes Mortars opened fire at a low flying aeroplane and drove it off.
    At 1.30 a.m. 40 rounds were fired in conjunction with the raid on our left.

    (d) <u>Machine Guns</u>. 2,000 rounds were fired onto M.30.a.

2. **OPERATIONS (German).**

    (a) <u>Infantry</u>. Nil.

    (b) <u>Artillery</u>. Hostile artillery was rather more active.
    During the morning 15 c.m. Hows. shelled the forward slopes of MONT NOIR intermittently. Retaliation for our bombardment in connection with the raid at 1.30 a.m. was fairly heavy on the REDOUBT and INTERMEDIATE lines.

3. <u>AIRCRAFT</u>. E.A. flew low over our lines several times.
    Two formations of five and one of three machines were seen. At 9 p.m. one German machine reconnoitred our Battery positions from a low altitude; this is the third night in succession that this has occurred.

4. <u>ENEMY'S DEFENCES</u>.

    (a) <u>Machine Guns</u>. An M.G. is suspected at M.30.a.4.7. Another M.G. fired on one of our patrols from M.28.d.9.4.

    (b) <u>Posts</u>. An enemy post is located at M.28.d.5.4. strongly wired with two rows of concertina. A sniper fires from here.

    (c) <u>Condition of Ground</u>. The ground east of the LOCRE - BAILLEUL Road about BURGRAVES FARM is reported to be marshy. "No Man's Land" in M.29.b. is also very wet. Weeds and grass are a foot high.

    (d) <u>Dumps</u>. A camouflaged ammunition dump is suspected at T.2.a.75.25

    (e) <u>Artillery</u>. (information from air photographs).
    Enemy has pushed five deep sapheads out of the wood on the top of KEMMEL HILL between 28 N.25.d.38.55. and d.82.75. thence trenches lead back through the wood to sunken road in N.25.d. These are evidently Artillery O.P's as they command a view of our lines in a N., N.W., and W. direction.
    The trench just behind the crest of the hill from N.26.c.18.65. to c.00.95. is used as a means of approach to an O.P. at N.26.b.03.90. which commands our lines to the N.W.

5. <u>MOVEMENT</u>. One horse transport was seen in M.36.d. proceeding towards DRANOUTRE. Movement of individuals was above normal and was chiefly observed round the Farm at T.2.c.4.6. where a dump is suspected and the house at T.1.d.9.9. which is marked with a red cross. The screened road in T.8.a. and the track in T.2.c. are used a good deal.

TURN OVER/

6. MISCELLANEOUS. At 1.30 p.m. one of our aeroplanes dropped a bomb on a German ammunition dump in the vicinity of MOUNT KEMMEL and blew it up.

7. GERMAN ORDER OF BATTLE. Three prisoners of the 23rd BAVARIAN R.I.R., 16th BAVARIAN DIVISION, captured about 1.30 a.m. this morning at N.14.c.1.2. by the Division on our left state that SAXON troops are in line South of their Division. This tends to confirm the relief of the 121st Division by the 58th (SAXON) Division.

H.Q. 35th Division,
19th July 1918.

A.J. Chesney
for Lieutenant-Colonel,
General Staff, 35th Division.

NOMENCLATURE. The following names have been approved and will be taken into use forthwith:-

CROSS ROADS at M.17.d.1.2. - STARFISH CROSS ROADS.
WOOD near REDAN CAMP, M.24.c. - REDAN CAMP.
Road from LOCRE to
BRULOOZE CABARET, M.24.a.8.3. - GORDON ROAD.

NEWS.
Wire from X Corps, timed 7.13 p.m. 18th July, reads:-

Progress of French attack on MARNE - SOISSONS front reported at midday as follows. BOURESCHES - TORCY - HAUTEVESNES - MONNES - NEUILLY - ST.FRONT - CHOUY - East edge of HAUTWISON WOOD (uncertain) east edge of MOLLOY WOOD - VIERZY - SACONIN) OSLY) HILL 140. No change on RHEIMS front. Situation at 2 p.m. unofficial. The French hold the whole of the MONTAGNE DE PARIS (S. of SOISSONS). In this region a French Corps took 4,000 prisoners and 30 guns. The French hold BERZY and are on line of CRISE RIVER where the German Artillery are retiring. The 1st and 16th French Armies have advanced 10 k.m.

SUMMER TIME.

	SUN.		MOON.	
Date.	Rises.	Sets.	Rises.	Sets.
July 20.	5.0 a.m.	8.45 p.m.	6.8 p.m.	1.25 a.m.(21st)
" 21.	5.1 a.m.	8.45 p.m.	6.59 p.m.	2.18 a.m.(22nd)

35th DIVISION
DAILY INTELLIGENCE SUMMARY No.65.
From 6 a.m. 17th July to 6 a.m. 18th July 1918.

Reference Sheet 28 S.W. 1/20,000.

1. OPERATIONS (British)
   (a) Infantry. The ground in front of our lines was steadily patrolled throughout the night. No enemy were encountered.
   (b) Artillery. Three bombardments of the enemy's lines were carried out last night and vigorous harassing fire was maintained from 10 p.m. to 3 a.m.
   On the afternoon of 17th July, 18-pounders engaged some camouflaged objects at S.6.d.8.4. and obtained several direct hits.
   (c) Trench Mortars.   Nil.

2. OPERATIONS (German)
   (a) Infantry. At 2 a.m. 17th July, the enemy opened a heavy bombardment of our front and support trenches and heavy machine gun fire on our front line.
   At 3 a.m. a party of Germans, the strength of which was estimated at 30, left the enemy's line at S.4.d.2.7. and advanced across 'No Man's Land'. The party was dispersed by our Lewis Gun fire with the exception of what appeared to be an officer and six men who apparently reached the British trenches at about S.4.central.
   (b) Artillery. The enemy's artillery was quiet and made little reply to our night bombardments except on our right subsector where retaliation was more intense.
   At 3.5 a.m. the enemy barraged the LOCRE - BRULOOZE (M.24.a.8.3.) Road, MONT ROUGE and CANADA CORNER (M.17.c.5.4.) for half an hour.
   During the day LOCRE was shelled intermittently, and the areas M.21.b. and M.22.a. were lightly shelled with Yellow Cross Gas shell and H.E. during the night.

3. AIRCRAFT. E.A. were rather more active than yesterday, chiefly in the early morning and just before dusk. At 8.30 p.m. a hostile machine flew exceptionally low over MONT ROUGE and MONT NOIR, the observer being distinctly seen, and was eventually driven off by Lewis Gun and rifle fire.

4. ENEMY DEFENCES.
   (a) Machine Guns. One gun suspected at M.30.a.7.5.
   (b) Trench Mortars. Recent air photographs show the following possible Trench Mortar positions. These positions should be carefully watched as confirmation is required:-

   M.30.b.15.75.   S.4.d.60.05.
   M.35.a.65.70.   S.4.d.65.40.
   M.35.a.90.98.   S.4.d.80.65.
   M.35.b.15.72.   S.4.d.85.55.
   S.4.d.28.18.   S.5.c.35.25.
   S.4.d.50.40.   S.10.b.18.95.

5. MOVEMENT.   Movement was again observed in T.1.d.

6. MISCELLANEOUS. During the German barrage this morning the enemy fired a number of double red lights both in the forward area and

TURN OVER/

from repeating stations behind.
      A large fire was seen at S.8.c.5.5. at 9 p.m.; it continued burning until midnight.

H.Q. 35th Division,   for   A. J. Chesney
18th July 1918.   Lieutenant-Colonel, Lieut
                                             General Staff, 35th Division.

   NOTE:- All samples of soap found on German prisoners should be forwarded to H.Q. 35th Division.

                        Summer Time.
        SUN.   MOON.
Dte.   Rises.   Sets.   Rises.   Sets.

19 July. 4.59 a.m. 8.49 p.m.   5.10 p.m.   1.25 a.m.(20th)
20 July. 5.0 a.m. 8.48 p.m.   6.8 p.m.   2.18 a.m.(21st)

FRENCH FRONT.

      X Corps wire, timed 1.3 p.m. 18th July, reads:-

           French Front.   This morning the French attacked between the AISNE and the MARNE.   First reports show the following objectives taken TORCY - BUSSIARES - HAUTEVESNES - ST.GENGOULPHE CHEVILLON - MONNES - MACOGNY - PASSY - MARIZY STE.GENEVIEVE NOROY - ANCIENVILLE LOUATRE - FERME - BEAUREBAIRS - MISSY - AUX - BOIS - SACONIN - BREVIL PERNANT - HILL 140 N. of FONTENOY. More than 1,200 prisoners are reported captured so far.

           There is no change on the remainder of the front.

35th DIVISION.
DAILY INTELLIGENCE SUMMARY No.64.
From 6 a.m. 16th July to 6 a.m. 17th July 1918.

Reference Sheet 28 S.W. 1/20,000

1. **OPERATIONS** (British)

(a) **Infantry.** A small patrol located an enemy post in the Trench at M.28.d.98.42. and attempted to rush it but were held up by a belt of new wire. Two Germans who were seen to hurriedly leave the post, were fired on and believed hit. The German trench was held by about 20 men. One man of our patrol failed to return and is missing.
   The northern point of the wood in N.29.c. was also reconnoitred, but no signs of occupation were seen.
   A German listening post was discovered at S.4.b.4.2. by one of our patrols; the garrison withdrew on the approach of our men.
   Further information concerning the enemy's defences was obtained by other patrols (See para.4.)

(b) **Artillery.** A bombardment of the enemy's lines was carried out at 3.10 a.m. 17th July, in retaliation for the activity of the enemy's artillery at that time.
   About 12.30 p.m. 16th July our artillery opened fire on the hostile trench in M.29.b. and obtained two direct hits; cries of wounded were heard.
   Throughout the night shell storms were fired onto selected targets.

(c) **Machine Guns.** 1,500 rounds were fired at a suspected Machine Gun nest in M.24.c.

2. **OPERATIONS** (German)

(a) **Infantry.** NIL.

(b) **Artillery.** The German artillery was quiet on the whole. MONT ROUGE and MONT NOIR were intermittently shelled during the 24 hours.
   Between 2.45 a.m. and 3.30 a.m. this morning the enemy put down an intense artillery and T.M. bombardment on the front of the LOCRE and SCHERPENBERG Sectors. A large proportion of Blue Cross gas shell was used.
   The vicinity of R.11.central was steadily shelled from 6 p.m. to 3 a.m.

(c) **Trench Mortars.** Hostile Trench Mortars took part in the bombardment at 2.45 a.m. and also fired a few rounds onto LOCRE HOSPICE(M.29.b.6.9.) during the day.

(d) **Machine Guns.** Exceptionally quiet.

3. **AVIATION.** No special activity. E.A. crossed our lines for the most part singly.

4. **ENEMY DEFENCES.**

(a) **Posts.** A post located at M.28.d.98.42. is protected by a belt of wire 4' high and 10' broad. Other posts were located at S.4.b.4.2., S.4.b.7.2., S.4.b.8.5., M.34.d.8.3., and M.34.b.3.7.

(b) **Wire.** The wire in front of the German outposts in S.4.b. is distributed and thin.

5. **MOVEMENT.** Movement was rather below normal. At 5.20 pm.six men were seen at T.1.b.6.0. They were fired on by our 4.5" Hows.and dispersed.
The following trains were observed:-
7.15 am. One steaming from ARMENTIERES to LILLE.
11.53 am. One shunting in ARMENTIERES.

6. MISCELLANEOUS.
During the bombardment at 2.45 a.m. lights were seen as follows:-
Double red, double green, double yellow, and white parachute lights. The latter burnt brilliantly for three minutes.

A. J. Chesney Lieut

H.Q. 35th Division,   for   Lieutenant-Colonel,
17th July 1918.   General Staff, 35th Division.

Date.	SUN. Rises.	Sets.	MOON. Rises.	Sets.
18 July.	4.56 am.	8.51 pm.	3.1 pm.	12.10 am. (19th)
19 July.	4.58 am.	8.50 pm.	4.6 pm.	12.44 am. (20th)

GENERAL NEWS.

Wire from X Corps, timed 10.35 a.m. 17th July :-

French Front situation. In CHAMPAGNE yesterday all enemy attacks were repulsed, and our line was advanced in places. Further South enemy attacked strongly in direction of EPERNAY. At 6 p.m. line here was approximately as follows:- BELVAL - Clearing in Wood S.W. of BELVAL - W. of BOURSAULT - S. of FESRIGNY - COMBLIZY - STAGNAN - CREZANCY - GLAND.

Wire from X Corps, timed 1.10 p.m. 17th July :-

French Front situation at 6 a.m. today. GLAND - N. of CREZANCY - S. of St.AGNAN - COMBLIZY - NESLE - LE REPONS - two kilometres N.W. of BOURSAULT - two kilometres E. of REVIL - N.W. of NANTEUIL Eastern edge of POURCY.

35th DIVISION
DAILY INTELLIGENCE SUMMARY No. 63.
From 6 a.m. 15th July to 6 a.m. 16th July 1918.

Reference Sheet 28 S.W. 1/20,000.

1. **OPERATIONS (British).**

   (a) **Infantry.** During the night patrols reconnoitred "No Man's Land" and the enemy's posts at several points, chief of these being:-
   (i) The road from M.28.d.7.7. - d.90.55
   (ii) M.29.c.10.80.
   (iii) Posts at M.34.d.90.15.
   In the case of (iii) our patrol was heard moving through the crops and fired on by a machine gun situated in the vicinity.

   (b) **Artillery.** Sensitive points and occupied areas were vigourously harassed by Field Artillery from 11 a.m. onwards throughout the day, and shell storms were directed on to similar areas at irregular intervals during the night.
   Hostile batteries in T.1.c., T.1.d., S.6.d and M.36.c. were engaged with gas and H.E. by 4.5" Howitzers, ammunition being set on fire at the position in S.6.d.
   An active battery at T.1.a.0.8 was also heavily bombarded by 4.5" Howitzers.

2. **OPERATIONS (German).**

   (a) **Infantry.** NIL.

   (b) **Artillery.** The usual activity was displayed by the German Artillery during the period under review.
   The forward slope of the ridge between MONT NOIR and MONT ROUGE was very persistently shelled during the day and considerable attention was paid to the village of LOCRE.

3. **AVIATION.** On four occasions single enemy aeroplanes flew over the Mts. ROUGE, VIDAIGNE and NOIR, and our lines were several times patrolled by machines which were engaged by Lewis Gun and Machine Gun fire.
   Hostile activity in the air has not been abnormal.

4. **HOSTILE DEFENCES.** NIL.

5. **MOVEMENT.** Slight individual movement was observed during the day in T.2, 7 and 8.
   The following movement of trains was seen:-
   One train from ARMENTIERES to LILLE.
   " " STEENWERCK to ARMENTIERES.
   " " ARMENTIERES to STEENWERCK.
   " " LAVENTIE to ARMENTIERES.

6. **MISCELLANEOUS.**

   (a) At 12.30 p.m. a German soldier belonging to the 41st Bn. LANDWEHR Foot Artillery approached our lines at M.34.d.5.0. and gave himself up.

   (b) The German Signal for "LENGTHEN RANGE" appears to be a rocket bursting into two red lights.

   C.W. Hodgkinson
   Capt.

H.Q. 35th Division,   Lieutenant-Colonel,
16th July 1918.   General Staff, 35th Division.

	SUN.			MOON.	
Date.	Rises.	Sets.		Rises.	Sets.
17 July.	4.56 am.	8.51 pm.		3.1 pm.	12.10 am.(18th)
18 July.	4.58 am.	8.50 pm.		4.6 pm.	12.44 am.(19th)

SUMMER TIME.   TURN OVER/

Annexe to 35th Division Intelligence Summary No.63 dated 16th July.

INTERROGATION of a PRISONER of the IInd. Battery, 41st
LANDWEHR FOOT ARTILLERY Battalion, who gave himself up at
M.34.d.5.0. (Sheet 28) about 12.30 p.m. 15th July 1918.

INTENTIONS.

Prisoner states that one of his Officers told him about 26th June that the offensive in this Sector was to start between the 15th and 20th July.

One of his comrades was also told the same thing by the O.C. IIIrd Battery.

Prisoner states that he returned from hospital on 12th July and saw a large number of troops concentrating round BAILLEUL by night and was told that sixteen Divisions were being assembled. Prisoner asserts, however, that the total ammunition at his battery position only numbers about 700 rounds, including 300 gas shell. The attack is to be launched on both sides of MOUNT KEMMEL, and is to be pushed through to a great depth.

ORDER of BATTLE.

Prisoner gives the order of battle from North to South as 118 I.R. (56 Division), 156 I.R., 10 R.I.R., 22 I.R.(11 Res.Division).

He is very vague and his statements do not appear to be at all reliable.

HEADQUARTERS.

The Battalion Headquarters of the line Battalions 156 I.R. and 10 R.I.R. are close together in T.7.c.

SPANISH INFLUENZA.

Spanish Influenza, which goes by the name of "SPANISCHE GRIPPE", has deprived his battery of about 50% of its effective strength for some weeks past, and all units have suffered from its effects.

Prisoner had not heard the rumours of the death of HINDENBURG.

35th DIVISION.
DAILY INTELLIGENCE SUMMARY No. 62.
From 6 a.m. 14th July to 6 a.m. 15th July 1918.

Reference Sheet 28 S.W. 1/20,000.

1. **OPERATIONS (British).**

   (a) **Infantry.** At 11.45 p.m. 14th July a small raid was carried out on the German positions North of LOCRE CAMP (M.24.d.) under cover of an Artillery, Stokes Mortar and Machine Gun barrage.

   Considerable difficulty was experienced on the right in forcing a way through the wire, but this was eventually overcome by means of a bangalore torpedo. On reaching the objective it was found that the enemy had evacuated his posts.

   (b) **Artillery.** Heavy and Field Artillery fired in support of our raid in M.24.d., the latter putting down a close barrage to cover the advance of the raiding Party, and the former bombarding selected targets to the rear and flanks of the objective.

   Harassing fire was directed on to roads, tracks and sensitive points by our Field Artillery at irregular intervals throughout the day and night.

2. **OPERATIONS (German)**

   (a) **Infantry.** - NIL.

   (b) **Artillery.** Hostile Artillery has displayed more activity than usual during the twenty-four hours. LOCRE and LOCRE HOSPICE (M.29.b.6.9.) have been subjected to bursts of fire, and the range of hills from MONT NOIR to SCHERPENBERG have been intermittently shelled with guns of all calibres up to 15 c.m.

   About thirty rounds of Blue Cross Gas shell were fired onto battery positions in M.20.b.& d. during the night by 7.7 c.m. guns.

   Retaliatory fire for our raid in M.24. was not heavy, but came down promptly and consisted of 7.7 c.m., 10.5 c.m. and T.M. shells.

   Between 11 a.m. and 1 p.m. our left Infantry Brigade Headquarters was bombarded by a species of Heavy Trench Mortar. The shell could not be heard travelling through the air, and the burst was very local.

3. **AVIATION.** Practically no activity was displayed by the enemy.

4. **HOSTILE DEFENCES.**

   Posts. A Patrol reports that a German Post exists at the undermentioned point :-

   M.29.d.23.95.

   On the night 13/14th July, two posts were discovered about 50 yards North West of the CABARET (M.34.d.9.2.)

5. **MISCELLANEOUS.**

   A large number of light signals were observed on the nights 13/14th and 14/15th July, but the meanings of the majority of them could not be ascertained.

   The golden rain rocket appears to be a signal for artillery fire, and at 3 a.m. 14th July a heavy barrage was put down in response to the following :-

   Two red over two yellow over two yellow fan-shaped lights.

   It was noticed that several of these signals were passed back by relay posts, one of the most important of these being the summit of MONT KEMMEL.

H.Q. 35th Division,
15th July 1918.

for Lieutenant-Colonel,
General Staff, 35th Division.

Summer Time.

Date	SUN Rises	Sets	Date	MOON Rises	Sets
16 July.	4.55 am.	8.52 pm.	17 July.	1.55 am.	11.44 am.
17 July.	4.56 am.	8.51 pm.	18 July.	3.1 am.	12.10 am.

35th DIVISION.
DAILY INTELLIGENCE SUMMARY No. 61.
From 6 a.m. 13th July to 6 a.m. 14th July 1918.

Reference Sheet 28 S.W. 1/20,000.

1. **OPERATIONS (British)**

   (a) **Infantry.** Several reconnaissances of German posts were made during the night.

   One patrol, consisting of one N.C.O. and ? men encountered a party of thirty Germans who were apparently forming up prior to carrying out a raid. Our patrol withdrew, with the intention of warning the garrison of the trench, but were pursued by the enemy into a barn or hut at about M.28.d.85.50. At this juncture, a short fight with bombs ensued: the patrol leader was wounded and the remaining three members of the patrol are missing.

   (b) **Artillery.** Vigourous harassing fire was carried out by our Field Artillery during the 24 hours.

   Bursts of fire were directed on known occupied areas at intervals throughout the day.

2. **OPERATIONS (German)**

   (a) **Infantry.** At 2 a.m. about twenty of the enemy attempted to raid our post at M.24.c.0.3. After throwing a number of bombs, the enemy rushed the post, but did not succeed in effecting an entrance, and were eventually forced to retire to their own line.

   (b) **Artillery.** Hostile artillery has been unusually active on our left and centre Subsectors during the period under review.

   At 1 a.m. 14th July an intense barrage was put down on LOCRE and our front line to the South-east of that village by guns of all calibres up to 15 c.m. Firing continued with less intensity until 3.55 a.m.

   Between 3 a.m. and 4 a.m., MONT ROUGE, CANADA CORNER (M.17.c.6.5) and the BRULOOZE (M.24.a.8.3.) - LOCRE Road were subjected to heavy shelling by 7.7 c.m. guns 10.5 and 15 c.m. Howitzers.

   At 10.30 a.m. 100 rounds were fired on to the area in M.16.d. by 15 c.m. Howitzers, and LOCRE and the SCHERPENBERG were shelled intermittently throughout the day.

3. **AVIATION.** Hostile aeroplanes attemtpted to cross our lines on several occasions, but the activity displayed by the enemy has not been unusual.

4. **HOSTILE DEFENCES**

   (a) **Machine Guns.** One M.G. located at M.24.d.1.2.

5. **MOVEMENT.** Slight individual movement was observed during the day in a field in T.13.b. and also in the vicinity of a camouflaged road at T.8.c.2.9.

   Three trains were observed on the LILLE - ARMENTIERES line, one travelling East and the remaining two in a Westerly direction.

   C.W. Hodgkinson
   Capt.
   for Lieutenant-Colonel,
   General Staff, 35th Division.

H.Q. 35th Division,
14th July 1918.

	SUN			MOON	
Date	Rises	Sets.	Date	Rises	Sets.
15 July.	4.54 am.	8.53 pm.	16 July.	12.50 am.	11.21 am.
16 July	4.55 am.	8.52 pm.	17 July.	1.55 am.	11.44 am.

Summer Time.

35th DIVISION,
DAILY INTELLIGENCE SUMMARY No. 60.
From 6 a.m. 12th July to 6 a.m. 13th July 1918.

Reference Sheet 28 S.W. - 1/20,000.

1. **OPERATIONS (British)**

   (a) Infantry. The Divisional front was patrolled throughout the night with the object of obtaining further information regarding the dispositions of the enemy.

   (b) Artillery. Throughout the day and night the enemy's roads and forward communications were intermittently harassed by our Field Artillery and bursts of fire were directed on known occupied areas.
   250 rounds were fired on to BIRMINGHAM CAMP WOOD (M.30.b.).

2. **OPERATIONS (German)**

   (a) Infantry. NIL.

   (b) Artillery. Hostile artillery has not been particularly active during the period under review.
   The crest and southern slopes of MONT ROUGE, the village of LOCRE and the SCHERPENBERG have been shelled at intervals.
   The road from CURRAGH CAMP (M.17.c.2.9.) to CANADA CORNER (M.17.c.6.4.) was shelled during the morning and with greater persistency during the afternoon.
   Between 9.45 p.m. and 11 p.m. the area in M.20.d. was shelled with H.E. and gas by 7.7 c.m.guns.
   About thirty gas shells (Blue Cross) were fired.

3. **AIRCRAFT.** Very slight activity.

4. **HOSTILE DEFENCES.**

   (a) Machine Guns. One gun was located by a patrol at M.29.d.40.90.
   A machine gun emplacement is also visible at N.25.b.90.25.

   (b) Trench Mortars. NIL.

   (c) Posts. BURGRAVE FARM (M.24.b.2.9.) was again found to be unoccupied.

   (d) Wire. The German wire at M.29.central is reported to consist of a single apron (with several gaps) and appears to be about ten yards from the enemy's parapet.

5. **MOVEMENT.** In spite of good visibility no movement was observed West of the line KEMMEL - DRANOUTRE.
   Trains were seen on the LILLE - ARMENTIERES Line as follows:-

   Three trains from ARMENTIERES to LILLE.
   One train from LILLE to ARMENTIERES.

   C.W. Hodgkinson
   Capt.

H.Q. 35th Division,   for Lieutenant-Colonel,
13th July 1918.   General Staff, 35th Division.

	SUN.			MOON.	
Date.	Rises.	Sets.		Rises.	Sets.
14 July.	4.53 am.	8.53 pm.		11.44 pm.	11.2 am.(15 July)
15 July.	4.54 am.	8.53 pm.		12.50 am.	11.21 am (16 July)

GENERAL NEWS. About 2 p.m. 11th July, a patrol of four men left our line S.W. of MERRIS to secure an identification, and returned with 15 prisoners. Other patrols then went out, and a total of 3 Officers 117 O.R. and 9 M.Gs. were captured.

FRENCH AVIATION. During June, 150 German aeroplanes were destroyed and 18 driven down damaged. Over 600 tons of bombs have been dropped.

ALBANIA. The advance of the Allied troops continues and the Austrians are reported to be falling back on the SKUMBI RIVER. French troops have occupied all the villages in the TOMERICA VALLEY upstream from DOBRENY.

35th DIVISION.
DAILY INTELLIGENCE SUMMARY No. 59.
From 6 a.m. 11th July to 6 a.m. 12th July 1918.

Reference Sheet 28 S.W. - 1/20,000.

1. **OPERATIONS (BRITISH).**

   (a) <u>Infantry</u>. In addition to several patrols which were carried out during darkness, a party of men went out with the object of locating a hostile working party in M.28.d. This having been done, a Lewis Gun was taken out and two drums fired into the party at close range causing all work to cease immediately. Definite results could not be obtained owing to the proximity of the workers to their own trench.

   (b) <u>Artillery</u>. Our Field Artillery vigorously harassed the enemy's tracks, roads and other sensitive points during the night.
   Movement among houses in M.36.b. was engaged during the evening and several casualties caused.

2. **OPERATIONS (GERMAN).**

   (a) <u>Infantry</u>. NIL.

   (b) <u>Artillery</u>. Hostile artillery has been unusually inactive.
   LOCRE was shelled at intervals during the morning, but this ceased shortly after noon.

   (c) <u>Trench Mortars</u>. Two bursts of Mortar fire were directed against our Left Subsector.

   (d) <u>Machine Guns</u>. Several attempts to open fire were made, but the guns so doing were immediately silenced by our Lewis Guns.

3. <u>AIRCRAFT</u>. No activity of importance was displayed.

4. <u>HOSTILE DEFENCE</u>. NIL.

5. <u>MOVEMENT</u>.

   Slight movement of men and vehicles observed South of KEMMEL HILL.
   Two wagons at T.2.c.4.7 were fired on and hit by our Artillery.
   The undermentioned movement of trains is reported:-
   From ARMENTIERES to LILLE - Seven trains at 5-5 a.m., 5-29 a.m., 5-55 a.m., 6-15 a.m., 4-20 p.m., 6-2 p.m., and 6-35 p.m.
   From LILLE to ARMENTIERES to LILLE - Three trains at 7 a.m., 12-45 p.m. and 3-50 p.m.
   From ARMENTIERES to ERQUINGHEM one train at 9-50 a.m.
   From ARMENTIERES to STEENWERCK - one train at 7-40 a.m.

H.Q: 35th Division,
12th July 1918.

C.W. Hodgkinson
for Capt.
Lieutenant-Colonel,
General Staff, 35th Division.

Date.	SUN. Rises.	Sets.	MOON. Rises.	Sets.
13th July.	4-52 am	8-54 pm	10-40 p.m.	10-44 a.m. (14th July).
14th July.	4-53 am	8-53 pm	11-44 p.m.	11-02 a.m. (15th July).

SUMMER TIME.

35th DIVISION
DAILY INTELLIGENCE SUMMARY No. 58.
From 6 a.m. 10th July to 6 a.m. 11th July 1918.

Reference Sheet 28 S.W. - 1/20,000.

1. **OPERATIONS (BRITISH).**

    (a) *Infantry.* Several patrols reconnoitred NO MAN'S LAND with the object of locating the positions of certain of the enemy's outposts and ascertaining the strength of the hostile wire (See para.4 below).
    In the early morning a small hostile working party was discovered in M.28.d. and a Lewis Gun team sent out to deal with it, but owing to the difficulty of communication by daylight, the results have not yet been reported.

    (b) *Artillery.* In addition to registration, our Field Artillery carried out several successful shoots during the period under review. A number of known occupied areas including the German dugouts at N.31.a.4.4 and N.26.c.20.75 and the cross roads at N.31.a.85.80 were shelled during the day. Fire was also directed on to the houses at S.6.c.70.25, S.5.d.75.20 and S.6.c.35.20, several direct hits being obtained.

2. **OPERATIONS (GERMAN).**

    (a) *Infantry.* NIL.

    (b) *Artillery.* Hostile artillery has shewn considerable activity, firing chiefly on to our Right Subsector. The increase of shelling on back areas by German Heavy Artillery has been marked.
    Roads and tracks on the Western slopes of MONT VIDAIGNE were continuously harassed from 9-30 p.m. to 12 midnight and MONT ROUGE was intermittently shelled throughout the day.
    15 cm Howitzers ineffectively fired 250 rounds on to one of our battery positions in M.7.b.

3. **AVIATION.**

    No unusual activity observed.

4. **HOSTILE DEFENCES.**

    (a) *Machine Guns.* One gun located at M.24.c.85.25.

    (b) *Trench Mortars.* None located.

    (c) *Posts.* An unoccupied shell hole which had apparently been organized for defence was found at M.24.d.15.35.

    (d) *Wire.* A patrol reports that a thin belt of wire has been erected in front of the enemy's posts in the vicinity of LOCRE Ch. P (M.24.d.0.1).

    (e) *Work.* New work (nature unknown) is visible at N.26.a.3.6.

5. **MOVEMENT.**

    Visibility good. Individual movement observed during the morning and afternoon particularly around the huts in AYRSHIRE CAMP (M.35.d.3.3) and dugout at T.7.a.55.30.
    Twelve trains were seen moving between WARNETON and ARMENTIERES during the day and some traffic was also observed on the ARMENTIERES - PONT DE NIEPPE and LILLE - ARMENTIERES lines.

H.Q. 35th Division,
11th July 1918.

C.W.Hodgkinson.
for Lieutenant-Colonel, Capt.
General Staff, 35th Division.

TURN OVER/

35th DIVISION.
DAILY INTELLIGENCE SUMMARY No. 57.
From 6 a.m. 9th July to 6 a.m. 10th July 1918.

Reference Sheet 28 S.W. - 1/20,000.

1. OPERATIONS (BRITISH).

   (a) Infantry. Patrolling was actively carried out along the whole Divisional front during the night. BURGRAVE FARM (M.34.b.2.9) and WESTULAAN DERN CABARET (M.34.d.9.2) were again reconnoitred. The former was, as previously reported, unoccupied by the enemy, but there was evidence of the latter being held in considerable force.

   (b) Artillery. Between 4.0 p.m. and 4.30 p.m. the Southern slopes of MONT KEMMEL were shelled by our Heavy Artillery. Field Artillery continued registration and in addition engaged and dispersed a working party at S.5.a.0.3.

   (c) Machine Guns. Fire was directed on the German forward communications by our Vickers Machine Guns at intervals throughout the night.

2. OPERATIONS (GERMAN).

   (a) Infantry. NIL.

   (b) Artillery. Hostile Artillery has been slightly more active than usual during the period under review.
   The mountain range from MONT NOIR to SCHERPENBERG (inclusive) was intermittently shelled throughout the day, particular attention being paid to MONT ROUGE during the afternoon by 15 cm Howitzers. LOCRE was shelled on several occasions during the period and at 1.0 pm in response to a single Green Light sent up from MONT KEMMEL, the same village was subjected to a heavy bombardment by guns and howitzers of all calibres up to 15 cm.

   (c) Machine Guns, harassed the forward areas of our Right and Centre Subsectors but were engaged with Rifle Grenades when possible.

3. AVIATION.

   A number of single aeroplanes patrolled our lines during the day, and several others attempting to fly in a Westerly direction were driven off by Lewis Gun and A.A. Gun fire.
   On the whole hostile air activity has been more noticeable than usual.

4. HOSTILE DEFENCES.

   (a) Machine Guns, were located by patrols at approximately the undermentioned points:-
   M.24.c.9.2 (2 guns)   M.2.c.85.80.
                         M.24.c.75.28.
   (b) Trench Mortars. None located.

   (c) Posts. Recently occupied listening posts with fresh tracks were located at M.34.d.55.75.

   (d) Guns. At 3-45 a.m. four flashes were observed at N.31.d.8.6.

War Diary

35th DIVISION.
DAILY INTELLIGENCE SUMMARY No.56.
From 6 a.m. 8th July to 6 a.m. 9th July 1918.

Ref: Sheet 28 S.W. 1/20,000.

1. **OPERATIONS (BRITISH).**

    (a) <u>Infantry</u>. Patrols reconnoitred the area in M.34.d and a disused trench at S.4.b.2.3. A French Light Machine Gun was found at the latter place and brought in.

    (b) <u>Artillery</u>. Field Artillery continued firing from new positions for purposes of registration.

    (c) <u>Machine Guns</u>, fired a large number of rounds during the night on hostile communications, with the object of harassing the enemy and in retaliation for the activity of the German machine guns.

2. **OPERATIONS (GERMAN).**

    (a) <u>Infantry</u>. NIL.

    (b) <u>Artillery</u>. The enemy artillery has not shown unusual activity during the period under review.
    The forward area was intermittently shelled during the day and between 11-30 A.M. and 12-15 P.M. LOCRE was subjected to a heavy and continuous bombardment with H.E. and Gas (believed Blue Cross) Shells.
    Bursts of fire were directed on to the roads on the Western slopes of MONT VIDAIGNE at intervals throughout the day. Considerable attention was paid to the SCHERPENBERG throughout the afternoon and evening.

    (c) <u>Machine Guns</u>, were unusually active throughout the night, firing continuously on to our roads and tracks East of the line MONT ROUGE - SCHERPENBERG.

3. **AVIATION.**

    Hostile aircraft have been slightly more active than usual. Several single machines and one formation of five machines patrolled our lines at various times of the day.

4. **HOSTILE DEFENCES.**

    (a) <u>Machine Guns</u>. There appear to be about four M.Gs. disposed at intervals along the road from M.24.d.0.9.40 to LOCRE CAMP (M.24.c.0.1)
    (b) <u>Trench Mortars</u>. One light T.M. was observed firing at 7 p.m. and 11-15 p.m. from a position at S.4.b.9.2.

    (c) <u>Posts</u>. Patrols report that trench at M.34.d.5.5 is held by the enemy.

    (d) <u>Wire</u>. One of our reconnoitring patrols encountered a hostile party at S.4.b.2.3, which was covering a further party of men who were at work, possibly on the erection of wire.

5. **MOVEMENT.**

    No movement was observed owing to ground mist.

    O.W. Hodgkinson Capt
    Lieutenant-Colonel,
    General Staff, 35th Division.

H.Q. 35th Division,
9th July 1918.

	SUN.		MOON.	
Date.	Rises.	Sets.	Rises.	Sets.
10th July	4-49 am	8-56 pm.	7-17 pm	9-47 am (11th July).
11th July	4-50 am	8-56 pm.	8-26 pm	10-7 am (12th July).

35th DIVISION.
DAILY INTELLIGENCE SUMMARY No. 55.
From 6 a.m. 7th July to 6 a.m. 8th July 1918.

Reference Sheet 28 S.W. - 1/20,000.

1. OPERATIONS (BRITISH).

   (a) Infantry. The Divisional front was actively patrolled during the night, reconnaissances being made of BURGRAVE FARM (M.34.b.2.9) WESTULAAN DERN CABARET and the bed of the small stream at M.29.a.15.25. In the case of the last named reconnaissance, the patrol worked Eastwards along the ravine, finding it to be of considerable depth (8 to 10 feet) and flanked by several shallow trenches.

   (b) Artillery. Field Artillery continued to register from new positions.

   (c) Trench Mortars. NIL.

   (d) Machine Guns. The enemy's tracks, roads and forward communications were subjected to harassing fire at intervals throughout the night.

2. OPERATIONS (GERMAN).

   (a) Infantry. NIL.

   (b) Artillery. The area East of the line MONT ROUGE - SCHERPENBERG was intermittently shelled during the day, particular attention being paid to M.22.b and d and LOCRE by 10.5 and 15 cm Howitzers.
   The roads immediately East of and the Western slopes of MONTS VIDAIGNE and NOIR were continuously shelled from 8 p.m. to 10-30 p.m. an unusually large proportion of shrapnel being used.

3. AVIATION.

   Hostile activity in the air has been very slight.
   At 4 a.m. 8th July one German machine flying at a great altitude dropped several bombs on MONT ROUGE.

4. HOSTILE DEFENCES.

   (a) Machine Guns. One gun was located by a patrol at M.29.d.5.7 (approx). Two emplacements are also suspected at M.24.c.75.20 and M.24.c.9.2.

   (b) Trench Mortars. None located.
   Several hostile mortars have been reported active, particularly one which fired 50 rounds during the day on LOCRE, M.23.d and M.29.b.

   (c) Posts and Occupied Areas. Patrols report that both the Southern building of BURGRAVE FARM (M.34.b.2.9) and WESTULAAN DERN CABARET (M.34.d.9.2) are unoccupied by the enemy.
   A post at M.34.b.3.7 was found to be occupied and well defended by wire.

5. MOVEMENT.

   Practically no hostile movement has been observed West of the line MONT KEMMEL - DRANOUTRE and visibility has not permitted observation to be carried out on back areas.

H.Q. 35th Division,
8th July 1918.

for Lieutenant-Colonel,
General Staff, 35th Division.

TURN OVER/

	SUN.		MOON.	
Date.	Rises.	Sets.	Rises.	Sets.
9th July.	4-48 a.m.	8-57 p.m.	6-06 p.m.	9-23 a.m. (10th July).
10th July.	4-49 a.m.	8-56 p.m.	7-17 p.m.	9-47 a.m. (11th July).

35th DIVISION.
DAILY INTELLIGENCE SUMMARY No.54.
From 6 a.m. 6th July to 6 a.m. 7th July 1918.

Reference Sheet 28 S.W.

1. OPERATIONS (BRITISH).

   (a) Infantry. Our patrols reconnoitred NO MAN'S LAND in front of the Right and Centre Subsectors, with the object of ascertaining the strength and positions of the enemy's wire and posts.

   (b) Artillery. Field Artillery continued to register from new positions.

2. OPERATIONS (GERMAN).

   (a) Infantry. At 4-15 a.m. a party of thirty Germans made a determined attempt to raid and obtain identification from one of our posts at M.29.b.8.8, but were driven off by rifle and Lewis Gun fire.
   None of our men are missing.

   (b) Artillery. Hostile artillery was moderately quiet during the morning of 6th July but became more active during the afternoon and evening.
   The area in M.23 was persistently shelled throughout the afternoon by 7.7 cm guns and 10.5 cm Howitzers and an area shoot was carried out on M.7, 8, 13 and 14. Particular attention was paid to one of our battery positions in M.7 by 15 cm howitzers, 400 rounds being expended.
   Bursts of fire were directed on to WESTOUTRE at intervals throughout the day, and at 3-20 p.m. the village of LOCRE was bombarded for forty minutes by 15 cm howitzers.

   (c) Trench Mortars. NIL.

   (d) Machine Guns. Slight activity during the night.

3. AIRCRAFT.

   The German aeroplanes were inactive throughout the period under review.

4. HOSTILE DEFENCES.

   (a) Machine Guns, have been located by ground observers at the undermentioned positions :-
   M.24.c.3.1
   S. 4.d.4.3

   (b) Wire. The enemy's wire between the points M.29.a.1.3 and M.29.a.5.3 was reconnoitred by a patrol and found to consist of plain concertina wire arranged in a series of small rows running approximately at right angles to the German front line.

5. MOVEMENT.

   No hostile movement was observed in the forward area, and owing to bad visibility it was not possible to observe the back area.

6. MISCELLANEOUS. A Red Cross Flag was observed at M.30.a.65.80.

W. Hodgkinson
Capt.

H.Q. 35th Division,   for Lieutenant-Colonel,
7th July 1918.   General Staff, 35th Division.

35th DIVISION.
DAILY INTELLIGENCE SUMMARY No. 53.
From 6 a.m. 5th July to 6 a.m. 6th July 1918.

Reference Sheet 28 S.W. - 1/20,000.

1. OPERATIONS (BRITISH).

   (a) Infantry. Patrols were active during the night chiefly for purposes of gaining touch with units on flanks.

   (b) Artillery. During the afternoon of 5th July British Field Artillery registered on various points from new positions.

2. OPERATIONS (GERMAN).

   (a) Infantry.   NIL.

   (b) Artillery. The German Artillery has been less active than usual. The usual harassing fire has been directed on to our front line by 7.7 cm guns and 10.5 cm Howitzers.
   The British Battery at M.16.b.4.9 was shelled at 11-30 a.m. and 6.0 p.m. by 10.5 cm Howitzers.
   In addition, the farm at M.10.c.95.40 and the ravine in M.17.d. were bombarded by 15 cm and 10.5 cm Howitzers respectively.

   (c) Machine Guns. Hostile machine guns showed considerable activity during the night, firing chiefly on to the forward slopes in rear of the Left Subsector.

3. AVIATION.

   Owing to bad visibility, activity in the air has been slight.

   One German aeroplane which crossed our lines at 4-30 p.m. was driven off by Lewis Gun fire.

H.Q. 35th Division,
6th July 1918.

Major-General,
Commanding 35th Division.

AO E 8 35 D
S1 32

August 18.

On His Majesty's Service.

Confidential.

The Officer in Charge,

D.A.D. Office,

At the Base

G3027.

ORIGINAL.

Army Form C. 2118.

WAR DIARY

INTELLIGENCE SUMMARY. (Page 1).

(Erase heading not required.)

H.Q. 35th DIVISION,
GENERAL STAFF.
1st to 31st August 1918.

Instructions regarding War Diaries and Intelligence Summaries are contained in F.S. Regs., Part II. and the Staff Manual respectively. Title pages will be prepared in manuscript.

Place	Date	Hour	Summary of Events and Information	Remarks and references to Appendices
LA MONTAGNE.	August 1918. 1st.		Fine day. On night 31st July/1st August 104th Infantry Brigade carried out a silent raid. No identifications were secured but some of the enemy were killed. 35th Division H.Q. moved to LA MONTAGNE; rear H.Q. remaining at TERDEGHEM. 27th Canadian Battalion, attached 104th Infantry Brigade, moved into line. 106th Infantry Brigade moved up to a position in the neighbourhood of Brigade H.Q. preparatory to the attack on DRANOUTRE RIDGE.	
	2nd.		Fine early; very wet all day after 10.30 a.m. X Corps Commander visited G.O.C. The attack which should have taken place on the night 2nd/3rd August is postponed on account of the weather.	
	3rd.		Fine day. 35th Division Operation Order No.185 issued. Front re-adjusted to form a two Brigade front. 104th Infantry on Left; 105th Infantry Brigade on Right. 106th Infantry Brigade in Divisional Reserve. G.O.C. visited Brigade H.Q. and returned to TERDEGHEM. 90th Infantry Brigade and 30th Bn. M.G. Corps rejoined the 30th Division.	O.O.185.
	4th.		Fine Day. G.O.C. attended Service at TERDEGHEM to commemorate the opening of hostilities. 104th Infantry Brigade raided enemy's trenches at 11.0 p.m. under Artillery and Machine Gun barrage; enemy fled; no identifications secured.	
	5th.		Fine generally; occasional slight drizzle. 35th Division Operation Order No.186 issued. 106th Infantry Brigade moved up to Support Position.	O.O.186.
	6th.		A very wet night compelled cancellation of operation against DRANOUTRE RIDGE ordered for August 7th. Fine day except for one heavy shower. His Majesty The King visited X Corps Area. X Corps Commander visited 35th Division H.Q. 35th Division Operation Order No.187 issued, re relief of 35th Division by 30th Division.	O.O.187.
TERDEGHEM.	7th.		Fine Day. 35th Division H.Q. opened at TERDEGHEM at 8.0 a.m. G.O.C. attended lectures and demonstrations at TERDEGHEM by Lieut-General Sir IVOR MAXSE, Inspector General of Training.	

ORIGINAL.

Army Form C. 2118.

WAR DIARY

of

~~INTELLIGENCE SUMMARY~~

(Erase heading not required.)

H.Q. 35th Division,
GENERAL STAFF.
1st to 31st August 1918.
(Sheet No.2.)

Instructions regarding War Diaries and Intelligence Summaries are contained in F.S. Regs., Part II. and the Staff Manual respectively. Title pages will be prepared in manuscript.

Place	Date	Hour	Summary of Events and Information	Remarks and references to Appendices
TERDEGHEM.	August 1918 8th.		Fine day. Reliefs according to 35th Division Operation Order No.187.	
	9th.		Fine and hot; strong Westerly wind. Lieut-General MAXSE'S demonstration at TERDEGHEM similar to that on 7th August. Reliefs according to 35th Division Operation Order No.187.	
CASSEL.	10th.		Fine day. 35th Division moved into X Corps Reserve with H.Q. at CASSEL. G.O.C. visited X Corps Schools. Army Commander visited G.O.C. 35th Division.	
	11th.		Fine Day. His Majesty The King attended a Parade Service at TERDEGHEM at 11.0 a.m. G.O.C. 35th Division was present.	
	12th.		Very hot. G.O.C. visited Tank Demonstration near ST POL.	
	13th.		Fine day. Training. Two Battalions and two Companies 35th Bn.M.G.C. go back to COLEMBERT Area for musketry.	
	14th.		Fine and hot. Training.	
	15th.		Fine and hot. G.O.C. goes on leave. Brigadier-General POLLARD takes over Command of 35th Division.	
	16th.		Hot and fine. Two Companies 35th Bn.M.G.C. return from COLEMBERT to OXELAERE.	
	17th.		Fine day. 35th Battalion M.G.C. attached to 30th Division; also one Brigade R.F.A. plus two Batteries R.F.A.	
	18th.		Fine day. 15th Bn.Cheshire Regiment and 18th Bn.Lancashire Fusiliers return from COLEMBERT Area their places being taken by 17th Bn.Royal Scots and 17th Bn.Lancashire Fusiliers.	

ORIGINAL.

Army Form C. 2118.

WAR DIARY
~~INTELLIGENCE SUMMARY~~

H.Q. 35th DIVISION,
GENERAL STAFF.
1st to 31st August 1918.
(Sheet No.3).

(Erase heading not required.)

Instructions regarding War Diaries and Intelligence Summaries are contained in F. S. Regs., Part II. and the Staff Manual respectively. Title pages will be prepared in manuscript.

Place	Date	Hour	Summary of Events and Information	Remarks and references to Appendices
CASSEL.	August 1918.			
	19th.		Fine Day. Training.	
	20th.		Fine Day. Training.	
	21st.		Very hot and fine. Orders received from X Corps for one Field Artillery Brigade, less one Battery, to be attached to 36th Division from 22nd August.	
	22nd.		Very hot. Army Commander inspects Infantry Brigades training.	
	23rd.		Fine day. Division training. 35th Bn.M.G.C. and one Field Artillery Brigade, lent to 30th Division for one week for operation; rejoined 35th Division.	
	24th.		Fine day. Two Battalions (one of 105 and one of 106 Infantry Brigades) to COLEMBERT Area for musketry; also portion of one battalion 104th Infantry Brigade. The 35th Division remains in X Corps Reserve with Division H.Q. at CASSEL. The General Staff 35th Division is now composed as follows:- Major-General A.H.MARINDIN, D.S.O., p.s.c., The Black Watch. Lieutenant-Colonel H.W.B.THORP, D.S.O., p.s.c., K.O.Y.L.I. Major Sir E.P.D.PAUNCEFORT-DUNCOMBE, Bart., D.S.O., Buckinghamshire Yeomanry. Captain R.P.HARRISON, General List, also Lieutenant A.I.CHESNEY, Intelligence Officer, and No.11489 Superintending Clerk A.S.MEYERS, Royal Engineers, Chief Clerk, Headquarters 35th Division.	
	25th.		Fine. Remaining three Companies of a battalion of 104th Infantry Brigade to COLEMBERT Area. 35th Division Operation Order No.188 issued. X Corps Operation Orders Nos.186 and 187 received.	O.O.188.
	26th.		Showery. Training.	
	27th.		Fine Day. Infantry Brigades training.	
	28th.		Heavy showers. Brigadier-General Commanding 35th Division attended a Conference held by the Corps Commander at TERDEGHEM.	

ORIGINAL.

WAR DIARY

H.Q. 35th DIVISION,
GENERAL STAFF.
1st to 31st August 1918.
(Sheet No. 4).

Army Form C. 2118.

Instructions regarding War Diaries and Intelligence Summaries are contained in F. S. Regs., Part II. and the Staff Manual respectively. Title pages will be prepared in manuscript.

(Erase heading not required.)

Place	Date	Hour	Summary of Events and Information	Remarks and references to Appendices
CASSEL.	August 1918. 29th.		Fine; cold. 35th Division Defence Scheme for ST JANS CAPPEL Area issued (copy in Appendix). Musketry parties returned from COLEMBERT. 105th Infantry Brigade and two Companies 35th Bn. M.G.C. moved in accordance with 35th Division Order No.188 to support positions ST JANS CAPPEL Area.	Defence Scheme.
	30th.		Fine. Numerous fires during the night made it clear that the enemy was retiring from BAILLEUL. Patrols established this fact and by 4.0 p.m. BAILLEUL was included in our lines. Relief of 36th (ULSTER) Division by 35th Division cancelled. 105th Infantry Brigade and two Companies 35th Bn.M.G.C. move back to Reserve Area. 35th Division, including Artillery, concentrated in original positions about CASSEL in X Corps Reserve.	
	31st.		Fine day. X Corps Operation Orders Nos. 189 and 190 received. 35th Division Operation Order No.189 issued. Orders received that 35th British Division is transferred from X Corps to II Corps with effect from 1st September. 35th Division Artillery to move into action 1st September on II Corps front, covering 14th British Division. The 35th Division to relieve the 30th American Division (H.Q. VOGELTJE) on the front VOORMEZEELE - ZILLEBEKE by 5th September. in Right Sector of II Corps front. 14th British Division (II Corps) on Left. 34th British Division (XIX Corps) on Right. 35th Division to move to HERZEELE - PROVEN - ST JAN TER BIEZEN Area on 2nd September.	O.O.189.

H.Q.35th Division,
31st August 1918.

[signature]

Brigadier-General,
Commanding 35th Division.

35th DIVISION.
DAILY INTELLIGENCE SUMMARY No. 79.
From 6 a.m. 31st July to 6 a.m. 1st August 1918.

1. OPERATIONS (BRITISH).

   (a) Infantry. A small raiding party succeeded in forcing an entry into an enemy post at M.24.c.94.31 and inflicted casualties on the garrison. Two prisoners were taken but the raiding party was counter-attacked in strength from the rear and forced to withdraw. The two prisoners were killed. No identification was secured.

   (b) Artillery. Harassing fire was carried out during the period on roads tracks and occupied areas.
   At 4-20 p.m. 50 rounds were fired on enemy battery at S.5.c.8.3 by 4.5" howitzers in answer to a N.F. call.

2. OPERATIONS (GERMAN).

   (a) Infantry. Nil.

   (b) Artillery. There was much shelling of MONT ROUGE by 7.7 cm guns, and 10.5 cm and 15 cm Hows. during the period, especially between 10-20 p.m. and midnight.
   M.21.c. was shelled by 15 cm Hows. at 10-55 a.m. and 11-15 pm.
   Some shelling of M.28.a. and M.29.b. by 10.5 cm and 15 cm Hows. during the day.

3. AVIATION.

   E.A. activity was above normal. One low-flying E.A. was engaged by anti-aircraft fire from M.Gs. and Stokes Mortars at 7-30 p.m. and was chased back over its own lines by two of our machines.

4. HOSTILE DEFENCES.

   Wire. The enemy is reported to be working on his wire opposite the Left Brigade Sector.

5. MOVEMENT. Visibility low.

6. MISCELLANEOUS.

   A hostile Field Gun position is suspected at T.8.a.7.6.

H.Q. 35th Division,
1st August 1918.

R. P. Harrison, Capt.
for Lieutenant-Colonel,
General Staff, 35th Division.

SUMMER TIME.

Date.	SUN. Rises.	Sets.	MOON. Rises.	Sets.
Aug.2.	5-14 a.m.	8-33 p.m.	0.30 a.m.	5-29 p.m.
3.	5-16 a.m.	8-32 p.m.	1-34 a.m.	6-18 p.m.

35th DIVISION.
DAILY INTELLIGENCE SUMMARY No. 80.
From 6 a.m. 1st August to 6 a.m. 2nd August 1918.

1. OPERATIONS (BRITISH).

   (a) Infantry. A patrol succeeded in penetrating the German trench about M.29.d.2.9 but found it unoccupied. Later on a second attempt was made and the sentry of a German post was shot. The enemy were on the alert and threw bombs. No identification was secured.

   (b) Artillery. We harassed the enemy's roads and tracks in M.30, M.36 and S.5.

   (c) Machine Guns. Our Lewis guns and Stokes Mortars engaged hostile M.Gs.

2. OPERATIONS (GERMAN).

   (a) Infantry. NIL.

   (b) Artillery. Activity below normal. Between 10 a.m. and 1 p.m. a shoot by 15 cm Hows. was carried out on R.17.d, 150 rounds being expended.
   From 11-35 p.m. to midnight, the enemy heavily bombarded the front system of our right Subsector with 7.7 cm, 10.5 cm and 15 cm. With the above exception the night was quiet.

   (c) Machine Guns. Quiet for the most part. From 2 a.m. to 3 a.m. intermittent bursts were fired down the DRANOUTRE - LOCRE Road. Bursts of overhead fire were directed at intervals on to MONT ROUGE. They mostly came from M.35.a.

3. AVIATION.

   E.A. active. At 8-45 p.m. one flew low over WESTOUTRE and was driven off by our Stokes Mortars.
   At 11-2 p.m. 1st August an aeroplane dropped a magnesia flare over our Right Subsector; it burnt for five minutes and drifted Westwards.
   Hostile A.A. guns were very active against our machines.

4. ENEMY DEFENCES.

   (a) Machine Guns. A M.G. fired from M.35.a.0.4.

   (b) Posts. An unoccupied post was discovered at M.29.b.30.15.

5. MOVEMENT.

   Movement at M.24.d.2.2 was engaged by our 18-prs.
   Visibility was poor throughout the day.

6. IDENTIFICATION.

   Four prisoners captured by the Division on our Right belong to the 5th Company 118 I.R. 56th Division (normal).

   FRENCH FRONT. The line now runs: CHAMBRECY (French), ROMIGNY (French), S. outskirts of VILLERS ARGON, 1 k.m. S. of GOUSSANCOURT, N. edge of BOIS MEUNIER, Hills N. of CIERGE and S. of NESLES, SERINGES, 500 metres S. of SAPONAY.

H.Q. 35th Division,
2nd August 1918.

for A.J. Chesney Lieut.
Lieutenant-Colonel,
General Staff, 35th Division.

SUMMER TIME.

Date.	SUN. Rises.	Sets.	MOON. Rises.	Sets.
Ag.3.	5-16 a.m.	8-32 p.m.	1-34 a.m.	6-18 p.m.
4.	5-18 a.m.	8-31 p.m.	2-38 a.m.	7-00 p.m.

35th DIVISION.
DAILY INTELLIGENCE SUMMARY No. 81.
From 6 a.m. 2nd August to 6 a.m. 3rd August 1918.

1. **OPERATIONS (BRITISH).**

   (a) Infantry. Patrols were out on the Divisional front. No Germans were encountered.

   (b) Artillery. Harassing fire on enemy roads and occupied areas was carried out during the period.

   (c) Machine Guns. Our M.Gs. fired harassing fire during the night, and our Lewis guns kept down the fire of enemy M.Gs.

2. **OPERATIONS (GERMAN).**

   (a) Infantry. NIL.

   (b) Artillery. A little shelling of MONT NOIR, MONT VIDAIGNE and MONT ROUGE during the period. LOCRE CHATEAU was shelled by 5.9 Hows. at three different times - about 30 shells in all. 7.7 cm. guns fired about 200 rounds into M.17.c., M.22.b., and M.23.a. between 9-30 p.m. and 12-30 a.m. About 20 rounds YELLOW CROSS Gas Shell fell in M.23.d.

   (c) Machine Guns. Frequent burst from hostile M.Gs. on the LOCRE-DRANOUTRE Road. The front line of Centre Brigade was swept by M.G. fire at intervals.

3. **AVIATION.**

   At 6-15 a.m. an enemy balloon was brought down in flames by two of our aeroplanes.
   One E.A. flew over our lines at 11.0 a.m. and was driven off by M.G.fire. Another which came over at 8-15 p.m. was driven off by fire from Stokes Mortars and M.Gs.

4. **HOSTILE DEFENCES.** No new work is reported.

5. **MOVEMENT.** Low visibility. No hostile movement seen.

6. **MISCELLANEOUS.**

   Double red flares repeated back by relay posts appear to be the enemy light signal for "Lengthen range".

P. P. Harrison
Capt.

H.Q. 35th Division,
3rd August 1918.

for Lieutenant-Colonel,
General Staff, 35th Division.

SUMMER TIME.

Date.	SUN. Rises.	Sets.	MOON. Rises.	Sets.
Aug. 4.	5-18 a.m.	8-31 p.m.	2-38 a.m.	7-00 p.m.
5.	5-19 a.m.	8-29 p.m.	3-45 a.m.	7-29 p.m.

35th DIVISION.
DAILY INTELLIGENCE SUMMARY No. 82.
From 6 a.m. 3rd August to 6 a.m. 4th August 1918.

Ref. Sheet 28 S.W. 1/20,000

1. **OPERATIONS** (British)
   (a) *Infantry*. The front was actively patrolled during the night. No German patrols were encountered.
   The reorganization of the Divisional front into two Brigade Sectors was completed during the night.
   (b) *Artillery*. Harassing fire was carried out on enemy roads and tracks, and concentrations were fired on sensitive points.
   18-pdrs. carried out a destructive shoot on an O.P. at N.26.c.1.8. Three "O.K's" were observed.
   At 10.28 a.m. and at 10.55 p.m. short bursts of fire were directed on enemy trenches in M.36.a. and M.30.d. in reply to the shelling of our front line.
   (c) *Machine Guns*. Our M.G's. harassed the enemy's tracks and occupied areas during the night.

2. **OPERATIONS** (German)
   (a) *Infantry*. Nil.
   (b) *Artillery*. Between 8.30 a.m. and 10.20 a.m. 7.7 c.m. guns fired about 80 rounds into LOCRE.
   About 100 rounds from 5.9 c.m. Hows. fell in M.10.c. between 10 a.m. and 12 noon. Five salvos from 5.9 Hows. fell in the same area between 6.30 p.m. and 6.45 p.m.
   Nearly 200 shells of calibres up to 15 c.m. fell in M.22. during the period, and LOCRE CHATEAU and MONT NOIR were intermittently shelled.
   Between 7 p.m. and 7.30 p.m. about 100 rounds 10.5 c.m. fell in M.16.b. and 20 more rounds in the same area at 10.0 p.m.
   (c) *Machine Guns*. Enemy Machine Guns were more active than usual during the night, sweeping our roads and tracks.

3. **AVIATION**. At 8.10 p.m. two E.A. flew low over our lines, and one E.A. flew over our battery positions; these were driven off by fire from Machine Guns and Stokes Mortars.
   Single E.A. were over our lines at 7.0 p.m., 4.50 p.m., and 9.30 p.m.
   At 4.30 a.m. and between 8.0 p.m. and 9.0 p.m. an E.A. fired his Machine Gun into our trenches. He was driven off by rifle and M.G. fire.

4. **HOSTILE DEFENCES**. Recently the enemy has repeatedly bombed his own wire, opposite our Left Brigade front, by night.

5. **MOVEMENT**. A little individual movement was observed in T.2.b. during the afternoon.
   Two trains were seen near ARMENTIERES, one going North at 9.15 a.m. and one going South-west at 9.35 a.m.

6. **MISCELLANEOUS**. At 9.15 p.m. the following was flashed by an enemy lamp, observed from M.22.d.0.9. on Magnetic bearing of 91° a long way away:- TNZITRDEN - KESNRVOTTETNG - BI - NTUUMIGNVGN3LN - MOTTN - O - OG.

R.P. Harrison Capt
Lieutenant-Colonel,
General Staff, 35th British Division,

H.Q. 35th Division,
4th August 1918.

FRENCH FRONT SITUATION:- At 10 p.m. 3rd. Line runs SOISSONS AISNE as far as SERMOISE S. of the VESLE to FISMES (which Americans have entered) HILL 236 BRANSCOURT ROSNAY GUEUX W. & N. of ST. BRICE. Cavalry have entered JONCHERY and MUIZON. MONTDIDIER FRONT:- The Germans have withdrawn from the S. of GRIVESNES to S.W. of MONTDIDIER. Line runs HILL 115 Wood S.W. of FONTAINE SOUS MONTDIDIER N.E. of MESNIL ST. GEORGES HILLS 60 and 98.

WAR DIARY

35th DIVISION.
DAILY INTELLIGENCE SUMMARY No. 83.
From 6 a.m. 4th August to 6 a.m. 5th August 1918.

1. **OPERATIONS (BRITISH).**

    (a) **Infantry.** At 11 p.m. under cover of our Artillery, Stokes Mortar and Machine Gun barrage, a raiding party consisting of two Officers and fifty other ranks entered the enemy's trenches at M.29.b.30.75, without difficulty. Bangalore torpedoes were used to destroy enemy wire. The trench was found to be unoccupied and no identification was secured. A set of German Infantry equipment was brought back. Our casualties were light.
    When our raiding party had been withdrawn the Officer Commanding the party went back to the point of entry and observed about twenty Germans approaching the deserted post from the rear. They were dealt with by rifle and Lewis Gun fire.
    The front of the right Subsector was actively patrolled. No Germans were encountered.

    (b) **Artillery.** Concentrations on enemy's defences and wire in M.34.b. and d. were fired at 8-30 a.m. and 4 p.m., also on enemy's posts in M.28.d. and M.29.c. at 10-30 a.m. 4.5" Hows. carried out a destructive shoot on M.Gs. in M.29.b. Between 2 a.m. and 4 a.m. harassing fire on M.29.c. and M.35.a.
    Barrages and diversions were fired at 11 p.m. in support of the raid by Left Infantry Brigade. Heavy Artillery carried out counter-battery work twice during the evening in response to hostile shelling of M.16.b.

2. **OPERATIONS (GERMAN).**

    (a) **Infantry.** At 2-30am an enemy patrol endeavoured to bomb our forward post at M.28.d.65.70 but were driven off by Lewis Gun fire.

    (b) **Artillery.** Enemy shelled M.16.b. persistently from 1 p.m. to 7-30 p.m. About 200 10.5 cm shells fell altogether.
    Particular attention was paid to Left Brigade H.Q. at M.16.b.2.9. Shelling at first consisted mainly of air bursts, but from 6-45 p.m. to 7-30 p.m. an intense fire was opened on M.16.b.2.9 by 10.5 cm guns.
    Enemy retaliation for our raid was slight, consisting of 7.7 cm and T.Ms. on front system.
    There was the usual intermittent shelling of forward areas.

3. **AVIATION.**
    Single E.A. crossed our lines at 6-15 a.m., 5-0 p.m., 5-15 p.m. 6-15 p.m., 8-45 p.m., and 4-30 a.m. They were driven off by fire from machine guns and Lewis Guns.

4. **HOSTILE DEFENCES.** Nothing to report.

5. **MOVEMENT.** Eight trains were seen near ARMENTIERES during the day.

6. **MISCELLANEOUS.** When our barrage began at 11 p.m. enemy sent up four red lights each of which burst into two red stars. On this signal enemy artillery opened fire. Two green lights of same type went up shortly afterwards and enemy fire became more intense.
    Light signals were repeated back to MONT KEMMEL.

H.Q. 35th Division,
5th August 1918.

Lieutenant-Colonel,
General Staff, 35th Division.

SUMMER TIME

Date.	SUN. Rises.	Sets.	MOON. Rises.	Sets.
Aug. 6.	5-21 a.m.	8-27 p.m.	4-56 a.m.	7-53 p.m. (New Moon).
7.	5-22 a.m.	8-25 p.m.	6-07 a.m.	8-17 p.m.

Ref. Sheet 28 S.W. - 1/20,000.
35th DIVISION
DAILY INTELLIGENCE SUMMARY No. 84.
From 6 a.m. 5th August to 6 a.m. 6th August 1918.

1. OPERATIONS (BRITISH).

   (a) Infantry. The Divisional front was actively patrolled during the night. No Germans were encountered.

   (b) Artillery. At 9-30 a.m., 12-30 p.m., 3-0 p.m. and 6 p.m. all active guns fired concentrations on enemy defences, dugouts and shelters in S.4.d., and S.5.c. and d. Harassing fire on tracks and occupied areas was carried out during the period. 4.5 Hows. exploded an enemy dump at S.18.a.7.3.

2. OPERATIONS (GERMAN).

   (a) Infantry. At 11 p.m. a strong enemy patrol approached one of our posts at about S.4.b.7.8 - it was dealt with by Lewis Guns.

   (b) Artillery. The usual intermittent shelling of forward areas was carried out. On three occasions during the morning the road and valley about M.16.d.5.4 were shelled by 10.5 cm Howitzers. 15 cm howitzers carried out an area shoot on M.21.d. at 5-5 p.m.
   The battery previously reported at about T.8.b.8.4 was active in the morning.
   At 6-15 p.m. the flashes of an enemy battery shelling the front of the Brigade on our left were observed. Grid bearing 96° from M.22.b.2.8.

   (c) Trench Mortars. A few light trench mortar shells fell on the front of left Brigade during the night.

3. AVIATION. One E.A. flew over our lines at 3-30 p.m.

4. ENEMY DEFENCES.

   (a) Machine Guns. Machine guns were reported firing from M.28.d.9.1, M.29.c.2.3, and M.29.c.25.90.

5. MOVEMENT.

   At 2-30 p.m. twenty men in twos and threes were seen in N.31.d. moving SOUTH towards the Red Cross Station at T.1.d.70.95. The artillery were informed.
   Several small parties of men were seen in T.8.a during the day.

6. MISCELLANEOUS.

   The enemy appeared to be very nervous opposite the left Subsector during the night; he fired an unusual number of Very Lights, and any movement between our posts provoked rifle grenade and small arms fire.

R. P. Harrison Capt
&
Lieutenant-Colonel,

H.Q. 35th Division,
6th August 1918.
General Staff, 35th Division.

SUMMER TIME.

Date.	SUN. Rises.	Sets.	Rises.	MOON. Sets.
Aug. 7.	5-22 a.m.	8-25 p.m.	6-07 a.m.	8-17 p.m.
8.	5-24 a.m.	8-24 p.m.	7-15 p.m.	8-37 p.m.

Ref. Sheet 28 S.W. - 1/20,000.

35th DIVISION.
DAILY INTELLIGENCE SUMMARY No.85.
From 6 a.m. 6th August to 6 a.m. 7th August 1918.

---

1. OPERATIONS (BRITISH).

   (a) Infantry. Patrols were out along the Divisional front. No Germans were encountered.

   (b) Artillery. Our Artillery carried out harassing fire on enemy communications during the period. An active trench mortar at M.30.a.5.5 was silenced by 4.5" howitzers.

   (c) Machine Guns. Our machine guns harassed the enemy tracks during the night and neutralized the fire of hostile M.Gs.

2. OPERATIONS (GERMAN).

   (a) Infantry. NIL.

   (b) Artillery. Hostile artillery activity was slightly below normal. There was the usual intermittent shelling of our forward areas.

   (c) Machine Guns. Enemy machine guns were active during the night opposite the left subsector.

3. AVIATION.

   Three E.A. flew over our line at 6-50 p.m. and one E.A. crossed our lines at 5-10 a.m. All were engaged by Lewis Gun fire.

4. HOSTILE DEFENCES.

   (a) Machine Guns. Hostile machine guns are suspected at M.24.c.9.3 and M.30.a.5.5.

   (b) Trench Mortars. An enemy trench mortar is suspected at M.29.d.6.4.

   (c) Wire. Enemy's wire in M.24.c. is reported by patrols to be weak.

5. MOVEMENT. A little individual movement on the Southern slopes of MONT KEMMEL was observed during the day.

6. MISCELLANEOUS. At 8-45 p.m. white lights changing to red were observed behind the enemy's line.
   Between 11.0 p.m. and 12.0 m.n. several parachute lights were put up to the North of MONT KEMMEL. They burnt for about 10 minutes.

R. P. Harrison Capt

H.Q. 35th Division,   Lieutenant-Colonel,
7th August 1918.   General Staff, 35th Division.
                    SUMMER TIME.

Date.	SUN. Rises.	Sets.	MOON. Rises.	Sets.
Aug.8th.	5-24 a.m.	8-24 p.m.	7-15 a.m.	8-37 p.m.
9th.	5-26 a.m.	8-22 p.m.	8-25 a.m.	8-54 p.m.

35th DIVISION
DAILY INTELLIGENCE SUMMARY No. 86.
From 6 a.m. 7th to 6 a.m. 8th August 1918.

Ref. Sheet 28 S.W. - 1/20,000.

1. OPERATIONS (BRITISH).

   (A) Infantry. Patrols were sent out to reconnoitre the enemy's dispositions. Six German posts were located and two working parties discovered; map references are given in paragraph 4.

   (B) Artillery. Our Field and Heavy Artillery co-operated in a concentration on the suspected Regimental H.Q. at T.7.c.6.1, gas shells, H.E. and thermite being fired. Occupied buildings in N.31 and T.1 were shelled and during the night shellstorms were fired on to sensitive points.

2. OPERATIONS (GERMAN).

   (A) Infantry. German working parties were at work at M.34.d.7.9, M.29.b.7.5 (wiring), and along the Northern edge of the wood in M.29.c. Our artillery were informed.

   (B) Artillery. Rather below normal. The enemy's night harassing fire was not very pronounced, and was chiefly directed against our roads and tracks on the reverse slopes of MONT ROUGE, MONT VIDAIGNE and MONT NOIR. Between 6 p.m. and midnight H.V. guns were very active on R.8., R.9., R.15.a.and b.

   (C) Machine Guns. Active during the night. Bursts were fired at the cross roads at M.22.d.6.8 and M.27.c.2.2.

3. AVIATION. E.A. were inactive.

4. ENEMY DEFENCES.

   (a) Machine Guns. M.Gs. are reported firing from M.29.c.00.42, S.4.b.5.3, S.4.b.8.5, S.4.b.9.8, M.24.c.40.05, M.30.a.8.6. The latter is probably the one previously reported at M.30.a.7.6.

   (b) Trench Mortars. A light T.M. fired from M.24.d.25.25. (Probably the T.M. already reported at M.24.d.3.3).

   (c) Posts. German post at M.24.c.7.1 was unoccupied. Patrols ascertained that the enemy was occupying posts at M.29.c.80.65 (on the LOCRE-DRANOUTRE Road), S.4.b.5.3, S.4.b.7.4, S.4.b.8.5, S.4.b.9.8, M.34.d.8.9.

   (d) Wire. The wire in front of the enemy post at M.24.c.7.1 consists of a strong belt, covered by a weaker one.

5. MOVEMENT. During the afternoon sentries were seen in the German post at M.24.c.65.00. A few rounds of 4.5" How. made them take cover.

6. MISCELLANEOUS. Very few Very Lights were observed during the night.

H.Q. 35th Division,
8th August 1918.

for A. J. Chesney Lieut.
Lieutenant-Colonel,
General Staff, 35th Division.

BRITISH ATTACK.
At 4-20 a.m. this morning an attack was launched by the 4th British and 1st French Armies on a front of 20 miles extending from North of MONTDIDIER to South of MORLANCOURT. Attack apparently a complete surprise and is progressing well and No news from the French at present but British Line now runs E. of DEMUIN, E. of MARCELCAVE, E. of WARFUSEE, W. of CERISY, E. of CHIPILLY, E. of BOIS GRESSAIRE. (2000 yds N.E. of CHIPILLY).

35th DIVISION.
DAILY INTELLIGENCE SUMMARY No. 87.
From 6 a.m. 8th August to 6 a.m. 9th August 1918.

Ref. Sheet 28 S.W. - 1/20,000.

1. **OPERATIONS (BRITISH).**

   (a) **Infantry.** Patrols were out along the Divisional front. On the Left Brigade front a strong Officer's patrol (1 Officer and 17 O.Rs.) proceeded to the enemy's wire at M.29.b.8.4 and placed a bangalore torpedo in position. When our artillery opened fire at 12 midnight (in connection with operation by the Division on our Left) the torpedo was exploded. When our artillery ceased to fire on the enemy's trench the patrol entered the trench and searched the ground for 80 to 90 yards in rear. No enemy was found. A patrol on the Right Brigade front which went out to reconnoitre enemy's posts and wire, found the enemy to be very alert.

   (b) **Artillery.** Our Left Brigade of Field Artillery fired diversion barrage in connection with the operation on our left. Harassing fire was actively carried out during the period. At 4.0 p.m. 4.5" Hows. fired a short concentration on an active hostile battery at T.2.d.9.3.

2. **OPERATIONS (GERMAN).**

   (a) **Infantry.** NIL.

   (b) **Artillery.** Enemy artillery activity was slightly above normal. Enemy replied to our shoot at 12 midnight by shelling our front and support lines and the forward areas.

3. **AVIATION.** One E.A. crossed our lines at 9.0 A.M., one at 9.0 P.M., one at 4-30 A.M. and one at 6.0 A.M. All were engaged by M.G. and Lewis Gun fire.

4. **HOSTILE DEFENCES.**

   (a) **Machine Guns.** A machine gun fired on one of our patrols from about M.24.c.70.15. This was reported by a patrol to be unoccupied on the night 7/8th August.

   (b) **Posts.** Enemy posts about M.35.a.0.0 were found to be on the alert.

5. **MOVEMENT.** A little individual movement was observed in N.31.b. and T.13.d.

   The smoke of trains was observed as follows:-
   1-50 p.m. Vicinity of ARMENTIERES.
   7-10 p.m. ARMENTIERES to LILLE.
   8-15 p.m. LILLE to ARMENTIERES.

6. **MISCELLANEOUS.**

   (a) When our artillery opened fire at midnight the enemy put up ordinary White Very Lights followed by double Red, double Golden and double Green Lights. At 4.0 A.M. Red lights were sent up from enemy front line. Enemy also sent up some White Lights bursting into three stars. All light signals were repeated by relays back to MONT KEMMEL.

   (b) During our artillery fire at midnight the enemy's light signals appeared to be fired from about 300 yards in rear of his front line.

   (c) The Brigade on our left obtained identifications of the 52nd Reserve Division during their operation.

R. P. Harrison Capt
for Lieutenant-Colonel,
General Staff, 35th Division.

H.Q. 35th Division,
9th August 1918.

Index

SUBJECT.

No.	Contents.	Date.
	GS 35th Division September 1918	

Original

WAR DIARY

Sheet No.1.
Headquarters 35th Division,
GENERAL STAFF,
September 1918.

Army Form C. 2118.

XXXXXXXXXXXXXXXXXXXXXXXXX
XXXXXXXXXXXXXXXXXXXXXXXX

(Erase heading not required.)

Place	Date	Hour	Summary of Events and Information	Remarks and references to Appendices
CASSEL	1		Fine day. 35th Division Artillery moves to HAMHOEK and HANDECOT Areas (H.Q. CLIFFORD CAMP F.19.d.7.2 Sheet 27). 159 Brigade R.F.A. goes into the line covering the 14th British Division. 35th Division O.O. 190 issued. Major-General A.H.MARINDIN,D.S.O. returns from leave.	O.O.190.
HERZEELE.	2		35th Division H.Q. closed at CASSEL at 10.0 a.m. opening at HERZEELE at the same hour. 35th Division moves by march route to HERZEELE (104th Infantry Brigade) – ROVEN (105th Infantry Brigade) – ST JAN TER BIEZEN (106th Infantry Brigade) Areas. The Major-General visited H.Q. 30th American Division. Fine day, windy. C.R.A. 35th British Division moves to GOUTHOVE CHATEAU (covering the front of 14th British Division).	
	3		Fine, windy day. The Major-General visits 30th American Division and the forward area in the morning. 106th Infantry Brigade relieved 119th American Regiment (30th American Division) in the Right Subsector of the CANAL SECTOR. Relief was completed without incident by 2-30 a.m. September 4th. Two companies 35th Bn. M.G.C. relieved two American M.G. companies in the Left Subsector. 106th Infantry Brigade and the Machine Gun companies proceeded to the forward area for relief, by light railway.	
	4		Command of the CANAL SECTOR (II Corps front) passed to G.O.C. 35th Division at 6.0 p.m. from G.O.C. 30th American Division. At 6.0 p.m. H.Q. 35th Division closed at HERZEELE opening at VOGELTJE at the same hour. 105th Infantry Brigade relieved 120th Infantry Brigade (30th American Division) in the Left Subsector of the CANAL SECTOR. Relief was completed without incident by 4-30 a.m. (Sept. 5th). Remaining M.G.Coys. of 35th Bn. M.G.C. relieved American M.G. Coys. in the Right Subsector. The front 35th British Division is covered by 66th Division Artillery. 41st British Division is in the line on the right flank (124th Infantry Brigade). 14th British Division is in the line on the left flank (43rd Infantry Brigade.). Rain during the night. II Corps Order No. 272 received. (Artillery reliefs).	
VOGELTJE				

5th/

WAR DIARY

XXXXXXXXXXXXXXXXXXXXX
XX
XXXXXXXXXXXXXXXXXXXXX

(Erase heading not required.)

Sheet No. 2.
Headquarters 35th Division, Army Form C. 2118.
GENERAL STAFF,
September 1918.

Instructions regarding War Diaries and Intelligence Summaries are contained in F. S. Regs., Part II. and the Staff Manual respectively. Title pages will be prepared in manuscript.

Place	Date	Hour	Summary of Events and Information	Remarks and references to Appendices
VOGELTJE	5		The Major-General visited all Brigade H.Q. and H.Q. 41st British Division. Fine day.	
	6		Mainly fine; thunder and rain during afternoon. The Major-General went out early and visited the Right front. II Corps Order 272 received (Artillery reliefs). 35th Division O.O. 191 issued (Infantry reliefs). 35th Division No. G. 3172 (CANAL SECTOR. Present Policy of Defences) issued. G.R.A. 35th Division assumed command of Artillery covering 35th Division front at 6-0 p.m. 66th Divisional Artillery is relieved on night 6/7th by 159th Brigade R.F.A. (Covering the Left Subsector) and 64th Army Brigade R.F.A. (Covering the Right Subsector). 157th Brigade R.F.A. remains under 14th Division. A daylight patrol of 105th Infantry Brigade (15th Cheshires) captured 6 prisoners - 4 unwounded, 2 wounded (all O.R.). Identifications normal, 236th Division, 148th I.R.	O.O.191
	7		Fine morning, heavy rain in afternoon. The Major-General visited the right front line.	
	8		Fine in the early morning, but heavy rain at intervals throughout the day. The Major-General visited Brigades and Field Ambulances. 104th Infantry Brigade relieved 105th Infantry Brigade in the left Subsector of the Divisional Sector. Relief was completed without incident by 11-15 p.m.	
	9		Cold windy day with rain at intervals. The Major-General visited Transport lines and the Reception Camp in the morning. In the afternoon he visited Brigades. Three men of the 17th Lancashire Fusiliers reported missing after a patrol encounter at about 6.0 a.m. (One wounded, two unwounded).	
	10		The Major-General visited the line (Right Brigade front). 35th Division O.O.192 issued (Relief of 105th Infantry Brigade by 105th Infantry Brigade and move of Brigade Headquarters). Rain fell at intervals during the day. The Army Commander visited Division H.Q. in the afternoon. Mutual relief of 157th Bde. R.F.A. and 64th Army Brigade R.F.A. began (One section per battery per night until completion).	O.O.192
	11		O.C. 157th Bde. R.F.A. took up command of the Artillery covering the Right Brigade Subsector of the CANAL SECTOR. Rain continued at intervals during the day. Patrols from 105th Infantry Brigade (on the Right Subsector) during the night 11/12th	find/

WAR DIARY

Sheet No. 3.
Headquarters 35th Division,
GENERAL STAFF,
September 1918.

Army Form C. 2118.

Place	Date	Hour	Summary of Events and Information	Remarks and references to Appendices
VOGELTJE	11		(Continued). find WHITE HORSE CELLARS unoccupied by the enemy.	
	12		The Major-General visited battery positions and YPRES in the morning. Daylight patrols from 106th Infantry Brigade found WHITE HORSE CELLARS unoccupied as on previous night. 105th Infantry Brigade relieved 106th Infantry Brigade in the Right Subsector. Relief was completed by 3-15 a.m. (Sept. 13th). Very heavy rain fell during the morning. II Corps Warning Order No. 276 received.	
	13		35th Division Order No. 193 issued (Extension of front Northwards, and relief of 104th Infantry Brigade by 106th Infantry Brigade on night 16/17th). Fine day. A noticeable increase of hostile Artillery activity. 104th Infantry Brigade (19th Durham L.I.) captured five prisoners (two wounded) in the Left Subsector at about 6.0 a.m. Identification:- 104th I.R. 40th (Saxon) Division. This was a new identification. The Major-General visited the forward area in the morning (O.Ps. etc.) with Corps Commander XIX Corps. 104th Infantry Brigade extended its front Northwards, taking over the line as far as I.21.a.0.7 (ZILLEBEK LAKE) from the 14th British Division. II Corps Order No. 277 received. 35th Division Artillery joined in a gas bombardment of HILL 60 at 10.0 p.m.	O.O.193
	14.		35th Division Order No. 194 issued. XIX Corps Order 192 received. Rain fell during the morning. In the afternoon the Major-General visited Infantry Brigades.	O.O.194
	15		35th Division Order No. 195 issued. 35th British Division was transferred from II British Corps to XIX British Corps with effect from 10.0 a.m. September 15th. 35th British Division continues to hold the CANAL SECTOR from VOORMEZEELE inclusive to ZILLEBEEK LAKE. At 6-15 p.m. the Major-General held a Conference of Infantry Brigadiers, C.R.A. etc. at Divisional H.Q.	O.O.195

WAR DIARY

Army Form C. 2118.

Sheet No. 4.

Headquarters 35th Division,
GENERAL STAFF,
September 1918.

Place	Date	Hour	Summary of Events and Information	Remarks and references to Appendices
VOGELTJE	15		(Continued). At 10-40 p.m. 105th Infantry Brigade and 104th Infantry Brigade advanced the line a distance of 1,000 yards along the whole front. There was not much resistance, 49 prisoners of 40th (Saxon) Division and 4 M.Gs. were captured. Our casualties were very light.	O.O.196
	16		Fine and very warm. 106th Infantry Brigade relieved 104th Infantry Brigade in the Left Subsector. Army Commander visited Division H.Q. 35th Division O.O.196 issued.	
WARATAH CAMP.	17		Heavy rain during the night. Fine day. Division H.Q. closed at VOGELTJE and opened at WARATAH CAMP at 1-0 p.m.	
	18		Fine. G.O.C. held a Conference at WARATAH CAMP at 5-30 p.m. Present:- G.O.C., C.R.A., three Brigadier-Generals commanding Infantry Brigades, A.A.& Q.M.G., D.A.Q.M.G., O.C. 35th Bn. M.G.C., O.C., 101st Bn. M.G.C., C.R.E., G.S.O.1, G.S.O.2, G.S.O.3.	
	19		Strong drying wind. 42nd Infantry Brigade (14th Division) relieved 105th Infantry Brigade in the Right Subsector. 42nd Infantry Brigade remained under command of G.O.C. 35th Division until 10.0 a.m. 20th September. On completion of relief 106th Infantry Brigade was holding the line in 35th Division Sector with 104th Infantry Brigade in support. 106th Infantry Brigade (less one Battn.) at SCHOOL CAMP, one battalion in Support Area. 35th Division Order No. 197 issued.	O.O.197
	20		Fine.	
	21		Fine. G.O.C. attended Corps Conference at 14th Division H.Q. Six guns 35th Bn.M.G.C. in 14th Division Area relieved during night 21/22nd September by guns of 14th Bn. M.G.C. 35th Division Order No. 198 issued.	O.O.198
	22		Stormy. Heavy rain in afternoon. Two companies 101st Bn. M.G.C. arrived in Division Area and came under orders of 35th Division. G.O.C. held a Conference at Division H.Q. Present:- Three B.Gs.C. Infantry Brigades, C.R.A., C.R.E., O.C., 35th Bn.M.G.C.	

Army Form C. 2118.

WAR DIARY

Headquarters 35th Division,
GENERAL STAFF,
September 1918.

Sheet No. 5.

(Erase heading not required.)

Place	Date	Hour	Summary of Events and Information	Remarks and references to Appendices
WARATAH CAMP.	23		Fine and clear. Hostile aircraft more active and night bombing. 35th Division Order No. 199 issued.	O.O.199
	24		Fine. Army Commander visited 35th Division H.Q.	
	25		Fine.	
	26		Fine after a wet night. 35th Division Order No. 200 issued.	O.O.200.
	27		Fine. Strong W. wind. All units of three Infantry Brigades moved to forward area during the night 26/27th.	
	28		Cold and dry. All troops moved to their assembly positions after dark during the night 27/28th. 35th Division attacked at 5-30 a.m. according to 35th Division Order No. 199 of the 23rd. 14th Division on the Right, 29th Division on the Left. The enemy did not offer serious resistance and all 1st objectives were captured. As the battle is proceeding it is not possible to forward an account now. A complete account will follow after the conclusion of operations.	
WOODCOTE HOUSE.	29		35th Division H.Q. moved forward to WOODCOTE HOUSE Sheet 28/I.20.c.	
	30		See Appendix (Account of Operations).	

H.Q. 35th Division,
30th September 1918.

Major-General,
Commanding 35th Division.

35 Division 'C' Register of Messages

Serial No	In or Out	From or To	Sender's Number	Time Sent	Time Recd.	PURPORT	Action Taken	Remarks
1	In	104 Bde	Bmg 12	0850	0955	The definite news is that our R.I.s have entered N.4.b. N.14.a on this front objectives consistent with rocket put up activity and slight opposition of N.30 and 34 seen reported told him at N.36.0 – N.19 pt. N.28.5 and BELLEGHEM.		
2	In	105	N.m.342	0950	1019	0835 Light of Goldfishes and 9th R.S. are held up on line N.12.d.8.2 – N.17.a.5.9. Try and get cleft forward from N.12.d.8.2 and 8.7.C.5.4 that attacks from N. showing confidently but sitrep report 08.30 states they are held up at about SNEVEGHEM Church at present. I see strong opposition on the front as shown in my first situation report assume through BDE Staff to front of Stafford of SLOXKEN [?]. H.366 from screen. Not to get from a firing over you right. Presume 40 or 50. Cannot communicate with 104 Bde — will you notify them from attack.		
3	Out	104 Bde 15 Corps	BC.9.1 Sitrep	1210	—	1132 Have got our lost arcades an hour the enclosing was boon for group. In the final objective I doubt if we can be on the spot sending come other Bn. now a great deal. I do not think it possible. I want it now to stop... I think we must be content with first [illegible]... KRUIPEL RIDGE... SVEVEGHEM supposed... [illegible].		
4	In	105 Bde	BC.S2	1215	1235	At 10.30 13 Cheshires still have not advanced then N.11.C.9.2 N.11.d.9.8 with advance parties at N.11 attacks N.W. side of stream and a post across stream at N.12 d.3.1. Enemy holding line of Rd to N.11 d.25 N.12 d.7.8 holds many mgs...		

35 Division "a" Register of Messages

Conseq. No.	In or Out	From or To	Sender's Number	Time Sent	Time Recd.	Purport	Action Taken	Remarks
5	In	104 Bde	Bm 766	1215	1245	Bombardment commenced in entrance to assault at attack of M.24. Col. Jacobs reports KRUPPE Ridge strongly held by hostile. Considerable numbers of enemy retired to sunken lane. Pretty numerous are the movement.		
6	Out	104 Bde	G.S.9	1300	—	A report been received from 1315 to 1330. 2½ as the assignment that a halt on batteries on left.		
7	Out	HQ C. 35 Div.	S.820	1345	—	9 Div. report to this line at 1300 near KROTE OP central to O.30. Central. Attack the advance near J.30. Central.		
8	Out	105 Bde	G.S.11	1400	—	Reports no 7 above.		
9	Out	2nd A.C.O.	G.S.12	1415	—	Night boundary 35 Div. run from M.20. Central to V.13. c.2.2. Report your troops may be up by [Day?] Boundary COURTRAI - COYGHEM Road then left boundary.		
10	In	105 Bde	Bm 323	1407	1422	The battle progresses right ahead of heavy rifle & mg M.M.G. N.L.C. N.6.C. N.6.L. at about our front of L and at. Have but Canal has not known and troops are marking a 1300 on HEUREM and D. Staffs report and received Crossed frost has taken refuge on our second Spanner has lost this Heavily positions of Sherwood.		
11	Out	3 Bde. 19 Corps. Gen. Res.	G.Q.13	1435	—	Nr. 7 Mbas. report contains four SUEVEGHEM state having left message 1500. Enemy group 8 of COURTRAI - BOSSUYT CANAL. Saw a few guns on Canal. Inconf. probably O.22.L. Absolute "Court" which had been cut under fire.		
12	In	104 Bde	Bm 970	1425	1512	Following message from 15 Sherwood, 4105 Bde. Holds up on enemies beyond Jam through SUEVEGHEM. Help and arty obs of message sent.		

N.E. Amis.

35 Division 'A' Register of Messages

Serial No	In or Out	From or To	Sender's Number	Time Sent	Time Recd.	PURPORT	Action Taken	Remarks
W.C.								
13	In	105 Bde	Bm 329/345	1315	1520	HQ 105 Bde closes M1 at 5.7 at 15.30 and opens H19 K7 3 at same hour. Communication by road established in M.I. sqr 3.		
14	In	105 Bde	Bm 326/507	1507	1550	15 Sherwoods have captured SWEVEGHEM and are apparently continuing advance.		
15	In	19 Corps	G.961	1590	1635	Div Comdrs Orders for pursuit of enemy.		
16	In	104 Bde	Bm 173/1324	1324	1624	JOCE report they have reached M N.W.C. and SIKU U.24.a and have orders for pursuance.		
17	Out	34 Div	G.17	1712		35 Div is attacking enemy 0.31 - 0.27 - 0.22 from tract to Bnl. 17.7 to day.		
18	In	122 9 Bde	5199	1600	1728	Bde HQ established H.33.c.o.6		
19	In	105 Bde	J.92	1635	1800	Situation 1390. Staff reported at Century Latrine 30/28 and DCR I. Enemy thought to be holding front against left hay at by five from across Canal. At 14.30 staff reported pushing through SWEVEGHEM Sherwoods front acct. HQrs and looking toward S of SWEVEGHEM astride the road W.7.& Cheshire road KEIBEEK 1600 pushing forward.		
20	In	41 Div	G.893	1650	1850	Warning Order for Conference of returns of 41 Division.		
21	In	41 Div.	G.694	1700	1944	Order for continue of pursuance of the enemy.		
22	In	106 Bde	BM.123	1920	1956	106 Bde HQ established at N.9.d.0.5 Château. Units en route in accordance with your G.H.T of to day.		
23	In	4 Div	G.695	1930	2020	Attachment 641 Division 96.94. (see McDonald) dated 26th.		
24	In	To Cow	J.599	1810	2035	Report of Staff. Reconnaissance of 20 Div front.		
25	Out	35 Div CW A	J.921	2105		30 Div line September 17.30. U.26 - COYEGHEM - U.19 - U.13.d -		

35 Division "A" Register of Messages

6/2/18

Serial No	In or Out	From or To	Sender's Number	Time Sent	Time Recd.	PURPORT	From Tickr	Remarks
797	Out	104/105 Bgd RFA	A10-21	0625	—	105- 2nd RFA report Scout at 10" Platoons N16.30.2 along road on N.E. boundary to O.13.B.20 and thence to O.13.B.33 where Patrol got in Bosch wire		
798	Out	106 IRB	908-87	06.57	—	1°- Ship worth Report Point 0602. 10°- Bn return 0645- Point B.61 in attempt entirely all our troops driven back. Further expansion H.N. State Examined 0645- B.62 Coys not H.W. State Examined 0645- B.62 Coys not yet in 614 contained Boches on O.14.A.		
799	In	105 IRB	Ben-202	6.51	06.52	Returned the whole Bn as was on Line of units advance of N. Staffs now pushed forward. Capture to O.14.B.62, Bosches on O.14.A. Believed captured by us but Capt. Hawker Reserve.		
799	In	2nd Dragons	9729	6906	0629	Morning Report.		
799	In	10 York	93-37	0916	1028	Situation on Report Front.		
799	In	CRA	Bn-16	0645	1010	HMR By. closed at HATHOEN at 1000 am 81°. 6th Section at NAPLES MT F.25 at Company Hour		
800	In	35 Div	G-241	0952	1025	Situation.		
801	In	106 IRB	J.2128	11.30	11.30	Division able to secure and reinforce 10 New a gap and will be to occupy this line ANT NERD. BRUGES. A line of units across the front of Ghent is reported to return to same vast N. and West of DESTRUYK. All troops across front of most adjacent sense at L'ESCAUT should now afford amuch. Line of L'ESCAUT to be on the country NW of L'ESCAUT to be handed a right of 105 further.		
802	In	10" SRFd Bgd	208	11.45	12.18	10"- 1RB close at 4.30 00 at 12.05 2000 and came from hour and H.30 up.		
803	In	106 IRB	1277	12.01		Before 0500 today the Bosche occupied Palace ACRATIS with British Patrols the road Lieucourt of Yvetot no say on forward Belgian on canal.		

War Diary

Ref.Sheets 28 N.W. & 28 S.W. 1/20,000.
35th DIVISION.
DAILY INTELLIGENCE SUMMARY No.88.
From 6 a.m. 4th September to 6 a.m. 5th September 1918.

---

1. OPERATIONS (British)

    (a) <u>Infantry</u>. The relief of the 120th American Regiment (30th American Division) by 105th Infantry Brigade (35th British Division) was carried out without incident.

    Our patrols were active, particularly on the front of the Right Infantry Brigade. No enemy patrols were encountered.

    At 4.15 a.m. one patrol went along the S.W. side of the CANAL as far as I.33.a.0.1. Here it came under M.G. and T.M. fire from SPOIL BANK - at least 3 M.G's. fired.

    The OLD FRENCH TRENCH is almost obliterated between BUS HOUSE and I.32.c.9.5.

    Enemy shells fell between I.32.d.0.3. and I.32.d.3.0. - apparently the area is unoccupied.

    Several of the enemy were seen between 0.2.a.2.4. and 0.2.a.4.5.

    (b) <u>Artillery</u>. Our Artillery carried out harassing fire during the night on enemy roads, tracks, and occupied areas.

2. OPERATIONS (German)

    (a) <u>Infantry</u>. Nil.

    (b) <u>Artillery</u>. Hostile Artillery was active on the roads in H.18.a.& b., H.23.b. and H.24.a.& b. between 6.45 p.m. and 11.45 p.m.

    40 rounds of Yellow Cross Gas Shell fell about H.18.central during the night.

3. AVIATION. At 4.10 p.m. two E.A. flew low over the enemy lines.

4. HOSTILE DEFENCES.

    (a) <u>M.G's</u>. There are several machine guns in SPOIL BANK and the ridge South of it.

    One M.G. fired on a patrol from ST.ELOI.

    (b) <u>T.M's</u>. A T.M. fired from behind SPOIL BANK on one of our patrols.

5. MOVEMENT. A good deal of movement was observed in O.14.d. during the day, and a little individual movement round the MOUND O.2.d.

6. <u>MISCELLANEOUS</u>. At 5.30 a.m. enemy sent up two red lights at several places along his front. Shelling of the front and support system of our right Brigade followed.

R. P. Hanson Capt

H.Q. 35th Division,
5th September 1918.

Lieutenant-Colonel,
General Staff, 35th British Division.

SUMMER TIME.

Date.	SUN. Rises.	Sets.	MOON. Rises.	Sets.
Sept. 6th.	6.9 a.m.	7.25 p.m.	7.17 a.m.	7.17 p.m.
Sept. 7th.	6.10 a.m.	7.23 p.m.	8.25 a.m.	7.35 p.m.

YELLOW CROSS GAS IN ABANDONED DUGOUTS (From G.H.Q. Summary).

A captured order of the 25th Reserve Division dated 29th July 1918 lays down that all abandoned dugouts will be contaminated by exploding a 10.5 c.m. howitzer Yellow Cross Gas Shell in them. A few dugouts will be left untouched for the use of rearguards, and, in order to deceive the enemy, will be marked as contaminated.

Ref.Sheets 28 N.W. & 28 S.W. 1/20,000.

35th DIVISION.
DAILY INTELLIGENCE SUMMARY No.89.
From 6 a.m. 5th September to 6 a.m. 6th September 1918.

1. OPERATIONS (British)
   (a) Infantry. Our patrols were very active along the whole front. No enemy patrols were encountered.
   A patrol went out at 2.0 a.m. and proceeded to BLAUWE POORT FARM I.27.b.5.4. which was found to be unoccupied.
   A Lewis Gun post was established at I.27.b.2.5. to watch the Farm and ascertain if the enemy attempted to occupy it by day.
   (b) Artillery Our Artillery fired concentrations and harassing fire on enemy roads, tracks and occupied areas, during the night.

2. OPERATIONS (German)
   (a) Infantry Nil.
   (b) Artillery. Hostile Artillery was intermittently active during the day and night. Special attention was paid to I.25.c.
   At about 11 p.m. I.31.a.& b. were shelled with about 30 rounds of Yellow Cross Gas Shell. The vicinity of LANKHOF CHATEAU I.26.c.d.0.0. was shelled by 10.5 c.m. Howitzers from 4 p.m. to 6 p.m.
   IRON BRIDGE I.26.c.3.6. and SWAN CHATEAU I.19.c.4.8. were shelled at intervals during the night.
   DOLL'S HOUSE I.19.b.2.5. was shelled by 10.5 c.m. and 15 c.m. Hows. between 10.45 p.m. and 1.0 a.m.
   A few rounds of Green cross gas shell fell in I.19.a. during the night.

3. AVIATION.   Three E.A. were over our front between 8.30 a.m. and 9.15 a.m.

4. HOSTILE DEFENCES.
   (a) Machine Guns. Enemy Machine Guns fired from about O.1.c.8.5.and I.27.d.5.7.

5. MOVEMENT.   2.30 p.m.   One man at O.2.c.08.40.
                 4.20 p.m.   One man at O.2.b.05.35.
                 5.13 p.m.   Two men at O.2.c.8.4.

P. P. Harrison
Capt

H.Q. 35th Division,
6th September 1918.
                                     Lieutenant-Colonel,
                              General Staff, 35th Division.

LATER. One of our daylight patrols captured four unwounded and two wounded Germans belonging to 11th Company 458th I.R. 236th Division (Normal) at I.28.a.0.4. at about 12 noon to-day.

SUMMER TIME.

Date.	SUN. Rises.	Sets.	MOON. Rises.	Sets
8th Sept.	6.12 a.m.	7.21 p.m.	9.31 a.m.	7.54 p.m.
9th Sept.	6.13 a.m.	7.19 p.m.	10.35 a.m.	8.19 p.m.

Preliminary interrogation of six prisoners of 11th Company 458 I.R. 236th Division captured about noon 6th September 1918 about I.28.a.0.4.

METHOD OF CAPTURE.

Prisoners together with two other men of their company were on outpost when our patrol approached. The sentry fired a couple of shots and ran for the dug-out, which was rushed by our men. The inmates with the exception of two men who ran away were captured by our patrol.

ORDER OF BATTLE.

Prisoners give the order of battle from North to South as -
458 I.R.
457 I.R.
459 I.R.

Prisoners cannot state what division is North of them.

DISPOSITIONS.

Prisoners have only been two days in the front line and are vague as to their dispositions. The IIIrd Battalion is in line with two companies in the front line and two companies in Support. The Ist Battalion is in Support and the IInd Battalion resting in GHELUWE.

About 2/3 of the men of the 11th Company are on outpost duty holding three posts roughly 100 yards apart. Each post has a light machine gun.

The outpost line runs 200 to 300 yards in front of MIDDLESEX ROAD. The remainder of the men and two light machine guns are at Company H.Q.

RELIEFS.

No word of the 236th Division being relieved.

WORK.

Prisoners' outpost consisted of a shell-hole containing the sentry post and a shelter about 20 yards in rear of it. Prisoners had no orders regarding work and all the wire in the vicinity was old.

One fresh row of concertina wire has been put out in front of MIDDLESEX ROAD. There are no shelters or concrete work along MIDDLESEX ROAD.

—o—o—o—o—o—o—o—o—

Ref. Sheets 28 N.W., & 28 S.W. 1/20,000.

35th DIVISION.
DAILY INTELLIGENCE SUMMARY No.90.
From 6 a.m. 6th September to 6 a.m. 7th September 1918.

1. OPERATIONS (British)
   (a) Infantry.   Our patrols were very active along the whole Divisional front both by day and night.
   The prisoners of 458th I.R. 236th Division (reported in 35th Division Summary No.89 dated 6th September) were captured at about 11.30 a.m. by a daylight fighting patrol consisting of one Officer and twelve other ranks at I.27.a.95.25. (NOT I.28.a.0.4) This patrol also discovered two unoccupied enemy listening posts at I.27.a.50.20. and I.27.a.50.25. The post at I.27.a.95.25. consisted of seven O.R's., six of whom were captured - the seventh escaped. (These were apparently manned by personnel from the post at I.27.a.95.25.)   A post at I.28.a.2.9. was evacuated by the enemy at the approach of one of our patrols.   A hostile L.T.Mortar fired on the evacuated post and a red flare was put up.
   An enemy working party at I.27.c.9.6. was dispersed by Lewis Gun fire.
   The Lewis Gun post established at I.27.b.2.5. (35th Division Summary No.89 para.1 (a)) returned to our lines at 10.0 p.m. having observed no enemy movement..
   CHESTER FARM I.33.a.75.55. was found to be unoccupied by day.
   During the evening of 6th September, the right battalion right brigade advanced its right company as far as the VOORMEZEELE SWITCH TRENCH.   We now hold the trench as far as its junction with OLD FRENCH TRENCH.
   A liaison post with the Division on our right has been established at Q.1.d.25.90.
   Enemy Artillery and M.G's. were active during the operation causing us a few casualties.
   OLD FRENCH TRENCH was reconnoitred by night from O.1.d.30.95 to O.1.b.8.0. and was found to be unoccupied.
   A daylight patrol (5.15 p.m.) proceeded to LOCK 7 I.32.b.7.3. and SPOIL BANK I.33.a.2.1.   A time fuze and a tunnel through the LOCK were found at LOCK 7.
   Our daylight patrols were expecially active from 5 p.m. onwards.
   Hostile balloons were up at this time, and one dropped a light signal, apparently the signal for Artillery fire which immediately began and was fairly heavy.
   A patrol entered an enemy post at I.33.a.4.6. and found a tunic and some letters.   Shoulder strap (457 I.R. 236th Division - Normal) was brought in.   The post is possibly occupied by night.
   (b) Artillery.   Our Artillery fired concentrations and harassing fire on enemy roads tracks and occupied areas during the period.

2. OPERATIONS (German)
   (a) Infantry.   Nil.
   (b) Artillery.   Hostile Artillery was very active on our front system from 5.15 p.m. for about an hour.   I.31.c. received much attention by day and night. . About 60 rounds of Yellow Cross Gas Shell from 15 c.m. and 10.5 c.m. Hows. fell in vicinity of Right Brigade H.Q. and ASSAM FARM H.22.a.2.8. during the night.
   Intermittent shelling of H.24.c. with Blue Cross Gas by 15 c.m. Hows. during the night.
   Between 9 p.m. and 2 a.m. roads in H.24.a., H.22.,

TURN OVER/

and H.29.a. were actively harassed with H.E. and Yellow Cross Gas Shell.
A few 7.7.c.m. shells were reported on our front line during the period, but most of the shelling was by 10.5 c.m. and 15 c.m. Hows.

3. AVIATION.   Hostile aerial activity was normal.

4. HOSTILE DEFENCES
   (a) Machine Guns.   Machine Gunss reported to have fired from I.27.d.3.5., I.27.b.6.5. and I.27.b.3.3.
   (b) Posts.   Occupied posts at I.27.a.95.25.(occupants captured) and I.28.a.2.9.
   (c) Wire.   Fairly thick concertina wire in front of the light railway between I.33.a.2.4. and I.33.a.5.5.

5. MOVEMENT.   Nil.

6. MISCELLANEOUS.
   (i) Smoke was seen coming from arachway under the road at I.33.a.30.35.
   (ii) At 8 p.m. four red rockets, each bursting into two red stars were put up from vicinity of ST. ELOI. No apparent action followed.

R.P. Harrison Capt
for
H.Q. 35th Division,   Lieutenant-Colonel,
7th September 1918.   General Staff, 35th British Division.

SUMMER TIME.

	SUN.		MOON.	
Date.	Rises.	Sets.	Rises.	Sets.
Sept. 9th.	6.13 a.m.	7.19 p.m.	10.35 a.m.	8.19 p.m.
" 10th.	6.15 a.m.	7.16 p.m.	11.40 a.m.	8.46 p.m.

Ref.Sheets 28 N.W., & 28 S.W. 1/20,000.

35th DIVISION.
DAILY INTELLIGENCE SUMMARY No.91.
From 6 a.m. 7th September to 6 a.m. 8th September.

War Diary

1. **OPERATIONS (British)**
   (a) **Infantry.** The dugouts in SPOIL BANK (I.33.a.& c.) were found to be unoccupied between 5.0 a.m. and 8.0 a.m. 7th. and LOCK No.7 is still mined.
   An officers' patrol approached CHESTER FARM (I.33.a.7.6.) and ascertained that it was held by an enemy M.G. post. A German patrol was then heard moving along the railway from I.32.b.8.9. to I.32.b.4.5. Our patrol opened fire and dispersed the enemy.
   The night was wet and dark and patrolling was hampered by the slippery condition of the ground.
   (b) **Artillery.** The suspected Inter-Battalion relief of the 458th I.R. was actively harassed in the early hours of the morning, heavy artillery co-operating.
   50 rounds 18 pdr. were fired at WHITE CHATEAU (O.4.d.)

2. **OPERATIONS (German)**
   (a) **Infantry.** None except the patrol encounter described in para.1(a).
   (b) **Artillery.** Enemy guns were fairly active during the day but quieter at night. Fire was mainly directed on to the approaches to VOORMEZEELE and our forward areas, H.30. and 36. and I.31. An increase was noticed in the use of 7.7 c.m. guns.
   During the night a few rounds were fired at the YPRES - VLAMERTINGHE Road by a long range gun.

3. **AVIATION.** E.A. practically nil.

4. **ENEMY DEFENCES.**
   (a) **Machine Guns.** M.G's. fired from:-
   I.27.b.60.45. (behind BLAUWE POORTE FARM)
   I.26.d.8.2.
   I.32.b.6.7.
   I.32.c.90.55. (suspected)
   I.33.c.10.45.
   O.2.a.4.6. (approx.) Fires down the BUS HOUSE - VOORMEZEELE Road.
   PICCADILLY FARM (O.8.a.4.8.) Fires at point where trench crosses road at O.1.d.3.9.
   Trench in I.32.d.
   (b) **Trench Mortars.** Nil.
   (c) **Snipers.** A sniper fires from BUS HOUSE (O.2.a.4.6.)
   (d) **Posts.** Unoccupied post at I.27.a.9.3.

5. **MOVEMENT.** Slight movement was seen in I.34.b. and d., and O.9.b.

R.P. Harrison Capt

Lieutenant-Colonel,
General Staff, 35th British Division.

H.Q. 35th Division,
8th September 1918.

SUMMER TIME.

Date.	SUN. Rises.	Sets.	MOON. Rises.	Sets.
Sept.11th.	6.16 a.m.	7.14 p.m.	12.44 p.m.	9.18 p.m.
" 12th.	6.18 a.m.	7.12 p.m.	1.45 p.m.	9.59 p.m.

Ref. Sheets 28 N.W. & 28 S.W. 1/20,000 .

35th BRITISH DIVISION.
DAILY INTELLIGENCE SUMMARY No.92.
From 6 a.m. 8th September to 6 a.m. 9th September 1918.

1. OPERATIONS (British)
   (a) Infantry.   Our patrols were active along the whole Division front.
   The VOORMEZEELE - ST.ELOI Road was reconnoitred as far as O.2.a.2.8. Very lights were observed to be sent up by the enemy from OLD FRENCH TRENCH at about O.2.a.2.4.
   OLD FRENCH TRENCH was reconnoitred by a daylight patrol from I.32.c.4.3. to I.32.d.8.4. No sign of the enemy was seen.
   A patrol crossed the ST.ELOI - LOCK 8 Road at I.32.d.0.7. and proceeded as far as I.32.d.3.7. No enemy were encountered.
   A daylight patrol (5.50 a.m.) reached and crossed the MIDDLESEX ROAD about 120 yards South west of LA CHAPELLE I.33.b.45.95.
   LA CHAPELLE and posts at I.27.d.60.45. were found to be occupied by the enemy and patrol was fired on from these places, also by machine guns from SPOIL BANK I.33.a., RAVINE WOOD I.34.a.& c., and I.27.d.8.2.
   Another daylight patrol (5.30 a.m. reconnoitred BLAUWE POORT FARM I.27.b.50.35. and found it unoccupied. A well-trodden path leading towards the enemy line was discovered.
   (b) Artillery   Enemy occupied areas and tracks were actively harassed. Concentrations were fired by all active guns on VERBRANDENMOLEN I.28.d., dugouts and tracks in I.34.a., and south Bank of the CANAL in I.33d.

2. OPERATIONS (German)
   (A) Infantry.   Nil.
   (b) Artillery.   The vicinity of VOORMEZEELE especially the road in I.31.c.& d. was intermittently shelled by 15 c.m. Howitzers most of the day. Shells appeared to come from the direction of BATTLE WOOD I.35., BELGIAN BATTERY CORNER H.24.a.4.8., was shelled by 15. c.m. Hows. during the night.
   The front line was intermittently shelled by 7.7.cm. guns.

3. AVIATION.   Aerial activity nil.

4. ENEMY DEFENCES.
   (a) Machine Guns.   Machine Guns fired from I.33.a., I.34.a., and I.27.d.8.2.
   A M.G. is suspected at BUS HOUSE O.2.a.4.7.

5. MOVEMENT.   At 8 a.m. five men seen at O.2.a.20.15.
   At 3.45 p.m. five men seen at O.2.a.20.15.
   One man observed to enter a dugout at about I.34.b.20.55.
   A little individual movement and smoke were observed in O.3.d.

P. P. Harrison Capt

H.Q. 35t Division,
9th September 1918.
Lieutenant-Colonel,
General Staff, 35th British Division.

SUMMER TIME.

Date	SUN. Rises.	Sets.	MOON. Rises.	Sets.
Sept.13th	6.19 a.m.	7.10 p.m.	2.40 p.m.	10.50 p.m.
" 14th	6.21 a.m.	7.7 p.m.	3.28 p.m.	11.52 p.m.

Ref.Sheets 28 N.W. & 28 S.W. 1/20,000.

35th BRITISH DIVISION.
DAILY INTELLIGENCE SUMMARY No.93.
From 6 a.m. 9th September to 6 a.m. 10th September 1918

----

1. OPERATIONS (British)
    (a) Infantry. At 11.30 p.m. 9th September a patrol left our lines at I.31.d.8.9. and having reached MIDDLESEX ROAD proceeded S.W. until it struck the VOORMEZEELE - ST.ELOI Road at O.2.a.20.80. They followed this road to BUS HOUSE which was thoroughly searched and the vicinity was reconnoitred but no sign of the enemy could be discovered.
    Another patrol left our lines at 6 a.m. 9th September and reached OLD FRENCH TRENCH at O.2.a.55.90. They crossed the trench and took up a position in a shelter at O.2.a.67.97. and remained there for some time. No enemy however appeared. They then moved forward and struck the ST.ELOI - LOCK 8 Road at O.2.a.95.90. and reconnoitred it for 100 yards on either side of this point without encountering any Germans.
    North of the YPRES - COMINES CANAL a daylight patrol examined a dugout E. of the point where MIDDLESEX ROAD crosses the Canal; it had evidently been originally used as an M.G. post.
    BLAUWE POORT FARM (I.27.b.5.4.) was also reconnoitred; the enemy has a post behind the Farm by day and a sniper fires from a Nissen Hut E. of the post.
    (b) Artillery. Our Artillery fired concentrations on the railway embankment in I.26.b., the concrete dugouts between I.28.d.0.8. and I.28.d.4.8. and CANAL WALK (I.33.d.). At 2.40 a.m. our Heavy Artillery shelled RAVINE WOOD (I.34.) Harassing fire was carried out on TRIANGULAR WOOD (O.3.b.), NORFOLK LODGE (I.33.c.80.60.) and tracks in I.33.c.

2. OPERATIONS (German)
    (a) Infantry. Nil.
    (b) Artillery. About normal. 100 rounds 10.5 c.m. were fired at the neighbourhood of SWAN CHATEAU (I.19.d.) about noon. At 1 p.m. the enemy fired another 35 rounds of the same calibre at KRUISTRAAT.
    The shelling of back areas increased somewhat and was mainly directed at the enemy's favourite targets H.30. and H.36. and VOORMEZEELE.
    Our front and support lines were intermittently shelled, especially on the left, by 7.7 c.m. and 10.5 c.m.
    The road in I.25.a. was shelled between 8 p.m. and 11 p.m. by 10.5 c.m. guns.

3. AVIATION. Weather conditions hindered aerial operations.

4. ENEMY DEFENCES.
    Posts. Occupied posts behind BLAUWE POORT FARM - Sniper's post close by. Another post at I.27.c.9.3. was also held. A post at I.27.d.25.45. opened fire on one of our patrols. Two unoccupied posts were discovered on the light railway at I.26.d.9.1. and one at I.27.c.4.3.

5. MOVEMENT. Movement was seen at SHELLEY FARM (O.2.b.9.1.), DOME HOUSE O.8.d.9.6.

H.Q. 35th Division,
10th September 1918.

A.J. Chesney Lieut.
for Lieutenant-Colonel,
General Staff, 35th British Division.

SUMMER TIME

	SUN		MOON	
Date.	Rises.	Sets.	Rises.	Sets.
Sept. 15th.	6.22 a.m.	7.5 p.m.	4.7 p.m.	0.59 a.m.
" 16th.	6.24 a.m.	7.3 p.m.	4.40 p.m.	2.16 a.m.

Ref.Sheets 28 N.W. & 28 S.W. 1/20,000.

War Diary

35th BRITISH DIVISION.
DAILY INTELLIGENCE SUMMARY No.94.
From 6 a.m. 10th September 1918 to 6 a.m. 11th September 1918.

1. OPERATIONS (British)
   (a) Infantry. Our patrols were active along the whole front.
   OLD FRENCH TRENCH was reconnoitred as far as O.1.b.8.0. On reaching this point the patrol was fired on by a machine gun and enemy sent up green light whereupon OLD FRENCH TRENCH and a post at O.1.d.35.95. were shelled by 7.7 c.m. guns.

   A patrol went along the light railway in I.32.c.& d. as far as MIDDLESEX ROAD and then proceeded along the north side of the road to about I.32.d.9.6. At this point two strongly wired enemy posts were discovered, one on each side of the road. These posts were occupied.

   Both banks of the CANAL from LOCK 8 to the point where MIDDLESEX ROAD crosses the CANAL I.33.a.2.2., were reconnoitred by a patrol (3.45 a.m. to 5.30 a.m.). This patrol then worked along the MIDDLESEX ROAD as far as CHESTER FARM I.33.a.6.7. CHESTER FARM was found to be unoccupied.

   Another patrol went along the railway from I.21.d.2.5. to I.27.b.8.8. No trace of the enemy was found.

   (b) Artillery. 18-pounders fired on hostile machine guns at I.27.b.70.32., I.27.d.3.2., and I.27.d.1.4.

   All active guns fired concentrations on dugouts at I.28.c.1.1., LARCH WOOD dugouts I.29.c.2.8. and dugouts from I.28.d.5.5. to I.28.d.5.7.

   Enemy tracks and occupied areas were actively harassed.

2. OPERATIONS (German)
   (a) Infantry. Nil.
   (b) Artillery. Intermittent shelling of our forward areas by 7.7 c.m. guns and 10.5 and 15 c.m. howitzers during the day and night.

   H.24.a.4.8. BELGIAN BATTERY CORNER was shelled by 15 c.m. howitzers (30 rounds). Direction of hostile battery T.B.120° from H.30.c.35.75.

   150 rounds from 15 c.m. howitzers fell about H.18.c.6.6. G.B. 135° from H.18.d.8.4.

3. AVIATION. Three E.A. were seen over our lines at 9.30 a.m. flying very high.

4. ENEMY DEFENCES. Two strongly wired occupied posts were located at I.32.d.9.6. and I.32.d.95.55.
   An hostile machine gun post located at I.27.c.9.3.

5. MOVEMENT. 3 p.m.   Three men seen at SPOIL BANK I.33.a.
   4.50 p.m.   One man seen near SHELLEY FARM O.2.b.9.0.
   4.50 p.m.& One man carrying a paper seen at WHITE
   6.20 p.m.   HORSE CELLARS O.2.a.95.30.

6. MISCELLANEOUS. At 6.15 a.m. several white lights bursting into two red lights were put up from I.33.d.
   Double red lights were put up from East of ST.ELOI during the night.

R.P.Harrison Capt
for Lieutenant-Colonel,
General Staff, 35th British Division.

H.Q. 35th Division,
11th September 1918.

SUMMER TIME.

Date.	SUN. Rises.	Sets.	MOON. Rises.	Sets.
Sept.17th.	6.25 a.m.	7.0 p.m.	5.11 p.m.	3.36 a.m. (18th)
" 18th.	6.27 a.m.	6.58 p.m.	5.35 p.m.	5.0 a.m. (19th)

Ref. Sheets 28 N.W. & 28 S.W. 1/20,000.

War Diary

35th BRITISH DIVISION.
DAILY INTELLIGENCE SUMMARY No.95.
From 6 a.m. 11th September to 6 a.m. 12th September.

1. OPERATIONS (British)
   (a) Infantry. Our patrols were again active both by day and by night.
   The crater at O.2.a.1.1. was found to be occupied, and a large duckboarded shell hole at O.1.d.95.95. appeared to have been recently occupied.
   A patrol (11.30 p.m. to 3.15 a.m.) left our lines at I.31.d.80.95. and proceeded to I.32.c.40.35. thence to cross roads at I.32.d.0.3. and thence to WHITE HORSE CELLARS O.2.b.0.3. WHITE HORSE CELLARS were searched but were unoccupied, and showed no signs of recent occupation. Patrol then waited for half an hour at about O.2.d.20.85. Very Lights went up from approximately O.3.c.05.55., O.2.d.05.10, and O.2.c.35.45.
   A daylight patrol reconnoitred trench and shelters at I.32.c.2.7.; these were found to be in good condition. A post of 1 Officer and 15 O.Rs. was established there at 4.0 a.m. 12th September.
   A patrol reconnoitred BLAUWE POORT FARM I.27.b.50.35. and found it occupied by the enemy. M.G's were fired from the Farm and lights sent up.
   CHESTER FARM I.33.a.6.7. was found to be unoccupied but LA CHAPELLE I.33.b.45.95. appears to be strongly held.
   An enemy post was located at I.27.d.2.7.
   (b) Artillery. Harassing fire was carried out during the period on enemy roads and occupied areas.
   All active guns fired concentrations on occupied areas in I.28.d. at 9.45 p.m. and 5.50 a.m., in I.29.c. at 9.15 p.m., and LARCH WOOD dugouts I.29.c.2.8. at 2.0 p.m.

2. OPERATIONS (German)
   (a) Infantry. A patrol of about seven men which approached our post at I.27.a.3.1. was dispersed by Lewis Gun fire.
   (b) Artillery. Our front line was intermittently shelled by 7.7 c.m. guns, particularly the front line of left battalion left Brigade from 3 a.m. to 5 a.m.
   The forward areas received the normal scattered shelling during the period. Particular attention was paid to IRON BRIDGE I.26.c.2.6.
   A few incendiary shells (7.7c.m.) were reported at H.24.b.7.7. at 5.45 a.m.

3. AVIATION. One E.A. flying high was seen at 9.0 a.m.

4. HOSTILE DEFENCES. Post located at I.27.d.2.7.
   Crater at O.2.a.1.1. found occupied.
   BLAUWE POORT FARM I.27.b.50.35. found to be occupied.
   LA CHAPELLE I.33.b.45.95. apparently strongly held.

5. MOVEMENT. 8.0 a.m. Two men left WHITE HORSE CELLARS O.2.b.0.3. and walked towards TRIANGULAR WOOD O.3.a.
   4.15 p.m. Six men left pill box at O.2.a.38.10. and disappeared over the ridge.
   7.0 p.m. Two men came over ridge and entered pill box at O.2.a.38.10.

6. MISCELLANEOUS. Two red lights fired several times by the enemy during the night. This is probably a signal for field guns to lengthen range.

H.Q. 35th Division,
12th September 1918.

Harrison Capt
Lieutenant-Colonel,
General Staff, 35th British Division.

Ref.Sheets 28 N.W. & 28 S.W. 1/20,000

35th BRITISH DIVISION.
DAILY INTELLIGENCE SUMMARY No.96.
From 6 a.m.12th September 1918 to 6 a.m.13th September 1918.

1. OPERATIONS (British)
   (a) Infantry. A daylight patrol (2.0 p.m. to 6.30 p.m.) went out to search WHITE HORSE CELLARS O.2.6.0.3. Patrol proceeded along N.E. side of VOORMEZEELE - ST.ELOI road to O.2.a.4.9. From this point two green lights followed by a green light were observed to be sent up from about O.8.a.5.5. and enemy artillery opened fire on a target well to the rear. Signal was repeated and enemy artillery again fired. Signal was repeated a second time and enemy artillery fire then opened on the VOORMEZEELE - ST.ELOI road in vicinity of the patrol. Patrol advanced to O.2.a.85.40. and was met with rifle fire from about O.3.c.10.55. and O.2.c.35.40. and was unable to advance further. No movement was observed at WHITE HORSE CELLARS and some enemy shells were falling around WHITE HORSE CELLARS.
   Another daylight patrol (2.45 p.m. to 6.45 p.m.) reached a point at about I.32.d.4.6.; from there it observed trench at I.32.d.4.2. A little enemy movement on the ridge was observed. Trench appeared to be in good condition and well wired. At 4.40 p.m. a single green light followed by two double green lights were sent up from about I.32.d.6.6. After about ten minutes enemy artillery opened fire, some shells falling near the patrol. Patrol was also fired on by rifles from I.32.d.4.2.
   A patrol reconnoitred some fortified shell holes at I.27.c.45.25. and found them unoccupied.
   At 3.30 a.m. an hostile patrol - strength five O.Rs.- approached our post at I.27.a.3.1. One of our N.C.Os. and two men dashed out of the post and captured the whole five. Two of the prisoners were wounded. Prisoners belong to 104 I.R. 40th Saxon Division. This is a new identification.
   (b) Artillery. Enemy communications and occupied areas were actively harassed throughout the period. All active guns fired concentrations on Trench and dug outs I.28.b.5.0. to I.28.b.8.2., HALT in I.22.c., VERBRANDENMOLEN and area west of THORN LANE I.34.b.

2. OPERATIONS (German)
   (a) Infantry. Nil, except for captured patrol (see 1 (a) above).
   (b) Artillery. Hostile artillery was more active than usual.
   From 5.45 p.m. to 6.5 p.m. heavy shelling by 7.7 c.m. guns along line from I.31.d.6.2. to I.32.b.1.5., and from I.31.d.6.2.to W. edge of VOORMEZEELE, by 15 c.m. howitzers.
   From 6.5 p.m. to 6.15 p.m. heavy shelling by 7.7 c.m. guns on our front line from I.31.d.9.9. to I.32.a.0.2. VOORMEZEELE was shelled by 15 c.m. Howitzers at the same time.
   The CAFE BELGE - KRUISTRAATHOEK road H.29.b. H.30.c. was intermittently shelled by H.V. guns during the night. About 160 shells fell altogether.
   BELGIAN BATTERY CORNER H.24.a.4.8. received a good deal of attention from 15 c.m. howitzers.
   The following areas were shelled at intervals during the day and night by 7.7 c.m. guns and 10.5 and 15 c.m. Howitzers :- H.18.a.& c., H.24.c., H.30.a.& c., I.31., I.19.c.
   About twenty rounds of yellow cross gas shell fell in H.29.b. during the night.

3. AIRCRAFT.   One E.A. flew over our lines at 7.15 p.m.

4. HOSTILE DEFENCES. LA CHAPELLE I.33.b.45.95. is apparently a platoon H.Q. and is held by one Sergeant Major(commanding a platoon) 12 other ranks and a machine gun.

TURN OVER

2.

<u>Hostile Defences</u> (cont'd)
Enemy also has posts at
I.27.d.20.35. - five men and one M.G.
I.27.d.70.45 - 1 Corporal and four men,
and two other posts South of LA CHAPELLE and about forty yards apart.

5. <u>MOVEMENT</u>.   A little movement was seen round trench in I.32.d.

Two men seen near the MOUND O.2.d. at 6.30 a.m.

R.P. Harrison Capt.

H.Q. 35th Division,   Lieutenant-Colonel,
13th September 1918.   General Staff, 35th British Division.

Ref.Sheets 28 N.W. & 28 S.W. 1/20,000.

35th BRITISH DIVISION.
DAILY INTELLIGENCE SUMMARY No.97.
From 6 a.m. 13th September to 6 am. 14th September.

1. OPERATIONS (British)

(a) Infantry. Patrols from the Right Infantry Brigade reconnoitred the old post at O.2.a.1.1., the VOORMEZEELE - ST.ELOI Road as far as BUS HOUSE, BUS HOUSE, the OLD FRENCH TRENCH between BUS HOUSE and junction with VOORMEZEELE SWITCH, cross roads at I.32.d.0.3. and the trenches N.W. and S.W. of these cross roads. At none of these points was there any sign of enemy occupation or movement.

A Very Light was fired from the CRATER at O.2.d.0.50. and a M.G. fired from approximately I.32.d.8.5.

A patrol proceeding along the South bank of the CANAL towards SPOIL BANK saw an enemy patrol of about five men near LOCK 7 (I.32.b.7.3.) Our patrol endeavoured to surround the enemy but they escaped and ran back towards SPOIL BANK. A M.G. then opened fire on our patrol from this point.

Patrols from the Left Infantry Brigade found CHESTER FARM unoccupied. Movement was heard S. of LA CHAPELLE (at about I.33.b.30.65.) No enemy movement was seen in the vicinity of BLAUWE POORT FARM (I.27.b.5.3.)

A patrol proceeded in a S.E. direction along the railway from I.21.d.3.4. and reached approximately I.28.a.4.6. without encountering any enemy.

A patrol located an enemy post in the belt of trees running from I.21.b.6.1. to about I.22.c.1.6. Red and white lights were fired from this point.

(b) Artillery. Harassing fire on roads and dugouts during the period.
At 10.0 p.m. 4.5" Hows. fired 120 rounds in a gas bombardment of HILL 60, in conjunction with Left Division Artillery and Corps Heavy Artillery.

2. OPERATIONS (German)

(a) Infantry. A German patrol of five men was seen in the vicinity of LOCK 7 (I.32.b.7.3.)

(b) Artillery. Enemy Artillery activity showed a marked increase, especially in the right subsector.

The area H.30. was heavily shelled throughout the period (during the day over 200 rounds, during the night up to 800) 21 c.m., 15 c.m., and 10.5 c.m. Hows. were employed.

Attention was paid at intervals to area H.29., H.36. and H.14.d. VOORMEZEELE was persistently shelled throughout the period. The vicinity of DOLL'S HOUSE I.19.b.2.5. was heavily shelled at intervals throughout the day by 15 c.m. Hows. A proportion of Blue Cross Gas was employed.

Other areas shelled were front line trench between the CANAL and VOORMEZEELE, Railway sidings in H.36.c. and d., CAFE BELGE - KRUISTRAATHOEK Road, SWAN CHATEAU (proportion of BLUE cross gas) DERBY ROAD and light railway in I.19.

Between 10.0 a.m. and 10.30 a.m. a 10.5 c.m. how. fired about 12 rounds of Blue cross gas into the area H.30.(Magnetic bearing 140° from H.30.a.8.8.)

(c) Machine Guns. Slight activity.
Patrols report M.Gs. firing from SPOIL BANK (I.33.a.) and I.32.d.8.5.

(d) T.Ms. At 1-30 p.m. about 20 T.M. shells fell on road at about O.1.b.7.5.

3. AVIATION. E.A. were seen over our lines at a great height on two occasions during the day.

TURN OVER. 4/

4. HOSTILE DEFENCES.

Occupied posts reported by patrols at I.32.d.8.5, crater at O.2.d.05.50, SPOIL BANK, in line of trees near I.22.c.1.6.

5. MOVEMENT.

Visibility generally poor.
Eight men were seen moving in crater at O.2.d.5.6 during the day.
At 3-15 p.m. movement of individuals was seen on the ridge in O.3.d,

H.Q. 35th Division,
14th September 1918.

a.E. Macdonald
for Lieutenant Colonel,
General Staff, 35th Division.

FURTHER INTERROGATION of five Prisoners of 11th Coy.
104th I.R., 40th (Saxon) Division captured about 6 a.m. 13th
September, about I.27.a.3.1.

METHOD OF CAPTURE. Prisoners were holding the right post of their Company front and were sent out to get touch with the 10th Coy. on their right. They lost their way and wandered towards our lines.

DISPOSITIONS. The 3rd Battalion has three companies in line as described in the preliminary interrogation. The remaining company (the 12th) is in close support in shelters about I.28.d.10.15. The joint company H.Q. of the 11th and 10th companies are also situated here.
        The 2nd Battalion is in support in the main line of resistance in I.34.a.& b. and the 1st Battalion is resting in all probability at GHELUWE.

RELIEFS. Inter-battalion reliefs take place every six days. On the 15/16th September the 2nd Battalion will move up to front line, being replaced in support by the 1st Battalion from GHELUWE. The 3rd Battalion on relief goes to GHELUWE. The routes are through the communication trenches in I.34.a.& b. and along the light railway from I.28.d.3.0. to MIDDLESEX ROAD and the tracks to the south of it in I.28.c., I.33.b. and I.34.a. Prisoners agree that the reliefs take place between midnight and 4 a.m.

INTENTION One prisoner thinks that the German Artillery is rather less active than usual in this sector.
        A British offensive is considered an unlikely contingency; a German one out of the question. A withdrawal to the MESSINES RIDGE is still considered possible but no definite orders had been issued on the subject. Prisoners company had received no definite orders as to action in the event of a British attack nor had they been ordered to work; no work had naturally been done and there was no wire either old or new in front of prisoners post.

TANKS. Prisoners were recently addressed by their Company Commander on the subject of British tanks. He said they must not take it for granted that immediately tanks appeared they were to evacuate their trenches, there were special revolver guns emplaced in rear to deal with them. The 104th I.R. has not been issued with any anti-tank rifles.

AUSTRIAN TROOPS. Prisoners saw Austrian Heavy Artillery in the neighbourhood of BAPAUME at the end of August and had heard that Austrian Infantry was in training at BEVERLOO.

AMERICAN TROOPS. When the 40th Division was recently in LORRAINE, the 2nd.Battalion 104th I.R. assisted by special storm troops and a trench mortar battery carried out a large scale raid against the Americans. Some of the latter emerged from their dugouts in their shirts and fought bitterly, the general impression gained being that they were by no means as untrained as they were made out to be by German officers.

LIGHT SIGNALS & PASSWORDS.   Green   S.O.S.
                             Red   - Lengthen range
                             Yellow - The outpost line has been
evacuated.
        The password at present in use in the 104th I.R. is "SEPTEMBER". Many of the men also use the word HEIMAT(Home)

TURN OVER/

PROPAGANDA.   Prisoners state that the leaflets dropped by our aeroplanes are much picked up, and are often sent home by the men. They are much discussed and commented on both by the men and their relations.

INTELLIGENCE.   Prisoners had been told that our posts were about 800 to 1,000 yards distant.   Apart from this they had no idea as to our whereabouts.

DRESS.   A German Army Order has now been issued to the effect that a distinction may now be worn by all ranks who have been wounded. This consists of a tin disc shaped like a pair of bursting grenades (crossed), surmounted by a German steel helmet.   The disc is worn on the left side of the stomach and is black for one wound or two and silver coloured for three or four wounds.

Ref.Sheets 28 N.W. & 28 S.W. 1/20,000.

War Diary

35th BRITISH DIVISION.
DAILY INTELLIGENCE SUMMARY No.98.
From 6 a.m. 14th September to 6 a.m. 15th September.

1. OPERATIONS (British)

   (a) Infantry. Patrols report that the enemy hold THE MOUND(O.2.d.) and CRATERS in the vicinity in some strength. A machine gun and Very Lights were fired from this point; a machine gun was also fired from a position about 50 yards S. of THE CRATER at O.2.d.55.60.

   No enemy were encountered between our front line and THE MOUND.

   A patrol (at night) found WHITE HORSE CELLARS (O.2.a.95.30.) unoccupied.

   A patrol going out at 9.0 p.m. found an unoccupied post at I.32.d.2.2. and saw no trace of the enemy in this vicinity; a later patrol (12.30 a.m.) reports that this post was then occupied. During this patrol a hostile M.G. fired from approximately I.32.d.80.60.

   The ground in "No man's Land" is reported to be difficult to cover owing to the recent heavy rain.

   (b) Artillery. Concentrations were fired on the following targets:-
   Dugouts I.28.a.5.2. - 8.4.
   Dugouts and tracks in I.29.c.
   VERBRANDENMOLEN and occupied areas in I.28.d.
   A small dump was exploded at VERBRANDENMOLEN.
   4.5" Hows. shelled Company H.Qs. at I.28.c.5.6.

2. OPERATIONS (German)

   (a) Infantry. Nil.

   (b) Artillery. The increased acticivty of the last few days was maintained and the usual areas were intermittently shelled throughout the period. Localities particularly affected were VOORMEZEELE, CHATEAU SEGARD (H.30.d.30.95.), the KRUISSTRAATHOEK - VOORMEZEELE Road, IRON BRIDGE (I.26.c.2.6), DOLL'S HOUSE (I.19.b.15.50), HUTS at I.19.a.9.2. G.H.Q. 1st.Line at about I.20.a.1.9.

   The greater part of the shelling was by 10.5 c.m. and 15 c.m. hows.

   During the day WOODCOTE HOUSE (I.20.c.45.20.) and SHRAPNEL CORNER (I.20.a.central) were heavily shelled, a proportion of Blue Cross Gas being employed.

   Between 2.45 p.m. and 3.15 p.m. MAIDA CAMP(H.30.a.1.1..) and road about H.29.b.8.4. was shelled by 7.7 c.m. guns.

   The following grid bearings are given, from H.30.c.30.75:-

   (i) 123°. 7.7 c.m. guns shelling H.30.c. at 8.50 a.m., H.29.d. at 9.30 a.m. and VOORMEZZELE at 11.53 a.m.
   (ii) 130°. 15 c.m. how. shelling CAFE BELGE Cross Roads (H.29.b.8.5) at 9.45 a.m. and 10 c.m. gun shelling H.30.c.35.75. at 2.30 p.m.

   (c) Trench Mortars. Nil.
   (d) Machine Guns. Normal activity.

3. AVIATION E.A. were more active than usual over our lines.
   At 7.30 a.m. and 9.10 a.m. formations of seven machines crossed at about 3,000 feet. At 9.10 a.m. the enemy formation attacked one of our machines which succeeded in escaping.

4. HOSTILE DEFENCES
   (a) Machine Guns fired from the CRATER at O.2.d.55.60. and from a position about 50 yards S. of this point.
   A M.G. is again reported firing from approx. I.32.d.8.6.
   (b) A post at I.32.d.2.2. is reported unoccupied at 9.30 p.m.; it was however, found occupied by the enemy shortly after midnight.

5. MOVEMENT. Slight individual movement was seen in O.9.a. and O.14.b.

H.Q. 35th Division,
15th September 1918.

for A.S. _____ Lt
Lieutenant-Colonel,
General Staff, 35th British Division.

War Diary

Ref. Sheets 28 N.W. & 28 S.W. 1/20,000.

35th BRITISH DIVISION.
DAILY INTELLIGENCE SUMMARY No.99.
From 6 a.m. 15th September to 6 a.m. 16th September 1918.

1. OPERATIONS (British)
   (a) Infantry. We advanced our outpost line last night, supported by fire from Heavy and Field Artillery, and established posts at the following points:-
   FRENCH TRENCH O.1.b.90.05.
   FRENCH TRENCH at O.2.a.15.40.
   BUS HOUSE O.2.a.4.7.
   FRENCH TRENCH at O.2.a.6.9.
   CROSS ROADS at I.32.c.95.25.
   MIDDLESEX ROAD at I.32.d.90.55.
   SPOIL BANK at I.33.a.4.2. (South of CANAL.)
   SPOIL BANK I.33.a.4.4. (North of CANAL.)
   CHESTER FARM. I.33.a.7.5.
   LA CHAPELLE. I.33.b.5.9.
   BLAUWE POORT FARM I.27.b.5.4.
   ROAD JUNCTION. I.28.a.1.9.
   MANOR HALT I.22.c.6.5.
   ZILLEBEKE LAKE I.22.a.7.0.

   In the right subsector no opposition was met with except at SPOIL BANK (South of CANAL) where an enemy post of seven men was encountered of whom five were killed and the other two captured.

   In the left subsector there was little opposition or M.G. fire from the enemy; forty one prisoners (including three wounded) were captured, and two machine guns. Total prisoners captured forty three, including three wounded.

   Prisoners belong to 181st I.R. (two) and 104th I.R. (forty one) 40th SAXON Division - Normal identifications.

   (b) Artillery. Field Artillery fired in conjunction with Heavy Artillery to support the infantry operation. Harassing fire was increased in view of suspected hostile relief.

2. OPERATIONS (German)
   (a) Infantry. Nil.
   (b) Artillery. There was intermittent shelling of the forward areas but hostile artillery was less active than on the three previous days.
   I.19.d. and I.25.b. received particular attention.
   In reply to our fire in connection with our operation the enemy put down a light barrage from 7.7 c.m. guns and 10.5 c.m. Hows. on our front and support lines.

3. AVIATION. E.A. crossed our lines as follows:-
   9.0 a.m. two E.A.
   1.20 p.m. two E.A.
   3.30 p.m. two E.A.
   4.0 p.m. one E.A.
   4.10 p.m. five E.A.
   5.20 p.m. two E.A.
   5.45 p.m. one E.A.
   6.30 p.m. two E.A.
   All were engaged by A.A. fire but were mostly too high to be engaged by small arms fire.
   One kite balloon up at G.B.145° from H.17.d.15.45.
   One kite balloon up at G.B.117° from H.18.d.8.4.

4. HOSTILE DEFENCES. Dug outs in SPOIL BANK I.33.a & c. on South side of CANAL are reported to be largely destroyed, except those in the western end of the BANK.

TURN OVER/

5. MOVEMENT.
   6 a.m. two men seen at O.9.a.O.4.
   8.30 a.m. two men seen at O.2.c.9.5.
   8.30 a.m. two men seen in O.9.a.

6. MISCELLANEOUS.
   Enemy sent up a few single red and green lights during our operation from about 400 or 500 yards away from our new outpost line.
   A few red lights bursting into two stars were also seen.

R.P. Hanson Capt
for Lieutenant-Colonel,
General Staff, 35th Division.

H.Q. 35th Division,
16th September 1918.

SUMMER TIME.

Date.	SUN. Rises.	Sets.	MOON. Rises.	Sets.
Sept.17th.	6.25 a.m.	7.0 p.m.	5.11 p.m.	3.36 a.m.
" 18th.	6.27 a.m.	6.58 p.m.	5.35 p.m.	5.0 a.m.

INTERROGATION of 41 Prisoners (38 unwounded and 3 wounded) of
2nd Battalion 104th I.R. 40th (SAXON) Division, captured about
10.30 p.m. 15th September 1918, between ZILLEBEKE LAKE and the
YPRES - COMINES CANAL.

OUR ATTACK. Prisoners are unanimous in stating that our barrage was very well placed and effectively kept their heads down; our Infantry were upon them before they could collect their wits.

RELIEFS. The 2nd Battalion 104th I.R. relieved the 3rd on the night 14/15th September, i.e. one day earlier than was scheduled, doubtless owing to our capture of five prisoners on 13th September.

The next relief is due for the 17/18th, when the 1st Battalion from support will relieve the 2nd Battalion in the front line. The relief is expected to take place between 10.0 p.m. and 11.0 p.m. The relief route is confirmed, i.e. the YPRES - COMINES Railway, light railway in I.28.c.& d. and I.27.d., and tracks to the S.W. of it.

DISPOSITIONS & LOSSES.

7th Company. (Company strength 40).
ZILLEBEKE LAKE to Road about I.28.a.5.7. Posts at
(a) I.22.b.4.1. M.G. and 5 men.
(b) about I.22.c.9.2. M.G. and 5 men.
(c) I.22.a.5.7. M.G. and 5 men.

Sentries are posted at night about midway between (a) and (b) and midway between (b) and (c). The remainder of the men are employed on bringing up rations. Out of the above (c) post was captured intact.

8th Company. (Company strength 25.)
Posts at
(a) I.28.a.5.5. (M.G. and 5 men.)
(b) I.28.a.1.2. (M.G. and 5 men.)
(c) I.27.d.8.6. (M.G. and 5 men.)

Two other posts between (a) and (b), and (b) and (c), each of 5 men. About 8 men were captured from the 8th Company and a few killed.

5th Company. (Company strength 29.)
Light railway at I.27.d.8.6. to road at I.33.b.2.5. This Company had posts at I.27.d.7.5., LA CHAPELLE and two others, and two machine guns. One post received a direct hit from a shell which smashed the M.G. and laid out all the crew; the garrisons of the other three posts were all captured with the exception of one man who was killed.

On the night 5/6th September, the 8th Coy. 104th I.R. lost 5 killed and 11 wounded from night bombing in LE QUESNOY.

INTELLIGENCE. The outgoing Battalion (3rd) informed the 2nd Battalion that we raided them on 13th September and captured five. Some of the prisoners thought Americans were opposed to them. One of the prisoners states that the password in his Battalion is VOGELWIESE (a shooting preserve) which is likely to be in use for some weeks.

MORALE. Prisoners morale is miserable. They state that not only the troops in the field but the people at home have given up hope of a German victory. It was a matter of complete indifference to the prisoners if they were raided and captured; consequently the majority of the posts had no sentry by day.

WORK. In no case have any orders been issued about work; none has been done and no attempt has been made to wire the posts.

Interrogation of two prisoners of 6th Coy. 181 I.R. 40th (Saxon)
Division captured about 10-30 p.m. 15th September 1918 at
I.33.a.6.0 (SPOIL BANK)

DISPOSITIONS.

The 181 I.R. has three companies in front line and one in close support (probably in the main line of resistance).
One company holds from the road at approximately H.33.b.2.6 to the Northern bank of the CANAL about H.33.a.9.0. The 6th company holds the Eastern end of SPOIL BANK. The 8th Company holds from H.33.c.7.8 to the road about H.33.c.40.25. The detailed dispositions of the 6th Company (Trench Strength about 70) are :-
One M.G. group (Light M.G. and nine men) on Northern bank of CANAL at H.33.a.90.05.
One M.G. Group on Southern bank at H.33.a.85.00.
One M.G. Group at H.33.c.70.80. A sentry is posted on the top of SPOIL BANK. The men of the company not accounted for by the above three M.G. Groups, about 40 men, are accommodated in dugouts on the North-Eastern face of the bank between H.33.c.90.95 and H.33.d.0.7. One Light Machine Gun is kept in reserve in these dugouts.

DEFENCES.

The LOCK at H.33.d.3.6 is defended by at least one heavy M.G. (silent). Prisoners confirm that the main line of resistance is the BLUFF - HILL 60 line and state that new wire on stakes has been put out in front of it.

ORDER OF BATTLE.

40th Division, N.to S.104th I.R., 181 I.R., 134 I.R. One prisoner is positive that a Bavarian Division is in line S. of the 40th Division. The same prisoner states that he saw men of the 23rd Bavarian Regiment in TOURCOING on the 7th September. Prisoner heard that the 236th Division on relief was destined for the TOURCOING area.

INTENTIONS.

Prisoner was warned by one of his Officers that an English Offensive in this Sector was expected shortly.

RELIEFS.

The 2nd. Bn. 181 I.R. came into line on the night 14/15th September and expects to be relieved on the 20/21st, by the 3rd Bn. which is now in support in the area I.34.d. and I.35.c. The regimental light T.Ms. are also in this area. After the 2nd Bn. has done six days in support it will go to rest at HOUTHEM, before returning to the line. The last relief took place early in the morning but this was doubtless due to the distance which had to be covered; the next relief will probably be carried out between 10.0 p.m. and 11.0 p.m. The route is along CANAL WALK from O.4.b. to H.33.d.5.6 thence across the CANAL to the S.W. bank and along footpaths to the forward posts.

HEADQUARTERS.

Battalion H.Q. at O.4.b.2.5. Divisional H.Q. MENIN.

TURN OVER.

Ref.Sheets 28 N.W. & 28 S.W. 1/20,000.

35th BRITISH DIVISION.
DAILY INTELLIGENCE SUMMARY No.100.
From 6 a.m.16th Septr. to 6 a.m.17th Septr.1918.

1. OPERATIONS (British)
   (a) Infantry. Our patrols were active along the whole front.
   Two prisoners, 181st I.R. 40th (SAXON) Division, were captured by one of our patrols at I.33.c.98.30. Normal identification.
   A patrol reconnoitred the CRATERS in O.2.d. getting as far as O.2.d.2.8. The CRATERS were found to be occupied by the enemy, apparently in some strength.
   (b) Artillery. Harassing fire was carried out on enemy's roads, tracks and occupied areas. Concentrations were fired on selected targets.

2. OPERATIONS (German)
   (a) Infantry. Two enemy patrols, one of six men and one of ten men, were seen in O.2.d.
   (b) Artillery. Hostile artillery was more active again, 15 c.m. and 10.5 c.m. Howitzers and 7.7 c.m. guns being used.
   About 220 rounds fell in H.30. and about 130 rounds in H.36. during the night.
   ST.DUNSTANS H.22.b.8.3. was shelled by 7.7 c.m. guns between 8.20 p.m. and 9.0 p.m. Position of gun firing was on a T.B. of 105° from H.22.b.8.3.
   Between 4.10 a.m. and 5.45 a.m. there was fairly heavy shelling of our forward areas, particular attention again being paid to H.30.
   At 10.30 p.m. vicinity of I.21.c.3.8. and area I.20.d. were heavily shelled.

3. AVIATION. E.A. were fairly active but their efforts to cross our lines were mostly stopped by our aeroplanes.
   Two enemy kite balloons were up during the day.
   An E.A. brought down one of our kite balloons S.E. of POPERINGHE at 7.15 p.m.

4. HOSTILE DEFENCES.
   (a) Posts. Hostile posts were located at O.2.d.2.6., O.2.d.6.6., O.2.c.8.7., and I.33.c.40.35.
   Three unoccupied dugouts were found at I.32.d.35.25.
   ARUNDEL HOUSE I.33.c.50.45. was found to be unoccupied. There is a strong point here with one row of barbed concertina wire and eight strands of trip wire immediately west of it.
   (b) Machine Guns. A M.G. fired down the road in T.26.d.
   (c) Wire. There is a belt of barbed concertina wire in front of the CRATERS at about O.2.d.5.7., but it has tracks through it and does not constitute a strong obstacle.

5. MOVEMENT. Individual movement seen in O.2.a. during the afternoon.
   At 6.40 p.m. one man left dugout at O.8.d.9.9.
   At 7.15 p.m. a cyclist seen in O.8.d. going S.E.

6. MISCELLANEOUS. Double red and green lights were sent up by the enemy during the night. No apparent action followed.

H.Q. 35th Division,
17th September 1918.

R.P. Harrison Capt
Lieutenant-Colonel,
General Staff, 35th British Division.

SUMMER TIME.

Date.	SUN Rises.	Sets.	MOON. Rises.	Sets.
Sept.18th.	6.27 a.m.	6.58 p.m.	5.35 p.m.	5.0 a.m. (19th)
19th.	6.28 a.m.	6.56 p.m.	5.58 p.m.	6.24 a.m.(20th)

INTERROGATION of eight prisoners of 7th and 8th Coys.104th.I.R. 40th (SAXON) Division, captured on 16th September 1918.

METHOD OF CAPTURE. Six of the prisoners were in a post near ZILLEBEKE LAKE during our attack, and did not come out until the dugout was searched by our men about 5 p.m. One man was on sentry by himself on the shore of the lake and fell asleep. When he woke up about noon he found himself just close to a British post, who captured him.
The remaining man was one of a post of about 12, (the remains of the 8th Coy.) which was on the light railway about I.27.d.70.55. He lost his way and wandered into our lines.

REINFORCEMENTS. One prisoner states that the enemy has brought up the 11th and 12th Companies of the 3rd Battalion (in support) to reinforce the front line between ZILLEBEKE LAKE and SANDBAG TRACK.

LOSSES. The 7th Coy. lost two machine guns in the attack on the night 15/16th, since when the prisoner (sentry on ZILLEBEKE LAKE) has not seen a sign of a single man of his Coy.
The 8th Coy. lost all three of the M.G's, which were forward. The remaining one in reserve had not yet been brought forward. Joint Company H.Q. of the 5th and 8th Coys. are at I.28.d.4.8, (Vide Air Photo No.10B.462.)

CONDITION OF GROUND. Prisoners state the ground in rear of the German outpost line is in worse condition than 'No man's Land' or the ground behind the British outposts. It is very marshy and cut up by shell fire. Prisoners have heard no word of a counter attack being intended.

INTERROGATION of three prisoners of 181st I.R., 40th (SAXON) Division, captured by our patrols on night 16/17th September.

METHOD OF CAPTURE Two of the prisoners belong to the 6th Coy. and maintain that they were on sentry at about I.33.c.95.98. At about 11.0 pm. they went into a dugout to eat their rations for the next day and were hauled out by one of our patrols.
The third prisoner (wounded) belongs to the 8th Coy. and was on duty with one other man at I.33.c.40.35. His companion was killed by a German shell shortly after capture.

MACHINE GUNS. The 6th Coy. has two machine guns, one heavy with a crew of eight men, at I.33.d.0.8., and one light M.G. manned by 4 men, about 15 yards south of the first. The remainder of the dispositions (men and machine guns) are confirmed. Vide Interrogation attached to Intelligence Summary No.99 dated 16th September. Coy. H.Q. are at O.4.a.30.97. (See Air photo No.10B.495).

ORDERS The orders are that the outposts are to resist until the S.O.S. (One red light) is sent up from the Coy.H.Q., upon which they withdraw to the main line of resistance. No work has been done on this line.

CASUALTIES. The 6th Coy. suffered a total of seven casualties on the 15/16th September.

AUSTRIAN TROOPS. One prisoner saw some Austrian Infantry on the ARRAS-CAMBRAI Road W. of CAMBRAI about the 7th September.

Ref.Sheets 28 N.W. & 28 S.W. 1/20,000.

35th BRITISH DIVISION.
DAILY INTELLIGENCE SUMMARY No.101.
From 6 a.m. 17th Septr. to 6 a.m. 18th Septr.
----

1. OPERATIONS (British)
    (a) Infantry.   A patrol proceeded towards the CRATERS in O.2.d. and reached a point approximately at O.2.d.20.95.   The enemy was doing much work in and around the CRATERS.   Two of the enemy approached our patrol.   One was captured and the other shot dead as he tried to escape.   Prisoner belongs to 181st I.R. 40th (SAXON) Division. Normal identification.

    SPOIL BANK in I.33.a. North of the CANAL was reconnoitred.   The dugouts were all found to be unoccupied and most of them have been destroyed.

    During the night our line of posts was advanced in the left Brigade Sector to an average depth of about 100 to 150 yards.

    Whilst a post was being established at I.28.a.45.20. six of the enemy were seen and attacked.   The enemy fled; one badly wounded prisoner belonging to 104th I.R. 40th (SAXON) Division, was captured. He died soon afterwards - Normal identification.

    Our patrols reconnoitred as far East as I.33.d.8.7. and I.34.a.2.4.   None of the enemy were encountered by these patrols.

    (b) Artillery.   Our artillery harassed the enemy's communications and occupied areas.   Harassing fire was increased owing to suspected hostile relief.

2. OPERATIONS (German)
    (a) Infantry.   Nil.
    (b) Artillery.   Hostile artillery was again very active.
    VOORMEZEELE was intermittently shelled by 15 c.m. Howitzers during the day..

    The CAFE BELGE - VOORMEZEELE and the CAFE BELGE - KRUISTRAAT Roads received much attention from 10.5 c.m. and 15 c.m. Howitzers and 7.7 c.m. guns during the period.

    36 rounds fell in I.25.a. at 10.30 a.m. from 10.5 cm. Howitzer firing from a position on a T.B. of 147° from H.30.c.8.8.

    At 8.30 p.m. flash of a 15 c.m. Howitzer firing on back areas was observed on a T.B. of 167° from H.30.c.8.8.

    Between 4.15 a.m. and 6.0 a.m. there was heavy shelling of the forward area of Left Brigade, apparently in response to enemy light signals double red double orange double green.

    The area H.30. was shelled throughout the period.

    At 9.45 p.m. 10 blue cross gas shell (7.7 c.m.) fell in H.23.d.

    Flash of 10 c.m. guns shelling roads in H.23.c. and H.29.b. between 12 midnight and 4.30 a.m. were observed on G.B's. of 115° and 127° from H.30.c.3.7.

3. AVIATION   E.A. were observed over our lines at the following times flying at about 1,000 feet :-
    7.30 a.m. (two)
    8.0 a.m. (one)
    12 noon   (one)

4. HOSTILE DEFENCES.
    (a) Work.   Much work was in progress on the MOUND and CRATERS in O.2.d.
    (b) Machine Guns. Machine guns were located at about O.2.d.5.6. and I.28.a.3.1.

5. MOVEMENT.   7.25 a.m.   Three men seen at O.2.d.5.6.

H.Q. 35th Division,
18th September 1918.

R. P. Harrison Capt
Lieutenant-Colonel,
General Staff, 35th British Division.

War Diary

ANNEXE to 35th Division Intelligence Summary No.101 - 18.9.18.

INTERROGATION of a prisoner of 5th Company 181st I.R. 40th (SAXON) Division, captured about 11.30 p.m. 17th September 1918, near WHITE HORSE CELLARS (O.2.b.0.2.)

METHOD OF CAPTURE   Prisoner states that he was visiting his posts when he saw a party of about 30 men approaching, whom he took to be a working party from the 134th I.R. on his left.   He approached them and was taken prisoner by the party (our patrol)

DISPOSITIONS.   Prisoner is unwilling to speak and his statements should be accepted with reserve.   He states that his Company (the 5th) holds from about I.33.c.2.2. to a point on the road leading North from ST.ELOI.   The Company has one platoon, 30 strong, in line.   The men are disposed in pairs, about 25 yards apart.   On the right touch is maintained with the 6th Company 181st I.R. at I.33.c.2.2. and on the left with the 134th I.R. on the above mentioned road.   The 5th Company has two light machine guns in line, one on the western side of the road and one about three quarters of the way across the Company front, i.e. about I.32.d.9.2.   Two other light M.G's. are in reserve at the transport lines.
          The line of posts mentioned by the prisoner is visible on air photo No.10B.498.
          The other two platoons of the Company are in reserve some distance in rear.

INTELLIGENCE.   Prisoner states that on coming into line his Company Commander told him that the troops opposite were the 35th British Division, a fighting Division, and that a sharp look out was to be kept.

ST.ELOI CRATERS.   Prisoner noticed that the large CRATER at O.2.d.1.6. was occupied.

Ref.Sheets 28 N.W. & 28 S.W. 1/20,000.

35th BRITISH DIVISION.

DAILY INTELLIGENCE SUMMARY No.102.
From 6 a.m.18th Septr. to 6 a.m.19th Septr.

1. **OPERATIONS (British)**
   (a) <u>Infantry</u>. A party was sent out to rush a German M.G. post at I.33.c.65.85, but found no trace of it.
   A patrol discovered the enemy holding posts about 200 yards S.E. of BUS HOUSE. These posts had been pushed forward since the return of our patrol last night. An endeavour was made to outflank the enemy, but they withdrew too quickly.
   (b) <u>Artillery</u>. Harassing fire was kept up on the MOUND and CRATERS in O.2.d., NORFOLK ROAD (O.3.b.), the CANAL BANK in O.4.a., and the area west of BATTLE WOOD. Concentrations were fired on VERBRANDENMOLEN.

2. **OPERATIONS (German)**
   (a) <u>Infantry</u>. At 2.45 a.m. a party of seven Germans approached our post at I.33.a.5.3. On being challenged they threw a bomb into the post and attempted to rush it. The sentry killed two by Lewis Gun fire and our post then pursued the enemy who in the darkness made good their escape. The identification secured show that the two dead men are a 2nd.Lieut.and a man of the 7th.Coy.181st I.R.(40th SAXON Division) normal.
   (b) <u>Artillery</u>. Increased activity is reported, especially of 10.5 c.m. and 15 c.m. Hows. Between 11.30 p.m. and 12.30 a.m. he bombarded the following places, which would appear to constitute a rear barrage line. I.21.b.1.4., TRASPORT FARM I.21.a.7.1., I.20.d.8.9., SHRAPNEL CORNER I.20.a., WOODCOTE HOUSE I.20.c.5.2., BEDFORD HOUSE I.26.a.,
   The whole of square I.26. received considerable attention throughout the day. VOORMEZEELE SWITCH was heavily shelled from 8.0 p.m. to 8.30 p.m.

3. **AVIATION.** At 3.15 p.m. a hostile 'plane attacked one of our balloons on the VLAMERTINGHE - YPRES Road and brought it down in flames.
   E.A. crossed our lines at frequent intervals during the day; their activity is becoming more pronounced.

4. **ENEMY DEFENCES.**
   (a) <u>Posts.</u> The ST.ELOI CRATERS are occupied. Shelters at I.33.b.6.5. were found unoccupied.
   ZILLEBEKE VILLAGE was searched and the cellars found unoccupied.
   An enemy post was located at I.23.c.5.5.and shots exchanged.
   (b) <u>Machine Guns.</u> A M.G. fired from I.22.d.7.4. Four M.G's.opened fire from about O.2.d.0.5.
   (c) <u>Wire.</u> Old British wire was encountered at I.33.b.6.4.

5. **MOVEMENT.** Occasional movement of individuals in O.2.c. and O.4.d. Visibility poor.

6. **MISCELLANEOUS.** Enemy artillery opened fire in response to red and green lights.

7. **GERMAN SUMMER TIME** German Summer Time, which began at 2.0 a.m.on the 15th April, ceased at 3.0 a.m. on the 16th September.
   Consequently Franco-British time will now be the same as German time, until Franco-British Summer Time ceases, when German time will again be one hour in advance of Franco-British Time.

8. **DISBANDING OF GERMAN DIVISIONS.** The German Officer mentioned in para.2 (a) above was recently transferred from the 107 R.I.R.24th (SAXON) Reserve Division, to the 181st I.R.40th(SAXON) Division. This tends to confirm the suspected disbanding of the 24th Reserve Division.

H.Q., 35th Division,
19th September 1918.

A.J. Chesney Lieut.
Lieutenant-Colonel,
General Staff, 35th Division.

Ref.Sheets 28 N.W. and 28 S.W. 1/20,000

35th BRITISH DIVISION.
DAILY INTELLIGENCE SUMMARY No.104.
From 6 a.m. 20th Septr. to 6 a.m. 21st Septr.

1. OPERATIONS (British)
   (a) Infantry. Our patrols were active but their movement was limited by the bright moonlight.
   One of our patrols was fired on by rifle fire and bombs were thrown at it from I.22.d.25.85. Our patrol returned the fire but could not deal further with the post as the ground at this point was impassable, the water at places being about four feet deep.
   (b) Artillery. Our Artillery carried out harassing fire on enemy communications and occupied areas during the night.

2. OPERATIONS (German)
   (a) Infantry. Nil.
   (b) Artillery. Hostile Artillery was less active during the period.
   Special attention was paid to SHRAPNEL CORNER I.20.a. and the S.W. corner of ZILLEBEKE LAKE.
   The southern bank of ZILLEBEKE LAKE from I.21.b.1.3. to I.22.a.0.1.was shelled at 2.15 a.m. with H.E and BLUE CROSS Gas.
   (c) Machine Guns. There was a considerable increase of machine gun activity during the night.

3. AVIATION   Hostile aerial activity was above normal. Between 6.30 p.m. and 7.30 p.m., two flights of E.A., one seven strong and the other eight strong, flew over our lines. They were heavily engaged by Anti-Aircraft fire.

4. HOSTILE DEFENCES.
   (a) Machine Guns. There is a machine gun at I.28.a.75.95. and there are three other machine guns near here, one on each flank of the M.G. at I.28.a.75.95. and one about 200 yards East of it.
   A machine gun fired from just south of point I.22.d.5.8., another fired from the vicinity of NORFOLK LODGE I.33.c., and another from I.28.c.65.40.
   (b) Posts.   Posts were located at I.22.d.25.85.and I.22.b.3.2.
   (HELL BLAST CORNER). Very Lights were sent up from I.22.d.4.9. and I.27.d.7.3. and rifles were fired from I.22.b.4.0.
   (c) Work.   An O.P. was observed in tree in TRIANGULAR WOOD at about O.3.a.87.09.
   Earth was seen to be thrown up at I.34.c.30.15
   Short length of new trench seen at 0.4.d.0.5. near WHITE CHATEAU.
   A slot of a M.G. or O.P. is visible at about I.28.c.6.1.

5. MOVEMENT.   There was a little individual movement in I.34., I.35., and O.2.d. during the day.

6. MISCELLANEOUS.   A new type of   light was observed apparently for use against aircraft.
   On reaching a height of about 1,000 feet it burst into many smaller lights.

H.Q. 35th Division,
21st September 1918.

Lieutenant-Colonel,
General Staff, 35th British Division.

SUMMER TIME

Date.	SUN. Rises.	Sets.	MOON Rises.	Sets.
Sept.22nd.	6.33 a.m.	6.49 p.m.	7.20 p.m.	10.39 a.m.(23
" 23rd.	6.34 a.m.	6.46 p.m.	7.53 a.m.	12 noon.(24th

Ref. Sheets 28 N.W. and 28 S.W. 1/20,000.

35th BRITISH DIVISION.
DAILY INTELLIGENCE SUMMARY No.105.
From 6 a.m. 21st Septr. to 6 a.m. 22nd Septr.

---

1. OPERATIONS (British)
   (a) **Infantry**. Our patrols were active. No hostile patrols were encountered.
   (b) **Artillery**. Selected targets were engaged by day. Harassing fire was carried out on enemy's road, tracks and occupied areas during the night.

2. OPERATIONS (German)
   (a) **Infantry** Nil.
   (b) **Artillery** Hostile artillery activity was above normal, special attention being paid to H.23.a.9.6., H.24.b., H.18.central., I.19.c.,
   At 11.40 p.m. there was heavy shelling of the South bank of ZILLEBEKE LAKE I.21.b.

3. AVIATION. E.A. crossed our lines at 9.15 a.m., 10.45 a.m., and 7.0 p.m.; there were five machines in each case. All were engaged by anti-aircraft guns and machine guns.

4. ENEMY DEFENCES.
   (a) **Machine Guns**. A machine gun fired from about I.22.b.8.8.

5. MOVEMENT. At 6.20 p.m. a working party seen at O.10.a.15.48. was engaged by our Artillery.

R. P. Harrison Capt
for
Lieutenant-Colonel,
General Staff, 35th British Division.

H.Q. 35th Division,
22nd September 1918.

SUMMER TIME.

Date.	SUN. Rises.	Sets.	MOON Rises	Sets.
Septr. 23rd.	5.34 a.m.	6.46 p.m.	7.53 p.m.	12 noon (24th)
" 24th	6.36 a.m.	6.44 p.m.	8.38 p.m.	1.9 p.m. (25th)

Ref.Sheets 28 N.W. and 28 S.W. 1/20,000.

35th BRITISH DIVISION.
DAILY INTELLIGENCE SUMMARY No.106.
From 6 a.m. 22nd Septr. to 6 a.m. 23rd Septr.

1. OPERATIONS (British)
   (a) Infantry.   Our Patrols were active during the night.
   (b) Artillery.   Our artillery harassed the enemy communications and occupied areas.

2. OPERATIONS (German)
   (a) Infantry.   Nil.
   (b) Artillery.   Hostile artillery was considerably more active both by day and night.
   BELGIAN BATTERY CORNER H.24.a.4.8. and the road from BELGIAN BATTERY CORNER to cross roads H.16.d.15.15. received much attention from 15 c.m. Howitzers and H.V. guns during the night.
   Others areas shelled were - I.19.c., I.20.a.& c., H.24.c.

3. AVIATION.   Two E.A. crossed our lines at 10.30 a.m.
   Four E.A.   "   "   "   " 11.0 a.m.
   Two E.A.   "   "   "   " 11.15 a.m.
   All were flying fairly high and were engaged by anti-aircraft guns.

4. HOSTILE DEFENCES. Two M.G's. fired from vicinity of I.28.b.00.85.

5. MOVEMENT.   Nil.

6. GENERAL   Except for artillery activity (para.2(b) above) the enemy was much quieter than during the preceding twenty-four hours.
   No Very lights were sent up opposite our left Brigade front and M.G. fire was below normal.

H.Q. 35th Division,
23rd September 1918.

for A.S. tracworth
Lieutenant-Colonel,
General Staff, 35th British Division.

SUMMER TIME.

Date.	SUN. Rises.	Sets.	MOON Rises.	Sets.
Sept.25th.	6.38 a.m.	6.42 p.m.	9.28 p.m.	2.9 p.m. (26th)
" 26th.	6.40 a.m.	6.39 p.m.	10.27 p.m.	2.55 p.m.(27th)

Ref. 28 N.W. and 28 S.W. 1/40,000

35th BRITISH DIVISION.

DAILY INTELLIGENCE SUMMARY No. 107.
From 6 a.m. 23rd Septr. to 6 a.m. 24th Septr.

---

1. **OPERATIONS (British)**
   (a) <u>Infantry</u>.   Our patrols were active but no Germans were encountered.
   (b) <u>Artillery</u>.   Shoots were carried out at 11 p.m., 11.15 p.m., and 11.50 p.m. About 500 rounds 18-pdr. and 150 rounds 4.5" How. were expended on harassing fire during the night.

2. **OPERATIONS (German)**
   (a) <u>Infantry</u>.   Nil.

   (b) <u>Artillery</u>.   Below normal.
   The enemy shelled his favourite targets, namely WOODCOTE HOUSE, BEDFORD HOUSE and square I.26., and also devoted a good many rounds to our posts near ZILLEBEKE LAKE.
   Between 10.0 p.m. and midnight Blue Cross Gas shells fell in vicinity of SWAN CHATEAU.
   The enemy carried out short but concentrated bombardments of the area North of the Divisional front at 12.30 a.m. and 1.32 a.m.

3. **AVIATION.**   Four E.A. were seen at 3.30 p.m. flying very high; they did not cross our line.
   Enemy bombing machines were active in the back areas by night.

4. **HOSTILE DEFENCES.**
   (a) <u>Machine Guns</u>. A German M.G. fired from I.22.b.8.8.
   (b) <u>O.P's</u>.   An O.P. is suspected at I.34.a.4.1. A slit in a shelter is visible at this point.
   Individual movement has recently been observed round EVANS FARM (O.14.b.3.2.) and a slit is also visible in this building. It may be used as an O.P.

5. **MOVEMENT.**   Occasional movement was observed on HILL 60 and round OAK DUMP (O.3.b.7.8.)

6. **MISCELLANEOUS.**   An enemy dump North of HILL 60 was set on fire by our gun fire at 1.30 a.m.

H.Q. 35th Division,
24th September 1918

for A.J. Cherry Lieut.
Lieutenant-Colonel,
General Staff, 35th Division.

SUMMER TIME.

Date.	SUN Rises.	Sets.	MOON Rises.	Sets.
Sept.26th.	6.40 a.m.	6.39 p.m.	10.27 p.m.	2.55 p.m.
" 27th.	6.42 a.m.	6.37 p.m.	11.33 p.m.	3.33 p.m.

Ref.Sheets 28 N.W. and 28 S.W. 1/20,000.

35th BRITISH DIVISION.
DAILY INTELLIGENCE SUMMARY No. 108.
From 6 a.m. 24th Septr. to 6 a.m.25th Septr.

1. OPERATIONS (British)
   (a) Infantry. Patrols were active along the front. No enemy patrols were encountered.
   (b) Artillery. Our field artillery harassed the enemy's communications and occupied areas. Concentrations were fired onto selected targets. Two enemy working parties reported by Infantry observers were engaged.

2. OPERATIONS (German)
   (a) Infantry. A party of the enemy attempted to rush our post at I.28.a.1.3. They threw bombs into an unoccupied post in front of our post and then tried to our post. They were dispersed by fire from rifles and a Lewis Gun and apparently suffered casualties. A search was made but no wounded or dead Germans were found.
   (b) Artillery. Artillery activity was below normal.
   Between 9.30 p.m. and 10.30 p.m. there was heavy shelling of I.19.d. and I.20.a & c. Some Yellow Cross gas was included in this shelling. Between 10.0 p.m. and 12.30 a.m. about 250 shells fell in H.18.a.& b. Most of the rounds were from 7.7 c.m. guns but a gun of a smaller calibre is reported to have participated in this shelling.
   The position of a H.V. gun was bisected at I.34.c.4.3. Our Heavy Artillery dealt with this and the gun ceased to fire.
   Batteries active at 3.20 a.m. were firing from O.6.c. and O.16.b.

3. AVIATION. Two of our aeroplanes were brought down by E.A. at 6.5 p.m. One fell in the vicinity of HILL 60 and burst into flames; the other fell behind TOR TOP TUNNELS I.24.d.
   Three E.K.B. were aloft at G.B. of 143°, 145°, and 164° from I.14.b.1.4.

4. ENEMY DEFENCES.
   (a) Work. A working party was located at night between I.34.a.3.5. and I.34.a.5.5. Nature of work unknown.
   (b) Machine Guns. A machine gun is suspected at I.29.c.2.8.

5. MOVEMENT Normal individual movement was observed.

6. MISCELLANEOUS. Enemy searchlights were active during the night.

R.P.Harrison Capt

H.Q. 35th Division,
25th September 1918.

Lieutenant-Colonel,
General Staff, 35th Division.

SUMMER TIME.

Dates.	SUN. Rises.	Sets.	MOON. Rises.	Sets.
Septr.27th.	6.42 a.m.	6.37 p.m.	11.33 p.m.	3.33 pm.(28th)
" 28th.	6.44 a.m.	6.34 p.m.		

R
Ref.Sheets 28 S.E. and 28 N.E. 1/20,000.

35th BRITISH DIVISION.
DAILY INTELLIGENCE SUMMARY No.109.
From 6 am. 25th Septr. to 6 am. 26th Septr.1918.

1. **OPERATIONS (British)**
   (a) <u>Infantry</u>. Our patrols encountered no Germans.
   (b) <u>Artillery</u>. Two minute concentrations were fired on the suspected battalion H.Q. at 0.4.b.05.65., railway embankment and occupied areas in I.29.c. and the road junction at I.35.a.4.1.
   Usual harassing fire during the night.

2. **OPERATIONS (German)**
   (a) <u>Infantry</u>   Nil.
   (b) <u>Artillery</u>   Rather below normal.
   The railway embankment between SHRAPNEL CORNER and I.21.c.4.7. received a good deal of attention throughout the day.
   During the evening the area between WOODCOTE HOUSE and SHRAPNEL CORNER and west of the SWAN CHATEAU was shelled with BLUE CROSS GAS SHELLS.
   About 7.0 p.m. a few 21 c.m. shells fell on CAFE BELGE.
   At 2.45 a.m. a heavy bombardment of the line south of the divisional front opened and lasted until 3.30 a.m.
   The enemy's long range guns were again active on our back areas.
   (c) <u>Machine Guns</u>   Enemy machine guns opened heavy fire at our aircraft. With this exception their activity was confined to the usual bursts during the night.

3. **AVIATION**.   Enemy activity below normal, during the day, but by night E A were again over our back areas.

4. **CONDITION OF GROUND**   A path runs across the bed of ZILLEBEKE LAKE from I.22.a.6.0. to I.22.a.75.30. The going is fairly good.

5. **LIGHT SIGNALS**.   At 7.40 p.m. a double red light was sent up by the enemy. This signal was repeated northwards along the enemy front. No consequent action was apparent.

H.Q. 35th Division,
26th September 1918.

A. J. Chevey Lieut.
Lieutenant-Colonel,
for General Staff, 35th British Division.

SUMMER TIME

Date	SUN Rises	Sets	MOON Rises	Sets
Septr. 28th.	6.44 a.m.	6.34 p.m.		
" 29th.	6.45 a.m.	6.32 p.m.	0.42 a.m.	4.2 p.m.

Ref.Sheet 28 N.W. and 28 S.E.   1/40,000

35th BRITISH DIVISION.

DAILY INTELLIGENCE SUMMARY No.110

From 6 a.m. 26th Septr. to 6 a.m. 27th Septr.

1. **OPERATIONS (British)**
   (a) <u>Infantry</u>.   Our patrols were active but encountered no Germans.
   (b) <u>Artillery</u>.   Harassing fire was carried out during the night and concentrations were fired on selected targets.

2. **OPERATIONS (German)**
   (a) <u>Infantry</u>.   Nil.
   (b) <u>Artillery</u>.   Hostile artillery activity was below normal.
   Our forward area in I.21. and I.27. received some shelling in the morning.

3. **AVIATION**.   Seven E.A. were seen during the morning flying high.
   Three E.A. flew over our lines at 3.30 p.m. and three more at about 5.30 p.m.
   Five Enemy Kite Balloons were aloft during the day.

4. **HOSTILE DEFENCES**
   (a) <u>Machine Guns</u>   A machine gun fired from approximately I.28.b.15.55.

5. **MOVEMENT**.   Normal individual movement was observed.

6. **HOSTILE BATTERIES**   Grid bearings on flashes of hostile batteries were taken from H.18.d.8.4. as follows:-

8.30 p.m.	174°
8.45 p.m.	156°
10.15 p.m.	130°
12.5 a.m.	110°
4.0 a.m.	144° 30'

H.Q. 35th Division,
27th September 1918.

P.P. Harrison
Captain
Lieutenant-Colonel,
General Staff 35th Division

G.S. 35th DIVISION   for Sep 18

Narrative of Operations
from 28th September to end of October, 1918.

First Phase - 28th September to October 3rd 1918.

1. On September 12th 35th Division was in the II Corps and held the line from Moated Grange, South of VOORMEZEELE to the YPRES-COMINES Canal where it is crossed by the YPRES-LILLE Road and thence to the road and railway crossing just South of the Western edge of ZILLEBEKE POND.

   Two Brigades were in line with H.Qrs. at ST.DUNSTANS and ASSAM FARM, and One Brigade in Reserve near BRANDHOEK with H.Qrs. put at WARATAH FARM and later at H.9.c.1.1. South of VLAMERTINGHE.

   Divisional H.Q. at VOGELTJE Convent, just South of CHATEAU LOVIE.

   41st Division was on the Right and 14th Division on the Left.

2. On the 12th September at 1800 hours the G.O.C. was sent for to XIX Corps and was told that the 14th and 35th Divisions were going to be transferred to the XIX Corps, that a big attack was pending, that no orders were to be issued in writing and that as few people were to be told of it as possible. XIX Corps was going to take over front up to ZILLEBEKE POND on the 15th. Meantime 35th Division was to take over 600 yards to the Left from 14th Division. General objective of attack was given, 35th Division to attack North of YPRES-COMINES Canal from the Bluff to TOR TOPS from its present Left Sector. The present Right Sector was to be handed over to 14th Division who would include from ST.ELOI to the Bluff in their attack.

3. On September 13th and 14th new administrative areas were allotted and Divisional H.Qrs. were ordered to move to WARATAH FARM. The proposed attack was communicated to Brigadiers and to C.R.A., C.R.E., and heads of "G" and "Q" Staffs only. All orders for movements of areas were camouflaged.

   Arrangements were made for the 105 and 106 Infantry Brigades to take and establish a line of posts on the night of 15/16th, and Operation Order No. 195 was issued.

4. On September 15th orders were brought verbally by B.G. G.S., XIX Corps that attack would take place on 22nd, and arrangements were made for relief by 14th Division of Right Sector.

   Later in the day the date of attack was postponed till 25th and all arrangements for relief were postponed for 48 hours.

   A further Divisional Conference was held at which the outlying scheme of attack was given.

   At 2223 hours the 105 and 104 Infantry Brigades carried out a minor operation and established a line of posts 500 to 800 yards in front of our line on the whole front of 4,000 yards and captured 49 prisoners and 4 machine guns. Two more prisoners and 2 of the enemy killed were accounted for next day. Our total casualties were 3 killed and 8 wounded.

   The objects of this operation were :-

Page 2.

(1) To give more room for deployment of Left and Centre Brigades in the attack near ZILLEBEKE.

(2) To enable machine guns to be brought within effective range for barrage purposes.

(3) To shorten the distance of attack by the 14th Division on the Bluff and ST.ELOI.

The new line of posts ran approximately along Old French Trench, Middlesex Road, to Eastern end of ZILLEBEKE POND and took in Western end of the SPOIL BANK, CHESTER FARM, BLAUWE POORT and MANOR FARM.

5. The Army Commander wired congratulations and came next day personally to convey congratulations and to discuss the plan of attack and of further exploiting the success as far as ZANDVOORDE.

He approved of the G.O.C's proposal that the attack should be carried out by three Brigades in depth instead of by two Brigades with One in reserve. The reasons given by the G.O.C. for this scheme were that, with the attack starting on a 1,700 yards front and ending on a 3,800 yards front, it would be easier to arrange for the extension by bringing battalions up than by leap frogging Brigades, also that the lines of attack were affected by the deep railway cutting between Hill 60 and the Dump and by the marshy ground between CANADA TUNNELS and OBSERVATORY RIDGE.

6. On this night (16th) the 106th Infantry Brigade relieved the 104th Infantry Brigade in the Left Sector, and the 105th Infantry Brigade extended its Left across the Canal to LANCKHOF CHATEAU, on the grounds that the Left Sector had extended to ZILLEBEKE POND but really with a view to the subsequent relief by the 14th Division. This subsequent relief was also ordered under the camouflage that one Brigade 14th Division had been placed at disposal of G.O.C. in order to give the troops of the 35th Division a rest, and would relieve the 105th Infantry Brigade on the 19/20th. These reliefs were carried out in accordance with O.O. 196 of 16th September and 197 of 19th September, and the 105th Infantry Brigade went back to SCHOOL CAMP, West of POPERINGHE.

The situation now was that the 35th Division held the front from which it was going to attack with the 106th Infantry Brigade, 104th Infantry Brigade was in camps about BRANDHOEK and 105th Infantry Brigade in SCHOOL CAMP.

Boundaries from rear to front were carefully arranged so that, nearer to the day of attack there should be 3 areas allowing a very narrow front to be taken over by each Brigade in which the final preparations for attack could be made, the remainder of the Brigades being in depth behind. Guns of all calibres were being brought in by night and the areas became very congested and required very careful Staff organization, vide Operation Order 198 of 21/9/18.

7. On the 17th Division H.Qrs. moved to WARATAH FARM. From the 18th to 23rd constant modifications of the scheme, of the rate of barrage, pauses in the barrage in order to suit the Belgians, etc. were made and the date of attack

was altered on the 22nd September to the 27th and then to the 28th. Battalions had already started moving up and had to be sent back.

Finally orders were issued on September 23rd, but these included a certain amount of vagueness as to when the second advance on ZANDVOORDE should commence, depending on hypothetical circumstances, and also included the 41st Division passing through the 35th before the reserves and guns of the 35th could get forward. As a result of a visit from the Army Commander and M.G., G.S., Army, and the B.G.G.S. of Corps these matters were modified and a definite time was laid down for the second advance in an amendment to orders.

The general scheme as finally amended was as follows:
Three Brigades to attack in line. 105 on Right, 104 in Centre and 106 on Left, each Brigade in depth. The attack to be covered by a creeping barrage at the rate of 100 yards in 3 minutes, with double pauses at 500, 1000, and 1500 yards. (Modifications of these pauses were made right up to the last and the rate of lift after 1500 yards was altered to 100 yards in 5 minutes). Special points were to be dealt with by Field Howitzers and, by arrangement with the Corps, Heavy Artillery was to deal with certain other special points further forward.

The first pause in the attack was to be on the line The Bluffs East of Hill 60-East of CANADA TUNNELS-East of TOR TOP TUNNELS-JAN LANE (J.19. central).

This would be reached in varying times by the different Brigades, the Brigade on the right reaching it about Zero, plus 48, the Brigade in the Centre at Zero plus 73, and the Brigade on the Left reaching it at Zero plus 118.

At Zero plus 96 the Artillery barrage covering the Right and Centre Brigades, which meantime had been searching forward and back, was to settle on its new line and at Zero plus 100 the Right and Centre Brigades (105 and 104 Brigades) were to resume the advance and capture the first objective, linking up with the Left Brigade which would still be pushing on. The first objective included BATTLE WOOD and KLEIN ZILLEBEEKE. It was anticipated that this objective would be reached at Zero plus 2 hours 20 minutes.

At Zero plus 4 hours and 20 minutes the advance was to be resumed by the Centre and Left Brigades (104 Infantry Brigade and 106 Infantry Brigade), the former capturing the high ground about ZANDVOORDE and the latter capturing ALASKA HOUSES to the North. The 105th Infantry Brigade was to stand fast and as soon as the 41st Division passed through, be reorganized to form the Divisional Reserve.

The two Brigades moving forward to ZANDVOORDE and ALASKA HOUSES were each to have one Battery 18 pdrs. and one section 4.5" Howitzers at the disposal of the B.G.C.

Two additional Brigades of Field Artillery were at disposal of 35th Division.

Orders were also issued for the immediate repair of certain roads as soon as the attack progressed.

8.   On the 25th and 26th September the G.O.C. took large parties of Officers, about 60 each day, to CASSEL and with the help of Major General PERCY (M.G.G.S.Second Army), and Captain HEYWOOD (G.3) explained the ground they were going to attack over on the large scale model at Second Army Headquarters, pointing out the marshy places, cuttings, land marks, dug-outs,etc., which all three Officers knew intimately from previous experiences. Afterwards the various Commanders of Battalions and Companies discussed their mutual co-operation and practically played a war-game of their portion of the attack. It is certain that this was responsible in a great degree for the smoothness with which the operations were subsequently carried out.

9. On the nights 25/26th and 26/27th, the three Brigades moved up and occupied the front in depth.

The G.O.C. visited the troops in front line and all Battalions, and found that the secret had been so well kept that troops in front line through which the others were going to attack did not know at 1200 on the day before the attack that an attack was going to take place. Officers were then going round the line telling them. This was due to the loyal way in which all Officers had kept the secret. Battalion Commanders had not been told till the 19th (it then being supposed that the attack was on the 22nd), and Company Commanders were not told till some days later.

On the night of 27/28th troops moved into assembly positions under cover of the posts which had been captured on 15th. Distribution of troops is shown in Map A. attached.

The two Right Brigades each had two Battalions in line and one in reserve, and Battalions attacked through their own troops. In the Left Brigade only one Battalion attacked and it attacked through a Company of another Battalion.

Brigade Headquarters of the two Right Brigades were established at WOODCOTE HOUSE and of the Left Brigade in the railway embankment near the triangular pond S.W. of ZILLEBEKE POND.

Divisional Headquarters remained at WARATAH FARM with Advanced Report Centre at ASSAM FARM.

10. The attack commenced at 0530 hours.
Order of attack was :-

		Objective.
Right Brigade.	4th N.Staffs.on Right.	From the Bluff.
105 Infantry) Brigade.)	15th Sherwood Foresters on Left.	(excl)to the Caterpillar
Brig.Genl.TURNER.	15th Cheshire Regt. in Reserve.	(excl.)
Centre Brigade.	18th Lancs. Fusiliers on Right.	From the Caterpillar (incl) to CANADA TUNNELS (incl.)
104 Inf. Bde. Brig.Gen.) SANDILANDS)	18th L.F.on Right. 19th D.L.I.on Left. 17th Lancs.Fusiliers in Reserve.	
Left Brigade.		
106th Inf.Bde.	12th H.L.I. attacking.	From CANADA TUNNELS to JAM LANE (incl).
	18th H.L.I.in support	
Brig.Gen.POLLARD.	17th R.Scots.in reserve.	

The attack started without a hitch, the enemy reply to our barrage being feeble, and was carried through up to pause line, and then to first objective exactly in schedule time. The advance was over very rough ground, pitted with shell-holes and covered with debris, but by 2 hours 20 minutes after Zero the first objective had been gained everywhere on a front of 4,000 yards and an average depth of 3,000 yards and large numbers of prisoners were coming in. By 1200 hours 750 prisoners had passed through Divisional Cage.

At 0950 hours the advance on ZANDVOORDE and ALASKA HOUSES by Centre and Right Brigades (17th Lancs.Fusiliers on ZANDVOORDE and 18th H.L.I. supported by 17th Royal Scots on ALASKA HOUSES commenced), and by 1430 hours reports were received at Divisional Headquarters that their objectives had been captured about 1230 hours. This added another 3,000 yards to the ground gained. A local counter-attack was made at 1830 hours to regain ZANDVOORDE was easily repulsed and left prisoners in our hands.

Meantime artillery had been pushing forward in spite of the bad ground. Pioneers and R.E. had been ordered up at 0740 hours to commence work on repair of roads. The 41st Division during the afternoon came through our Right Brigade.

At 1605 hours orders were issued to Brigades to make good the ground gained, to put out Outposts and push out patrols to exploit success, reorganize, bring up affiliated guns and machine-guns, and bring up food and ammunition and be prepared for further action at short notice.

Transport lines were moved forward to near ZILLEBEKE POND and rations and ammunition were sent up by pack train which worked admirably during this and succeeding days.

Late in the evening the G.O.C. visited the battle ground and saw Brigadiers at TOR TOP TUNNELS and WOODCOTE HOUSE. Prisoners continued coming in. A large amount of guns, trench mortars, and machine guns had been captured, but were not salved until later.

At 2355 hours orders were issued to the following effect :- 35th Division to advance on following morning to TENBRIELEN and thence on WERVICQ, with 29th Division of the II Corps advancing on Left, and 41st Division advancing on COMINES on the Right. 104th Infantry Brigade to take over the defence down to CANAL and to remain in reserve about ZANDVOORDE and old final objective: 105th Infantry Brigade to move via ZANDVOORDE using any route between Hill 60 and TOR TOP, and to make good the line TENBRIELEN-BLAGNAERT FARM and thence, if all went well, on both flanks, to capture WERVICQ: one Battery 18 pdrs. and one section 4.5 howitzers were placed at disposal of Brigadier-General Commanding 105th Infantry Brigade. Heavy artillery was to bombard intermittently the line TENBRIELEN-BLAGNAERT FARM and LA FACON FARM at 1000 hours: 106th Infantry Brigade to be in support: if both Brigades became involved Brigadier-General POLLARD to assume command of combined 105th and 106th Brigades.

11. On the 29th Advanced Divisional H.Qrs. moved to WOODCOTE HOUSE. No news was received all the morning from 105th Infantry Brigade, but at 1300 hours a message was received from Brigadier-General SANDILANDS (commanding 104th Infantry Brigade with H.Qrs. near Hill 60) to say that 105th Infantry Brigade had lost direction in the mist, and moved towards HOLLEBEKE instead of North of ZANDVOORDE and then moved up towards ZANDVOORDE and were held up by machine-guns from South-Eastern spur of ZANDVOORDE. The G.O.C. spoke to General POLLARD on the telephone at 1325 hours and instructed him that, if the 105th Infantry Brigade was held up, the 106th Infantry Brigade must push on through them to TENBRIELEN and BLAGNAERT FARM, otherwise 106th were to support and push on the 105th Infantry Brigade. General POLLARD to take command of all advanced troops.

G.O.C. proceeded to 104 H.Qrs. near Hill 60, where he

Page 6.

he was able to speak to General POLLARD and then on to
KLEIN ZILLEBEKE to see the situation. At 1540 hours
he telephoned back through Advanced Divisional H.Qrs.
to Corps that the 15th Cheshire Regiment had been held up
East of ZANDVOORDE and that the N.Staffords. and 15th
Sherwoods were attacking ZANDVOORDE. General POLLARD
was with General TURNER and was sending one Battalion
106th Infantry Brigade with two Battalions in close
support, on to TENBRIELEN regardless of what was taking
place at ZANDVOORDE. The G.O.C. in consultation on the
telephone with General POLLARD arranged that all available
artillery should be turned on TENBRIELEN up to 1730 hours.

At 1800 hours detailed information was brought
in by a Staff Officer who had been sent forward, that at
1245 hours the 105th Infantry Brigade had been held up,
but had attacked the Eastern spur of ZANDVOORDE again with
two Battalions, and had been successful, and that troops
were seen at 1630 hours advancing towards TENBRIELEN.

At 1634 hours reports were received from General
POLLARD that one Battalion 106 and one Battalion 105 were
on their objectives at TENBRIELEN, that it was too dark
to continue advance that night, but that he proposed
attacking WERVICQ at 0550 hours the following morning.
He asked for artillery bombardment from 0550 hours to
0650 hours on WERVICQ and reported that he had two
Battalions of his own Brigade and one Battalion of 105th
Infantry Brigade to support the attack.

At 1920 hours a message was sent to General
POLLARD approving his proposals, informing him that
arrangements had been made to give Artillery support
of Heavies and Divisional Artillery as requested, and
that Group Commanders of both D.A.Brigades were affiliated
to him for direct orders during the operation, also that
41st Division had been asked to carry out their attack on
COMINES at the same time.

B.G.C. 104th Infantry Brigade was told that the
BATTLE WOOD line -(Triangular Bluff O.5.a. - Railway Trench)
need no longer be held, that the Brigade was to be collected
and given as much rest as possible.

At 2050 hours in consequence of telephonic conversation with Corps the following order was issued.

" Battalions of 105th and 106th Infantry Brigades
" are on TENBRIELEN SPUR.
" 105th and 106th Infantry Brigades both under
" orders of General POLLARD will move off at 0550 hours
" tomorrow morning 30th, and attack Northern outskirts of
" WERVICQ, forming a bridge-head on ridges overlooking
" WERVICQ.
" 104th Brigade will hold ZANDVOORDE and ALASKA
" HOUSES with Right on PAUPER TRENCH (P.2.d.) and Left
" about J.34. central. Two Battalions 104th Brigade will
" be held in readiness to support attack on WERVICQ and will
" be located near ZANDVOORDE. All available heavy and
" field artillery will bombard ridges just North of WERVICQ-
" COMINES railway and Northern outskirts of WERVICQ from
" 0550 to 0650 hours on 30th. 41st Division is attacking
" COMINES at same time."

At 2220 hours in consequence of telegraphic
orders received from Corps the following additional
orders were sent :-

"   In continuation of G.A.75 .35th Division will
" penetrate to Railway North of WERVICQ and then push
" forward patrols to line of river. Right of 35th Division
" and Left of 41st Division will be directed on LES
" CASERNES (P.29.b.)".

SUMMARY OF THE DAY'S FIGHTING.

Two things contributed to the difficulty of the day's fighting.(1) ZANDVOORDE is on a kidney shaped hill and the village is completely destroyed. When the 104th Infantry Brigade reported they had captured ZANDVOORDE on the 29th they had captured all the Western part and the Western spur,but had not taken the Eastern spur which still had strong pill-boxes and machine-guns. (2) The wood just East of KLEIN ZILLEBEKE forks, one portion which was nearly obliterated at this point going to ZANDVOORDE and the other was much better defined going towards HOLLEBEKE CHATEAU. The leading Battalion 105th Infantry Brigade(15th Cheshire Regiment) in the mist took the Right-hand fork and before the mistake was rectified had nearly reached HOLLEBEKE CHATEAU. General TURNER then decided that it was too late to go back and moved on ZANDVOORDE from the West, thus coming under fire from 10 machine-guns in the South-East spur of ZANDVOORDE. The attack at 1245 hours by the 15th Cheshires was hung up and it was not till an attack by two Battalions was made at 1545 hours that this spur was cleared. If the 105th Infantry Brigade had passed between ZANDVOORDE and ALASKA HOUSES as ordered the delay would not have happened.

General POLLARD, on receiving orders to take command of the situation, finding that the 105th Infantry Brigade was making a second attack deferred action beyond ordering the 17th Royal Scots to operate on their Left and the 12th and 18th H.L.I. to support. 17th Royal Scots advanced at 1510 hours on the Left flank of 4th North Staffs. through ZANDVOORDE. Subsequently 105th Infantry Brigade advance appeared to be going well but their support Battalion was not moving. General POLLARD therefore at 1700 hours ordered the 18th H.L.I. to advance supported by 12th H.L.I. and assumed command of the operation. The result was that,by nightfall, the line TENBRIELEN-BLAGNAERT FARM was occupied by the 106th Infantry Brigade with one Battalion of the 105th Infantry Brigade while the remainder of the 105th Infantry Brigade was in support, 17th Royal Scots and a company of 12th H.L.I. having done particularly good work during the advance.

The advance to this line brought our troops forward a further 3,500 yards.

Total prisoners up to 2230 hours for the two days amounted to 1013.

12.   During the night of 29/30th and all day on the 30th heavy rain fell. A good deal of discussion went on during the night as to whether we actually occupied TENBRIELEN and as to the exact position of our line,but it was eventually made quite clear that TENBRIELEN had been occupied by the 12th H.L.I. the previous night. Messages were much delayed including one from General POLLARD asking that the attack should be put off till 0615 hours; it being too late to alter the commencement of the

bombardment, the bombardment was kept up rather longer. The attack started at 0615 hours and at 0745 hours news was received that it was progressing well and had already advanced 1500 yards. At 0905 hours a verbal report was received from General POLLARD that "a prisoner taken on the outskirts of WERVICQ said that Germans retreated during the night to a position 5 kilometres East of the Canal.".

At 1000 hours a message was sent to 104th Infantry Brigade to be ready to move towards MENIN. At 1109 hours a message was received from XIX Corps that the 29th Division was reported East of GHELUWE and ordering that Reserve Brigade of 35th Division should be pushed on between WERVICQ and GHELUWE to link up with 29th Division in direction of MENIN.

At 1110 hours the following order was dispatched to all Brigades :-

" 29th Division reported just East of GHELUWE.
" 104th Infantry Brigade will move in the first instance
" to line of road WERVICQ-GHELUWE (Q.4.c.) and thence to
" line WERVICQ-MENIN gaining touch with Right of 29th
" Division between WERVICQ and MENIN. Right of 104th
" Infantry Brigade to connect with General POLLARD's force
" at REEKE (Q.20.b.). 104th Brigade will move as soon
" as possible, reporting hour. General POLLARD'S force
" will hold lightly the line LES CASERNE (P.29.b.) -
" REEKE (Q.20.b.) his remaining troops being collected into
" support on a two Brigade front. Suggested route for
" 104th Brigade is ZANDVOORDE-TENBRIELEN-Eastern tracks
" towards AMERICA CABARET (P.12.b) and GHELUWE advancing
" S.E. from that line."

At 1134 hours G.S.O. 3 who had gone forward as Liaison Officer reported that at 1030 hours 12th and 18th H.L.I. were on line of railway North of WERVICQ with two Companies Royal Scots pushing up on Left of 18th H.L.I. and two companies Cheshires on Right of 12th H.L.I.; remainder of 105th Infantry Brigade in close support. 159th Brigade R.F.A. moving towards WERVICQ from vicinity of TENBRIELEN.

G.O.C. went to General SANDILAND'S H.Qrs. near Hill 60 and amplified the instructions given in the wire ordering his advance. 104th Infantry Brigade commenced to move at 1230 hours.

At 1205 hours a message was received that the 29th Division had been driven out of GHELUWE but were attacking again that afternoon. This message was sent on to G.O.C. at General SANDILAND'S Hd.Qrs. and communicated to General SANDILANDS, who was instructed to get in touch with his neighbouring Brigadiers as soon as possible and arrange concerted action.

At 1300 hours the following forecast of movements was communicated to G.O.C by B.G.G.S. XIX Corps :-
(A) 30th Division relieves 35th Division on 1st October from LES CASERNES P.29.b. to WERVICQ ST.JANS BEEKE.
(B) 35th Division hold WERVICQ to MENIN.
(C) 34th Division move to ZANDVOORDE Area on 1st October.
(D) 34th Division relieves 104th Brigade WERVICQ-MENIN on 2nd October.
(E) 41st Division go behind 35th Division and take over MENIN to WEVELGHEM.

AT 1340 hours a detailed message was received from General POLLARD giving the situation at 1030 hours showing that the 106th Infantry Brigade supported by 105th Infantry Brigade had had heavy fighting in front of WERVICQ and was held up by a line of trenches and pill-boxes just North of the railway. Casualties were reported heavy and no further advance could be made without artillery support.

This message was confirmed and amplified later by G.S.O. 3 showing that most of the troops at General POLLARD'S disposal were in . line and becoming very weak. Later the following definite line was given showing that General POLLARD had reached his point of junction with the 41st Division at LES CASERNES.

" Line now runs P.24.b.85.80 - P.24.d.70.75 - P.24.d.
" 25.00 - P.30.a.70.50 - P.30.a.00.30 LES CASERNES with
" forward posts at P.24.d.75.00 and Q.19.c.10.55. Enemy
" reported trying to dribble round left of Royal Scots about
" P.24.c.8.1. Field guns of 157 and 159 now in action."

At 1530 hours a message was sent to General POLLARD that heavy artillery would bombard trench in Q.20.a. from 1600 hours to 1630 hours also the LYS Bridges in WERVICQ. It was also arranged that 157 Artillery Brigade should be affiliated to 104 Infantry Brigade and 159 Artillery Brigade to 106th Infantry Brigade and act under direct instructions of Brigadiers. C.R.A. sent a mounted Officer to ensure that proper liaison had been secured and G.S.O. 2 sent up to keep touch with the situation.

At 1615 hours a message was received from General POLLARD that under the circumstances it would not be possible to distribute his forces on a two-Brigade front or to extend his Left to REEKE. Accordingly the following message was sent at 1640 hours :-

" Make best arrangements possible for tonight.
" Essential to join up to REEKE by tomorrow to enable us to
" hand over line to another Division. SANDILANDS coming
" up on your Left may lessen pressure and enable you to
" extend. German retirement tonight probable. Our heavy
" artillery will bombard WERVICQ South of railway tonight. "

A letter was sent by Special D.R. (mounted) to General POLLARD regarding situation and future movements.

At 2000 hours in consequence of a report brought back by G.S.O.2 regarding progress of 104th Infantry Brigade and of weakness of the mixed force under General POLLARD caused by heavy casualties the following message was sent:-

" Boundary between 104th Brigade and General POLLARD'S
" force will be the beeke in Q.14.d. and Q.20.a. Hill
" between this beeke and REEKE Q.20.b. will be taken by 104th
" Brigade. Left of 104th Brigade must be in touch with 29th
" Division about Q.17.c. 1,000 yards West of CONCOU."

At 2130 hours a message was received from General SANDILANDS to the effect that the situation was not clear on his Left. Part of 29th Division had been met North of AMERICA CABARET and others had been seen coming back from still further North (Q.1.c.) Heavy enemy machine gun fire had been encountered from Q.7.b. just East of the CABARET. There was no chance of reaching the final objective that night.

At 2215 hours a wire was sent to Corps giving situation and explaining that Left of 104th Infantry Brigade would be unable to extend further East than 1,000 yards West of CONCOU, and asking that 29th Division should join up at that point.

No. 10.

SUMMARY OF LYS OPERATIONS.

General POLLARD'S report on the operations is as follows:--

"The advance was resumed at 0615 hours in the following order:--

12th H.L.I. (Right) and 18th H.L.I. (Left) to attack.
Cheshire Regt. (Right) and 17th Royal Scots (Left) in support.
Sherwood Foresters and N.Staffords (in that order) in reserve.

The weather was bad with heavy rain and strong wind. The attack progressed well up to TERVICQ, some elements entering the outskirts of that town, but the enemy opened an exceedingly severe M.G. fire, having waited to let us get well in, and, in some places, through his line and his very strong wire. About 0900 hours Brigade Hd.Qrs. having arrived at P.10.a.6.3. and communication to the rear being through I proceeded forward with B.G.C. 105th Infantry Brigade to investigate the situation.

Finding that the attack was held up by severe machine gun fire and many casualties incurred, I ordered the advance not to be resumed without artillery support and returned to P.10.a.6.3 to arrange. The line was then on the ridge N. of WERVICQ about the railway line. Support from such artillery as was available was arranged but the advance was unable to be resumed without undue loss. The line was maintained during the night."

From other reports it appears that there are strong defences around WERVICQ forming part of the GHELEUWE Switch and that there were a large number of machine guns firing from the upper storeys of houses in WERVICQ.

Meantime the 104th Infantry Brigade moving via TENBRIELEN and AMERICA CABARET towards GHELEUWE with the intention of moving from a line East of AMERICA CABARET, South Eastwards to the WERVICQ-GHELEUWE road as a first objective, found that the 29th Division were not as far forward as believed and eventually encountered heavy opposition just East of AMERICA CABARET, thus at nightfall being checked in a line facing East instead of South East and with their left flank in the air.

Owing to the bad weather artillery had great difficulty in getting forward but eventually both Brigades were up in close support in positions near TENBRIELEN and BLAEGNAERT FARM. Rationing and the evacuation of the wounded was a very serious problem, the carrying for the latter being a very long one through ZANDVOORDE and KLEIN ZILLEBEKE and down to MIDDLESEX Road, the road between ZANDVOORDE and KLEIN ZILLEBEKE being thigh deep in mud.

13. On October 1st the weather improved. G.S.O.1 went up early to visit the two Right Brigades and G.S.O.3 to visit the Left Brigade.

At 0148 hours a message was received from XIX. Corps that 41st Division would be passing through 35th Division in order to come in position on our Left, passing behind our line. At the same time the 30th Division was moving in, ready to relieve our Right Brigade. Consequently the country all day was full of troops moving from West to East in full view of the enemy on PAUL BUCQ and other heights on the other side of the river, but he took little notice and concentrated all his shelling on the forward troops.

At 0712 hours the 29th Division reported that they were on the line Q.15.a.5.9. - Q.9.d. in touch with 35th Division on the Right, enemy apparently holding high ground in Q.15.d. and Q.16.

At 0905 a message dated 0705 hours gave the situation of 104th Infantry Brigade at 0545 hours "18th Lancs". advancing in close touch with Border Regt. 29th Division last seen going from through Q.8.a.1.4. 19th D.L.I. making ground by strong patrols."

At 1115 hours G.S.O. 3 reported from General SANDILAND'S Headquarters that 104th Brigade H.Q. was at BLAGNAERT FARM, 18th Lancs. Fus. on Left, 19th D.L.I. on Right, 17th Lancs. Fus. in support at BLAGNAERT FARM. Left Company 18th Lancs. Fus was in touch with Right Company Border Regt.(29th Division)at AMERICA during the night. Advance started at 0545 hours. 19th D.L.I. were up to ST.JANS BEEKE in Q.20.a. and in touch by patrols with 106th Infantry Brigade. A wire from 29th Division had been received at 0920 hours stating their Right was in Q.15.d.5.3. Head of 41st Division was passing Headquarters of 104th Infantry Brigade (BLAGNAERT FARM) at 0645 hours moving East. Liaison with artillery satisfactory.

This information was passed to 41st Division.

At 1130 hours a message from 104th Infantry Brigade gave the situation at 0830 hours Line now runs through Q.13.d. and Q.14.c. Progress still being made. Continued M.G. opposition which is being overcome."

At 1240 hours the following message was received from Corps.

It is of the greatest importance to the general operations that progress should be made by XIX Corps towards MENIN without delay. 41st Division leading troops who have reached AMERICA at 0740 hours will do their utmost to push forward South of GHELUWE and capture TERHAND line between the WERVICQ - MENIN Railway and the GHELUWE - MENIN road. 35th Division will make every effort to maintain touch with the Right of the 41st Division."

Meantime G.S.O. 1 had reached General POLLARD at 0740 hours with instructions about extension of Left to ST.JANS BEEKE, also about relief of 105th and 106th Infantry Brigades by 30th Division, the cross move of the 41st Division by TENBRIELEN and AMERICA and the orders for the advance of the 104th Brigade. General POLLARD said the extension of Left to ST.JANS BEEKE could not be done before night, casualties were heavy, strength of 105th Brigade was 900 and of 106th Brigade 500.

G.O.C. went up about 1000 hours and saw Generals POLLARD and TURNER in Headquarters just South of ZANDVOORDE and found that there was little prospect of General POLLARD'S force being able to carry out a further attack before being relieved. He arranged that WERVICQ should be bombarded with Heavy and Divisional artillery from 1600 hours to 1700 hours and that patrols should be sent in after dark to see if enemy had cleared, before handing over the line to 30th Division.

He then visited 104th Infantry Brigade at BLAGNAERT FARM and found that the attack in the morning had been checked and another attack was then in progress but owing to bad communications and the heavy going it was very difficult to co-ordinate the times of attack with the 29th Division. The area was full of troops of 41st and 30th Divisions.

Page 12.

G.O.C. got back about 1615 hours and at 1810 hours a message was received from General SANDILANDS dated 1650 hours saying

" D.L.I. mistaken in saying they hold high ground between
" ST. JANS BEEKE and REEKE. Their Right is on high ground
" in Q.19.a (instead of Q.20.a. as previously
" reported). I have no doubt that we are up against
" GHELUWE Switch which is reported by Colonel JEWELS
" as consisting of heavily wired trenches and pill-boxes
" which could only be taken by Infantry with Tanks or
" systematic wire-cutting by artillery in case of frontal
" attack. Failing this it must be turned by an advance
" through GHELUWE."

The Corps Commander came about 1800 hours and said it had been decided at an Army Conference that there should be a combined attack of 104th Infantry Brigade, 41st Division, 29th Division on morning of 2nd at 0700 hours with half an hour's preliminary bombardment. After discussing the situation and seeing General SANDILAND'S message he agreed that the objective of 104th Infantry Brigade should be defined as the KNOLL in Q.20.a. and c. and the spur in Q.15.d. where a post would be established to connect with the 41st Division.

Accordingly a telegraphic order was sent by wire at 1920 hours and a Staff Officer was sent with written instructions amplifying the above as follows:-

" At an Army Conference today Army Commander set
" great importance on line WERVICQ-MENIN being taken at
" once. A simultaneous attack is to be made by 104th
" Infantry Brigade, 41st Division, and 29th Division.
" Bombardment to commence at 0630 hours, attack at 0700
" hours Wednesday morning 2nd October. Objective of
" 104th Brigade is Q.20.c.2.8. & Q.20.d.3.8. - road as
" far as Q.15.c.2.2. and afterwards establish a company
" on the end of the spur Q.15.c.95.20. That is to say
" that the main objective is to gain possession of the
" whole of the high ground in Q.20.a. and c. and to
" establish a post on the spur in Q.15.c. and d. to connect
" up with the 41st Division. Heavy artillery will
" bombard the high ground in Q.20. a. and c. and WERVICQ
" tonight. The barrage of the D.A. to cover your own
" front will be arranged by you direct with Colonel COWAN
" who should make it as intense as possible and may use up
" all the ammunition in his positions. Telegram G.A.136
" timed 1920 of 1st October has been sent to you on this
" subject.
" Sent by hand of Lieut. MacIVER M.C. 17th L.F.
" starting from 35th Division H.Q. at 2000 hours 1st
" October."

At 1930 hours the relief of the 105th and 106th Infantry Brigades and 157 R.F.A. Brigade by the 30th Division was commenced. On relief they withdrew to near KRUISEECKE cross-roads where transport and cookers met them.

? 159 see
159 Bde diary

SUMMARY of the 1st OCTOBER.

All day great uncertainty prevailed as to the exact position of the 104th Infantry Brigade and the 29th Division, and it is clear from subsequent events that neither were as far forward as they thought. Both made various attacks during the day but were in the end held up by the GHELUWE Switch which was heavily wired and had a very strong machine gun defence.

The 105th and 106th Infantry Brigades under General POLLARD maintained their line in front of WERVICQ during the day and collected and evacuated wounded, but had suffered heavy casualties and were not strong enough to extend their line to the Left or make any attack in that direction. They were relieved by 21st Brigade 30th Division and moved to bivouacs at KRUISEEKE. Before being relieved strong patrols attempted to get into WERVICQ but found it still strongly held with machine guns covered by artillery.

R.E. and Pioneers worked on the road leading through KLEIN ZILLEBEKE to ZANDVOORDE but it was in a deplorable condition. Beyond ZANDVOORDE the road was good. The A.D.M.S. shifted his line of evacuation bringing the motor ambulances by the LILLE Road and HOLLEBEKE to TENBRIELEN thus greatly shortening the carry.

All ammunition and supplies had to be brought by pack train which did admirable work.

As exemplifying the difficulty of communication and the issues of orders it may be noted that the Staff Officer taking the order to B.G.C. 104th Brigade, who started at 2000 hours with two trained Observers and who knew the road perfectly, did not reach 104th Headquarters till 0225 hours.

14. At 1032 hours on October 2nd a message dated 0900 hours was received from General SANDILANDS :-
" Attack on high ground Q.20.a. stopped. All lost at
" once by heavy M.G. fire inflicting heavy casualties.
" High ground even if taken would be impossible to hold as
" it is machine gunned from three sides including houses
" in WERVICQ. Enemy artillery and M.G's increasing."

In consequence of message received from 29th Division the following message was sent to 104th Infantry Brigade at 1140 hours. :-
" 29th Division . 0940 hours and at MILL Q.5.c.4.4. .
" South East of GHELUWE. This turns GHELUWE Switch
" and should lessen pressure on your front."

Reports received from a prisoner captured by 29th Division were to the effect that enemy was ordered to hold GHELUWE Switch. His company of 50 strong with 4 M.G's was holding about 100 yards.

At 1325 hours a message was received from Corps that a large number of enemy troops had been seen moving on the roads West and North-West of MENIN, and that between 0800 hours and 1200 hours 16 trains had been seen to enter MENIN.

This message was passed to 104th Infantry Brigade and orders were issued to consolidate positions held at present.

At 1415 hours a message timed 1315 hours from 104th Infantry Brigade said :-
" 41st Division attacked through our Left last night
" advanced about 400 yards and were stopped by M.G.fire.
" Attack was resumed at 0700 hours this morning but
" according to my information no appreciable progress was
" made by Brigade on our Left. Believe my men are also
" up against GHELUWE Switch. H.Q. Right Company 41st
" Division Q.8.c.5.3. Our Left Company H.Q. at Q.7.d.8.0.
" 18th L.F. at post Q.8.c.0.3. which is now our extreme
" left since 41st Division have attacked."

At 1427 hours a long message was received from 41st Division showing that they were definitely held up and that a heavy bombardment and organised attack would be necessary before the Switch could be carried.

In the afternoon appearances pointed to a counter attack from the direction of MENIN being imminent and messages were received from XIX Corps that arrangements had been made with X Corps to support XIX Corps with two Brigades if the situation required it.

G.S.O.1. 34th Division came in to arrange about relief if ordered.

Corps Commander came in and said that there would probably be a stand-fast for a few days to allow guns being brought up and roads made, and that 35th Division would probably be pulled out to refit.

At 1630 hours orders were issued for 105th and 106th Infantry Brigades with transport and attached M.G. Companies to march at 0200 hours on Thursday October 3rd from present billets round KRUISEEKE to accommodation in bivouacs and shelters South and West of YPRES, and for 104th Infantry Brigade - if relieved - to move to KRUISEEKE Area on relief and subsequently to march on October 3rd at an hour to be decided by the Brigadier commanding to an area South of YPRES.

At 1805 hours definite orders were issued for relief of 104th Infantry Brigade by a Brigade of 34th Division, the 41st Division being relieved at the same time.

At 2150 hours orders were issued for relief of 157 Brigade R.F.A. by artillery of 34th Division.

SUMMARY of the DAY.

The combined attack of the 104th Infantry Brigade, 41st Division and 29th Division at 0700 hours failed, though progress was made in some places. The GHELUWE Switch was strongly held and during the afternoon strong hostile reinforcements arrived at MENIN and a counter-attack appeared imminent. A strong attack actually did take place on a Division on our Left.

The Army Commander decided to call a halt till preparations could be made for an organised offensive, and the 35th and 41st Divisions were relieved by the 34th Division and proceeded to bivouacs and shelters South of YPRES and to KRUISTRAAT respectively.

15. This ends the first phase of the operations, lasting from September 28th to October 2nd.

During this phase the 35th Division attacked and captured the high ground on the South of the YPRES salient on a frontage of 4,000 yards and made a total advance of 8 miles.

The total number of prisoners taken was 1,105, of which the greater number were taken on the first day.

42 guns were brought in, of which 30 were captured in the first advance, the remainder being in debatable ground through which other Divisions subsequently passed. There were still some guns unsalved when the Division left the area. A large number of heavy and medium trench mortars and machine guns and a great quantity of signalling and other stores was captured.

The weather was bad from soon after the start of the attack to the end, with the exception of a few fair intervals. The difficulties of movement of guns and transport have been referred to in earlier in this Report.

Page 15.

Our casualties were as follows :-

By dates.

Date.	Officers.			Other ranks.			Total.		
	K.	W.	M.	K.	W.	M.	K.	W.	M.
Sept. 28th.	-	21	-	57	464	31	57	485	31
" 29th.	5	15	--	61	406	37	66	421	37
" 30th.	5	8	1	80	253	43	85	261	44
Oct. 1st.	-	4	-	47	128	4	47	132	4
Oct. 2nd.	-	1	-	9	66	2	9	67	2
	10	49	1	254	1317	117	264	1366	118

By Units.

Unit.	Officers.			Other ranks.		
	K.	W.	M.	K.	W.	M.
104 Inf.Bde.						
17th L.F.	-	4	-	16	123	7
18th L.F.	-	7	-	30	107	2
19th M.L.I.	-	2	-	16	123	7
104 T.M.B.	-	-	-	-	2	-
105 Inf.Bde.						
15th Cheshires	1	2	-	13	116	2
15th Sherwoods	-	3	-	28	89	8
4th N.Staffs.	1	8	-	27	180	32
106th Inf.Bde.						
17th R.Scots.	2	7	1	55	195	38
12th H.L.I.	3	2	-	26	154	4
18th H.L.I.	1	9	-	22	105	12
106 T.M.B.	-	-	-	-	3	-
19th N.F. (Phrs.)	-	-	-	2	12	-
35th M.G.C.	2	3	-	12	45	4
R.A.	-	2	-	5	49	1
R.E.	-	-	-	2	8	-
R.A.M.C.	-	-	-	-	6	-
	10	49	1	254	1317	117

H.Q., 35th Division,
28th December, 1918.

Major General,
Commanding 35th Division.

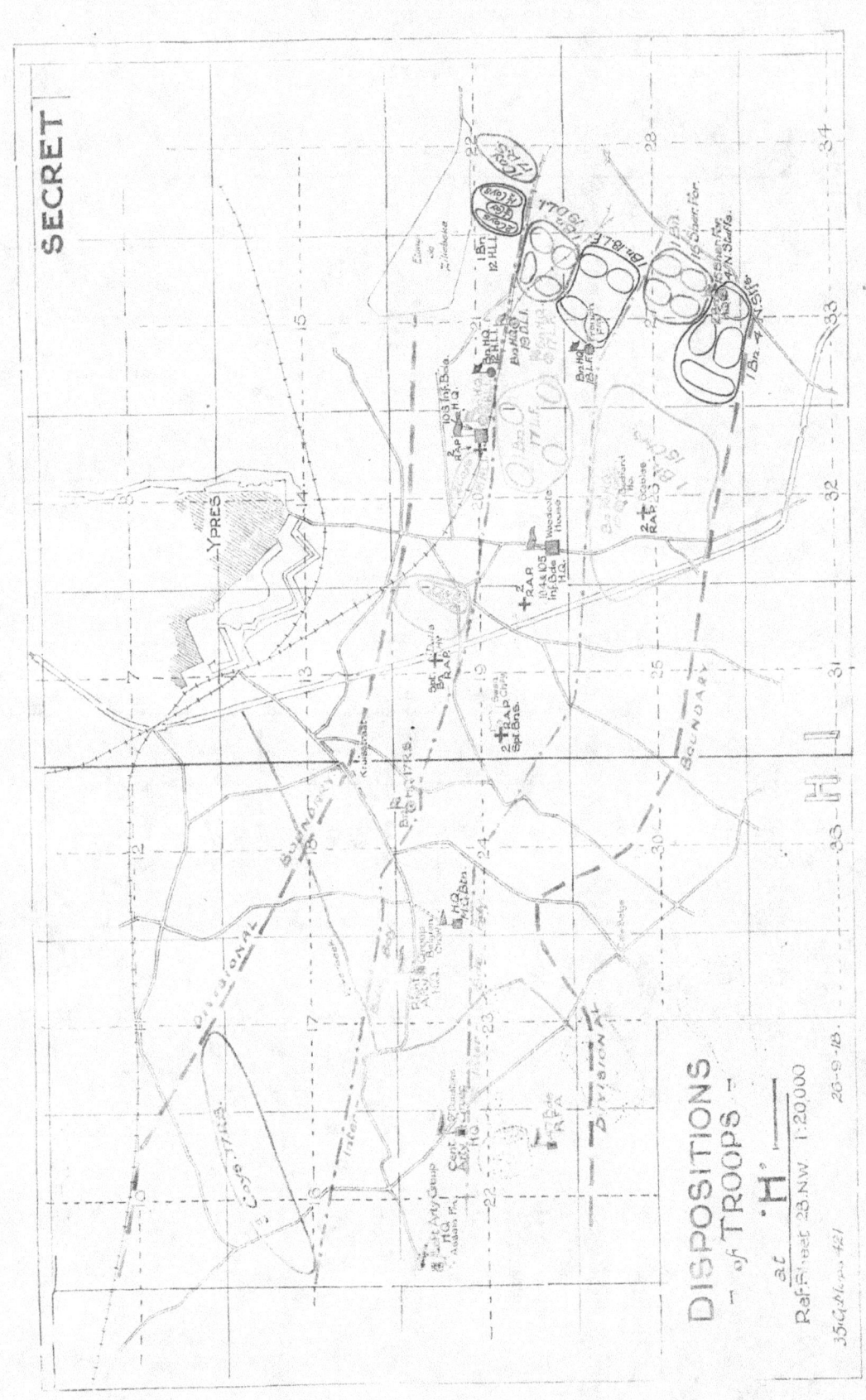

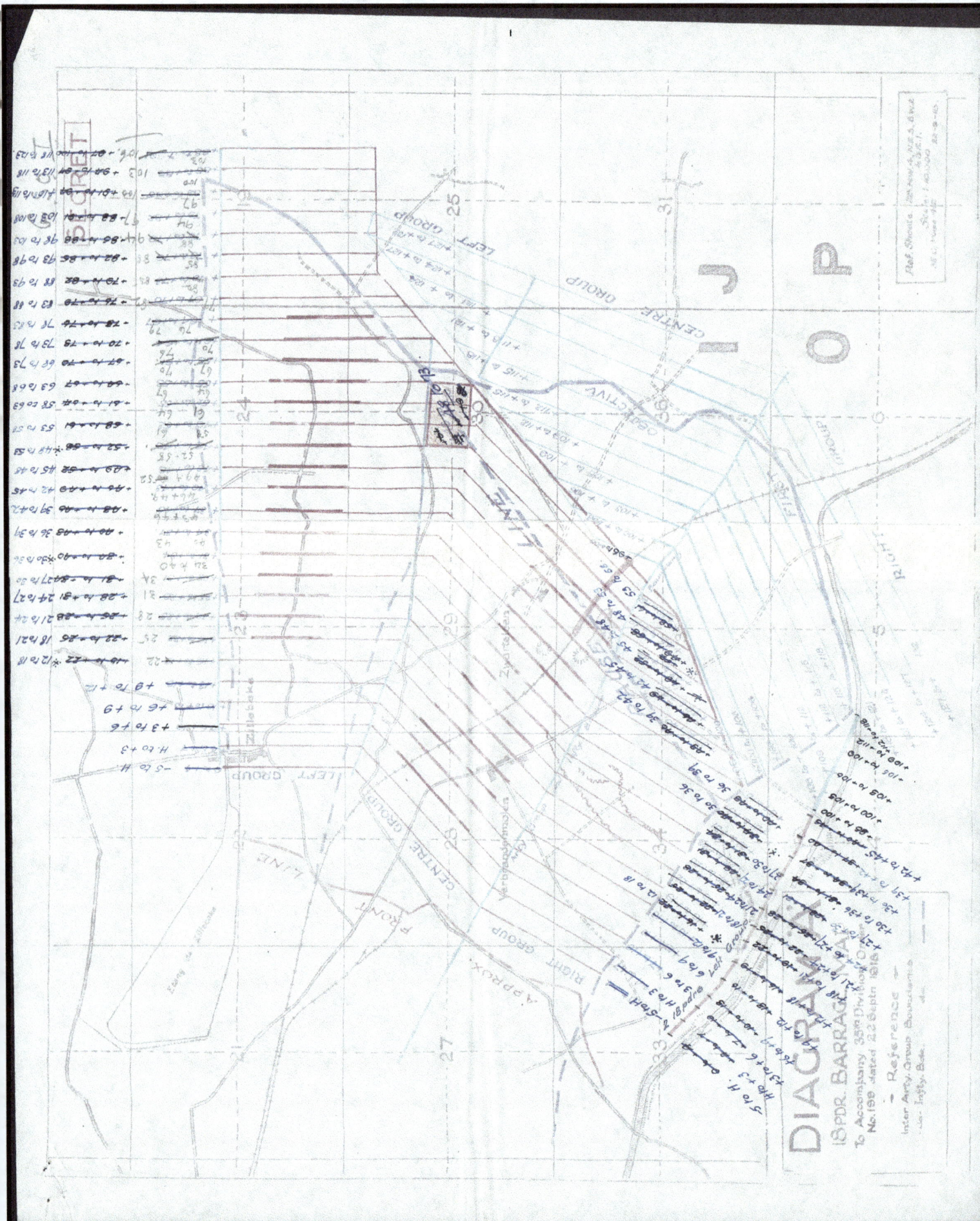

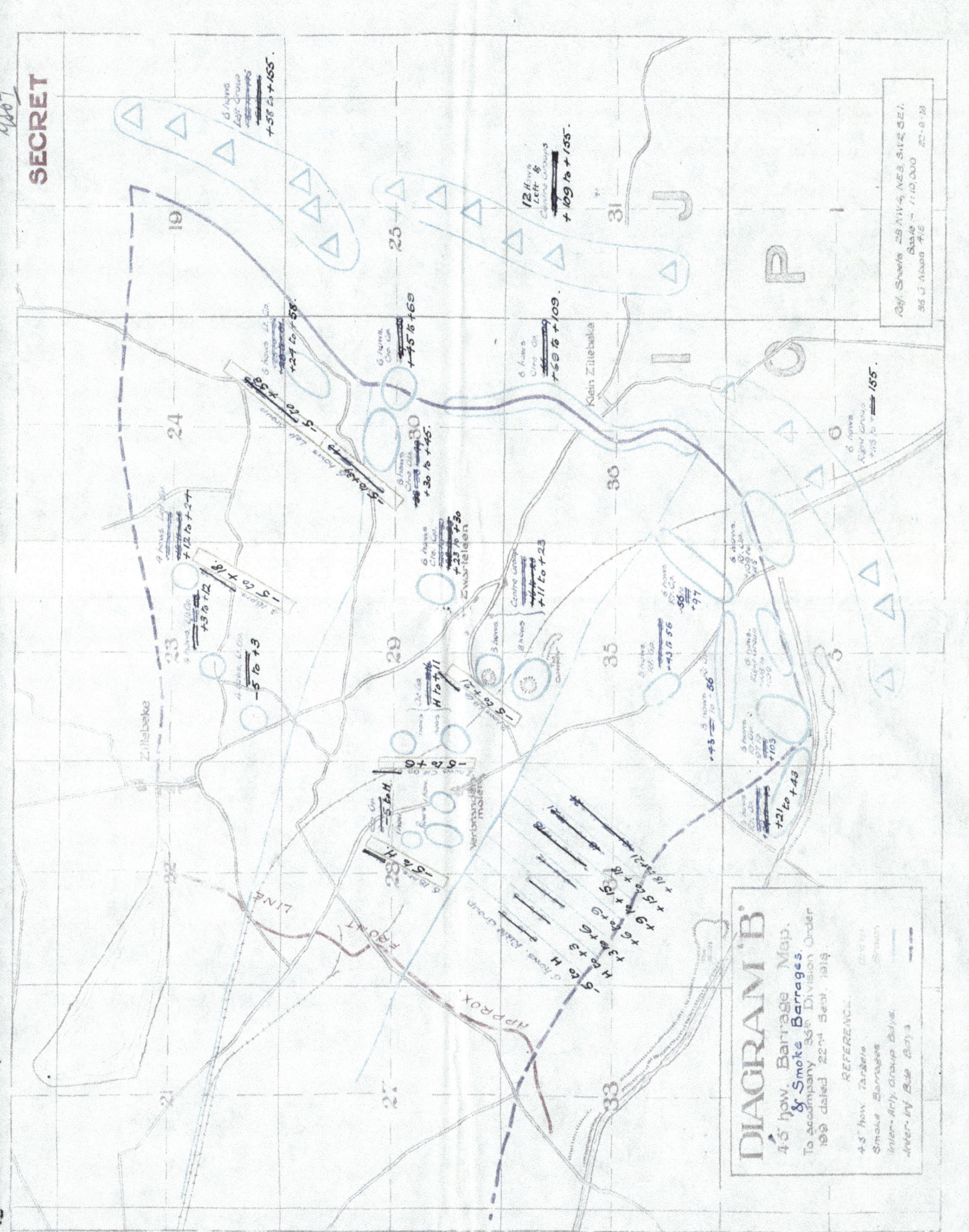

War Diary

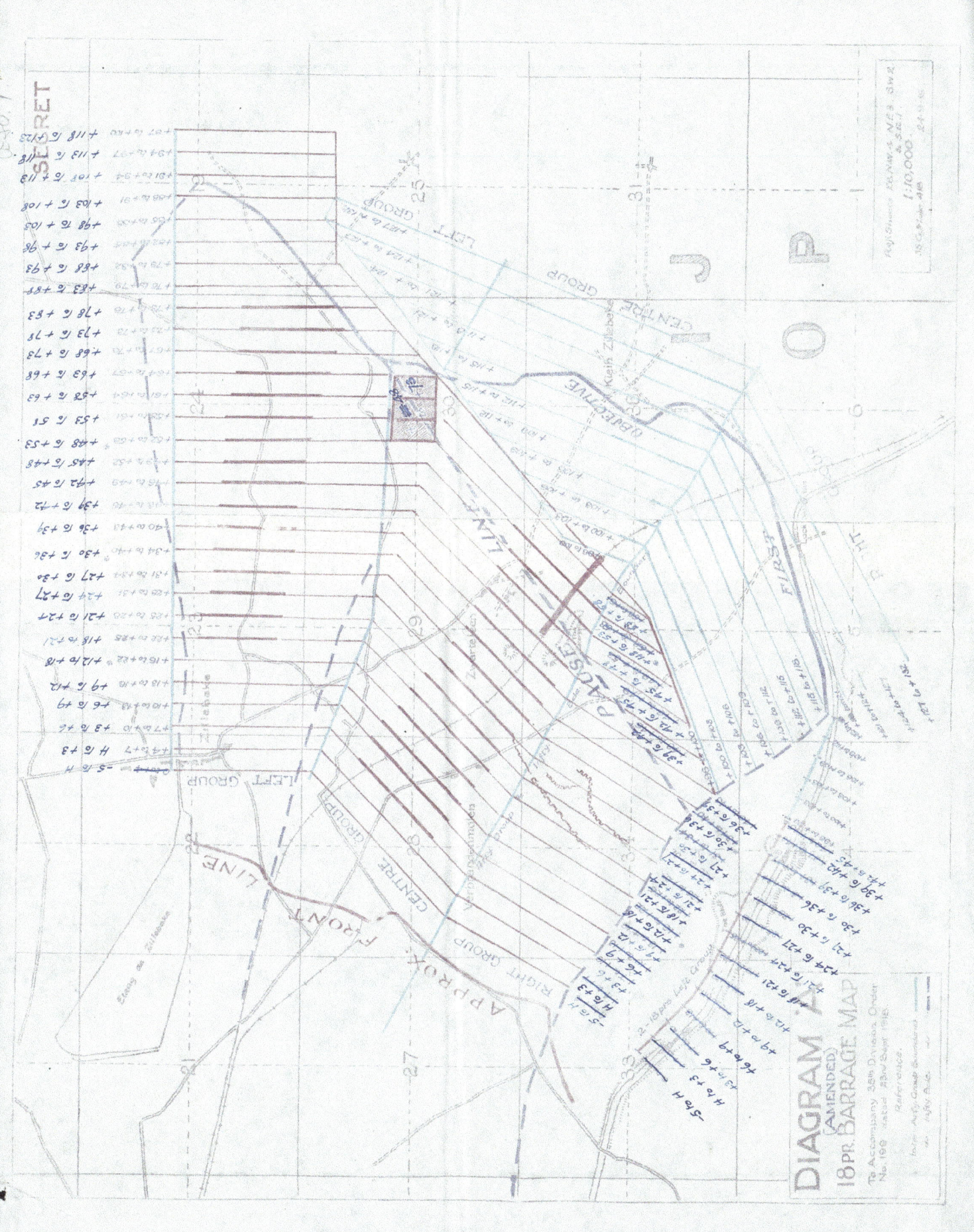

ENEMY DISPOSITION MAP No 73

Reference:
- Companies in Line
- Batt.n Support
- Head Quarters
- Main Roads in Use
- Minor Roads and Tracks
- Div. Boundaries
- Regt Boundaries
- Coy. Boundaries
- Collected from prisoners statements
- Confirmed by Aeroplane Photos

Date 24.9.18
Scale 1/20,000

FOR INFORMATION EAST of THIS LINE SEE MAP No 74

- 12. BAV. DIV
  - 28. BAV. I.R.
- 40. DIV
  - 104. I.R. — Resting Batt at GHELUWE
  - 181. I.R. — Resting Batt AMERIKA No 1
  - 134. I.R. — Resting Batt in KRUITHEM
- 12. BAV. DIV
  - Resting Batt at LEDEGHEM, WINKEL, ST ELOI
- 6. BAV. RES. DIV
  - 25. BAV. I.R.

ENEMY FRONT LINE
SUPPORT LINE

Artillery 25th Sept

WAR DIARY

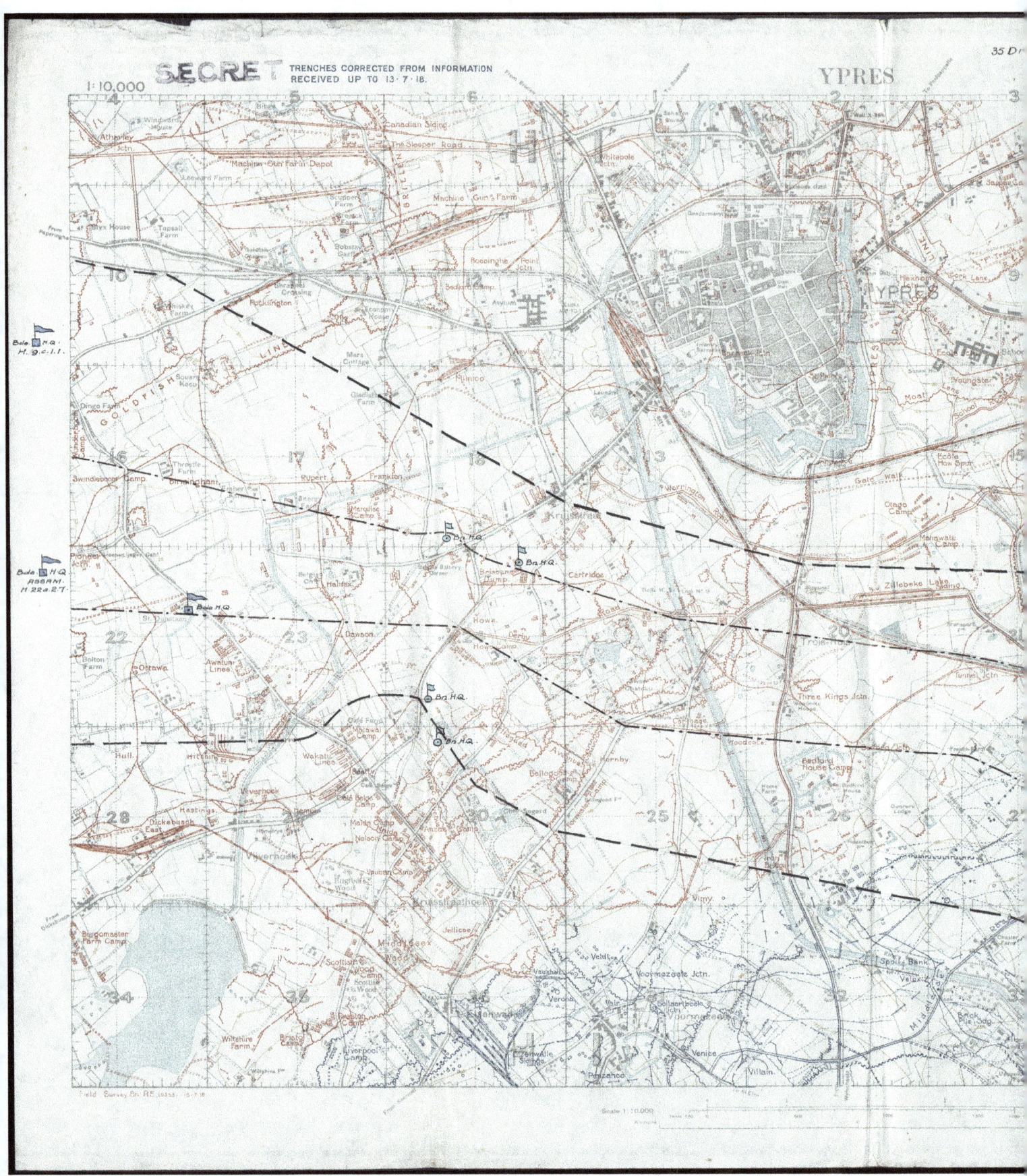

War Diary

War Diary

War Diary
G.S. 35th Divn.
October 1918.

Original

Sheet No.1.
Headquarters 35th Division,
GENERAL STAFF.
October 1918.

Army Form C. 2118.

WAR DIARY

(Erase heading not required.)

Instructions regarding War Diaries and Intelligence Summaries are contained in F. S. Regs., Part II. and the Staff Manual respectively. Title pages will be prepared in manuscript.

Place	Date	Hour	Summary of Events and Information	Remarks and references to Appendices
WOODCOTE HOUSE.	1		During the night 1/2nd October 104 and 105 Infantry Brigades were relieved by 30th Division and moved on relief to neighbourhood of KRUISSEECKE. 41st Division was relieved the same night and moved round to the North of 104 Infantry Brigade in line.	
	2		104 Infantry Brigade and 35th D.A. were relieved by 34th Division in the line during the night 2/3rd October.	
	3		Command of WERVICQ-GHELUWE front passed to G.O.C. 34th Division at 7 a.m. 104, 105 and 106 Infantry Brigades also 35th D.A. moved back to areas between ST DUNSTANS and ZILLEBEKE LAKE.	
	4		Fine day. Verbal instructions received during the morning that 35th Division will take over the line North of the 41st Division on night 5/6th October. G.O.C. attended Conference at XIX Corps H.Q. 7-30 p.m. G.S.O.1 with G.O.C.	
	5		Cold. Showers. XIX Corps Order No.200 dated 4th October received. 35th Division takes over the line from one Brigade of 36th Division N. of GHELUWE. 105th Infantry Brigade on the right, 104th Infantry Brigade on the left. 106th Infantry Brigade remains for the present at ST DUNSTANS. One Company 35th Bn.M.G.C. relieves one Company 36th Bn.M.G.C. in line. 35th Division Order No. 201 issued.	O.O.201.
	6		Fine. No change in the situation. G.O.C. attended Church Parade at 106th Infantry Brigade.	
	7		Fine, cold. Wet afternoon. G.O.C. visited 104 and 105 Infantry Brigades in the line. 106th Infantry Brigade relieves 104th and 105th Infantry Brigades. 104th Infantry Brigade moves into support and 105th Infantry Brigade into Reserve W. of YPRES.	
	8		Fine. Army Commander visited Division H.Q.	
	9		Fine, cold. A post was established on our Left Boundary about 300 yards East of our line, thus connecting more closely with the right of the 36th Division on our left.	
	10		Fine. 35th Division Order No. 202 issued.	O.O.202.

WAR DIARY / INTELLIGENCE SUMMARY

Headquarters 35th Division,
GENERAL STAFF,
October 1918.

Sheet No.2. Army Form C. 2118.

Place	Date	Hour	Summary of Events and Information	Remarks and references to Appendices
WOODCOTE HOUSE.	11		Fine. 36th Division on left captured GOLD FLAKE FARM at 10.0 a.m. but were ejected by a counter-attack at 6-30 p.m. 104th and 105th Infantry Brigades relieved 106th Infantry Brigade in the line, 104th Infantry Brigade on the left.	
JACKDAW CAMP.	12		Fine morning, wet afternoon. 35th Division Advanced H.Q. moved to JACKDAW CAMP opening at 2.0 p.m. Conference at Division H.Q. 5.0 p.m. Present:- G.O.C., C.R.A., C.R.E., B.G.C. 106th Infantry Brigade, G.S.O.1. 35th Division Order No. 203 issued.	O.O.203.
	13		Wet day. Troops moved to Assembly Positions after dark. 35th Division Order No.204 issued.	O.O.204.
	14.		35th Division attacked at 5-35 A.M. with 105th Infantry Brigade on right and 104th Infantry Brigade on the left. 41st Division was on the right of 35th Division and 36th Division on the left. Hostile barrage was put down very promptly. Much difficulty was experienced in keeping direction owing to a thick ground mist. An advance of 6,500 yards was made on a 1200 yards front. The 36th Division was held up W. of GULLEGHEM by M.G. fire and our left flank was turned back in consequence. Enemy resistance was considerable. 14 Officers and 439 O.R. were captured also many guns and machine guns. The day was very fine and the going good. Full details of the operation are attached as Appendix.	
	15		Dull and fine. The attack was renewed at 9.0 a.m. in conjunction with the 36th Division on the left. All objectives were gained and prisoners captured. 43 guns have been captured since 14th October. Orders issued for 106th Infantry Brigade to attack through 104th and 105th Infantry Brigades at 5-30 a.m. 16th October; objective the LYS River crossings. 34th Division relieved 41st Division on right of 35th Division.	
	16		Rain all night. 35th Division attacked at 5-30 a.m. in conjunction with 36th Division on the left. By 4 p.m. our left flank was on the river LYS and the remainder of the line an average of 450 yds from the river completely commanding all crossings.	

Sheet No. 3.
Headquarters 35th Division,
GENERAL STAFF,
October 1918.

WAR DIARY

INTELLIGENCE SUMMARY

(Erase heading not required.)

Instructions regarding War Diaries and Intelligence Summaries are contained in F. S. Regs., Part II. and the Staff Manual respectively. Title pages will be prepared in manuscript.

Place	Date	Hour	Summary of Events and Information	Remarks and references to Appendices
JACKDAW CAMP	16 (Continued).		Troops prevented crossing by M.G. fire from huts and railway embankment on right bank of LYS. Since 14th October 35th Division has captured 12 15cm Hows., 19 10.5cm Hows., and 12 7.7cm guns.	
TERHAND.	17		35th Division H.Q. opened near TERHAND at 11.0 a.m. Orders received from 19th Corps at 7.5 p.m. to be ready to bridge the LYS at short notice. G.A.480 issued 7-45 p.m.:- Orders for 106th Infantry Brigade to push patrols across the LYS and cover bridging operations by R.E. Attempts not to be made to force a passage in the face of strong opposition. This operation was successfully carried out during the night, and it was made possible for troops to cross on the left of the Divisional front. Elsewhere enemy M.Gs. hindered operations.	
HERTHOEK.	18		35th Division H.Q. closed at TERHAND at 12 noon opening at HERTHOEK (L.28.central) at the same hour. "A" and "Q" moved up from ASSAM FARM and opened at the same place. At 12-50 p.m. G.16 was received from XIX Corps (in confirmation of a previous telephone message from the B.G.G.S.) instructing 35th Division to endeavour to secure MARCKE as early as possible. Orders were issued to 106th Infantry Brigade to carry out this operation at night; 104 Bde. was moved forward and 105 instructed to be ready to attack. The attack was carried out at 10.0 p.m. All objectives were gained and 104th Inf. Bde. succeeded in taking more ground than originally planned. The R.E. were successful in throwing bridges across the LYS.	
	19		Fine. 122nd Inf. Bde. (41st Division) placed at disposal of 35th Division. Orders issued for continuation of the advance at 7.0 a.m. 20th October. During the night 19/20th October 105th Infantry Brigade moved N.E. and came into position with its left on the BOSSUYT CANAL. 104th Infantry Brigade on the right, 106th Infantry Brigade in Reserve. 122nd Infantry Brigade (41st Division) also in Reserve in area S. of COURTRAI.	
	20		35th Division attacked on a 6000 yards front (whole of XIX Corps front) 34th Division (X Corps) on the right, 29th Division (II Corps) on left. 41st Division (less 1 Inf. Bde.) in XIX Corps Reserve. 35th Division Report Centre opened at MARCKE at 7.0 a.m. the G.O.C. and G.S.O.2 going forward. The day opened wet, and then cleared up, only to return to very wet conditions in the evening and throughout the night.	

WAR DIARY

Headquarters 35th Division
GENERAL STAFF.
October 1918.

Sheet No.4.
Army Form C. 2118.

Place	Date	Hour	Summary of Events and Information	Remarks and references to Appendices
HERTHOEK	20		(Continued). The enemy put up a stubborn resistance in the centre and left. SWEVEGHEM was captured at 1-55 p.m. 104th Infantry Brigade on the right reached the objective early. After stiff fighting all day and night the first objective was reached throughout the 35th Division front by 6.0 p.m. 21st October.	
			106th Infantry Brigade made a strenuous attack to gain the final objective attacking from a flank but was unable to do so. This effort calls for special mention. At 8-30 a.m. 30th Division passed through the 34th Division.	
MARCKE.	21.		Wet. At 7-30 a.m. 41st Division, to whom 122nd Infantry Brigade reverted passed through the line held by 35th Division and continued the advance. Troops of 35th Division marched back to an area South of COURTRAI. 35th Division H.Q. opened at MARCKE at 12 noon.	
	22.		Showers. Corps Commander visited Division H.Q.	
	23.		Fine. 15th Cheshires and 15th Sherwoods specially mentioned in the C. in C's. despatch, concerning the retreat in March 1908.	
COURTRAI.	24.		Fine, cold. Division H.Q. closed at MARCKE and opened at the CHATEAU between COURTRAI and SWEVEGHEM at 1200 hours. 106th Infantry Brigade placed at disposal of 41st Division and moved to East side of SWEVEGHEM.	
	25.		Fine, cold and dull. Refitting. Orders from XIX Corps received to relieve 41st Division on night 26/27th October.	
	26.		Very fine clear day. Army and Corps Commanders visited Division H.Q. G.O.C. held conference at Division H.Q. at 10-30 a.m. Present:- C.R.A.; three Inf. Bde. Commanders, O.C., 35th Bn. M. G. C. 35th Division Orders 205 and 206 issued. 35th Division relieves 41st Division during night 26/27th October. 106th Infantry Brigade on the right, 104th Infantry Brigade on left, 105th Infantry Brigade in Reserve. 30th Division is relieving the 34th Division on the right during the same night and 34th Division relieving the 9th Division on the left. The line now runs practically North and South from the River SCHELDT just East of AVELGHEM which was captured this morning.	O.O. 205 & 206.

Sheet No. 5.
Headquarters 35th Division
GENERAL STAFF,
October 1918.

WAR DIARY

Place	Date	Hour	Summary of Events and Information	Remarks and references to Appendices
SWEVEGHEM	27		Fine. Some drizzle in afternoon. 35th Division H.Q. opened at SWEVEGHEM at 10.0 a.m. 104th Infantry Brigade captured three prisoners of 11th Division during the night.	
	28		Fine bright day. G.O.C., G.S.O.1, and A.A.& Q.M.G. attended formal reception by the BELGIAN Authorities in COURTRAI. XIX Corps O.O. No. 204 received.	
	29		Very fine. Quiet day, very little Artillery fire. G.O.C. visited 31st Division to make arrangements about the next attack. 35th Division Order No. 207 issued.	O.O.207.
	30.		Fine day. Preparations for the continuation of the attack completed.	
	31.		Mist and drizzle in afternoon. 35th Division attacked in accordance with orders issued at 5.25 a.m. 104th Infantry Brigade attacked with three Battalions in line. 31st Division II Corps was on the left. All objectives were gained by 11-25 a.m. Captures 6 Officers 223 O.Rs. Information received from XIX Corps that 35th Division will probably be relieved in the line on 1st/2nd November.	

Major-General,
Commanding 35th Division.

H.A. 35th Division,
1st November 1918.

14th October 1918.   35? Division "G"

		From or To	Sender's Number	Time Sent	Time Received	
1	In	Wamo (106)	BR 53	0500	0530	H.Q estab
2	In	B.G.G.S. 19 Corps	Phone		0607	B.G.G.S asked whether there Told him one and that bo
3	In	Wamo (106)	BR 54	0608	0625	No informati at Zero.
4	In	35 Div. Signals	Phone		0635	35 Div Signals down. In
5	Out	104 + 105 IBdes	GA 301	0700		Send short you
6	In	Wapu (105)	BM 180	0713	0717	Assembly co fairly thick
7	In	B.G.G.S	Phone		0720	Asking for n him wires a
8	Out	19 Corps. 36, 41 Divs.	GA 302	0720		Both Bdes opened promp
9	In	Wabo (104)	BM 903	0555	0735	Assembly co fell at once
10	In	Wabo (104)	BR 704	0720	0736	No news rec Few prisoners vicinity Bde prisoners belong

REGISTER OF MESSAGES

PURPORT	Action taken	Remarks
...ched K21.b.0.7		
...of troops had formed up all right, and ...was much shooting before 'H'. ...Bde had reported forming up complete ...th Bdes reported situation quiet.		
...n received yet. 12th H.L.I moved off		
...report all lines forward of TERHAND are ...touch with 104 Bde by wireless		
...report by wireless. No news yet 0700 from		
...et. Enemy barrage artillery M.G. fire		
...ws. Rptd BM 18C from 103 Bde. Till ...down		
...lld well. Enemy barrage and M.G. ...y. No aeroplane report yet.		
...lled satisfactorily. Enemy barrage ...about LEADHALL COPSE		
...yet. Still considerable hostile shelling ...coming back. Heavy enemy gas shelling ...from approximately 0600 to 0645. Some ...100th Saxon Regt.		

35th DIVISION "G" No. 1.

14th October 1918.   REGISTER OF MESSAGES

No.	In or out.	From or To	Senders number	Time sent	Time recd.	Purport.
1	In	WAMO (106)	B.R.53	6500	0530	H.Q. established K.21.b.0.7.
2	In	B.G.G.S. 19 Corps.	Phone		0607	B.G.G.S. asked if troops had formed up all right and whether there was much shooting before "H". Told him one Bde. has reported forming up complete and that both Bdes. reported situation quiet.
3	In	WAMO (106)	B.R.54	0608	0625	No information received yet. 12th H.L.I. moved up at Zero.
4.	In	35 Div.Sig.	Phone.		0635	35 Div. Signals report all lines forward of TERHAND are down. In touch with 104 Bde. by wireless.
5	Out	104 and 105 Inf. Bdes.	G.A.301	0700		Send short report by wireless. No news yet 0700 from you.
6.	In	WAPU (105)	B.M.180	0713	0717	Assembly correct. Enemy barrage Artillery M.G. fire fairly thick.
7	In	B.G.G.S.	Phone		0720	Asking for news. Repeated B.M. 180 from 105 Bde. Tell him wires all down.
8	Out	19 Corps, 36, 41 Divs.	G.A.302	0720		Both Bdes. started well. Enemy barrage and M.Gs. opened promptly. No aeroplane report yet.
9	In	WABO (104)	B.M.903	0555	0735	Assembly completed satisfactorily Enemy barrage fell at once about LEADHALL COPSE.
10	In	WABO (104)	B.M.704	0720	0736	No news received yet. Still considerable hostile shelling. Few prisoners seen coming back. Heavy enemy gas shelling vicinity Bde H.Q. from approximately 0600 to 0645. Some prisoners belong 100 Saxon Regt.

....

105th. Inf: Bde: /G. 1939.

Headquarters,

35th. Division.

H.Q.
35TH DIVISION
(GENERAL STAFF).
No. G3876
Date 15/10/18

SHORT SUMMARY OF OPERATIONS.

The enemy put down a heavy barrage ½ hour before H, causing a certain number of casualties. The Cheshires attacked, and in the early stages of their attack met considerable opposition. The fog helped them, which at early stages was not so thick as it became later.

They reached their objective and pushing forward consolidated on line MUTWAL FARM, HILARY FARM, VISCOUNT FARM and L.27.b.7.2.

Direction of this Battalion generally well kept. They got in touch with Units on Right and Left.

The Sherwood Foresters continued the attack, and direction generally had too Southern a trend and the fog lifting they saw they had reached the line of their objective, - about CABIN COPSE, but found their Right entirely uncovered, and had to push forward as far South as ADMIRAL FARM, in the vicinity of which they were somewhat severely handled by enemy Field Guns South of HANGMAN FARM firing point blank. The Teams and detachments of two of these guns while getting away were shot and the guns captured. The remaining guns got away under cover of Machine Gun fire. The Sherwood Foresters were unable to make ground towards KLOEFHOEK and KAPPELHOEK, the North Staffordshire Regiment pushed through them on their Left. Finally a line was reached - ADMIRAL FARM - BADGER CROSS ROADS - Junction of roads in KLOEFHOEK at M.1.a.4.9, - thence along the KLOEFHOEK - MOORSEELE ROAD to G.31.c.0.9. - thence North in front of ADVANCE FARM, with their Left at G.25.a.80.25. - their Flank uncovered.

Troops of 104th. Infantry Brigade were interspersed amongst the North Staffords on the North. Beyond this line they have been unable to advance owing to Machine Gun fire.

During the forenoon the enemy apparently worked through the buildings on the WIJNBERG ROAD, and the present line held runs BADGER CROSS ROADS - in front of ADLER FARM to road at about L.36.c.90.55. - thence as before. Later on the troops of the 41st. Division took over ADMIRAL FARM, BADGER CROSS ROADS and placed a post at HANGMAN FARM.

The troops in front area - the North Staffords and Sherwood Foresters are a bit mixed up, the Sherwood Foresters generally hold the Right on a Front of two Companies; the remainder about TAMIL FARM and ACORN FARM. The North Staffords have got two and a half Companies from the MOORSEELE ROAD - WEVELGHEM ROAD to their Northern Limit, with remaining troops in CABIN COPSE and BAIT JUNCTION. The Machine Gunners have 8 guns about CABIN COPSE facing S.E. and 4 guns in Reserve in position about VISCOUNT FARM.

Casualties estimated at about 100 per Battalion, including 5 Officers per Battalion. Two Platoons of the Sherwood Foresters lost touch in the fog, and are believed to have lost direction Southwards.

Number of captured guns not counted, but estimated at 14 guns known, it is believed about 130 to 150 prisoners.

H.Q., 105th. Inf: Bde:
14th. October, 1918.

Brigadier-General,
Commanding, 105th. Infantry Brigade.

33rd DIVISION "G"

Serial No	In or Out	From or To	Sender's Number	Time Sent	Time Received	
11	Out	104, 115, 106 Bdes CRA 35 Div	GA 303	0740	—	Aeroplane rep... House
12	In	BGGS	Phone		0725	BGGS 19 C... that at 063... proper pract... contents of...
13	In	10 Squad RAF	Phone		0738	At 6.30 a... — L 20 b 7 a — L 26 a 2 8 L 32 a 6 7
14	In	CRA	Phone	—	0740	Asking fo... message f... firing from... are dealing...
15	Out	19 Corps H1 & 36 Div	GA 304	0747		Left Bde... Heavy gas... from 0600... Regt.
16	In	36 Div.	Phone		0750	36 Div say... & their batt... have some... in their ca...
17	In	35 Div I.O	C 56	0735	0755	First batch... to 1st & 2nd B... (normal.)

REGISTER of MESSAGES.

PURPORT	Action taken	Remarks.

...ts 0630 our troops on line MURRAY
FLUTE FARM.

...told GSO 1. that aeroplane reported
...the 35 Division had reached then
...for that hour. GSO 1 told BGGS
...GA 302

our men seen at L 21 a 3.7 - L 21 a 4 3
L 27 a 2 2 - L 27 a 2. 6 - L 26. b 6 5
- L 26 c. 1. 3 - L 26. d. 5. 6 -
L 32. a 2. 3 - L 31. b 5 3. - L 31 c 6. 6

...news. Said he had a wireless
...105 Bde. asking for 5.9 battery
...HEWIN to be neutralized. Heavier
...with it.

...ports hostile barrage fell at once.
...elling of Bde. H.Q. & neighbourhood
...to 0645. Prisoners of 100 Saxon

...their Bdes. are progressing well
...ion H.Q. have gone forward. They
...prisoners of 1st Bav. Res. Div.

...f 15 prisoners arrived 0730. Belong
...100 Resᵗ Gren. Regᵗ 23ʳᵈ Res. Div

File

35th DIVISION "G". No. 2.

14th October 1918.   REGISTER OF MESSAGES.

No.	In or out	From or To.	Senders No.	Time sent	Time recd.	Purport.
11	Out	3 Bdes. C.R.A.35 Div.	G.A.303	0740		Aeroplane reports 0630 our troops on line MURRAY HOUSE - FLUTE FARM.
12	In	B.G.G.S.	Phone		0725	B.G.G.S. 19 Corps told G.S.O.1 that aeroplane reported that at 0630 the 35th Div. had reached their proper position for that hour. G.S.O.1 told B.G.G.S. contents of our G.A.302.
13	In	10 Sqdn. R.A.F.	Phone		0738	At 6-30 am our men seen at L.21.a.3.7 - L.21.a.4.3. - L.20.b.7.4 - L.27.a.2.2 - L.27.a.2.6 - L.26.b.6.5 - L.26.a.2.8 - L.26.c.1.3 - L.26.d.5.6 - L.32.a.6.7 - L.32.a.2.3 - L.31.b.5.3 - L.31.c.6.6.
14	In	C.R.A.	Phone		0740	Asking for news. Said he had a wireless message from 105 Bde. asking for 5.9 Bty. firing from MENIN to be neutralized. Heavies are dealing with it.
15	Out	19 Corps. 41,36 Divs.	G.A.304	0747		Left Bde. reports hostile barrage fell at once. Heavy gas shelling of Bde. H.Q. and neighbourhood from 0600 to 0605. Prisoners of 100 Saxon Regt.
16	In	36 Div.	Phone		0750	36 Div. say their Bdes. are progressing well and their Battn H.Q. have gone forward. They have some prisoners of 1st Bav. Res. Div. in their Cage.
17	In	35 Div.I.O.	G.56	0735	0755	First batch of 15 prisoners arrived 0730. Belong to 1st and 2nd Bns. 100 Res. and Grendr. Regt. 23 Res. Div. (Normal).

....

35th DIVISION G

Consec. No.	In or Out	From or To	Sender's Number	Time Sent	Time Received	
18	In	WAPU (105)	BM/181	0550	0850	Enemy Arty... but his M... progress y...
19	In	19 Corps I	Phone	—	0802	10 Squad... L.22.c.1.9 — L.25.b.1.7. R.3.o.2.8.
20	In	105 Bde	BM/182	0617	0814	Hostile b... ceased ...
21	In	CRA	Phone		0815	(1) At 0655... No news f... (2) Shelling MENIN ROAD considerably (3) Thy amm... arrived over ROAD (4) No new...
22	In	35 Div IO	C 57	0750	0820	Total pris... 2" & 3" Bns 39 Div. (...
23	Out	104, 105, 106 Bde 36 Div & 35 DA	GA 305	0807	—	10 Squad L.22.c.1.9 — L.25.b.1.7. and R.3.c.2...

REGISTER of MESSAGES

3

PURPORT	Action taken	Remarks

...barrage has quietened down considerably.
6 five pounds active. No news of
...

RAF report 0650 our men seen at
L27 b 2.3 - L33.a.2.8 - Q.6.a.7.4 -
At 0715 red flares seen at L35 a 7.1

...barrage much decreased & M.G. fire
...nd assembly area.

41 Div. report right attack going well
centre or left
which was heavy on cross roads
east of CHELUVELT has slackened

...tion Officer who is near CHELUVELT
500 prisoners coming along MENIN

...from batteries yet. Lines still down.

...now 46 O.R. Further identification
132 I.R. and 2nd & 3rd 172 I.R. both
(...mal)

RAF report our men seen at 0650 at
L27 b 2.3 - L33 a 2.8 - L32 c 2.8 - Q 6 a 7.4
At 0715 red flares seen at L35 a 7.1
8.

File

35th DIVISION "G". No. 3.

14th October 1918. REGISTER OF MESSAGES.

No.	In or out.	From or To	Senders numbers	Time sent	Time recd.	Purport.
18	In	WAPU (105)	B.M.181	0550	0850	Enemy artillery barrage has quietened down considerably but his M.G. fire sounds active. No news of progress yet.
19	In	19 Corps I.	Phone		0882	10 Sqdn. R.A.F. report 0650 our men seen at L.22.c.1.9 - L.27.b. 2.3 - L.33.a.2.8 - Q.6.a.7.4 - L.25.b.7.7. At 0715 red flares seen at L.35.a.7.1, R.3.c.2.8.
20	In	105 Bde.	B.M.182	0617	0814	Hostile barrage much decreased and M.G. fire ceased round assembly area.
21	In	C.R.A.	Phone		0815	(1) At 0655 41 Div. report Right attack going well. No news from Centre or Left. (2) Shelling which was heavy on cross roads of MENIN ROAD East of GHELUVELT has slackened considerably. (3) My ammunition Officer who is near GHELUVELT counted over 500 prisoners coming along MENIN ROAD. (4) No news from batteries yet. Lines still down.
22	In	35 Div.I.O.	C.57	0750	0820	Total prisoners now 46 O.R. Further identification 2nd and 3rd Bns. 132 I.R. and 2nd and 3rd 172 I.R. both 39 Div. (normal).
23	Out	3 Bdes. 36 Div. 35 D.A.	G.A.305	0807		10 Sqdn R.A.F. report our men seen at 0650 at L.22.c.1.9 - L.27.b.2.3 - L.33.a.2.8 - L.32.c.2.8 - Q.6.a.7.4 - L.25.b. 7.7. At 0715 red flares seen at L.35.a.7.1 and R.3.c.2.8.

....

33rd DIVISION G

Consec No	In or Out	From or To	Sender's Number	Time Sent	Time Received	
14/10/18 24	In	X army	G/x 3	07.00	08.25	Morning
25	In	105 Bde	AM 178	04.50	08.33	Enemy a Heavy Sh
26	In	104 Bde	BM 906	07.55	08.40	Comm seen to On a brig passed impos Wireless by Gag the Aeroplan on line
27	In	105 Bde	BM 179	05.00	08.40	Very hea Especial from our Battery
29	In	33 DA	Phone	—	08.50	All Bat forward
28	In	106 Bde	Phone	—	08.43	Asking if forward to told them from Div.
30	In	19 Corps	?	08.38	08.55	07.12 seven Rouler. Explosion

REGISTER of MESSAGES. 4

PURPORT	Action taken	Remarks

Situation report

...ty active on forward area
...elling about K29

...nication very bad. Wounded
...free that everything is going
...it. A few prisoners have
...own. Ground mist so thick
...ble to see what is going on.
...put out of action temporarily
...lle bursting in own way.
...just reported 06.30 troops
...urray farm & Hule Farm

...y shelling on our front,
...y forward area. Fire coming
...ection of Menin. Counter-
...asked for.

...teries 157 Bde RFA moved
...at 07.30

...Gen Pollard may now move
...pre-arranged place viz K13a.4.6.
...to wait until orders sent

...large fires burning in
...07.52. four large fires & one
...in Wervicq.

File

35th DIVISION "G".   No. 4.

14th October 1918.   REGISTER OF MESSAGES.

No.	In or out	From or To	Senders number	Time sent	Time recd.	Purport.
24	In	2nd Army	G.223	0700	0825	Morning situation report.
25	In	105 Bde.	B.M.178	0450	0833	Enemy's artillery active on forward area. Heavy shelling about K.29.
26	In	104 Bde.	B.M.706	0755	0840	Communication very bad. Wounded seem to agree that everything is going on alright. A few prisoners have passed down. Ground mist so thick impossible to see what is going on. Wireless put out of action temporarily by Gas Shell bursting in doorway. Aeroplane just reported 0630 troops on line MURRAY FARM and FLUTE FARM.
27	In	105 Bde.	B.M.179	0500	0840	Very heavy shelling on our front, especially forward area. Fire coming from direction of MENIN. Counter Battery asked for.
28	In	106 Bde.	Phone		0843	Asking if Gen. POLLARD may now move forward to prearranged place viz:- K.13.a.4.8. Told them to wait until orders come from Div.
29	In	35 D.A.	Phone		0850	All batteries 157 Bde R.F.A. moved forward at 0730.
30	In	19 Corps I	I.G.6	0838	0852	0712 several large fires burning in ROULERS. 0752 four large fires and one explosion in WERVICQ.

....

35th DIVISION 'G'

	Corps No	In or Out	From or To	Sender's Number	Time Sent	Time Received	
14/10/18	31	In	19 Corps	G/5	08.41	09.07	Contact pa... at L22c... Q6a.y4... seen at
	32	In	41 Div	G/58	08.45	09.14	Prisone...
	33	In	105 Bde	BM186	08.35	09.14	B.G.P. mo... situation Commun...
	34	In	105 Bde	BM185	08.00	09.14	No further Still ve... at K29 t... up to p... 3 MGs f... House.
	35	In	Lt McIver	Phone	—	09.15	HQ 159 Bde in action moved fo...
	36	In	AQ 36 Div	QM5	08.50	09.16	Man of 3...
	37	In	CRA	Phone		09.18	All Bdes going well Shelling Sixty pri... Regt bro... Same R... Bearers (...

REGISTER OF MESSAGES.   5

PURPORT	Action taken	Remarks

trol reports 06.50 - our men seen
1.q - L27.B.23 - L33 a.2.8 - L32 c.2.8
L25 B 7.7 - at 07.15 red flares
L35 a 7.1 & R.3 c.2.8.

identified up to 06.30.

ing forward to find out
with Wireless Set. Other
nication to Division cut.

news from forward. First
y flick. Am remaining
ll information comes in.
ent one Officer 57 prisoners
assed thro' from Ponsonby

R.7A. at L30 c 7.3. with Guns
along Rly. 104 Bde HQ
rward about 30 minutes ago.

Bn 1st Bav: Res: Inf Regt identified

have moved forward. Inf reported
up to time at 07.30. Light
erhand continues 07.3.0.
oners 1st Bav Res Div & 100 Saxon
right cir. Many more of
egt left behind as stretcher
rom 15 q Bde R.7A).

35th DIVISION "G".   No. 5.

14th October 1918.   REGISTER OF MESSAGES.

No.	In or Out.	From or To	Senders number	Time sent	Time recd.	Purport.
31	In	19 Corps I	I.G.5	0841	0902	Contact patrol reports 0650 our men seen at L.22.c.1.9 - L.27.b.2.3 - L.33.a.2.8 - L.32.c.2.8 - Q.6.a.7.4 - L.25.b.7.7 -. At 0715 red flares seen at L.33.a.7.1 and R.3.c.2.6
32	In	41 Div.	G.585	0845	0914	Prisoners identified up to 0830.
33	In	105 Bde.	B.M.186	0835	0914	B.G.C. moving forward to find out situation with wireless set. Other communication to Div. cut.
34	In	105 Bde.	B.M.185	0800	0914	No further news from forward. Mist still very thick. Am remaining at K.29 till information comes in. Up to present one Officer 57 prisoners. 3 M.Gs. passed through from PONSONBY HOUSE.
35	In	Lt. McIVER	Phone		0915	H.Q. 159 Bde. R.F.A. at L.20.c.7.3 with guns in action along railway. 104 I.Bde.H.Q. moved forward about 20 mins. ago.
36	In	D.I.O. 36 Div.	I.M.5	0850	0916	Man of 3rd Bn. 1st Bav.Res. Inf. Regt. identified.
37	In	C.R.A.	Phone		0918	All Bdes. have moved forward. Infantry reported going well and up to time at 0730. Light shelling TERHAND continues 0730. 60 prisoners 1st Bav. Res. Div. and 100 Saxon Regt. brought in. Many more of same Regt. left behind as Stretcher Bearers (from 159 Bde. R.F.A.).

....

35th DIVISION

Date	Serial No	In or Out	From or To	Sender's Number	Time Sent	Time Received	
14/10/18	38	In	35 A.D.O	C58	0645	09.19	Total u... identifi...
	39	Out	106 Bde	GA306	09.25	-	106 Inty... from ... cross.
	40	In	ADO 36 Div	MM	08.30	09.27	New id...
	41	In	35 M.G.B.	NV11	08.40	09.28	Disposit...
	42	In	19 Corps	SY7	09.01	09.30	New ide...
	43	Out	19 Corps, 36 & 41 Divs	GA308	09.30	-	Reserve... Terhand... 35 Div. C... & 71.
	44	In	36 Div	GT57	08.40	09.38	Advance ... moving K... 50 prison...
	45	Out	106 Bde	GA311	09.40	-	As reques... Terhand...
	46	Out	106 Bde	P116M	09.43	-	106 Bde HQ Pollard to move
	47	Out	19 Corps, 36 & 41 Div.	GA310	09.43	-	Ref: 35 Div now mov...

REGISTER OF MESSAGES.

PURPORT	Action taken	Remarks
...ow 2 Offr & 71 OR. Fresh ...tion 132 Signal Section 132 IR.		
...de HQ will move forward now ...er hand to K 23 a 4. 8. Poulteveu		
...ntifications.		
...ous 35 Bn M.G.B.		
...ntifications by 3rd Division		
...nfy Bde HQ now moving from ...to K 23. a 4.7. Prisoners in ...ge 08.45 number 20/pec io		
...ogressing favourably 1st Siniosks ...l to Rockstone Farm L15 A Over ...rs by this Bn.		
...ed by you, 106 Bde HQ will remain. Cancel my GA 306.		
...may move to K 23 a 4 7. Gen ...l now says he does not wish ...his HQ without his Bde.		
...GA 308. Res. Infy Bde HQ is not ...ing.		

File

35th DIVISION "G". No. 6.

14th October 1918.   REGISTER OF MESSAGES.

No.	In or out.	From or To	Senders number	Time sent	Time recd.	Purport.
38	In	35 D.I.O.	C.58	0845	0919	Total now 2 Officers and 71 O.R. Fresh identification 132 Signal Section, 132 I.R.
39	Out	106 Bde.	G.A.306	0925		106 Inf. Bde. H.Q. will move forward now from TERHAND to K.23.a.4.8 PEULTEVIN WOOD.
40	In	D.I.O.36 Div.	I.M.4	0830	0927	New identifications.
41	In	35 M.G.C.	N.V.11	0840	0928	Dispositions 35th Bn.M.G.C.
42	In	19 Corps I.	I.G.7	0901	0930	New identifications by 34 Div.
43	Out	19 Corps, 36, 41 Divs.	G.A.308	0930		Reserve Inf. Bde. H.Q. now moving from TERHAND to K.23.a.4.7. Prisoners in 35 Div. Cage 0845 number 2 Officers and 71.
44	In	36 Div.	G.T.57	0840	0938	Advance progressing favourably. 1st Innissks. moving H.Q. to ROCKSTONE FARM L.15.a. Over 50 prisoners by this Battalion.
45	Out	106 Bde.	G.A.311	0940		As requested by you, 106 Bde. H.Q. will remain TERHAND. Cancel my G.A.306.
46	Out	106 Bde.	Phone	0943		106 Bde. H.Q. may move to K.23.a.4.7. Gen. POLLARD now says he does not wish to move his H.Q. without his Bde.
47	Out	19 Corps 36, 41 Divs.	G.A.310	0943		Ref. 35 Div. G.A.308, Res. Inf. Bde. H.Q. is not now moving.

....

35th DIVISION G

Date	Comsec No	In or Out	From or To	Sender's Number	Time Sent	Time Received	
14/10/18	48	In	Plane	BM156	09.00	09.44	08.30 Ca waived L28.c.9 at 09.00 Building Big explo
	49	In	19 Corps	G.9	09.13	09.48	10 Squadron heavy g scattere road at Halluin
	50	In	105 Bde	C26	09.25	09.59	Ref G.A. SH 07.05 .08. 08.30 now But but well. H heavy n forward House. 105 round further
	51	Out	3 Bdes CRA 106 Div	GA312	10.00	—	at 08.30 J33.d.5.9 J28.d.4.6 lines on
	53	In	BGGS 19 Corps	Phone	—	10.05	aeroplan waving J32 d.5.9 behind en

PURPORT	Action taken	Remarks

...lled for flares - our troops
...white paper from L29 a 2.8 -
...L33 A 5.9 - L28. d 9 8. Red flares
...from about L28 d 9 8. All farm
...s on fire behind enemy's lines
...on N. side of Menin at 08.42.

...Report - 06.15 visibility very bad
...ound mist in valley. 07.55
...parties enemy infantry along
...R 20 & 21. MG's active from

...Situations sent Jon 05.50, 06.17
...0, 08.35. Dense fog until
...clear. No definite report from
...all wounded state attack going
...tile Arty & MG Barrage fairly
...ntil 06.00. B.G.B. moving
...09.15 to establish HQ Murray
...until this established HQ
...is Cavandar K 29 B until
...notice.

...our troops at Lg a 2.8 L28 c 8 9
...- Red flares 09.00 about
...Farm buildings enemy
...bove from aeroplane reports.

...08.30 reports. Troops seen
...white paper at L29 a 2.8 L28 c 8 9
...L 28 d. 9 8 all farm buildings
...my lines seen burning

File

35th DIVISION "G". No. 7.

14th October 1918.   REGISTER OF MESSAGES.

No.	In or Out.	From or To	Senders number.	Time sent	Time recd.	Purport.
48	In	Plane	B.4156	0900	0944	0830 Called for flares. Our troops waved white paper from L.29.a.2.8 - L.28.c.8.9 - L.33.d.5.9 - L.28.d.9.8 - Red flares at 0900 from about L.28.d.9.8. All farm bldgs on fire behind enemy's lines. Big explosion N. side of MENIN at 0842.
49	In	19 Corps.	I.G.9	0913	0948	10 Squadron report 0815 visibility very bad. Heavy ground mist in valley. 0755 scattered parties enemy infantry along road at R.20 and 21. M.Gs. active from HALLUIN.
50	In	105 Bde.	C.26	0925	0959	Ref. G.A.343. Situations sent you 0550, 0617, 0705, 0800 and 0835. Dense fog until 0830; now clear. No definite report from Battalions but all wounded state attack going well. Hostile Artillery and M.G. barrage fairly heavy until 0600. B.G.C. moving forward 0915 to establish H.Q. MURRAY HOUSE. Until this established H.Q. 105 remains CAVANDAR K.29.b. until further notice.
51	Out	3 Bdes. C.R.A. & 36 Div.	G.A.312	1000		At 0830 our troops at L.29.a. 2.8, L.28.c.8.9, L.33.d.5.9. Red flares.0900 about L.28.d.9.6. Farm buildings enemy lines on fire Above from aeroplane reports.
52	In	B.G.G.S. 19 Corps.	Phone		1005	Aeroplane 0830 reports troops seen waving white paper at L.29.a.2.8, L.28.c.8.9, L.32.d. 5.9 - L.28.d.9.8. All farm buildings behind enemy lines seen burning.

....

35th DIVISION 'G'

	Consec No	In or Out	From or To	Sender's Number	Time Sent	Time Received	
14/10/18	53	Out	H Div 104-1 106 Bde & CRA	GA314	10.09		105 Bde re... at 09.15 at Cavan... at Murr...
	54	In	104 Bde	A7504	09.50	10.11	Message... of 18.5.7.17 Road f... 7.30 am. J.F. Kin... Cars work...
	55	In	19 Corps S.	Y10	09.51	10.12	Prisoners... Ledeghem
	56	In	19 Corps S.	Y11	09.52	10.20	10 Squad... seen at...
	57	Out	19 Corps 36th Divs + CRA	GA315	10.20	—	Following message...
	58	Out	35 Div Q	GA650	10.45		Arrange for 20 Men of... from 15th...
	59	In	5 Army	G5024	08.40	10.50	Situation...
	60	In	Q 35 Div	C60	09.55	10.50	Interrogat...
	61	In	Q 35 Div	C59	09.30	10.50	Fresh iden...

REGISTER of MESSAGES.

PURPORT	Action taken	Remarks.
ports timed 09.20. Bde H.Q moving to Murray House, but remains ...der K.29 B until established ...ay.		
...timed 08.10 from 18/.7 Troops ...g D.2.9 beyond Golden Cross ...c. & Herts Cross Roads L28.c at Opposition slight K.21.y & 18 at Elba Corner. Ambulance ...ing from Railway L2.D.		
...of 2nd Bav: R I R captured N of		
report 08.30 British troops ...d 5.5 & L29 B.7.7.		
from 10 Bde begins. (Repeats 0.5.H).		
...C.C to ration at Assam about ...s Div: Sig: Co now at Assam		
report.		
...ion of prisoners.		
...tifications & interrogations.		

File

35th DIVISION "G". No. 8.

14th October 1918.   REGISTER OF MESSAGES.

No.	In or Out.	From or To	Senders number	Time sent	Time recd.	Purport.
53	Out	41 Div. 104 & 105 Bdes. C.R.A.	G.A. 314	1009		105 Bde. reports timed 0920 Bde H.Q. moving at 0915 to MURRAY HOUSE but remains at CAVANDER K.29.b. until established at MURRAY.
54	In	104 Bde.	A.F.504	0950	1011	Message timed 0810 from 18 L.F. Troops of 18 L.F. and 19 D.L.I. beyond GOLDEN CROSS ROADS L.22.c. and HERTS CROSS ROADS L.28.c. at 7-30 a.m. Opposition slight. H.Q. 17 and 18 L.F. then at ELBA CORNER. Ambulance Cars working from railway L.2.d.
55	In	19 Corps I.	I.G.10	0921	1012	Prisoners of 2nd Bav. R.I.R. captured N. of LEDEGHEM.
56	In	19 Corps I.	I.G.11	0932	1020	10 Sqdn. report 0830 British troops seen at L.21.d.5.5 and L.29.b.7.7.
57	Out	19 Corps. 36 & 41 Divs. C.R.A.	G.A.315	1020		Following from 104 Bde. begins (repeats message No.54).
58	Out	35 Div.Q.	G.A.650	1045		Arranged for C.C. to ration at ASSAM about 20 men of 35 Div. Signal Coy. now at ASSAM from 15th.
59	In	2nd Army	G.224	0840	1050	Situation report.
60	In	I.O.35 Div.	C.60	0955	1050	Interrogation of prisoners.
61	In	I.O.35 Div.	C.59	0930	1050	Fresh identifications and interrogations.

....

REGISTER of MESSAGES.   9

PURPORT	Action taken	Remarks.

report "forming up" carried out
...torily & attack launched.
...tive reached & attack reported
... Noops of 154 & 23 Inf Bdes
...FA reported passed KD6 c 4.3

...o 3 Offrs + 80 O.R.   Fresh
...ation 132 Minenwerfer Coy.

... from Contact Plane 08.30 –
...oke Screen over most of area
...ndered observation impossible.
...oops seen at L31. d 5.5 +
... Hares called for but not
... L.X. HQrs at K 31 c 8.7
... Panel out.

...ging in on line of second pause at 0800
... FARM L 27c. and in touch with 104 Bde
...T with 41 Div. on right. Sherwoods
...sed through Cheshires by 0830 but
...ot known owing to dense fog – HQ 105
... CAVENDER. Many M.G. one field gun two
... captured

...als. Operation progressing favourably
... is occupied, prisoners over 200 including
... also a number of MGs taken – Belong to 172 IR
... and 100 RIR. Enemy arty. very active with
... the Corps front. Visibility impossible owing

35th DIVISION. G.

Serial No	In or Out	From or To	Sender's Number	Time Sent	Time Received	
62	In	19 Corps I	IG14	1015	1105	Signs turning on the first phase to ground floors 132 IR. 168 IR do . H.E. shells te dine smoke
63	In	105 Bde	G28 1625	1105	15 Cheshires dig with HQ. Duffers on left No 9 Staffords second on right No 7 mid Lanh join Shore – Bopham
64	In	111 Bde	4554 DE 58	10.53	Josseroire bathdesie
63	In	30 35 RA	G81	10.00	10.53	Jotal no Casualties 1140 82R 08.75 Satisfa Just 8th Preceden
14/10/18 62	In	111 Bde	4554 DE 58	10.50	

File

35th DIVISION "G". No. 9.

14th October 1918.　　REGISTER OF MESSAGES.

No.	In or Out.	From or To	Senders number	Time sent	Time recd.	Purport.
62	In	41 Div.	G.584	0858	1050	122 Inf. Bde. report "forming up carried out satisfactorily and attack launched. First objective reached and attack reported proceeding. Troops of 124 and 123 Inf. Bdes. and 190 Bde. R.F.A. reported passed K.26.c.4.3 - 0825.
63	In	35 D.I.O.	C.61	1000	1053	Total now 3 Officers and 380 O.R. Fresh identification 132 Minenwerfer Coy.
64	In	41 Div.	G.587	0858	1053	Following from Contact Plane 0830 - Dense smoke screen over most of area which rendered observation impossible. British troops seen at L.21.d.5.5, and L.27.b.7.7. Flares called for but not shown. LX Hd.Qrs. at K.31.c.8.7. POPHAM PANEL out.
65	In	105 Bde.	C.28	1025	1105	15 Cheshires digging in on line of 2nd Pause at 0800 with H.Q. DUKES FARM L.27.c. and in touch with 104 Bde. on left but NOT with 41 Div. on right. Sherwoods and Staffords passed through Cheshires by 0830 but their success not known owing to dense fog. H.Q. 105 Bde. still at CAVANDER. Many M.G. one Field Gun, 2 Anti-tank guns captured.
66	In	19 Corps I.	I.G.14	1015	1105	Pigeon message reads - Operation progressing favourably. The first PAUSE line is occupied. Prisoners over 200 including several Officers also a number of M.Gs. taken. Belong to 172 I.R., 132 I.R., 168 I.R., and 100 R.I.R. Enemy artillery very active with gas and H.E. along the Corps front. Visibility impossible owing to dense fog.

....

35th Division.

Date	Consec. No	In or Out	From or To	Sender's Number	Time Sent	Time Received	
14/10/18	67	Out	41 Div	GA 316	11.10	—	Repeat to
	68	In	19 Corps	DG 16	10.40	11.10	No 10 Squa... at Lga... 29 ch 9... large groups of a.a. M.G
	69	In	35 DA	BM 4510	26	11.10	HQ 15g also two near HQ L22A 7.4
	70	In	19 Corps	Phone	11	14	35 Div HQ move on 15th to arrange
	71	In	90—36 Div	M 6	09.35	11.10	Number
	72	Out	19 Corps, CRA 35 Div, 106 Bde 36 Div, 141 Div	GA 317	11.15	—	105 Infy Bd line Se... Farm on left 08.30. Through prevented many anti-

REGISTER OF MESSAGES.

PURPORT	Action taken	Remarks

Message No 60.

report 09.00 our troops seen
8 - J.23.c.8.9. - J.33.D.5.9 - J.28.d.9.8
Red flares at J.28.D.6.8. 09.00
fires in Wervicq. 08.38 three
French Cavalry J.16.D & J.17.c.
fire at R.3 & R.33.

Established J.20.c.y.8 at 09.00 -
18pdrs & one 4.5 Btty in action
15.9. One How Btty in action
at 09.15.

Fighting portion will anyhow
forward on 16th & possibly
D army is coming round

of prisoners & units.

a report 15 Cheshires 08.00 on
cono Pause with HQ Dukes
L.27.c. & in touch with 10th Bde
but not with H Div on right.
Sherwood & Staffords passed
Cheshires but dense fog
view of their progress.
M.Gs one field gun two
Tank guns captured.

File.

35th DIVISION "G". No. 10.

14th October 1918.   REGISTER OF MESSAGES.

No.	In or Out.	From or To	Senders number	Time sent	Time recd.	Purport.
67	Out	41 Div.	G.A.316	1110		Repeats message No. 60.
68	In	19 Corps I	I.G.16	1040	1110	No. 10 Sqdn. report 0900. Our troops seen at L.29.a.2.8 - L.23.c.8.9 - L.33.d.5.9 - L.28.d.9.8 - L.29.c.4.9. Red flares at L.28.d.6.8. 0700 large fires in WERVICQ. 0838 three groups of French Cavalry L.16.d. and L.17.c. A.A.M.G. fire at R.3. and R.33.
69	In	35 D.A.	B.M.45	1026	1110	H.Q. 159 Bde. established L.20.c.7.8 at 0900, also two 18-prs. and one 4.5 bty. in action near H.Q. 159. One How. Bty in action L.22.a.1.4 at 0915.
70	In	19 Corps	Phone	1114		35 Div. H.Q. fighting portion will anyhow move forward on 16th and possibly on 15th. D.A.& Q.M.G is coming round to arrange.
71	In	36 D.I.O.	I.M.6	0935	1110	Number of prisoners and units.
72	Out	19 Corps. C.R.A.35 Div. 106 Bde. 36 & 41 Divs.	G.A.317	1115		105 Inf. Bde. report 15 Ches. 0800 on line second pause with H.Q. DUKES FARM L.27.c. and in touch with 104 Bde. on left but NOT with 41 Div. on right. 0830 Sherwoods and Staffords passed through Cheshires but dense fog prevented view of their progress. Many M.Gs. one Field Gun, two Anti-tank guns captured.

....

	Consec N°	In or Out	From or To	Sender's Number	Time Sent	Time Received	
14/10/16	73	In	36 Div	GT63	10.54	11.17	First line...
	74	In	36 Div.	GT61	10.15	11.27	Message...
	75	In	36 Div	2.O.July	11.00	11.30	One man...
	76	In	35 D.A.	BM46	11.15	11.36	157th Q...
	77	In	Lt Thacker	AM110	11.45	11.40	Hicks...

REGISTER of MESSAGES.   11

PURPORT	Action taken	Remarks

niskillings HQ Penny Corner,
moving to Rockstone farm.
...is holding line o/road
to Elizabeth Ridge, held up
will report timed 08.5.5.

from 6 A.M.1. timed 09.45 states
... just returned from L22c19.
...ct. moved forward from there
Man bringing back about
...ners states they were taken
...skirts of Moorseele about
About 80 prisoners passed
... WABO apparently held
... is sending to Res Batt to
... situation & take action
...iew to forming defensive flank.

1st Bav. Pioneer Coy taken at
... One man 2nd Bav Res Inf
...att. also Moorseele.

...vander House moving to
House 10.15. 119 A Bde Btys
... G35 at 10.00 — not yet
... action. Two 18pdr Btys.
...tion L22B at 09.40 —
... reported very difficult.

...pats 10.00 ZOV1 on their
08.30 — Repats left Div. were
...seele. Hicks is at Golden
...ds.

File

35th DIVISION "G". No. 11.

14th October 1918.   REGISTER OF MESSAGES.

No.	In or out.	From or To	Senders number.	Time sent	Time recd.	Purport.
73	In	36 Div.	G.T.63	1054	1117	First Innissks. H.Q. PENNY CORNER, 2nd Innis. moving to ROCKSTONE FARM. Later 1st Innis. holding line of road L.19.a.9.5 to ELIZABETH RIDGE, held up at SACK MILL. Report timed 0855.
74	In	36 Div.	G.T.61	1015	1127	Message from WAMI timed 0945 states M.G. Officer just returned from L.22.c.1.9. Mobile Section moved forward from there 0830. Man bringing back about 20 prisoners states they were taken on Western outskirts of MOORSEELE about 0800. About 80 prisoners passed en route. WABO apparently held up. WANI is sending to Res. Bn. to ascertain situation and take action with regard to forming defensive flanks.
75	In	36 D.I.O.	I.M. 7	1100	1130	One man 1st Bav. Pioneer Coy. taken at MOORSEELE. One man 2nd Bav. Res. Inf. Regt. 3rd Bn. also MOORSEELE.
76	In	35 D.A.	B.M.46	1115	1136	157 H.Q. CAVANDER HOUSE moving to MURRAY HOUSE 10-15. 119 A Bde. Batteries moving to G.25 at 1000. Not yet reported in action. Two 18-pr Batteries 159 in action L.22.b. at 0940. Observation reported very difficult.
77	In	Lt.MACIVER	A.M. 1	1045	1140	Hicks reports 1000 ZOVI on their objective 0830. Reports Left Div. were through MOORSEELE. Hicks is at GOLDEN CROSS ROADS.

33rd DIVISION

Serial No	In or Out	From or To	Sender's Number	Time Sent	Time Received	
78	In	104 Inf Bde	BM 707	11-20	1140	Arrived Pill... not yet seen... round me... DUKE FARM... timed 0815... direction in... going throu... with 80... Arty. H.Q.
79	In	104 Inf Bde	—	—	11-50	Troops movi... Coys 19 DL... to final ob... out from 19... LYS through... Enemy shell... Estaminet
80	In	106 Inf Bde	BR 60	11-26	1200	106 Bde... depth in... 18 HLI to... to L.19c... reporting to... 106 Bde... of units... they pass
81	In	Meteor	—	1012	1200	Weather
82	Out	19 Corps 36 & 41 Divs 35 Div Arty	GA 319	1200	—	Repeats 104...

REGISTER OF MESSAGES

PURPORT	Action taken	Remarks

Box 200 yds S. of ELBA CORNER. Have
a dead British soldier. 17 L.F all
say everything went well. HQ Cheshires
also say everything alright. Sherwoods
beyond HERTS CROSS ROAD, rather lost
fog. Cheshires timed 0909 saw British
southern edge of MOORSEELE. Coat
and yellow grenade here, apparently
Field. Arty. 80 Regt. 1 Battn.

through without opposition about 3
I and 3 Coys. 18 L.F believed through
picture. Exploiting platoons now pushing
MOORSEELE – WOLVEGHEM Road towards
G.25 b. and G.31 b. and into WEVELGHEM
WEVELGHEM. Civilians released at
G.29. b 8.9.

will move at once and be formed up in
positions of readiness for further moves.
L.20.c. W of Railway. 17 R. Scots
A & C Coys M G Bn. to join 12 HLI
O C. 12 H.L.I at DEBENHAM HOUSE.
Q moving to K 23 a 3 8. Representatives
report at Bde H.Q. K 23 a 3.8. as

forecast.

wire (message No. 79).

File

35th DIVISION "G". No. 12.

14th October 1918.   REGISTER OF MESSAGES.

No.	In or Out.	From or To	Senders number	Time sent	Time recd.	Purport.
78	In	104 Bde.	B.M.707	1120	1140	Arrived pill box 200 yds S. of ELBA CORNER. Have not yet seen a dead British soldier. 17 L.F. all round me say everything went well. H.Q. Cheshires DUKE FARM also say everything alright. Sherwoods timed 0815 beyond HERTS CROSS ROADS; rather lost direction in fog. Cheshires timed 0909 saw British going through Southern edge of MOORSEELE. Coat with 80 and yellow grenade here, apparently Artillery H.Q. Field Arty. 80 Rgt. 1st Bn.
79	In	104 Bde.			1150	Troops moving through without opposition about three coys. 19th D.L.I. and three coys. 18 L.F. believed through to final objective. Exploiting platoons now pushing out from MOORSEELE - WULVEGHEM Road towards Lys through G.25.b. and G.21.b. and into WEVELGHEM. Enemy shelling WEVELGHEM. Civilians released at Estaminet G.29.b.8.9.
80	In	106 Bde.	B.R.60	1126	1200	106 Bde. will move at once and be formed up in depth in positions of readiness for further moves. 18 H.L.I. to L.20.c. West of railway, 17 R.Scots. to L.19.c. A and C Coys. M.G. Bn. to join 12 H.L.I. reporting to O.C. 12th H.L.I. at DEBENHAM HOUSE. 106 Bde H.Q. moving to K.23.a.3.8. Representatives of units to report at Bde H.Q. K.23.a.3.8 as they pass.
81	In	Meteor.		1012	1200	Weather Forecast.
82	Out	19 Corps, 36 & 41 Divs. 35 D.A.	G.A.319	1200		Repeats 104 Bde wire (Message No. 79.

....

35th DIVISION "G"

Serial No	In/Out	From or To	Sender's Number	Time Sent	Time Received	
83	In	19 Corps	G915	1100	1205	Confirmation of 35 Div
84	In	36 Div	G764	1130	1215	WANI report MOORSEELE on right be BRIDGE intac Roads excel MOORSEELE there. Th
85	Out	19 Corps	G323	1215	—	Brigadier 104 1120 report yet
86	In	35 Div Obs. Gp.	WH1	1020	1223	KEZELBERG forward. I have see
87 & 8	In	19 Corps I	IG17	1051	12.23	10 Squad of MENIN fam. build
88	In	35 Div Arty	Phone		1227	A Battery Infantry in E. of HOOKS
89	In	35 Div IO.	C62	1155	1235	Total 10 off Fresh identif
90	In	IO. 36 Div	IM7	1101	1235	Identification

REGISTER of MESSAGES.

13

PURPORT	Action taken	Remarks.

of telephone message, ordering move
HQ. (message No. 70).

to QOBI consolidated line just E of
All 3 Bn. HQs. near SILVER FARM. Line
ids back. JOANS BRIDGE and ELIZABETH
t. QOZE coming up & going through
hat. Liaison Officer has been in
and reports plenty of drinking water
ssage timed 0945.

Inf Bde. at ELBA CORNER L 27 b.
advance progressed well but no details

useless at present. Am going further
All state attack going very well.
120 prisoners pass through.

Reports. 0841 Big explosion on N. side
MG fire drawn from Q 29 c 8 5. All
gs behind enemys lines are on fire.

of 157 Bde. RFA reports at 1015 that
med them that troops of 36 Div were
ELE.

am 206 6R. including Bn. Commander
inkins

File

35th DIVISION "G".   No. 13.

14th October 1918.   REGISTER OF MESSAGES.

No.	In or Out.	From or To	Senders number.	Time sent	Time recd.	Purport.
83	In	19 Corps.	G.915	1100	1205	Confirmation of telephone message ordering move of 35 Div. H.Q. (Message No. 70).
84	In	36 Div.	G.T.64	1130	1215	WANI reports QOBI consolidated line just E. of MOORSEELE. All three Bn. H.Q. near SILVER FARM. Line on Right bends back. JOANS BRIDGE and ELIZABETH BRIDGE intact. QOZE coming up and going through. Roads excellent. Liaison Officer has been in MOORSEELE and reports plenty of drinking water there. Message timed 0945.
85.	Out	19 Corps.	G.A.323	1215		Brigadier 104 Inf. Bde. at ELBA CORNER L.27.b. 1120 reports advance progressed well but no details yet.
86	In	35 Div. Obs.Group.	W.H.1	1020	1223	KEZELBERG useless at present. Am going further forward. All state attack going very well. I have seen 120 prisoners pass through.
87	In	19 Corps I	I.G.17	1051	1223	10 Sqdn reports 0841 big explosion on N. side of MENIN. M.G. fire drawn from Q.29.c.8.5. All farm buildings behind enemy's lines are on fire.
88	In	35 D.A.	Phone		1227	A Battery of 157 Bde. R.F.A. reports at 1015 that Infantry informed them that troops of 36th Div. were East of MOORSEELE.
89	In	35 D.I.O.	C.62.	1155	1235	Total 10 Officers 206 O.R. including Bn. Commander. Fresh identifications.
90	In	36 D.I.O.	I.M.7	1101	1235	Identifications.

....

35 DIVISION G

Date	Serial No.	In or Out	From or To	Sender's Number	Time sent	Time received	
14/10/18	91	In	35 Div. 06 Group	104	11.15	12.41	19 DL ? M.G fire They are collected have coll
	92	In	104 Bde	A7505	11.00	12.41	Following 10.45. H pushing with OC going
	94	Out	19 Corps, 36 & 41 Div, 106 Bde CRA	GA375	12.50	-	19 DLI a L55 d 10.45 Bdgs - all Prisoners includin
	93	Out	105, 106 Bdes	GA374	11.45	-	Repeats 10
	95	In	36 Divn	G167	12.16	12.58	109 Bde ref L16 d 5.9 t L17 a 8.6 - by M.G fi Elizabeth How pa Penny C slight - about 10 on flank
	96	In	106 Bde	-	13.00	13.55	204 Field Co me.

Register of Messages.   14

Purport.	when taken	Remarks.
...eld up outside Gullegham by ...om farms on western outskirts. ...reparing to move forward with ...reinforcements. They claim to ...ected 30 guns.		
...received from OC 19 D.L.I at ...ve arrived Dragoman Farm ...on to Damik Buildings. Am ...18 F. in touch with Coys, all ...ell.		
...ived at Dragoman Farm ...& advancing to L39 B Damik ...going well. In 35 Division ...Cage 11.50, 10 Offrs & 206 Others ...one B'n Commander.		
...& Bde message No 79.		
...out Hogu reports situation ...ined 1120. Hogu reached line ...L23 a 8.9 at 08.00 - was held up ...e from Moorseele but reached ...Bridge L 17 d 2.2 at 09 30. ...ssed Kro' at 1000. Hoha passed ...over 1005. Hogu casualties ...prisoners about 150 captured ...field guns & 5 horses. Touch ...is maintained.		
...E is with me. Shall I proceed with		

File

35th DIVISION "G". No. 14.

14th October 1918.   REGISTER OF MESSAGES.

No.	In or Out.	From or To	Senders number.	Time sent	Time recd.	Purport.
91	In	35 Div. Obs. Group.	104	1115	1241	19 D.L.I. held up outside GULLEGHEM by machine gun fire from farms on Western outskirts. They are preparing to move forward with collected reinforcements. They claim to have collected 30 guns.
92	In	104 Bde.	A.F.505	1100	1241	Following received from O.C. 19 D.L.I. at 1045. Have arrived DRAGOMAN FARM. Pushing on to DAMK BUILDINGS. Am with O.C. 18th L.F. In touch with Coys. All going well.
93	Out	105 & 106 Bdes.	G.A.324	1145		Repeats 104 Bde. Message No.79.
94	Out	19 Corps. 36 & 41 Divs. 106 Bde. C.R.A.	G.A.325	1250		19 D.L.I. arrived at DRAGOMAN FARM L.22.d.10.45 and advancing to L.29.b. DAMK BUILDINGS. All going well. In 35 Div. Prisoners Cage 1150 10 Officers and 206 others including one Bn. Commander.
95	In	36 Div.	G.T.67	1216	1258	109 Bde. HOQU reports situation L.16.d.5.9 timed 1120. HOQU reached line L.17.a.8.6 - L.23.a.8.9 at 0800. Was held up by M.G. fire from MOORSEELE, but reached ELIZABETH BRIDGE L.17.d.2.2 at 0930. HOWO passed through at 1000. HOHA passed PENNY CORNER 1005. HOQU casualties slight. Prisoners about 150. Captures about 10 Field Guns and five horses. Touch on flanks maintained.
96	In	106 Bde.		1200	1255	204 Field Coy.R.E. is with me. Shall it proceed with me.

....

35th DIVISION "G

	Serial No	In or Out	From or To	Sender's Number	Time Sent	Time Received	
14/10/18	97	In	35 Div	O.663	12.40	12.55	Fresh ide of 1st Bav
	98	Out	19 Corps, 36th Div, 106 Bde+CRA	GA326	13.00	-	19 A.C.I. 11 by Germa west side. preparato
	99	In	104 Bde	BMg10	12.30	13.08	Have seen Consider already + suggest in any
	100	Out	104 Bde	GA328	13.15	-	Ref: BM q Reserve Situation Call in
	101	In	41 Div	G598	13.15	13.15	Prisoner
	102	In	105 Bde (Lt Marrindin)	Phone	13.25	-	Beating BG at th objective 41 Divn Keeping
	103	In	9.O.36 Div.	9O.q	12.55	13.27	Identified
	104	Out	104, 105, 106 Bdes (By hand of G.S.O.2)	GA329	13.30	-	106 Infy Bde to move for 35 Div: but real emerge objectives + pr

REGISTER of MESSAGES.   15

PURPORT	Action taken	Remarks

...tifications - Minenwerfer Coy
...R.I.R. 1st Bav Res Div - Normal.

...s reported checked at Fullegheim
...in M.G. fire from farms on
...They were then collecting reserves
...ly to advancing again.

... nothing of Gen. Pollard.
Valuable time is being lost. Have
ordered 12H LI to line of Rly
106 Bde should close up to him
... case.

... 106 Bde remain in Div
under orders from Army. It
is critical one Bn is at your
case of necessity.

... with Div Cage 2 O/Rs 13H O.R.

... from K3q B2q Hodgkinson &
Murray House. Bde on final
more or less. Not in touch with
... who do not appear to be
... up.

...

... in Div Res. + by Army order is not
...ward E. of Rly without orders from
... one Bn is at call of 101 Bde in case of
...cy only. 104 & 105 Bdes to reach their final
...ith patrols towards LRS, but not to call on 106 Bde to assist.

File

35th DIVISION "G". No. 15.

14th October 1918.   REGISTER OF MESSAGES.

No.	In or Out.	From or To	Senders number.	Time sent	Time recd.	Purport.
97	In	35 D.I.O.	G.63.	1240	1255	Fresh identifications. Minenwerfer Coy of 1st Bav.R.I.R., 1st Bav. Res. Div. (normal).
98	Out	19 Corps, 36 & 41 Divs. 106 Bde. C.R.A.	G.A.326	1300		19 D.L.I. 1115 reported checked at GULLEGHEM by German M.G. fire from farms on W. side. They were then collecting reserves preparatory to advancing again.
99	In	104 Bde.	B.M.910	1230	1308	Have seen nothing of General POLLARD. Consider valuable time is being lost. Have already ordered 12th H.L.I. to line of railway and suggest that 106 Bde should close up to him in any case.
100	Out	104 Bde.	G.A.328	1315		Ref. B.M.910. 106 Bde. remain in Div. Reserve unders from Army. If situation is critical one Bn is at your call in case of necessity.
101	In	41 Div.	G.598	1215	1315	Prisoners in 41 Div. Cage 2 Officers 134 O.R.
102	In	105 Bde. (Lt.MARINDIN)	Phone		1325	Speaking from K.29.b.2.9. HODGKINSON and B.G.C. at MURRAY HOUSE. Bde on final objective more or less. Not in touch with 41 Div. who do not appear to be keeping up.
103	In	36 D.I.O.	I.O.9	1255	1327	Identifications.
104	Out	3 Bdes. (By hand of G.S.O.2).	G.A.329	1330		106 Inf. Bde. is in Div. Reserv and by Army Order is not to move forward E. of rlwy without orders from 35 Div.; but one Bn. is at call of 104 Bde. in case of real emergency only. 104 and 105 Bdes. to reach their final objectives and push patrols towards LYS; but not to call on 106 Bde to assist.

....

OPERATIONS OF 35th DIVISION
from September 28th to November 11th 1918.
SECOND PHASE.

October 3rd to October 31st.

1. On October 3rd 105th and 106th Infantry Brigades marched at 0200 to bivouac area near KRUISSTRAAT and SWAN CHATEAU and 104th Infantry Brigade marched later in the day to bivouacs round ZILLEBEKE POND.

On October 4th the G.O.C. 35th Division was sent for by the Corps Commander in the morning to discuss whether, in view of casualties, the Division would be fit to go into another attack. The Corps Commander said he was anxious to keep the Division and the G.O.C. assured him that the Division was in good fettle, and only needed some reinforcements to be quite ready for further operations.

A Conference was held at Corps Headquarters at 1930 at which objectives and boundaries for the new attack were given. The date of attack was to be the 7th, and the 35th Division was to go into the line East of TERHAND on the night of 5/6th.

On October the 5th a Conference of Infantry Brigadiers and C.R.A. was held at WOODCOTE HOUSE, at which the new scheme was discussed, boundaries between Brigades were fixed, and reliefs arranged. 105th and 104th Infantry Brigades were to attack and 106th Infantry Brigade was to be in Reserve. During the day the date of the attack was postponed first for one day, then for 6 days, and then for 7 days.

105th and 104th Infantry Brigades went up and took over the battle front from 107th Infantry Brigade (36th Division), with 1½ and 2 battalions respectively, and with Headquarters in old buildings and pillbox just South of TERHAND (K.21.b. and K.21.c.).

The Northern Divisional Boundary followed the TERHAND - WIJFWEGEN - MOORSEELE Road, skirted South of MOORSEELE and then followed the road to POESELHOEK.

The Southern Boundary ran from K.27.central to K.29.central and then to L.35.b.6.2.

The Southern Boundary between the area taken over by 41st Division and the X Corps ran along the bottom of K.33. - K.36 and then turned South to R.3.c.0.2.

The line taken over consisted of a series of posts just East of the GHELEUWE - WIJFWEGEN Road as shewn on the Map. The Corps Objective ran through R.3.c.0.2 through 35th Division boundary at L.35.b.6.2. to G.21.d.0.3, near POESELHOEK.

The Divisional Objective therefore was rather more than double the length of the initial line (about 3,200 yards), and was diagonal to the boundary line between Brigades, which ran from the Cross Roads in K.22.c. through SLUNSEHOEK FARM - HERTHOEK Cross Roads to G.25.d.9.4.

On hearing of the postponement of the attack till the 14th it was decided that the 106th Infantry Brigade should take over the whole front on the night 7/8th, and that the 105th Infantry Brigade should come back into rest near ZILLEBEKE POND, and the 104th Infantry Brigade into Support Area in J.20, astride the MENIN ROAD at the head of the BASSERBILLEBEEKE. Accordingly the other battalions of 105 and 104 Infantry Brigades were stopped from moving up.

2. Pioneers and R.E. were employed on the road from GHELUVELT to TERHAND and also in building Divisional Headquarters at JACKDAW TUNNELS near STIRLING CASTLE.

3. The Division was mentioned in the G.H.Q. communique of the 6th, for distinguished service in the attack of September 28th and subsequent days.

4. On the night of the 7/8th October the 106th Infantry Brigade relieved 105th and 104th Infantry Brigades, Brigadier-General POLLARD going into Headquarters at ZUIDHOEK.
Just before relief the Division and especially the 105th
Infantry/

Brigade suffered a heavy loss in the death of Lieutenant-Colonel CRELLIN, Commanding the 15th Sherwood Foresters, who was killed while reconnoitring passages in the wire.

5. On October 8th preliminary instructions for the attack (G.3773) were issued.
The B.G.G.S. XIX Corps came to discuss a minor operation and points connected with the barrage, areas etc., and on the next day General COFFIN, Commanding 36th Division, came to discuss the minor operation on GOLDFLAKE FARM (L.19.c), which was on the boundary between the Divisions, it being finally decided that this should be carried out by the 36th Division alone on the morning of the 11th. Several meetings were held on the 9th, 10th, and 11th to settle points about areas, lines of barrage, routes etc., and late on the 11th orders were received that if the attack was successful it was to be exploited, and a bridgehead formed on the other side of the LYS.
As a result of this on October 12th various conferences were held with B.G.G.S., General LAWFORD, Commanding 41st Division, and later with General POLLARD, Commanding 106th Infantry Brigade, C.R.A. and C.R.E. It was decided that the 106th Infantry Brigade was to go through the other Brigades to carry out the second operation.

6. On the night of the 11/12th October, the 105th and 104th Infantry Brigades relieved the 106th Infantry Brigade on the battle front and were distributed in depth, Headquarters 105th Infantry Brigade being at TERHAND and of 104th at PEULTEVIN WOOD (K.22.b.).
The 106th Infantry Brigade moved back to the shelters occupied by the 104th Infantry Brigade at the head of BASSEVILLEBEEK, with Headquarters just North of the MENIN ROAD.
On the 12th the 1st Echelon of Divisional Headquarters moved to JACKDAW TUNNELS and the 2nd Echelon remained at ASSAM FARM.
The attack of the 36th Division on GOLDFLAKE had only been partially successful in spite of being carried out under a heavy bombardment. A good deal of retaliation came back on the 35th Division and there were several casualties between the 11th and 14th.
On the 13th G.O.C. 35th Division visited the attacking Brigade and found all in good fettle. The area was very congested with guns of three Divisions and heavy Artillery, as the TERHAND SPUR formed the only good cover.

7. The scheme for attack was made difficult by two things:-
(1) The objective was diagonal to the line of advance, thus forcing the left Brigade to push out its left into a sharp corner, and also causing the barrage line to be diagonal to the line of advance. No method of overcoming this could be devised, as in the previous attack, as the whole Army front was similarly situated.
In order to obviate the infantry being drawn off their proper line of advance by the crooked barrage and losing direction Southwards, it was decided to mark the Divisional right boundary by a Thermite shell fired at each minute during the advance and during the first five minutes of the pauses.

(2) The length of the attack (7000 to 8000 yards) making it impossible for the Artillery to cover the whole advance with barrage fire without shifting position. This was made the more difficult as the only suitable road for the advance of the Artillery of both the 35th and 36th Divisions was the road common to both on the boundary. Two Brigades of Artillery

of Artillery, each less one battery and one section, were detached to fire from behind the TERHAND - MOLENHOEK SPUR, with a limit of range reaching to about the second pause, i.e. 3000 yards from the first line of barrage. Superimposed on these the 119th Army Brigade R.F.A. was to fire up to the limit of its range, i.e. about half way between the third and fourth pause. As soon as the advance started the two detached batteries and two detached sections of howitzers were to move off to a position to carry on the barrage from the line reached by the 119th Army Brigade to the final objective. These were to be followed by the remaining batteries of the Divisional Artillery as soon as they had reached the limits of their range.

This worked admirably, as described later and the barrage was kept up throughout the whole infantry advance.

The rate of barrage was 100 yards in two minutes with an additional pause of fifteen minutes (i.e. 17 minutes) at every 1500 yards.

4.5" Howitzers were in the first instance to fire on the enemy's trench running from L.2.c to L.9.d. and on certain farms and pillboxes, and were then to join in the creeping barrage, being specially directed on probable strong localities.

Heavy Artillery besides doing counter-battery work was to fire on certain farms in advance of the barrage of the field artillery.

The attack was to be carried out by the 105th Infantry Brigade on the right and the 104th Infantry Brigade on the left, each Brigade on a one battalion front. At the second pause (3000 yards) the leading battalions was to consolidate, while the remaining battalions were to leapfrog and continue the advance.

Special orders were given with a view to assisting the Division on our left if it had any trouble with MOORSEELE or GULLEGHEM.

The 106th Infantry Brigade forming the Divisional Reserve was to move up on the night before the attack to positions of readiness West of the TERHAND SPUR. At Zero it was to push forward one battalion into our old front line, ready to give immediate support, if required.

These orders were embodied in the preliminary instructions issued on October 8th; in operation order No.203 issued on 12th October (in which modifications were made in the barrage); and in Operation Order No.204 of 13th October, in which the following additions to the original scheme were made :-

(1) As soon as 105 and 104 Infantry Brigades had reached their final objectives, they were to push forward strong patrols with supporting troops to the crossings of the LYS, and were, if possible, to clear BISSEGHEM of the enemy.

(2) Field Artillery were to move to position from which they could shell the country to a depth of 1000 yards on the far side of the LYS.

(3) The B.G.C. 106th Infantry Brigade was to close up his rear battalion on his leading battalion and establish his Brigade in depth between the TERHAND SPUR and the railway running through L.26.

(4) On the order being received from XIX Corps "Establish Bridgeheads" B.G.C. 106th Infantry Brigade was to meet Artillery Brigade Commanders at the Headquarters of 104th Infantry Brigade at ELBA CORNER (L.27.b.), learn the situation, and arrange with Artillery Commanders for the support of his attack. He would have the support of all three Artillery Brigades less the batteries and sections at the direct call of 105th and 104th Infantry Brigades.

(5) The above will be the procedure, presuming the order "Establish Bridgeheads" was received in time for immediate action. If the order was received to do so on the following day, the scheme of attack and bombardment would be arranged by Divisional Headquarters.

8. About 1730 Operation Orders of 36th Division were received, and it was noticed that at the third pause they were going to halt an additional hour, in order to get up guns, instead of 17 minutes. As this would leave the flank of 107th Infantry Brigade exposed during its advance past GULLEGHEM, XIX Corps was communicated with, who in turn communicated with II Corps. A considerable discussion on the telephone followed, and it was ascertained that the Division North of the 36th Division was going on in the same manner as the 35th Division after the 17 minutes pause. It was however decided that it was too late to alter the order of the 36th Division, unless the whole operation was to be postponed.

Information of this was sent to General SANDILANDS, and he was told that he would have to watch his left flank. General POLLARD was also warned that he might have to support him on this flank.

On October 14th the assembly was carried out successfully, in spite of a heavy counter preparation put down by the enemy half an hour before Zero, which caused a considerable number of casualties.

The attack started at 0535 in a thick white mist.

105th Infantry Brigade on the right:-
  15th Cheshires leading with two Companies in line.
  15th Sherwood Foresters in Support at 500 yards distance with orders to pass through the Cheshires at the second pause and capture the final objective.

  4th North Staffordshire Regiment in reserve.

104th Infantry Brigade on the left:-
  17th Lancashire Fusiliers on a four platoon front carrying out the attack up to the second pause.

  18th Lancashire Fusiliers on the right.

  19th D.L.I. on the left behind the 17th Lancashire Fusiliers with orders to pass through at the second pause and capture final objective.

  (N.B. Two battalions were employed for this purpose owing to the widening of the objective).

106th Infantry Brigade in Reserve.
  12th H.L.I. was sent forward to TERHAND to occupy old front line at Zero and the other two battalions were kept in hand, the Brigadier moving up into the Headquarters at TERHAND vacated by the 105th Infantry Brigade.

All went according to programme. News came in steadily both from Brigades and aeroplane, but observation was very difficult owing to the mist.

The line/

The line of Second Pause was reached in schedule time and direction had been well kept the leading battalions consolidated and the remainder went through them. In the second advance the Sherwoods bore away a little to the Southward, but reached the Southern part of their objective and overlapped into 41st Division Area. This was partly due to the fog and partly owing to the left of the 41st Division being held up by a nest of machine guns and a field gun on their which it had passed over. The Sherwoods finding opposition right were drawn away towards it, and had to push as far South as ADMIRAL FARM (L.35.c.), in the vicinity of which they were somewhat severely handled by enemy field guns South of HANGMAN FARM (L.35.a.) firing point blank. The teams and detachments of two of these guns were shot, and the guns captured. The remaining guns got away under cover of machine gun fire. The North Staffords pushed up on the left of the Sherwoods to make good the objective up to the junction with the 104th Infantry Brigade.

Finally a line was reached ADMIRAL FARM - BADGER CROSS ROADS (L.35.d.) - Junction of Roads in KLOEFHOEK at M.1.b.4.9, thence along the KLOEFHOEK - MOORSEELE ROAD to G.31.d.0.9, thence North in front of ADVANCE FARM with their left at G.25.b.80.25. For a time our right flank was in the air but later on the left of the 41st Division drew up level and took over ADMIRAL FARM, and BADGER CROSS ROADS, and placed a post at HANGMAN FARM.

Meantime in the Left Brigade area the second advance had gone forward equally satisfactorily till the left flank became exposed owing to the halt of the Division on our left near MOORSEELE. Never-the-less they pushed on up to near GULLEGHEM about 2000 yards beyond MOORSEELE. At 1241 a message timed 1115 was received from the Divisional Observation Group at ELBA CORNER:- "19th D.L.I. held up outside GULLEGHEM by machine gun fire from farms on Western outskirts. They are preparing to move forward with collected reinforcements. They claim to have collected 30 guns."

At 1330 in consequence of indications that direct calls were being sent to 106th Infantry Brigade to assist 104th Infantry Brigade, and in consequence of orders from Second Army that one Brigade was to be kept in hand for the second operation, the following message was sent in writing to all Brigades by G.S.O.2, amplifying a wire sent at 1315 to 104th Infantry Brigade:-

"106th Infantry Brigade is in Divisional Reserve, and by orders from Army is not to move forward East of Railway without orders from 35th Division but one battalion is at call of 104th Infantry Brigade in case of real emergency only. 104th and 105th Infantry Brigades are to reach their final ovjective and push patrols towards the LYS; but not to call on 106th Infantry Brigade to assist."

From messages received from 36th Division and from 159th Brigade R.F.A. about 1500 it appeared that the 36th Division was held up West of GULLEGHEM.

At 1532 a message was received from C.R.A. giving positions of all batteries, showing that they had carried out programme and were well up close to the front and ready to engage the Crossings of the LYS.

At 1542 a message was received from 104th Infantry Brigade showing that we were well on our objective and as far forward as KLOEFHOEK on the right, but that our left was held back by fire from GULLEGHEM. Efforts were being made to push the left on towards SCHOONWATER.

At 1610 in consequence of a message from 105th Infantry Brigade, asking if they might call on 106th Infantry Brigade to protect their right flank which was still in the air owing to the check of 41st Division, a message was sent as follows:-

"Not use 106 Infantry Brigade. Cheshires available. Understand 41st Division now join you at L.35.d. 106 Brigade will not attack tonight remains Divisional reserve."

At 1610/

At 1610 a telephone message was received from B.G.G.S. saying that Army Commander had ordered that GULLEGHEM must be taken that night, and that 35th Division was to assist 36th Division to do so by working round the South of GULLEGHEM. A battalion of the Reserve Brigade was to be used if necessary.

At 1620 orders were sent to 104th Infantry Brigade to push on to SCHOONWATER, and to co-operate with 36th Division in the capture of GULLEGHEM, and that if necessary one battalion 106th Infantry Brigade might be used.

Further repeated messages came from 105th Infantry Brigade asking for reinforcements to be sent to their right flank, but at 1733 information was received that the 41st Division had come up on the right and had taken over from the 105th Infantry Brigade the posts in their area (ADMIRAL FARM to L.36.a.).

At 1857 a message was received from G.S.O.2, who had gone forward giving detailed positions, and approximate strengths of all units, from which it appeared that on our right we were well in front of our objective, with posts close to WEVELGHEM, that our left was still held back, and that our guns were all up and in action on the crossings of the LYS.

At 1900 orders were received from Corps that the secondary operation for forming a bridgehead across the LYS was not to be carried out.

At 1940 touch was obtained with 36 Division, and it was found that they had given up all idea of taking GULLEGHEM that night, but were going to do an organized attack on the following morning, and wanted 35th Division to co-operate by moving East within their own boundary but not to join in the attack on GULLEGHEM itself.

In consequence of the above and further messages received from Corps by 36th Division, the following orders were telegraphed at 2035 to 104th Infantry Brigade:-

"Division on our left intend to attack GULLEGHEM under cover of a barrage on morning of 15th time not yet settled. 104th Infantry Brigade will at same time attack Eastwards within our boundary, capturing the SCHOONWATER SPUR, and the SPUR in G.28.a., and will consolidate the general line in touch with 105th Infantry Brigade. Two F.A. Brigades at disposal of 104th Infantry Brigade to cover attack. Also one battalion 106th Infantry Brigade if necessary. 36th Ulster Division Scheme will be wired when known. Brigadier 104 will get touch with Brigadier 36th Division at ASHMORE FARM L.15.c.8.0 and arrange details of co-operation." And at 2230 to 104th Infantry Brigade:-

"36th Division is attacking GULLEGHEM at 0900 15th. Assist by capturing SPURS in G.27.a. and b. and in G.28.a. within our boundary. Consolidate and hold these; if opportunity occurs push patrols to LYS crossings within our boundaries." And at 2240 to 105th Infantry Brigade:-

"The full objectives contained in Square G.32.a. will be secured and consolidated on morning of 15th by 105th Infantry Brigade and touch obtained with 104th Infantry Brigade. Apparently your line runs behind KAPPELHOEK G.32.a.2.6 instead of in front. Essential that all high ground overlooking the LYS be occupied. If opportunity occurs push patrol to LYS crossings within our boundaries."

Summary of the day.

The attack went like clockwork up to the second pause, when the rear battalions went through the leading battalions, and thence onwards up to the final objective, and beyond it in the right Brigade. The right Brigade had its right exposed for some hours but held on till the Division on the right came up. The left went equally well past MOORSEELE, and nearly up to GULLEGHEM, but then got checked owing to its left being in the air, due to the unfortunate pause of the Division on the left at the line of the third pause, just on the

Eastern/

Eastern outskirts of MOORSEELE.

The Artillery carried out its part of covering by barrage an advance of 7,000 yards admirably, the rear Echelons passing the front Echelons and being in position to take up the barrage exactly to Schedule time at the point where the first Echelon had reached their limit of range.

43 guns were captured on this day, as detailed later, and an immense quantity of machine guns, trench mortars, signalling stores etc.

The enemy were evidently surprised by the attack and in many places hot breakfasts were found as the attacking troops got in.

The attack was carried out in a very thick white mist, and the direction was extraordinarily well kept considering how difficult this country is even on a clear day.

As appeared later undue importance was given to the SPURS at KAPPELHOEK and SCHOONWATER owing to their prominence on the layered map. They are barely distinguishable from the rest of the country which is very flat, the Church at WEVELGHEM being the only dominating point for observation.

10. On 15th October the 104th and 105th Infantry Brigades attacked under a barrage at 0900, in co-operation with an attack by 36th Division on our left. Satisfactory reports were received, and by 1300 it was clear that the Sherwoods and Staffords were established on the SPURS and high ground between KLOEFHOEK and KAPPELHOEK, with posts on the outskirts of WEVELGHEM, and that the 19th D.L.I. had gained all objectives, and had established posts on the Spur in G.28.a., SCHOONWATER SPUR in G.27.a., and the road in G.26.d., and were in touch with the 18th Lancashire Fusiliers about G.26.d.central. The 36th Division was reported to be through GULLEGHEM (vide messages 243 and 249).

At 1350 orders were sent to Brigades to consolidate the line and exploit vigorously with strong patrols towards the LYS, using affiliated artillery (vide message 252).

At 1445 a message was received and repeated to 104th Infantry Brigade, that the 36th Division were attacking again at 1500, with the object of securing the passages of the LYS, but it was too late to arrange co-operation beyond the general instructions already issued.

Provisional orders were issued for the relief of 104th and 105th Infantry Brigades by 106th Infantry Brigade, but at 1900, as a result of an Army Conference, telephonic orders came to clear the area within our boundary down to the LYS. These were confirmed by telegraphic orders received at 2020 giving boundaries and hour of attack, 0530. (vide message 291).

Orders were issued for relief to be cancelled, 106th Infantry Brigade to attack through 104th and 105th Infantry Brigades, all artillery to be at disposal of B.G.C., 106th Infantry Brigade, and C.R.A. was sent up to arrange details of barrage (vide messages 289 and 299).

At 2220 a report was received that patrols of the 105th Infantry Brigade had reached WEVELGHEM CHURCH without encountering the enemy, and that further patrols had been ordered to push on to the LYS, though outside our area.

A report from 104th Infantry Brigade at 2340 giving detailed line held by both Brigades showed that the enemy was holding the light railway running North-east from WEVELGHEM in some strength (vide messages 305 and 308).

Written orders were sent at 2230 (a copy to General POLLARD was taken by C.R.A.)., giving boundaries and hour of attack and line of heavy artillery barrage. Line and rate of field artillery barrage to be fixed by General POLLARD, three Artillery Brigades and two Machine Gun Companies being

placed/

placed at his disposal. Troops of 104th and 105th Infantry Brigades to stand fast till further orders (vide G.3081).

11. On the 16th October a message was received from 105th Infantry Brigade that a patrol of the North Staffords moving through WEVELGHEM had reached the LYS at M.8.d.8.0. without encountering the enemy. Bridge at this point was found destroyed.

At 0530 G.O.C. and G.S.O.1 went to TERHAND. Leaving G.S.O.1 to open a report centre G.O.C. went on and saw General POLLARD (106th Infantry Brigade) and waited at his Headquarters at ELBA CORNER for news of the attack, then visited 104th and 105th Infantry Brigades and gave orders for each to withdraw two battalions into Reserve West of the railway, and leave one battalion East of the railway at the call of 106th Infantry Brigade (message No. 337 at 1020). G.O.C. then returned to Advanced Report Centre at TERHAND, where he saw B.G.G.S. Corps. So far no definite news had been obtained except that 106th Infantry Brigade had reached the line of the river, but were held up by machine gun fire from the opposite bank, from the direction of MARCKE and from the outskirts of COURTRAI. Later information showed that enemy machine guns were also firing from the tile works in M.10.b. and from the high ground East of the river.

At 1101 a message was received from Corps that 35th Division would repair the crossings over the LYS, and push sufficient troops across to provide for the immediate protection of the bridges.

C.R.E. was sent up to arrange about crossings, and parties of the R.E. Companies working on the forward roads were collected ready for bridge work.

Touch was eventually gained with the divisions on the flanks. The 36th Division after trying to get into COURTRAI was relieved by the 41st Division, which thus crossed over from our right flank to our left flank, while the 34th Division came up on our right.

G.O.C. and G.S.O.1 returned to Headquarters at JACKDAW TUNNELS.

About 1630 and again at 2200 reports were received that the 106th Infantry Brigade was definitely all along the river and in touch with divisions on the flanks, but could not get down to the banks or to the crossings owing to machine gun fire from the opposite banks.

Two additional machine gun companies were sent up to General POLLARD.

12. The results of the fighting from the 14th October to night of the 16th was that the Division had reached the banks of the LYS, (11,000 yards), and had captured 14 Officers and 438 other ranks, also 12 - 5.9" Howitzers, 19 - 4.2" Howitzers, 12 - 77mm field guns, making a total of 43, and a very large quantity of signalling and Artillery equipment, several teams of horses and some wagons.

The 5.9" Howitzers were complete and in good condition, with large quantities of ammunition, and were at once used on the enemy.

13. On 17th October the first Echelon of Divisional Headquarters moved to new H.Q. just West of TERHAND SPUR where huts were being built,

All efforts of patrols to cross the LYS during the night had been stopped by machine gun fire. News was also received that /

that the troops of the Division on our left which had got into COURTRAI had had to come back.

G.O.C. went to General POLLARD'S Headquarters at ELBA CORNER and held a Conference with him, C.R.A., C.R.E., and O.C., M.G. Battalion, and arranged that a barrage should commence on a line 1,000 yards on the other side of the river, creep towards the river down to the bank, and then forward again, and that this should be followed by a crossing of patrols and the construction of bridges. All details were worked out and embodied in G.3887. Time of operation was to be between 1800 and 2200, and was to be notified later.

After visiting 105th Infantry Brigade G.O.C. returned to new Headquarters, and found them only partially made and very inaccessible and decided to move forward the following day. During the day various reports were received that troops of the 34th Division were in MARCKE across our front, where our barrage was going to fall; (this report afterwards proved inaccurate); also that civilians were in MARCKE waving to airmen.

After discussion with Corps it was decided that in view of there being civilians in MARCKE the barrage arrangements should be modified.

G.O.C. went again to General POLLARD'S Headquarters and had a further Conference at 1800, modifying the barrage so as not to fall on MARCKE.

At 1905 the following instructions were received from Corps:-

"35 and 41 Divisions will maintain their present positions and rest and economise troops as much as possible. Every endeavour will be made to drive off enemy detachments from the vicinity of the river LYS and COURTRAI. All preparations will be made to bridge the river at as many points as possible as soon as this is practicable, but attempts to effect a passage are not to be made in face of serious opposition. Points selected for bridges to be reported."

At 1945 the following instructions were sent to 106th Infantry Brigade, C.R.A. and C.R.E, and the gist notified to Corps and flank Divisions:-

"Artillery will barrage as arranged at Conference area between canal and railway between M.10.a.5.9 and G.36.a.6.9 and siding in H.31.c.3.2 for 50 minutes beginning 2200 17th October. No shooting South of railway. 106th Infantry Brigade will push patrols across and if all is clear R.E. will make footbridges at selected points. Under orders from Corps attempts to force a passage in face of strong opposition are not to be made but if all is clear small standing patrols may be left on far bank."

Reports received during the night and early morning of the 18th were to the effect that after the bombardment our troops were held up by machine gun fire from MARCKE and buildings not dealt with in the modified barrage. In the centre a bridge was reported repaired and on the left a bridge partially made. A few men were reported over the river.

Orders were sent to C.R.E. to get up material for extensive bridging and to C.R.A. to get up ammunition and move guns to forward positions.

Divisional Headquarters of both Echelons moved to HERTHOEK, South-west of MOORSEELE.

G.O.C. visited General POLLARD at ELBA CORNER and
discussed/

discussed how crossings were to be secured, while waiting for report from Brigade Major who had gone forward to ascertain exact situation. The report was not very satisfactory as to the amount of bridging which had been done, the R.E. having been driven off by heavy gas shelling.

While there the G.O.C. received the following transmitted message from Corps 1215 p.m. "Endeavour to secure MARCKE today. X Corps are trying to make good the line of the COURTRAI - AELBEKE Road with their left on the high ground in M.18. No Artillery fire will be directed within danger limits of the Northern grid line of Squares M.16, 17, 18."

G.O.C. discussed plans with General POLLARD and sent him and C.R.A. in a car to BISSEGHEM to meet C.Os. of battalions in the 106th Infantry Brigade and R.A. Brigade Commanders and fix up details.

Wires were sent to 104th Infantry Brigade to move forward early in the afternoon to any accommodation near and West of their original objective i.e. line KLOEFHOEK - SCHOONWATER, and to 105th Infantry Brigade to be prepared to carry out an attack at short notice.

At 1755 orders were received from Corps not only to capture MARCKE and secure the crossings of the river but also to advance and capture an objective about 4,000 yards East of the river (see message 537).

On receipt of this message General SANDILANDS, C.R.A. and later on General TURNER were collected at Divisional Headquarters and verbal orders were issued to them to work on to the following effect:-

106th Infantry Brigade to dribble across by Eastern footbridge and attack MARCKE at 2200 from the South-west under cover of a barrage moving North-east through MARCKE towards COURTRAI. 106th Infantry Brigade to gain the line of HELLEBEKE, from G.36 to M.11.d.

R.E. to make three bridges for Infantry before 0200.

104th Infantry Brigade to move by the GULLEGHEM - BISSEGHEM Road, meet guides, cross the river at three points and attack the line of the COURTRAI - ROLLEGHEM Road under a barrage moving Eastwards at the rate of 100 yards in two minutes with pauses of 10 minutes at 700 yards and at 1700 yards.

The 105th Infantry Brigade to move to line of the WEVELGHEM - BISSEGHEM Road and to be ready to cross the river to the line of the AELBEKE - POTTELBERG Road as soon as the attack begins and to support the 104th Infantry Brigade, one battalion being specially detailed to guard the left flank and watch the outskirts of COURTRAI.

Written orders (G.3090) embodying the above and giving details of the barrage were issued.

About 1900 telephonic orders came from the Corps that if G.O.C. 35th Division wished he might send one Brigade to attack MARCKE through 34th Division area. At first the G.O.C. was reluctant to alter the orders issued but later decided to make the following modifications and sent G.S.O.1 to arrange details with 34th Division.

105th Infantry Brigade instead of following 104th Infantry Brigade across the river by the three bridges and taking up a defensive line along the POTTELBERG RIDGE was ordered to move through the 34th Division area, cross the river and move through LAUWE to a position of readiness near from which it could carry out one of the following roles:-

(1) If original plan was successful it would move into a position on the POTTELBERG RIDGE to support 104th Infantry Brigade and watch the left flank.

(2) If the crossings of the river were not completed in time the 105th Infantry Brigade would take on the task of the 104th Infantry Brigade and moving into position North of MARCKE would carry out the attack on the POTTELBERG RIDGE and the COURTRAI - ROLLEGHEM Road.

(3)   If the 106th Infantry Brigade failed in its attack
on MARCKE the 105th Infantry Brigade would be in a
position to attack MARCKE at dawn from the South-west.
Alternative barrages were arranged accordingly.
These modifications were explained to General TURNER
on the telephone and alterations were made in the orders.
General POLLARD attacked at 2200 and gained all objectives
the 17th Royal Scots capturing MARCKE.
Generals SANDILANDS and TURNER having got their troops on
the move, came to Divisional Headquarters and were kept there
till news was received at 0130 that the construction of bridges
was progressing satisfactorily. They were then sent off to their
Brigades with final instructions.
At 1256 on October 19th the following message had been
received from the 106th Infantry Brigade "MARCKE occupied.
All objectives gained right and left battalions in touch.
Boche running fast and apparently far."
At 0315 a wire was sent to Corps. 106th Infantry Brigade
report timed 0145. "All bridges completed."
At 0530 orders were sent to C.R.E. to convert one and
if possible two of the bridges into Artillery bridges as soon
as possible after the attacking troops have crossed.

14.   By dawn on the 19th 104th Infantry Brigade were
completely across the river and attacked at 0530 under a
creeping barrage which paused just East of POTTELBERG RIDGE
and then moved forward again.
The attack was entirely successful and not only reached
the final objective but pushed on to the COURTRAI - HOOGHE Road.
105th Infantry Brigade moved into support on the POTTELBERG
RIDGE.
Patrols from both Brigades belonging to the 15th Sherwood
Foresters and 19th D.L.I. entered COURTRAI and brought out
prisoners and machine guns.
By 0755 it was possible to wire to Corps and flank
Divisions that all objectives had been gained and at 0800
orders were sent to C.R.A. to get Artillery across the river
as soon as the bridge was ready. Artillery began crossing
1100.
G.O.C. went at 0800 across the river to MARCKE and
reconnoitred from POTTELBERG RIDGE after seeing the Brigadiers
from 104th and 105th Infantry Brigades. About 1145 the
enemy started shelling the bridges but without effect.
About this time the following messages were received from
Corps and sent on to G.O.C. by S.D.R.
(1) "From General WATTS: Well done 35th Division.   The
Command Leadership and Staff work of all concerned and
the action of the troops must have been admirable."
(2) "The eventual objective of the XIX Corps is the line
of the SCHELDT between CANAL JUNCTION at V.13.c.9.2 and
P.34.central, the approximate area of the operations
being that included within straight lines drawn from the
XIX Corps boundary on the LYS to these points.   The
advance will be resumed tomorrow the 20th as follows.
35th Division pivoting on its right will establish the
line ROLLEGHEM - KNOCK N.20.b. to N.10.b. and as the
left moves forward will prolong this line to the left
through squares N.5 and H.35 as far as the BOSSUYT CANAL
by pushing forward fresh troops.   If the enemy are still
in COURTRAI pickets will be dropped to cover South and
East exits.   Time of advance to be settled by 35th
Division and reported as soon as the above line has been
established.   The advance will be continued on the
whole front and a line from road junction in N.29.c.,
O.9.c.central, CANAL inclusive will be secured;   the
latter point is right of II Corps final objective of
20th October.   G.O.C. 41st Division will place one
Infantry/

Infantry Brigade at the disposal of G.O.C. 35th Division as a reserve and this Brigade will cross the LYS in 35th Division area as soon as possible under orders of G.O.C. 35th Division. 41st Division will also place two Field Companies R.E. and all pontoon equipment at disposal of 35th Division for improvement of bridges. 41st Division will cross the LYS North of COURTRAI tonight 19/20th October as already ordered and will clear the area between the COURTRAI - BOSSUYT CANAL and IX Corps boundary. 41st Division will eventually pass through 35th Division at a later date."

The three Brigadiers and C.R.A. were all at MARCKE and G.O.C. was able to hold a Conference at once, communicate those messages and issue verbal instructions as follows:-

"104th Infantry Brigade to pivot on its right, 105th Infantry Brigade to move North of 104th Infantry Brigade and extend to the left of 104th Infantry Brigade facing South-east, 106th Infantry Brigade to concentrate at MARCKE and thence move on in Divisional Reserve following the two leading Brigades, the Brigade of the 41st Division to cover the South-eastern exits of COURTRAI. One Brigade of Artillery to be at the disposal of each of the leading Infantry Brigades. Brigade to commence the advance from a starting line MARIONETTEBERG CANAL near STACEGHEM at 0700 and to move in open warfare without pre-arranged barrage.

G.O.C. returned to Divisional Headquarters at HERSHOEK.

About 0200 Major-General LAWFORD Commanding 41st Division came in to discuss arrangements for move of his Brigade about 0245. Corps Commander and M.G.G.S. Second Army came.

At 0600 further orders were received from Corps modifying the previous orders chiefly as regarding the boundary of II Corps, II Corps undertaking to clear the area East of the BOSSUYT CANAL in H.21., 22, 27, 28, 29, and 35th Division undertaking to clear the areas in H.36, I.31, I.32 and O.2. Remainder of 41st Division was ordered to cross the LYS and concentrate in an area South-west of SWEVEGHEM with a view to passing through 35th Division on 21st.

Objective was further extended to the ridges O.31, O.27 and O.23 (afterwards called the HOOGESTRAATJE RIDGE), 2000 to 3000 yards further than the original objective. N.29.c. - O.9.c. afterwards called the KREUPEL RIDGE).

Operations Orders G.3092 confirmation of verbal orders were issued at 0640.

During afternoon and evening Brigades moved into suitable positions for advance next morning.

Summary of 18th and 19th October.

Orders for the above operations were received at 1755 18th. At 2200 106th Infantry Brigade attacked and gained MARCKE and formed a bridgehead, capturing some prisoners and machine guns; during the night bridges were made and 104th Infantry Brigade crossed over by them and 105th Infantry Brigade crossed over in 41st Division area; at 0530 104th Infantry Brigade attacked Eastward and reached the line of COURTRAI - HOOGHE Road while 105th Infantry Brigade moved into support on POTTELBERG RIDGE and both Brigades sent patrols into COURTRAI; at 1100 transport and Artillery began crossing and by evening the whole of the Artillery and first line Transport of Infantry Brigades were across also the Field Companies and bridging material.

Orders for fresh operations were received at 1145 and preparations made for carrying them out, one Brigade of 41st Division was brought over. Incidentally the Mayor and some members of the Corporation of NOTTINGHAM arrived at 1400 on the 19th and were sent over the new pontoon bridge to visit the 15th Sherwood Foresters on the outskirts of COURTRAI and came in for rather a heavy gas shelling at the river crossing on their return.

15. Early on the 20th October G.O.C. with a Staff Officer moved to an advanced report centre at the Convent MARCKE the remainder of Divisional Headquarters remaining at HERTHOEK.

The attack started at 0700. Information was very slow at first but prisoners began to arrive in early. The 4th North Stafford Regiment were checked at the outset before reaching their assembly position on the starting line by strong machine gun opposition at BLOKKEN and by artillery firing over the sights, but eventually overcame this capturing the guns and got into line on our extreme left. The 15th Sherwood Foresters fought their way into SWEVEGHEM as far as the Church but had heavy casualties and were driven out by a counter-attack and held up for some time on the North-west of SWEVEGHEM. The 15th Cheshire Regiment forming the right of the 105th Infantry Brigade and the 19th D.L.I. forming the left of the 104th Infantry Brigade were held up along the line of the KEIBEEK by heavy machine gun fire from the glacis slopes at KREUPEL RIDGE which was apparently strongly held. The 18th Lancashire Fusiliers were echeloned forward of the D.L.I. in square N.23. Meantime the 17th Lancashire Fusiliers on the extreme right had met with practically no opposition and had got right forward at the outset to the junction of the two main ridges of KREUPEL and HOOGSTRAAT in N.35.d. - N.36.a.

Orders were sent to the Reserve Brigade R.F.A. to shell the KREUPEL RIDGE till 1200 and to 105th Infantry Brigade to push on when the bombardment stopped. A further bombardment by Reserve Brigade R.F.A. and by Heavy Artillery was ordered to be carried out between 1315 and 1330 on square N.24. Before this the line of the second objective, the HOOGSTRAAT RIDGE, had been bombarded intermittently.

At 1300 the Divisional Commander went to General POLLARD at HOOGHE with C.R.A. and took him to General SANDILANDS at MARIONETTEBERG N.14.d. and then to General TURNER at H.34.d. on the SWEVEGHEM Road. As it then appeared that the 18th Lancashire Fusiliers and 19th D.L.I. were beginning to get forward on to the KREUPEL RIDGE and the 15th Cheshires were also beginning to gain ground, also that the 15th Sherwood Foresters had captured SWEVEGHEM after hard fighting and the 4th North Staffords had reached the BOSSUYT CANAL (capturing two 5.9" Hows.) and were over on the left of the Sherwoods, the Divisional General decided that he would leave the 104th and 105th Infantry Brigades to complete the capture of first objective and would send the 106th Infantry Brigade by a flank march down the COURTRAI - GOYGHEM Road round the right to attack the second objective, the HOOGSTRAAT RIDGE, from West to East, believing that this would lessen the opposition on the first ridge and that the intervening ground between the ridges would be cleared automatically. On the way back to General POLLARD'S Headquarters the Divisional General saw the Brigadier General Commanding the 122nd Infantry Brigade (41st Division) and told him to stand fast and that his Brigade would in all probability not be used. At General POLLARD'S Headquarters plans were arranged with him and C.R.A. Attack was to take place at 1715. A barrage of all available Artillery was to start on the grid line West of O.31 and move Eastwards to CANAL at 100 yards in two minutes with a 20 minutes pause on the road in O.26.c. On return to Advanced Headquarters in MARCKE orders were issued confirming the above and C.R.A. arranged details with Artillery Brigade Commanders. News of the attack on first objective arrived slowly but about 2000 it appeared that the left of 104th Infantry Brigade was on the KREUPEL RIDGE, that the 15th Cheshire Regiment had not yet got their portion of the ridge, that the Sherwoods had reached the top of the ridge on the line O.7.d.0.0 to O.8.c.2.7 but were held up by a very strong nest of machine guns firing up a glacis slope of about 800 yards from the large

farm/

farm buildings of KAPPELLE MILAENE, that the Staffords were gaining ground on the left.

Orders were sent to the 105th Infantry Brigade that the Cheshires must get on to the ridge, that a bombardment would be arranged at 2315 on KAPPELLE MILAENE and the area up to the CANAL, and that the Sherwoods and Staffords must then push on.

Very little definite information was received during the night as to the progress of General POLLARD'S flank attack, except that owing to the bad weather and other causes it had not started the attack along the ridge till 2 hours after the barrage had commenced at 1715. The 12th H.L.I. followed by the 18th H.L.I. each accompanied by a machine gun company, had attacked along the ridge at 1915 and at first had made good progress, but considerable machine gun fire had been met about O.31.b. and O.36.c. When the attack was nearing O.36.c. General POLLARD ordered the 17th Royal Scots to advance from N.18 through the 15th Cheshires and join hands with the 12th H.L.I. and push along the ridge.

At 0400 the final line known to be occupied had to be telegraphed to the 41st Division, and was given as O.31.b.2.4 - O.31.a.7.3 - O.25.central - O.19.central with posts of Royal Scots in O.19.d.4.0 - along KOSTELBEEK - then just North of KAPPELLE MILAENE - PONT LEVIS No.2 in O.9.d.

Subsequently, however, it turned out that the Sherwood Foresters had captured KAPPELLE MILAENE and that by 0400 the 105th and 104th Infantry Brigades had got the whole of the first objective, while the Royal Scots had pushed along the second ridge, captured HOOGSTRAAT, and pushed patrols to the CANAL by 0540.

Thus the whole of the first and second objectives had been secured after 23 hours continuous fighting. The advance of General POLLARD'S Brigade, made in the dark in heavy rain, after a flank march of 3 miles resulted in clearing 6,000 yards of ridge some two to three thousand yards in front of where the main fighting was going on.

The BOSSUYT CANAL was heavily wired, as also were the approaches to SWEVEGHEM, and the Western end of the KREUPEL RIDGE, which was strongly held by machine guns. All the wire and defences were prepared for an attack from the West; consequently our attack moving Southward met most opposition on its left, and the two left battalions, 4th North Staffords and 15th Sherwoods, had the brunt of the fighting.

The total advance of 6,000 yards, in addition to the approach march, over heavy ground and in bad weather, was in itself a test of physical endurance, without the continuous fighting which lasted for 23 hours.

At 0700 21st October the 41st Division passed through 35th Division, and the troops of the latter moved into rest billets by Brigade Groups in areas South the of the railway through COURTRAI.

G.O.C. returned at 0700 to Divisional Headquarters at HERTHOEK. Later in the day the whole of Divisional Headquarters moved to MARCKE.

16. On the 22nd and 23rd October the troops rested and refitted. On the 23rd an order was received to put one Brigade at the disposal of 41st Division and to be prepared to relieve the 41st Division after an operation which was to be carried out on the 25th October.

On the 24th Divisional Headquarters first echelon moved to a CHATEAU on the COURTRAI - SWEVEGHEM Road, and the remainder to Offices and billets in COURTRAI.

106th Infantry Brigade moved up to the neighbourhood of SWEVEGHEM in support of the 41st Division.

On/

On October 25th the 41st Division reached its first objective, but not beyond, and orders were received to relieve the 41st Division on the night of the 26th/27th.

The total of prisoners taken from 14th October to 26th October was as follows:-

	Officers.	O.R.
UnWounded	19	529
Wounded	5	110
	24	639

also 3 - 5.9" Hows.

17. On the 26th October the B.G.G.S. came and explained the situation. A Conference of Brigadiers was held and boundaries and reliefs were settled. 106th Infantry Brigade was to go into the line on the right, the 104th Infantry Brigade on the left, both on a narrow front in depth, 105th Infantry Brigade to remain in reserve North-east of SWEVEGHEM. (Operation Orders Nos. 205 and 206).

Verbal orders were received from the Corps to attack North-east with the right on the river SCHELDT, and the left on the 9th Division so as to outflank the heights which were checking the 9th Division.

The Army Commander came and gave a forecast of a big attack along the banks of the SCHELDT.

G.O.C. visited 9th Division to arrange co-operation.

In consequence of a report that the 9th Division before relief had pushed patrols into HOFFDRIES and WAERMAERDE orders were sent at 1915 to 104th Infantry Brigade to secure the line WAERMAERDE(Q.19.c.),- OKKERWIJK (P.10.d.), and to push on patrols to TIEGHEM and TENHOVE.

The relief took place without incident, but the line taken over was very ill defined, and the relief was a kind of battle relief. The approximate line was AUTRYVE - AVELGHEM - P.24.a.0.0 - P.16.c.

On October 27th Divisional Headquarters complete moved to SWEVEGHEM.

104th Infantry Brigade had found that the line of SCHEEBEEK RIVER was strongly held by machine gun posts, and that an advance to WAERMAERDE without a prepared attack was impossible. Their patrols had captured one machine gun and four prisoners. 104 Brigade Headquarters were at BANHOUT BOSCH, 106th Infantry Brigade Headquarters at KAPPELLE MILAENE. Large numbers of civilian refugees came in from AVELGHEM, who had been badly shelled and gassed. Divisional Ambulances and stretcher bearers were sent to help them.

On 28th October the Corps Commander made a state entry into COURTRAI, and received the Freedom of the City. Representatives and detachments of the 35th Division attended.

Verbal orders were received at 1600 to prepare to attack Eastwards with the right on the SCHELDT and the left on the 31st Division, who had relieved the 9th Division.

G.O.C. visited General SANDILANDS and gave him an outline of the plan.

Early on the 29th the XIX Corps orders for attack were received. The attack was practically an attack up a defile with high ground and a large number of machine guns across the river on our right, and high ground which was being attacked by the 31st Division on our left. Special arrangements were required for neutralizing fire and smoke barrage on our right. These were undertaken by the Corps while the Division arranged its own frontal barrage and the movement forward of Artillery Brigades to assist the smoke barrage after reaching the original limit of range.

Conferences/

Conferences were held with Major-General J. CAMPBELL, 31st Division, at HARLEBEKE, with G.O.C.R.A. Corps, with C.R.A., Brigadier-General SANDILANDS, and with the Brigadier-General Commanding 94th Infantry Brigade on our left, also with Os.C. 35th and 101st Bns. M. G. C.

A reconnaissance was made by the G.O.C. of the ground from KLEINE RUS HILL, East of OOTEGHEM.

Operation Order No.207 was issued embodying the following points:-

(a) The attack was to be carried out by 104th Infantry Brigade with its right on the SCHELDT and its left on the boundary, P.15.d.central - P.16.a.4.0 - P.11.c.0.0 - Q.7.d.5.6 - Q.3.d.0.0.

The first objective was to be the line WAERMAERDE - P.12.d.5.1; the second objective was to be the line Q.15.central - Q.9.a.0.5.

(b) G.O.C.R.A. XIX Corps arranged to neutralize enemy's batteries and machine guns and to mask with smoke the attack from observation from the high ground on the right bank of the SCHELDT. The masking was to be carried out by three blocks of smoke in the first part of the attack, and by two blocks of smoke in the second part. A very large quantity of artillery was allotted for this purpose.

(c) The attack was to be supported frontally by a barrage moving at the rate of 100 yards in 3 minutes, with a double pause at 1200 yards, a pause of 2 hours and 3 minutes at first objective, and a double pause at Zero plus 231 minutes.

6" Hows. were to piquet certain farms and cross roads. Arrangements were made for the two R.F.A. Brigades carrying out the barrage in the first phase to move forward and come under the orders of the G.O.C.R.A. Corps for the smoke screen, and for the third Brigade to take up the barrage in the second phase.

(d) The Infantry attack was to be under the B.G.C., 104th Infantry Brigade, who was to arrange drop parties and machine guns as the attack progressed, to hold the banks of the SCHELDT.

Two machine gun companies were placed at his disposal, one for forming the defensive flank, the other for assisting the attack by consolidating the first and second objectives.

One Brigade R.F.A. was to be affiliated to him as soon as the barrage was over.

The 106th Infantry Brigade was to take over the River line up to P.29.b.9.8 as soon as the attack started, and was to be ready to be relieved on the night 31st October/1st November.

105th Infantry Brigade was to move one battalion forward, to be at the tactical call of 104th Infantry Brigade.

In addition to the two Machine Gun Companies mentioned above, two companies between AUTRYVE and AVELGHEM were to supplement the XIX Corps Artillery firing on the right bank, and three companies were to fire as long as it was safe on certain groups of houses and road junctions in front of the attack.

On the 29th Divisional Headquarters were bombed by aeroplanes and on the 30th SWEVEGHEM was shelled. A large number of casualties amongst horses were caused.

On the 30th final preparations were made and the G.O.C. visited Brigades.

18.   On 31st October the G.O.C. moved with Advanced Report Centre to BANHOUT BOSCHE.

The barrage and attack began at 0525. The barrage and smoke screen were excellent and completely obscured the opposite side of the river.

The attack was carried out as follows:-
- 19th D.L.I. on the right.
- 17th Lancashire Fusiliers in Centre.
- 18th Lancashire Fusiliers on left.

Two companies in each battalion were used for the first objective, and two companies for the second objective.

19th D.L.I. and one company M.G.Bn. dropped parties along the river to form a defensive flank at points laid down in 104th Infantry Brigade Orders.

The attack progressed satisfactorily, the first objective, WAERMAERDE - TIEGHEM being reached in schedule time. After a two hours pause the attack pushed on to the final objective which was also secured. A considerable amount of machine gun resistance was met from the farms and villages in this very densely populated country, but the barrage fire was excellent and the attack carried all before it. After the attack a very unusual number of enemy dead was found in proportion to the number of prisoners. During the pause the Artillery Brigades changed position and were ready to fire again at schedule time. The 106th Infantry Brigade took over the ground as far as RUGGE (inclusive) immediately after that place was taken by the D.L.I.

At 0700 the G.O.C. visited General SANDILANDS at Advanced Headquarters (P.13.c.) where news was received of the Centre battalion being on its first objective. The G.O.C. then returned to Divisional Headquarters. News and prisoners came in by degrees during the morning. By 1155 it was clear that we were on our final objective.

At 1210 orders were received from Corps to exploit beyond the line of the second objective and sieze EEUWHOEK if possible. This was wired to 104th Infantry Brigade.

At 1345 a report was received from 104th Infantry Brigade giving the exact line held on the final objective and stating that the enemy was retreating towards AUDENARDE.

At 1430 the G.O.C. sent G.S.O.2 with written instructions (G.100) to General SANDILANDS to the following effect:-
(1)   To exploit success to EEUWHOEK.
(2)   That Corps reported that there might be two German Divisions West of the SCHELDT for counter-attack.
(3)   That he would have two machine gun companies, two Brigades R.F.A., and one Brigade R.G.A. covering him, and that an Artillery Liaison Officer representing all Artillery would join him.
(4)   That if his men were very exhausted he could put in the 15th Cheshires to hold his Eastern front, but that he was not to do so if it could be avoided, as the G.O.C. wished to keep the whole of 105th Infantry Brigade intact.

At 1600 congratulations were received from Army and Corps Commanders and communicated.

At 1920 a Warning Order for the relief of the 35th Division by the 41st Division on the night of the 1/2nd November was received, arrangements already having been made for the relief of the 106th Infantry Brigade by the 41st Division on the night of 31st October/1st November.

During the night EEUWHOEK was occupied, and during the following morning (November 1st) a very valuable and daring reconnaissance, made by a Staff Officer close up to KWAADESTRAAT and ELSEGHEM, brought back valuable information from the inhabitants, that the enemy was in full retreat,

but/

but was still holding these places with machine guns.

On November 1st the Army Commander came and congratulated all concerned.

As a result of the flank attack made by the 35th Division, and two Divisions to the North, the enemy had fallen back in front of the French, and a very big forward advance was made on 1st November, by troops to the North of 35th Division.

Captures of 35th Division in this fight were -

	Officers.	O.R.
Unwounded prisoners	6	227
wounded ,,	2	42
	8	269

3 Field Guns
2 Motor Ambulances with patients.
A very large number of trench mortars and machine guns and a certain amount of transport and horses.

On the night of November 1/2nd the relief of the 35th Division was completed and the whole Division moved to rest billets in areas South of COURTRAI, 105th Infantry Brigade near MARCKE, 106th near CHEVAL ROUGE, and 104th Infantry Brigade near STACEGHEM.

On the night of 1st November SWEVEGHEM was bombed by aeroplanes, "Q" Office damaged and a good many casualties inflicted on Pioneers and Machine Gunners.

19.

18a.

Our casualties were as follows:---

By dates.

Date.	Officers.			Other ranks.			Total.		
	K.	W.	M.	K.	W.	M.	K.	W.	M.
Oct.3 to 13.	2	7	1	15	94	2	17	101	3
Oct. 14th.	-	8	-	27	98	27	27	106	27
" 15th.	4	11	-	65	334	55	69	345	55
" 16th.	3	11	-	32	214	23	35	235	23
" 17th.	-	-	-	1	10	-	1	-	-
" 18th.	-	4	-	1	24	2	1	28	2
" 20th.	-	3	-	27	103	9	27	106	9
" 21st.	1	11	1	21	83	17	22	94	18
" 22nd to 30th.	1	8	-	34	182	13	35	190	13
" 31st.	5	16	-	51	283	73	56	299	73
Nov.1 to 11th.	3	6	-	3	36	-	6	42	-
Total Oct. 3rd to Nov. 11th.	19	85	2	277	1461	221	296	1546	223

By Units.

Unit.	Officers.			Other ranks.			Total.		
	K.	W.	M.	K.	W.	M.	K.	W.	M.
104 Inf. Bde.									
17th L.F.	5	9	-	34	248	44	39	257	44
18th L.F.	1	9	-	45	193	55	46	202	55
19th D.L.I.	1	8	-	25	168	41	26	176	41
105 Inf. Bde.									
15th Cheshires.	3	9	-	37	159	19	40	168	19
15th Sherwoods.	2	16	2	38	171	40	40	187	42
4th N.Staffs.	2	10	-	28	170	7	30	180	7
106 Inf. Bde.									
17th D.Scots.	-	1	-	8	54	-	8	55	-
12th H.L.I.	-	2	-	4	46	7	4	48	7
18th H.L.I.	1	2	-	18	46	-	19	48	-
19th N.F. (Pnrs.)	2	4	-	12	37	-	14	41	-
35th Bn.M.G.C.	1	5	-	12	100	5	13	105	5
R.A.	-	5	-	6	39	3	6	44	3
R.E.	1	5	-	10	24	-	11	29	-
R.A.M.C.	-	-	-	-	1	-	-	1	-
R.A.S.C.	?	-	-	-	3	-	-	3	-
232 Emp. Compy.	-	-	-	-	2	-	-	2	-
Total.	19	85	2	277	1461	221	296	1546	223

20. The following is a summary of the attacks carried out by the Division in those first two phases of the operations which commenced on September 28th:-

		Attacking Bdes.
Sept. 28th.	Attack on VERBRANDENMOLEN RIDGE	104
	BLUFF to TOR TOP TUNNELS	105
	including HILL 60	106
	Exploiting to ZANDVOORDE	104
	& ALASKA HOUSES	106
Sept. 29th.	Attack to TENBRIELEN -)	105
	BLEGNAERT FARM)	106
Sept. 30th.	Attack to WERVICQ)	105
	)	106
Oct. 1st & 2nd	Attacks towards GHELEUWE SWITCH	104
Oct. 14th.	Attack from TERHAND towards	104
	COURTRAI	105
Oct. 15th.	Attack to SCHOONWATER SPUR	104
	and KLOEFHOEK	105
Oct. 16th.	Clearing BISSEGHEM and area) down to LYS.)	106
Oct. 18th.	Capture of MARCKE and crossing) over the LYS)	106
Oct. 19th.	Attack to COURTRAI - HOOGE Road	104
Oct. 20th. 21st.	Attack S.E. from COURTRAI on KREUPEL and HOOGSTRAATJE RIDGE	104
		105
	Flank attack	106
Oct. 31st.	Attack along banks of the SCHELDT	104

SUMMARY OF CAPTURES DURING THIS PERIOD.

	Officers.	O.R.	Guns.
28th Sept. to 2nd Oct.	35	1070	42
14th Oct. to 22nd Oct.	24	639	46
31st Oct. to 1st Nov.	8	269	3
	67	1978	91

H.Q., 35th Division.
29th December, 1918.

Major-General.
Commanding 35th Division.

WAR DIARY

35th Division No. G. 3709.

The Major-General takes the opportunity of this pause in the operations to congratulate all ranks for their share in the recent victory. He wishes especially to thank the Infantry and Artillery for the magnificent endurance and resolution with which they pushed forward and brought up the guns during the bad weather on the second and third days of the operations, also the transport pack trains and medical services for the determination with which they overcame all difficulties of weather and mud in bringing up rations and ammunition and in getting away the wounded.

Total prisoners captured by 35th Division amount to 1091.

(Signed) A.H. MARINDIN,

H.Q. 35th Division,
3rd October 1918.

Major-General,
Commanding 35th Division.

(2).

C.R.A. 35th Division.
104th Infantry Brigade.
105th   do.
106th   do.
A.D.M.S.
35th Div. Train, A.S.C.
A.A.& Q.M.G.

The above minute by the Major-General Commanding is forwarded for communication to all concerned.

H.W.B. Thorp

H.Q. 35th Division,
3rd October 1918.

Lieutenant-Colonel,
General Staff, 35th Division.

BELGIUM AND PART OF FRANCE

1:40,000

INSTRUCTIONS AS TO THE USE OF THE SQUARES.

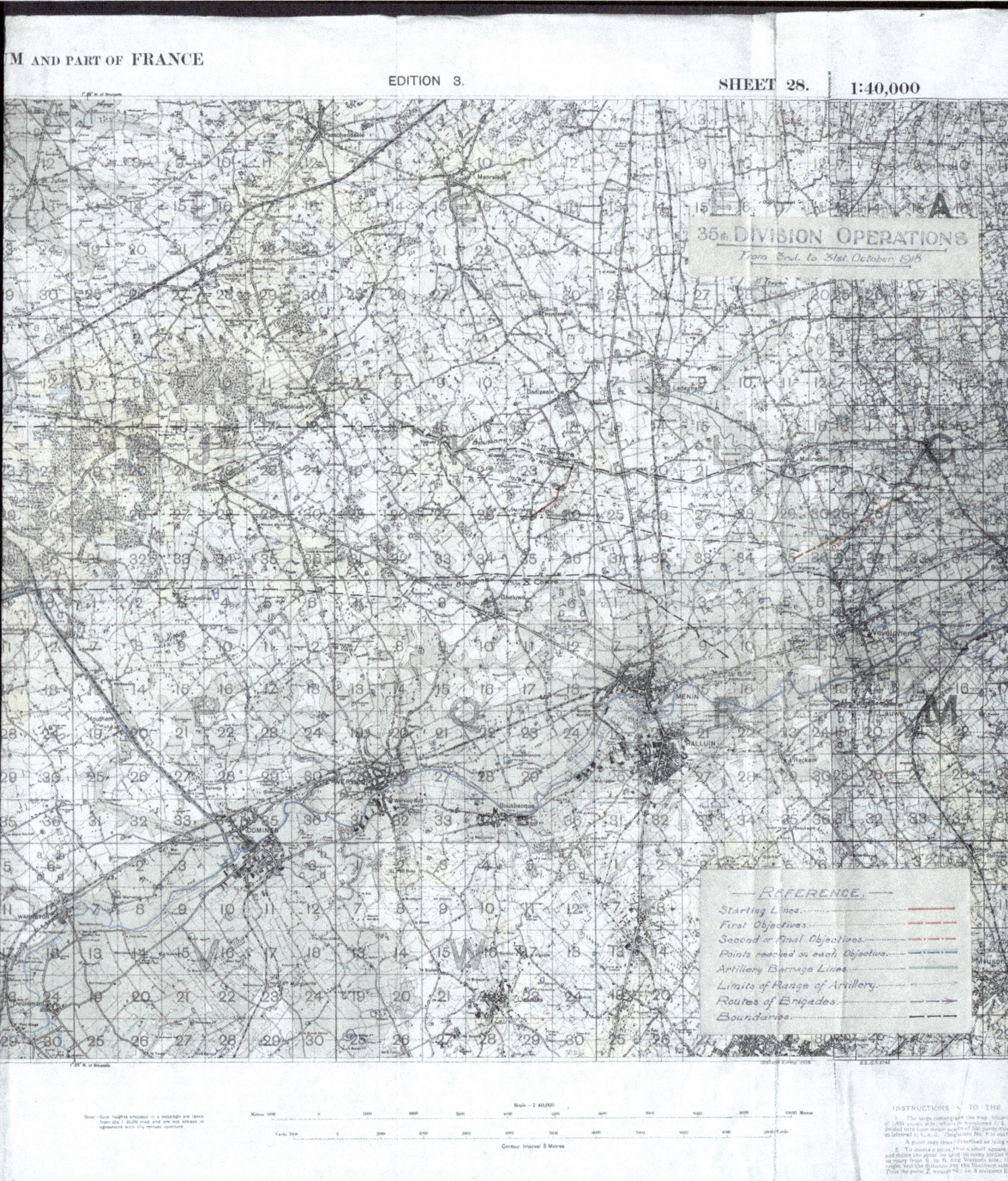

35

25th Div.

Narrative of Opns
28/9 — to end Oct. '18

35th DIVISION

Narrative of Operations
from 28th September to end of October, 1918.

First Phase - 28th September to October 3rd 1918.

1. On September 12th 35th Division was in the II Corps and held the line from Moated Grange, South of VOORMEZEE LE to the YPRES-COMINES Canal where it is crossed by the YPRES-LILLE Road and thence to the road and railway crossing just South of the Western edge of ZILLEBEKE POND.

    Two Brigades were in line with H.Qrs. at ST.DUNSTANS and ASSAM FARM, and One Brigade in Reserve near BRANDHOEK with H.Qrs. put at WARATAH FARM and later at H.9.c.1.1. South of VLAMERTINGHE.

    Divisional H.Q. at VOGELTJE Convent, just South of CHATEAU LOVIE.

    41st Division was on the Right and 14th Division on the Left.

2. On the 12th September at 1800 hours the G.O.C. was sent for to XIX Corps and was told that the 14th and 35th Divisions were going to be transferred to the XIX Corps, that a big attack was pending, that no orders were to be issued in writing and that as few people were to be told of it as possible. XIX Corps was going to take over front up to ZILLEBEKE POND on the 15th. Meantime 35th Division was to take over 600 yards to the Left from 14th Division. General objective of attack was given, 35th Division to attack North of YPRES-COMINES Canal from the Bluff to TOR TOPS from its present Left Sector. The present Right Sector was to be handed over to 14th Division who would include from ST.ELOI to the Bluff in their attack.

3. On September 13th and 14th new administrative areas were allotted and Divisional H.Qrs. were ordered to move to WARATAH FARM. The proposed attack was communicated to Brigadiers and to C.R.A., C.R.E., and heads of "G" and "Q" Staffs only. All orders for movements of areas were camouflaged.

    Arrangements were made for the 105 and 106 Infantry Brigades to take and establish a line of posts on the night of 15/16th, and Operation Order No. 195 was issued.

4. On September 15th orders were brought verbally by B.G. G.S., XIX Corps that attack would take place on 22nd, and arrangements were made for relief by 14th Division of Right Sector.

    Later in the day the date of attack was postponed till 25th and all arrangements for relief were postponed for 48 hours.

    A further Divisional Conference was held at which the outlying scheme of attack was given.

    At 2223 hours the 105 and 104 Infantry Brigades carried out a minor operation and established a line of posts 500 to 800 yards in front of our line on the whole front of 4,000 yards and captured 49 prisoners and 4 machine guns. Two more prisoners and 2 of the enemy killed were accounted for next day. Our total casualties were 3 killed and 8 wounded.

    The objects of this operation were :-

Page 2.

(1) To give more room for deployment of Left and Centre Brigades in the attack near ZILLEBEKE.

(2) To enable machine guns to be brought within effective range for barrage purposes.

(3) To shorten the distance of attack by the 14th Division on the Bluff and ST.ELOI.

The new line of posts ran approximately along Old French Trench, Middlesex Road, to Eastern end of ZILLEBEKE POND and took in Western end of the SPOIL BANK, CHESTER FARM, BLAUWE POORT and MANOR FARM.

5. day The Army Commander wired congratulations and came next personally to convey congratulations and to discuss the plan of attack and of further exploiting the success as far as ZANDVOORDE.

He approved of the G.O.C's proposal that the attack should be carried out by three Brigades in depth instead of by two Brigades with One in reserve. The reasons given by the G.O.C. for this scheme were that, with the attack starting on a 1,700 yards front and ending on a 3,800 yards front, it would be easier to arrange for the extension by bringing battalions up than by leap frogging Brigades, also that the lines of attack were affected by the deep railway cutting between Hill 60 and the Dump and by the marshy ground between CANADA TUNNELS and OBSERVATORY RIDGE.

6. On this night (16th) the 106th Infantry Brigade relieved the 104th Infantry Brigade in the Left Sector, and the 105th Infantry Brigade extended its Left across the Canal to LANKHOF CHATEAU, on the grounds that the Left Sector had extended to ZILLEBEKE POND but really with a view to the subsequent relief by the 14th Division. This subsequent relief was also ordered under the camouflage that one Brigade 14th Division had been placed at disposal of G.O.C. in order to give the troops of the 35th Division a rest, and would relieve the 105th Infantry Brigade on the 19/20th. These reliefs were carried out in accordance with O.O. 196 of 16th September and 197 of 19th September, and the 105th Infantry Brigade went back to SCHOOL CAMP, West of POPERINGHE.

The situation now was that the 35th Division held the front from which it was going to attack with the 106th Infantry Brigade, 104th Infantry Brigade was in camps about BRANDHOEK and 105th Infantry Brigade in SCHOOL CAMP.

Boundaries from rear to front were carefully arranged so that, nearer to the day of attack there should be 3 areas allowing a very narrow front to be taken over by each Brigade in which the final preparations for attack could be made, the remainder of the Brigades being in depth behind. Guns of all calibres were being brought in by night and the areas became very congested and required very careful Staff organization, vide Operation Order 198 of 21/9/18.

On the 17th Division H.Qrs. moved to WARATAH FARM. From the 18th to 23rd constant modifications of the scheme, of the rate of barrage, pauses in the barrage in order to suit the Belgians, etc. were made and the date of attack was altered on the 22nd September to the 27th and then to the 28th. Battalions had already started moving up and had to be sent back.

Finally orders were issued on September 23rd, but these included a certain amount of vagueness as to when the second advance on ZANDVOORDE should commence, depending on hypothetical circumstances, and also included the 41st Division passing through the 35th before the reserves and guns of the 35th could get forward. As a result of a visit from the Army Commander and M.G., G.S., Army, and the B.G.G.S. of Corps these matters were modified and a definite time was laid down for the second advance in an amendment to orders.

The general scheme as finally amended was as follows:

Three Brigades to attack in line. 105 on Right, 104 in Centre and 106 on Left, each Brigade in depth. The attack to be covered by a creeping barrage at the rate of 100 yards in 3 minutes, with double pauses at 500, 1000, and 1500 yards. (Modifications of these pauses were made right up to the last and the rate of lift after 1500 yards was altered to 100 yards in 5 minutes). Special points were to be dealt with by Field Howitzers and, by arrangement with the Corps, Heavy Artillery was to deal with certain other special points further forward.

The first pause in the attack was to be on the line The Bluffs-East of Hill 60-East of CANADA TUNNELS-East of TOR TOP TUNNELS-JAN LANE (J.19. central).

This would be reached in varying times by the different Brigades, the Brigade on the right reaching it about Zero, plus 48, the Brigade in the Centre at Zero plus 73, and the Brigade on the Left reaching it at Zero plus 118.

At Zero plus 96 the Artillery barrage covering the Right and Centre Brigades, which meantime had been searching forward and back, was to settle on its new line and at Zero plus 100 the Right and Centre Brigades (105 and 104 Brigades) were to resume the advance and capture the first objective, linking up with the Left Brigade which would still be pushing on. The first objective included BATTLE WOOD and KLEIN ZILLEBEEKE. It was anticipated that this objective would be reached at Zero plus 2 hours 20 minutes.

At Zero plus 4 hours and 20 minutes the advance was to be resumed by the Centre and Left Brigades (104 Infantry Brigade and 106 Infantry Brigade), the former capturing the high ground about ZANDVOORDE and the latter capturing ALASKA HOUSES to the North. The 105th Infantry Brigade was to stand fast and as soon as the 41st Division passed through, be reorganized to form the Divisional Reserve.

The two Brigades moving forward to ZANDVOORDE and ALASKA HOUSES were each to have one Battery 18 pdrs. and one section 4.5" Howitzers at the disposal of the B.G.C.

Two additional Brigades of Field Artillery were at disposal of 35th Division.

Orders were also issued for the immediate repair of certain roads as soon as the attack progressed.

8. On the 25th and 26th September the G.O.C. took large parties of Officers, about 60 each day, to CASSEL and with the help of Major General PERCY (M.G.G.S.Second Army), and Captain HEYWOOD (G.3) explained the ground they were going to attack over on the large scale model at Second Army Headquarters, pointing out the marshy places, cuttings, land marks, dug-outs, etc., which all three Officers knew intimately from previous experiences. Afterwards the various Commanders of Battalions and Companies discussed their mutual co-operation and practically played a war-game of their portion of the attack. It is certain that this was responsible in a great degree for the smoothness with which the operations were subsequently carried out.

9.   On the nights 25/26th and 26/27th, the three Brigades moved up and occupied the front in depth.

The G.O.C. visited the troops in front line and all Battalions, and found that the secret had been so well kept that troops in front line through which the others were going to attack did not know at 1200 on the day before the attack that an attack was going to take place. Officers were then going round the line telling them. This was due to the loyal way in which all Officers had kept the secret. Battalion Commanders had not been told till the 19th (it then being supposed that the attack was on the 22nd), and Company Commanders were not told till some days later.

On the night of 27/28th troops moved into assembly positions under cover of the posts which had been captured on 15th. Distribution of troops is shown in Map A. attached.

The two Right Brigades each had two Battalions in line and one in reserve, and Battalions attacked through their own troops. In the Left Brigade only one Battalion attacked and it attacked through a Company of another Battalion.

Brigade Headquarters of the two Right Brigades were established at WOODCOTE HOUSE and of the Left Brigade in the railway embankment near the triangular pond S.W. of ZILLEBEKE POND.

Divisional Headquarters remained at WARATAH FARM with Advanced Report Centre at ASSAM FARM.

10.   The attack commenced at 0530 hours.
Order of attack was :-

		Objective.
Right Brigade. 105 Infantry) Brigade.) Brig.Genl.TURNER.	4th N.Staffs.on Right. 15th Sherwood Foresters on Left. 15th Cheshire Regt. in Reserve.	From the Bluff (excl) to the Caterpillar (excl.)
Centre Brigade.	18th Lancs. Fusiliers on Right.	From the Caterpillar (incl) to CANADA TUNNELS (incl.)
104 Inf. Bde. Brig.Gen.) SANDILANDS)	18th L.F.on Right. 19th D.L.I.on Left. 17th Lancs.Fusiliers in Reserve.	
Left Brigade. 106th Inf.Bde.	12th H.L.I. attacking.	From CANADA TUNNELS to JAM LANE (incl).

18th H.L.I.in support
Brig.Gen.POLLARD. 17th R.Scots.in reserve.

The attack started without a hitch, the enemy reply to our barrage being feeble, and was carried through up to pause line, and then to first objective exactly in schedule time. The advance was over very rough ground, pitted with shell-holes and covered with debris, but by 2 hours 20 minutes after Zero the first objective had been gained everywhere on a front of 4,000 yards and an average depth of 3,000 yards and large numbers of prisoners were coming in. By 1200 hours 750 prisoners had passed through Divisional Cage.

At 0950 hours the advance on ZANDVOORDE and ALASKA HOUSES by Centre and Right Brigades (17th Lancs.Fusiliers on ZANDVOORDE and 18th H.L.I. supported by 17th Royal Scots on ALASKA HOUSES commenced), and by 1430 hours reports were received at Divisional Headquarters that their objectives had been captured about 1230 hours. This added another 3,000 yards to the ground gained. A local counter-attack was made at 1830 hours to regain ZANDVOORDE was easily repulsed and left prisoners in our hands.

Meantime artillery had been pushing forward in spite of the bad ground. Pioneers and R.E. had been ordered up at 0740 hours to commence work on repair of roads. The 41st Division during the afternoon came through our Right Brigade.

At 1605 hours orders were issued to Brigades to make good the ground gained, to put out Outposts and push out patrols to exploit success, also to bring up affiliated guns and machine-guns, and bring up food and ammunition and be prepared for further action at short notice.

Transport lines were moved forward to near ZILLEBEKE POND and rations and ammunition were sent up by pack train which worked admirably during this and succeeding days.

Late in the evening the G.O.C. visited the battle ground and saw Brigadiers at TOR TOP TUNNELS and WOODCOTE HOUSE. Prisoners continued coming in. A large amount of guns, trench mortars, and machine guns had been captured, but were not salved until later.

At 2355 hours orders were issued to the following effect :- 35th Division to advance on following morning to TENBRIELEN and thence on WERVICQ, with 29th Division of the II Corps advancing on Left, and 41st Division advancing on COMINES on the Right. 104th Infantry Brigade to take over the defence down to CANAL and to remain in reserve about ZANDVOORDE and old final objective: 105th Infantry Brigade to move via ZANDVOORDE using any route between Hill 60 and TOR TOP, and to make good the line TENBRIELEN-BLAGNAERT FARM and thence, if all went well, on both flanks, to capture WERVICQ: one Battery 18 pdrs. and one section 4.5 howitzers were placed at disposal of Brigadier-General Commanding 105th Infantry Brigade. Heavy artillery was to bombard intermittently the line TENBRIELEN-BLAGNAERT FARM and LA FACON FARM at 1000 hours: 106th Infantry Brigade to be in support: if both Brigades became involved Brigadier-General POLLARD to assume command of combined 105th and 106th Brigades.

11. On the 29th Advanced Divisional H.Qrs. moved to WOODCOTE HOUSE. No news was received all the morning from 105th Infantry Brigade, but at 1300 hours a message was received from Brigadier-General SANDILANDS (commanding 104th Infantry Brigade with H.Qrs. near Hill 60) to say that 105th Infantry Brigade had lost direction in the mist, and moved towards HOLLEBEKE instead of North of ZANDVOORDE and then moved up towards ZANDVOORDE and were held up by machine-guns from South-Eastern spur of ZANDVOORDE. The G.O.C. spoke to General POLLARD on the telephone at 1325 hours and instructed him that, if the 105th Infantry Brigade was held up, the 106th Infantry Brigade must push on through them to TENBRIELEN and BLAGNAERT FARM, otherwise 106th were to support and push on the 105th Infantry Brigade. General POLLARD to take command of all advanced troops.

G.O.C. proceeded to 104 H.Qrs. near Hill 60, where he

he was able to speak to General POLLARD and then on to KLEIN ZILLEBEKE to see the situation. At 1540 hours he telephoned back through Advanced Divisional H.Qrs. to Corps that the 15th Cheshire Regiment had been held up East of ZANDVOORDE and that the N.Staffords. and 15th Sherwoods were attacking ZANDVOORDE. General POLLARD was with General TURNER and was sending one Battalion 106th Infantry Brigade with two Battalions in close support, on to TENBRIELEN regardless of what was taking place at ZANDVOORDE. The G.O.C. in consultation on the telephone with General POLLARD arranged that all available artillery should be turned on TENBRIELEN up to 1730 hours.

At 1800 hours detailed information was brought in by a Staff Officer who had been sent forward, that at 1245 hours the 105th Infantry Brigade had been held up, but had attacked the Eastern spur of ZANDVOORDE again with two Battalions, and had been successful, and that troops were seen at 1630 hours advancing towards TENBRIELEN.

At 1654 hours reports were received from General POLLARD that one Battalion 106 and one Battalion 105 were on their objectives at TENBRIELEN, that it was too dark to continue advance that night, but that he proposed attacking WERVICQ at 0550 hours the following morning. He asked for artillery bombardment from 0550 hours to 0650 hours on WERVICQ and reported that he had two Battalions of his own Brigade and one Battalion of 105th Infantry Brigade to support the attack.

At 1920 hours a message was sent to General POLLARD approving his proposals, informing him that arrangements had been made to give Artillery support of Heavies and Divisional Artillery as requested, and that Group Commanders of both D.A.Brigades were affiliated to him for direct orders during the operation, also that 41st Division had been asked to carry out their attack on COMINES at the same time.

B.G.C. 104th Infantry Brigade was told that the BATTLE WOOD line -(Triangular Bluff O.5.a. - Railway Trench) need no longer be held, that the Brigade was to be collected and given as much rest as possible.

At 2050 hours in consequence of telephonic conversation with Corps the following order was issued.

" Battalions of 105th and 106th Infantry Brigades
" are on TENBRIELEN SPUR.
" 105th and 106th Infantry Brigades both under
" orders of General POLLARD will move off at 0550 hours
" tomorrow morning 30th, and attack Northern outskirts of
" WERVICQ, forming a bridge-head on ridges overlooking
" WERVICQ.
" 104th Brigade will hold ZANDVOORDE and ALASKA
" HOUSES with Right on PAUPER TRENCH (P.2.d.) and Left
" about J.34. central. Two Battalions 104th Brigade will
" be held in readiness to support attack on WERVICQ and will
" be located near ZANDVOORDE. All available heavy and
" field artillery will bombard ridges just North of WERVICQ-
" COMINES railway and Northern outskirts of WERVICQ from
" 0550 to 0650 hours on 30th. 41st Division is attacking
" COMINES at same time."

At 2220 hours in consequence of telegraphic orders received from Corps the following additional orders were sent :-

"   In continuation of G.A.75 .35th Division will
" penetrate to Railway North of VERVICQ and then push
" forward patrols to line of river, Right of 35th Division
" and Left of 41st Division will be directed on LES
" CASERNES (P.29.b.)".

SUMMARY OF THE DAY'S FIGHTING.

Two things contributed to the difficulty of the day's fighting.(1) ZANDVOORDE is on a kidney shaped hill and the village is completely destroyed. When the 104th Infantry Brigade reported they had captured ZANDVOORDE on the 28th they had captured all the Western part and the Western spur, but had not taken the Eastern spur which still had strong pill-boxes and machine-guns. (2) The wood just East of KLEIN ZILLEBEKE forks, one portion which was nearly obliterated at this point going to ZANDVOORDE and the other which much better defined going towards HOLLEBEKE CHATEAU. The leading Battalion 105th Infantry Brigade(15th Cheshire Regiment) in the mist took the Right-hand fork and before the mistake was rectified had nearly reached HOLLEBEKE CHATEAU. General TURNER then decided that it was too late to go back and moved on ZANDVOORDE from the West, thus coming under fire from 10 machine-guns in the South-East spur of ZANDVOORDE. The attack at 1245 hours by the 15th Cheshires was hung up and it was not till an attack by two Battalions was made at 1545 hours that this spur was cleared. If the 105th Infantry Brigade had passed between ZANDVOORDE and ALASKA HOUSES as ordered the delay would not have happened.

General POLLARD, on receiving orders to take command of the situation, finding that the 105th Infantry Brigade was making a second attack deferred action beyond ordering the 17th Royal Scots to operate on their Left and the 12th and 18th H.L.I. to support. 17th Royal Scots advanced at 1510 hours on the Left flank of 4th North Staffs. through ZANDVOORDE. Subsequently 105th Infantry Brigade advance appeared to be going well but their support Battalion was not moving. General POLLARD therefore at 1700 hours ordered the 18th H.L.I. to advance supported by 12th H.L.I. and assumed command of the operation. The result was that, by nightfall, the line TENBRIELEN-BLAGNAERT FARM was occupied by the 106th Infantry Brigade with one Battalion of the 105th Infantry Brigade while the remainder of the 105th Infantry Brigade was in support, 17th Royal Scots and a company of 12th H.L.I. having done particularly good work during the advance.

The advance to this line brought our troops forward a further 3,500 yards.

Total prisoners up to 2230 hours for the two days amounted to 1013.

12.   During the night of 29/30th and all day on the 30th heavy rain fell. A good deal of discussion went on during the night as to whether we actually occupied TENBRIELEN and as to the exact position of our line, but it was eventually made quite clear that TENBRIELEN had been occupied by the 12th H.L.I. the previous night. Messages were much delayed including one from General POLLARD asking that the attack should be put off till 0615 hours, it being too late to alter the commencement of the

bombardment, the bombardment was kept up rather longer. The attack started at 0615 hours and at 0745 hours news was received that it was progressing well and had already advanced 1500 yards. At 0905 hours a verbal report was received from General POLLARD that "a prisoner taken on the outskirts of WERVICQ said that Germans retreated during the night to a position 5 kilometres East of the Canal."

At 1000 hours a message was sent to 104th Infantry Brigade to be ready to move towards MENIN. At 1109 hours a message was received from XIX Corps that the 29th Division was reported East of GHELUWE and ordering that Reserve Brigade of 35th Division should be pushed on between WERVICQ and GHELUWE to link up with 29th Division in direction of MENIN.

At 1110 hours the following order was dispatched to all Brigades :-

" 29th Division reported just East of GHELUWE.
" 104th Infantry Brigade will move in the first instance
" to line of road WERVICQ-GHELUWE (Q.4.c.) and thence to
" line WERVICQ-MENIN gaining touch with Right of 29th
" Division between WERVICQ and MENIN. Right of 104th
" Infantry Brigade to connect with General POLLARD's force
" at REEKE (Q.20.b.). 104th Brigade will move as soon
" as possible, reporting hour. General POLLARD'S force
" will hold lightly the line LES CASERNE (P.29.b.) -
" REEKE (Q.20.b.) his remaining troops being collected into
" support on a two Brigade front. Suggested route for
" 104th Brigade is ZANDVOORDE-TENBRIELEN-Eastern tracks
" towards AMERICA CABARET (P.12.b) and GHELUWE advancing
" S.E. from that line."

At 1134 hours G.S.O. 3 who had gone forward as Liaison Officer reported that at 1030 hours 12th and 18th H.L.I. were on line of railway North of WERVICQ with two Companies Royal Scots pushing up on Left of 18th H.L.I. and two companies Cheshires on Right of 12th H.L.I.; remainder of 105th Infantry Brigade in close support. 159th Brigade R.F.A. moving towards WERVICQ from vicinity of TENBRIELEN.

G.O.C. went to General SANDILAND'S H.Qrs. near Hill 60 and amplified the instructions given in the wire ordering his advance. 104th Infantry Brigade commenced to move at 1230 hours.

At 1205 hours a message was received that the 29th Division had been driven out of GHELUWE but were attacking again that afternoon. This message was sent on to G.O.C. at General SANDILAND'S Hd.Qrs. and communicated to General SANDILANDS, who was instructed to get in touch with his neighbouring Brigadiers as soon as possible and arrange concerted action.

At 1300 hours the following forecast of movements was communicated to G.O.C. by B.G.G.S. XIX Corps :-
(A) 30th Division relieves 35th Division on 1st October from LES CASERNES P.29.b. to WERVICQ ST.JANS BEEK
(B) 35th Division hold WERVICQ to MENIN.
(C) 34th Division move to ZANDVOORDE Area on 1st October.
(D) 34th Division relieves 104th Brigade WERVICQ-MENIN on 2nd October.
(E) 41st Division go behind 35th Division and take over MENIN to WEVELGHEM.

AT 1340 hours a detailed message was received from General POLLARD giving the situation at 1030 hours showing that the 106th Infantry Brigade supported by 105th Infantry Brigade had had heavy fighting in front of WERVICQ and was held up by a line of trenches and pill-boxes just North of the railway. Casualties were reported heavy and no further advance could be made without artillery support.

This message was confirmed and amplified later by G.S.O. 3 showing that most of the troops at General POLLARD'S disposal were in . line and becoming very weak. Later the following definite line was given showing that General POLLARD had reached his point of junction with the 41st Division at LES CASERNES.

" Line now runs P.24.b.85.80 - P.24.d.70.75 - P.24.d.
" 25.00 - P.30.a.70.50 - P.30.a.00.30 LES CASERNES with
" forward posts at P.24.d.75.00 and Q.19.c.10.55. Enemy
" reported trying to dribble round left of Royal Scots about
" P.24.c.8.1. Field guns of 157 and 159 now in action."

At 1530 hours a message was sent to General POLLARD that heavy artillery would bombard trench in Q.20.a. from 1600 hours to 1630 hours also the LYS Bridges in WERVICQ. It was also arranged that 157 Artillery Brigade should be affiliated to 104 Infantry Brigade and 159 Artillery Brigade to 106th Infantry Brigade and act under direct instructions of Brigadiers. C.R.A. sent a mounted Officer to ensure that proper liaison had been secured and G.S.O. 2 sent up to keep touch with the situation.

At 1615 hours a message was received from General POLLARD that under the circumstances it would not be possible to distribute his forces on a two-Brigade front or to extend his Left to REEKE. Accordingly the following message was sent at 1640 hours :-

" Make best arrangements possible for tonight.
" Essential to join up to REEKE by tomorrow to enable us to
" hand over line to another Division. SANDILANDS coming
" up on your Left may lessen pressure and enable you to
" extend. German retirement tonight probable. Our heavy
" artillery will bombard WERVICQ South of railway tonight."

A letter was sent by Special D.R. (mounted) to General POLLARD regarding situation and future movements.

At 2000 hours in consequence of a report brought back by G.S.O.2 regarding progress of 104th Infantry Brigade and of weakness of the mixed force under General POLLARD caused by heavy casualties the following message was sent:-

" Boundary between 104th Brigade and General POLLARD'S
" force will be the beeke in Q.14.d. and Q.20.a. Hill
" between this beeke and REEKE Q.20.b. will be taken by 104th
" Brigade. Left of 104th Brigade must be in touch with 29th
" Division about Q.17.c. 1,000 yards West of CONCOU."

At 2130 hours a message was received from General SANDILANDS to the effect that the situation was not clear on his Left. Part of 29th Division had been met North of AMERICA CABARET and others had been seen coming back from still further North (Q.1.c.) Heavy enemy machine gun fire had been encountered from Q.7.b central just East of the CABARET. There was no chance of reaching the final objective that night.

At 2215 hours a wire was sent to Corps giving situation and explaining that Left of 104th Infantry Brigade would be unable to extend further East than 1,000 yards West of CONCOU, and asking that 29th Division should join up at that point.

SUMMARY OF LYS OPERATIONS.

General POLLARD'S report on the operations is as follows:--

"The advance was resumed at 0615 hours in the following order:--
12th H.L.I. (Right) and 18th H.L.I. (Left) to attack.
Cheshire Regt. (Right) and 17th Royal Scots (Left) in support.
Sherwood Foresters and N.Staffords (in that order) in reserve.

The weather was bad with heavy rain and strong wind. The attack progressed well up to WERVICQ, some elements entering the outskirts of that town, but the enemy opened an exceedingly severe M.G. fire, having waited to let us get well in, and, in some places, through his line and his very strong wire. About 0900 hours Brigade Hd.Qrs. having arrived at P.10.a.6.3. and communication to the rear being through I Proceeded forward with B.G.C. 105th Infantry Brigade to investigate the situation.

Finding that the attack was held up by severe machine gun fire and many casualties incurred, I ordered the advance not to be resumed without artillery support and returned to P.10.a.6.3 to arrange. The line was then on the ridge N. of WERVICQ about the railway line. Support from such artillery as was available was arranged but the advance was unable to be resumed without undue loss. The line was maintained during the night."

From other reports it appears that there are strong defences around WERVICQ forming part of the GHELUVE Switch and that there were a large number of machine guns firing from the upper stoReys of houses in WERVICQ.

Meantime the 104th Infantry Brigade moving via TENBRIELEN and AMERICA CABARET towards GHELUWE with the intention of moving from a line East of AMERICA CABARET, South Eastwards to the WERVICQ-GHELUWE road as a first objective, found that the 29th Division were not as far forward as believed and eventually encountered heavy opposition just East of AMERICA CABARET, thus at nightfall being checked in a line facing East instead of South east and with their left flank in the air.

Owing to the bad weather artillery had great difficulty in getting forward but eventually both Brigades were up in close support in positions near TENBRIELEN and BLAEGNAERT FARM. Rationing and the evacuation of the wounded was a very serious problem, the carrying for the latter being a very long one through ZANDVOORDE and KLEIN ZILLEBEKE and down to MIDDLESEX Road, the road between ZANDVOORDE and KLEIN ZILLEBEKE being thigh deep in mud.

13. On October 1st the weather improved. G.S.O.1 went up early to visit the two Right Brigades and G.S.O3 to visit the Left Brigade.

At 0148 hours a message was received from XIX. Corps that 41st Division would be passing through 35th Division in order to come in position on our Left, passing behind our line. At the same time the 30th Division was moving in, ready to relieve our Right Brigade. Consequently the country all day was full of troops moving from West to East in full view of the enemy on PAUL BUCQ and other heights on the other side of the river, but he took little notice and concentrated all his shelling on the forward troops.

At 0712 hours the 29th Division reported that they were on the line Q.15.a.5.9. - Q.9.d. in touch with 35th Division on the Right, enemy apparently holding high ground in Q.15.d. and Q.16.

At 0905 a message dated 0705 hours gave the situation of 104th Infantry Brigade at 0545 hours "18th Lancs. advancing in close touch with Border Regt. 29th Division last seen going strong through Q.8.a.1.4. 19th D.L.I. making ground by strong patrols "

At 1115 hours G.S.O. 3 reported from General SANDILAND'S Headquarters that 104th Brigade H.Q. was at BLAGNAERT FARM, 18th Lancs. Fus. on Left, 19th D.L.I. on Right, 17th Lancs. Fus. in support at BLAGNAERT FARM. Left Company 18th Lancs. Fus was in touch with Right Company Border Regt.(29th Division) at AMERICA during the night. Advance started at 0545 hours. 19th D.L.I. were up to ST.JANS BEEKE in Q.20.a. and in touch by patrols with 106th Infantry Brigade. A wire from 29th Division had been received at 0920 hours stating their Right was in Q.15.d.5.8. Head of 41st Division was passing Headquarters of 104th Infantry Brigade (BLAGNAERT FARM) at 0900 hours moving East. Liaison with artillery satisfactory.

This information was passed to 41st Division.

At 1130 hours a message from 104th Infantry Brigade gave the situation at 0930 hours
"Line now runs through Q.13.d. and Q.14.c. Progress still being made. Continued M.G. opposition which is being overcome."

At 1240 hours the following message was received from Corps.
"It is of the greatest importance to the general operations that progress should be made by XIX Corps towards MENIN without delay. 41st Division leading troops who have reached AMERICA at 0740 hours will do their utmost to push forward South of GHELUWE and capture TERHAND line between the WERVICQ - MENIN Railway and the GHELUWE - MENIN road. 35th Division will make every effort to maintain touch with the Right of the 41st Division."

Meantime G.S.O. 1 had reached General POLLARD at 0740 hours with instructions about extension of Left to ST.JANS BEEKE, also about relief of 105th and 106th Infantry Brigades by 30th Division, the cross move of the 41st Division by TENBRIELEN and AMERICA and the orders for the advance of the 104th Brigade. General POLLARD said the extension of Left to ST.JANS BEEKE could not be done before night, casualties were heavy, strength of 105th Brigade was 900 and of 106th Brigade 500.

G.O.C. went up about 1000 hours and saw Generals POLLARD and TURNER in Headquarters just South of ZANDVOORDE and found that there was little prospect of General POLLARD'S force being able to carry out a further attack before being relieved. He arranged that WERVICQ should be bombarded with Heavy and Divisional artillery from 1600 hours to 1700 hours and that patrols should be sent in after dark to see if enemy had cleared, before handing over the line to 30th Division.

He then visited 104th Infantry Brigade at BLAGNAERT FARM and found that the attack in the morning had been checked and another attack was then in progress but owing to bad communications and the heavy going it was very difficult to co-ordinate the times of attack with the 29th Division. The area was full of troops of 41st and 30th Divisions.

Page 12.

G.O.C. got back about 1615 hours and at 1810 hours a message was received from General SANDILANDS dated 1650 hours saying

"D.L.I. mistaken in saying they hold high ground between ST.JANS BEEKE and REEKE. Their Right is on high ground in Q.19.a (instead of Q.20.a. as previously reported). I have no doubt that we are up against GHELUWE Switch which is reported by Colonel JEWELL as consisting of heavily wired trenches and pill-boxes which could only be taken by Infantry with Tanks or systematic wire-cutting by artillery in case of frontal attack. Failing this it must be turned by an advance through GHELUWE."

The Corps Commander came about 1800 hours and said it had been decided at an Army Conference that there should be a combined attack of 104th Infantry Brigade, 41st Division, 29th Division on morning of 2nd at 0700 hours with half an hour's preliminary bombardment. After discussing the situation and seeing General SANDILAND'S message he agreed that the objective of 104th Infantry Brigade should be defined as the KNOLL in Q.20.a. and c. and the spur in Q.15.d. where a post would be established to connect with the 41st Division.

Accordingly a telegraphic order was sent by wire at 1920 hours and a Staff Officer was sent with written instructions amplifying the above as follows:-

"At an Army Conference today Army Commander set great importance on line WERVICQ-MENIN being taken at once. A simultaneous attack is to be made by 104th Infantry Brigade, 41st Division, and 29th Division. Bombardment to commence at 0630 hours, attack at 0700 hours Wednesday morning 2nd October. Objective of 104th Brigade is Q.20.c.2.8. & Q.20.d.3.8. - road as far as Q.15.c.2.2. and afterwards establish a company on the end of the spur Q.15.e.95.20. That is to say that the main objective is to gain possession of the whole of the high ground in Q.20.a. and c. and to establish a post on the spur in Q.15.c. and d. to connect up with the 41st Division. Heavy artillery will bombard the high ground in Q.20. a. and c. and WERVICQ tonight. The barrage of the D.A. to cover your own front will be arranged by you direct with Colonel COWAN who should make it as intense as possible and may use up all the ammunition in his positions. Telegram G.A.136 timed 1920 of 1st October has been sent to you on this subject.

Sent by hand of Lieut. MacIVER M.C. 17th L.F. starting from 35th Division H.Q. at 2000 hours 1st October."

At 1930 hours the relief of the 105th and 106th Infantry Brigades and 157 R.F.A. Brigade by the 30th Division was commenced. On relief they withdrew to near KRUISEECKE cross-roads where transport and cookers met them.

SUMMARY of the 1st OCTOBER.

All day great uncertainty prevailed as to the exact position of the 104th Infantry Brigade and the 29th Division, and it is clear from subsequent events that neither were as far forward as they thought. Both made various attacks during the day but were in the end held up by the GHELUWE Switch which was heavily wired and had a very strong machine gun defence.

The 105th and 106th Infantry Brigades under General POLLARD maintained their line in front of WERVICQ during the day and collected and evacuated wounded, but had suffered heavy casualties and were not strong enough to extend their line to the Left or make any attack in that direction. They were relieved by 21st Brigade 30th Division and moved to bivouacs at KRUISEEKE. Before being relieved strong patrols attempted to get into WERVICQ but found it still strongly held with machine guns covered by artillery.

R.E. and Pioneers worked on the road leading through KLEIN ZILLEBEKE to ZANDVOORDE but it was in a deplorable condition. Beyond ZANDVOORDE the road was good. The A.D.M.S. shifted his line of evacuation bringing the motor ambulances by the LILLE Road and HOLLEBEKE to TENBRIELEN thus greatly shortening the carry.

All ammunition and supplies had to be brought by pack train which did admirable work.

As exemplifying the difficulty of communication and the issues of orders it may be noted that the Staff Officer taking the order to B.G.C. 104th Brigade, who started at 2000 hours with two trained Observers and who knew the road perfectly, did not reach 104th Headquarters till 0225 hours.

14. At 1032 hours on October 2nd a message dated 0900 hours was received from General SANDILANDS :-
" Attack on high ground Q.20.a. stopped. All lost at
" once by heavy M.G. fire inflicting heavy casualties.
" High ground even if taken would be impossible to hold as
" it is machine gunned from three sides including houses
" in WERVICQ. Enemy artillery and M.G's increasing."

In consequence of message received from 29th Division the following message was sent to 104th Infantry Brigade at 1140 hours. :-
" 29th Division . 0940 hours and at MILL Q.5.c.4.4.
" South East of GHELUWE. This turns GHELUWE Switch
" and should lessen pressure on your front."

Reports received from a prisoner captured by 29th Division were to the effect that enemy was ordered to hold GHELUWE Switch. His company of 50 strong with 4 M.G's was holding about 100 yards.

At 1325 hours a message was received from Corps that a large number of enemy troops had been seen moving on the roads West and North-West of MENIN, and that between 0800 hours and 1200 hours 16 trains had been seen to enter MENIN.

This message was passed to 104th Infantry Brigade and orders were issued to consolidate positions held at present.

At 1415 hours a message timed 1315 hours from 104th Infantry Brigade said :-
" 41st Division attacked through our Left last night
" advanced about 400 yards and were stopped by M.G.fire.
" Attack was resumed at 0700 hours this morning but
" according to my information no appreciable progress was
" made by Brigade on our Left. Believe my men are also
" up against GHELUWE Switch. H.Q. Right Company 41st
" Division Q.8.c.5.3. Our Left Company H.Q. at Q.7.d.8.0.
" 18th L.F. at post Q.8.c.0.3. which is now our extreme
" left since 41st Division have attacked."

At 1427 hours a long message was received from 41st Division showing that they were definitely held up and that a heavy bombardment and organised attack would be necessary before the Switch could be carried.

In the afternoon appearances pointed to a counter attack from the direction of MENIN being imminent and messages were received from XIX Corps that arrangements had been made with X Corps to support XIX Corps with two Brigades if the situation required it.

G.S.O.1. 34th Division came in to arrange about relief if ordered.

Corps Commander came in and said that there would probably be a stand-fast for a few days to allow guns being brought up and roads made, and that 35th Division would probably be pulled out to refit.

At 1630 hours orders were issued for 105th and 106th Infantry Brigades with transport and attached M.G. Companies to march at 0200 hours on Thursday October 3rd from present billets round KRUISEEKE to accommodation in bivouacs and shelters South and West of YPRES, and for 104th Infantry Brigade - if relieved - to move to KRUISEEKE Area on relief and subsequently to march on October 3rd at an hour to be decided by the Brigadier commanding to an area South of YPRES.

At 1805 hours definite orders were issued for relief of 104th Infantry Brigade by a Brigade of 34th Division, the 41st Division being relieved at the same time.

At 2150 hours orders were issued for relief of 157 Brigade R.F.A. by artillery of 34th Division.

SUMMARY of the DAY.

The combined attack of the 104th Infantry Brigade, 41st Division and 29th Division at 0700 hours failed, though progress was made in some places. The GHELUWE Switch was strongly held and during the afternoon strong hostile reinforcements arrived at MENIN and a counter-attack appeared imminent. A strong attack actually did take place on a Division on our Left.

The Army Commander decided to call a halt till preparations could be made for an organised offensive, and the 35th and 41st Divisions were relieved by the 34th Division and proceeded to bivouacs and shelters South of YPRES and to KRUISTRAAT respectively.

15. This ends the first phase of the operations, lasting from September 28th to October 2nd.

During this phase the 35th Division attacked and captured the high ground on the South of the YPRES salient on a frontage of 4,000 yards and made a total advance of 8 miles.

The total number of prisoners taken was 1,105, of which the greater number were taken on the first day.

42 guns were brought in, of which 30 were captured in the first advance, the remainder being in debatable ground through which other Divisions subsequently passed. There were still some guns unsalved when the Division left the area. A large number of heavy and medium trench mortars and machine guns and a great quantity of signalling and other stores was captured.

The weather was bad from soon after the start of the attack to the end, with the exception of a few fair intervals. The difficulties of movement of guns and transport have been referred to in earlier in this Report.

Page 15.

Our casualties were as follows :—

By dates.

Date	Officers			Other ranks			Total		
	K.	W.	M.	K.	W.	M.	K.	W.	M.
Sept. 28th.	-	21	-	57	464	31	57	485	31
" 29th.	3	15	-	61	406	37	66	421	37
" 30th.	5	8	1	80	253	43	85	261	44
Oct. 1st.	-	4	-	47	128	4	47	132	4
Oct. 2nd.	-	1	-	9	66	2	9	67	2
	10	49	1	254	1317	117	264	1366	118

By Units.

Unit	Officers			Other ranks		
	K.	W.	M.	K.	W.	M.
104 Inf.Bde.						
17th L.F.	-	4	-	16	123	7
18th L.F.	-	7	-	30	107	2
19th D.L.I.	-	2	-	16	123	7
104 T.M.B.	-	-	-	-	2	-
105 Inf.Bde.						
15th Cheshires	1	2	-	13	116	2
15th Sherwoods	-	3	-	23	89	8
4th N.Staffs.	1	8	-	27	180	32
106th Inf.Bde.						
17th R.Scots.	2	7	1	55	195	38
12th H.L.I.	3	2	-	26	154	4
18th H.L.I.	1	9	-	22	105	12
106 T.M.B.	-	-	-	-	3	-
19th N.F. (Pnrs.)	-	-	-	2	12	-
35th M.G.C.	2	3	-	12	45	4
R.A.	-	2	-	5	49	1
R.E.	-	-	-	2	8	-
R.A.M.C.	-	-	-	-	6	-
	10	49	1	254	1317	117

H.Q., 35th Division,
28th December, 1918.

Major General,
Commanding 35th Division.

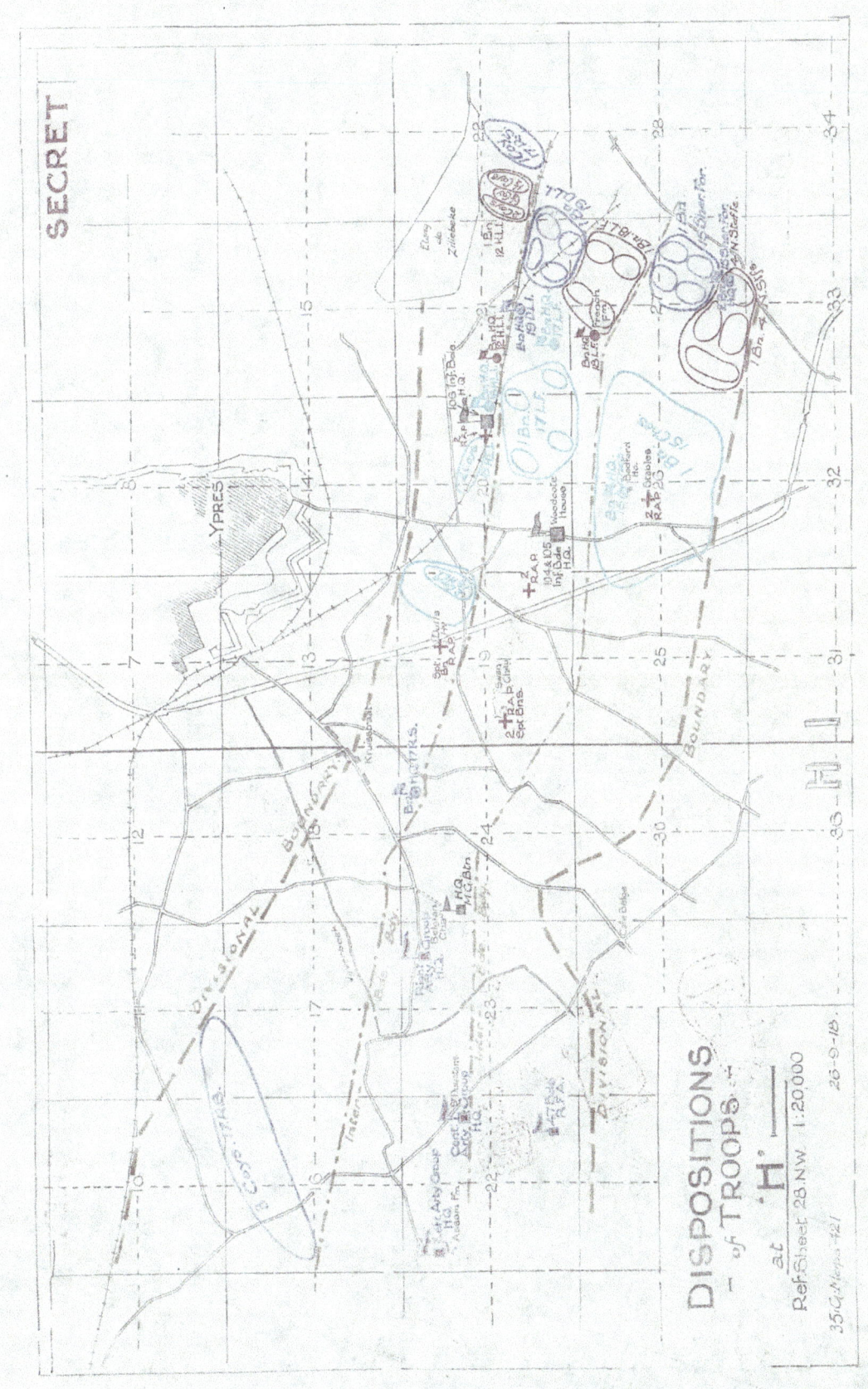

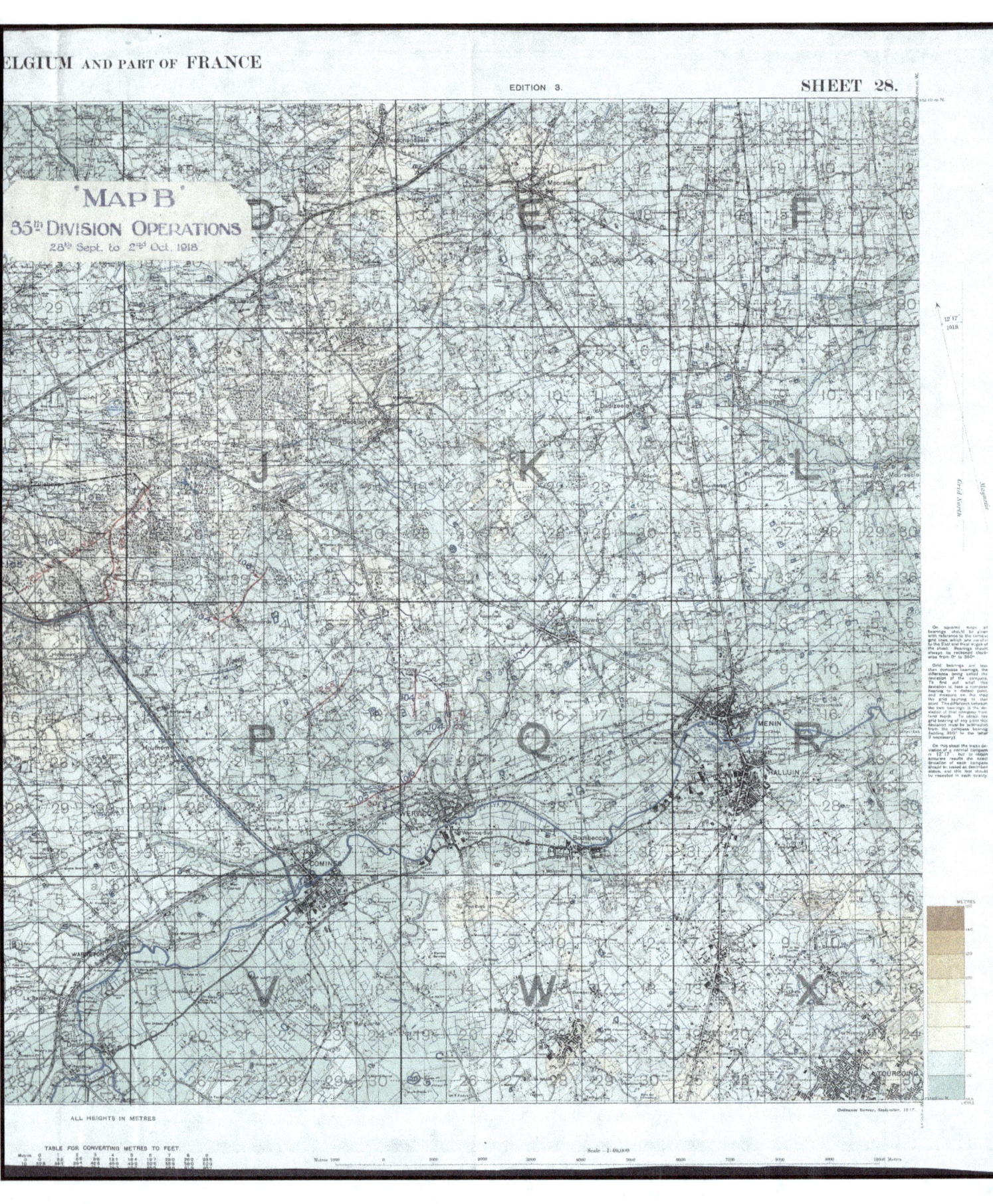

(6392) Wt. W6192/P875 1,500,000 4/18 McA & W L.td (E 2815) Forms W3091/4. Army Form W.3091.

Cover for Documents.

Nature of Enclosures.

Narrative of Operations
31st October 1918
by
35th British Division.

To accompany War Diary, Headquarters 35th Division, General Staff, October 1918.

Notes, or Letters written.

CONFIDENTIAL.

35th Division No.G.122/2.

WAR DIARY.

Headquarters 35th Division General Staff.

NOVEMBER 1918.

Contents.

WAR DIARY (Army Form C.2118. Sheets 1 to 5.)

Volume 4 of Narrative of Operations by 35th British Division covering period 2nd to 11th November 1918.

-o-o-o-o-o-o-o-

CONFIDENTIAL.

35th Division No. G. 122/2.

WAR DIARY.

Headquarters 35th Division General Staff.

NOVEMBER 1918.

Contents.

WAR DIARY (Army Form C.2118. Sheets 1 to 5.).

Volume 4 of Narrative of Operations by 35th British Division covering period 9th to 11th November 1918.

-o-o-o-o-o-o-o-

Original

WAR DIARY

Sheet No.1.
Headquarters, 35th Division, Form C. 2118.
GENERAL STAFF.
November 1918.

(Erase heading not required.)

Place	Date	Hour	Summary of Events and Information	Remarks and references to Appendices
SWEVEGHEM	1		Fine and Hot. Army Commander visited Division H.Q. 41st Division took over bank of river SCHELDT from 106th Infantry Brigade during night 31st Oct/1st Nov. 35th Division relieved by 41st Division during night 1/2nd November. The 41st French Division is now on the left of the 41st British Division along the SCHELDT towards AUDENARDE. 35th Division Order No. 208 issued.	O.O.208
	2		Dull day. Division Commander held a Conference at 6.0 p.m. Brigadiers Commanding 105th and 106th Infantry Brigades and C.R.A. attended. Light Infantry joined the Division, appointed Major A.E.SANDERSON, D.S.O., Oxf. & Bucks. Light Infantry joined the Division, appointed G.S.O.2 vice Major Sir E.P.D.PAUNCEFORT-DUNCOMBE, Bart, D.S.O. (Acting) who proceeds to rejoin the 165th Infantry Brigade as Brigade Major. xix Corps Special Instructions G.213/15/27 of 1.11.1918.	G127. G127/2
	3		Dull but fine. XIX Corps Commander and Major-General attended a Demonstration of bridging with portable bridges over River LYS at COURTRAI. 35th Division Warning Order No. G.127/2 for the crossing of L'ESCAUT and occupation of high ground on Eastern side including MONT L'ENCLUS issued. (Appendix). Preliminary Instructions with reference to Warning Order No. G. 127/2 of today issued. (Appendix).	G127/3
	4		Fine bright day. Good visibility. Wire (Signal) received from XIX Corps at 1205 that 35th Division would relieve 41st Division tonight from P.30.d.0.0 to Q.20.a.8.8. MARCKE, SWEVEGHEM, OOTEGHEM and TIEGHEM allotted to the Division and giving the direction of the right of the 35th Division in case they can advance unopposed as W.7.central with Inter-Divisional boundary between 35th and 41st Divisions who will be on our left Q.20.a.8.8 to W.5.c.0.0. The 30th Division will be on the right. 35th Division No. G.137 orders for relief issued. 35th Division No. G.137/1 issued giving a general forecast of moves in connection with relief. (Appendix). 35th Division Order No. 209 issued.	O.O.209. G137 G137/1
	5		Wet. Visibility indifferent. Relief of 41st Division between P.30.d.0.0 and Q.20.a.8.8 by 106th Infantry Brigade with one battalion 105th Infantry Brigade attached reported completed at 1.0 a.m. G.O.C. 35th Division assumed command of the front from P.20.d.0.0 to Q.20.a.8.8 at 0645. During night Germans fired occasional bursts of M.G. fire from E. bank of river on 106th Bde. Sector. Major-General visited 106th Bde. Brigades continue practise of bridging over the LYS at COURTRAI. Major-General attended Conference at Corps Headquarters at 4-30 p.m. Lt-Col. SHERBROOKE, D.S.O., R.A. arrived to take over the duties of G.S.O.1 vice Lt-Col.THORPE,	

Instructions regarding War Diaries and Intelligence Summaries are contained in F.S. Regs., Part II. and the Staff Manual respectively. Title pages will be prepared in manuscript.

WAR DIARY

Headquarters, 35th Division.
GENERAL STAFF.
November 1918.

Sheet No. 2.
Army Form C. 2118.

Place	Date	Hour	Summary of Events and Information	Remarks and references to Appendices
SWEVEGHEM	5	(Continued).	D.S.O., appointed G.S.O.1 Tank Corps.	
	6		Very wet. Rained all day without ceasing after 1100 hours. Major-General held a Conference at Division H.Q. at 1200 hours on future operations. The Brigadiers Commanding Brigades attended. Wire received from XIX Corps that 35th Division would take over a further part of the front held by 41st Division tonight as far North as Q.21.a.8.6. 35th Division Order No.210 issued. 3 Field Companies moved to area round INCOYGHEM.	O.O.210.
ST LOUIS.	7		Dull but fine. Visibility poor. Lieutenant-Colonel SHERBROOKE, D.S.O., R.A., took over the appointment of G.S.O.1 from Lieutenant-Colonel THORPE, D.S.O., K.O.Y.L.I. at 0900. The latter left to assume his appointment of G.S.O.1 (Head of "G" Branch) Headquarters Tank Corps, to be Temp. Colonel while so employed. Divisional Headquarters closed at SWEVEGHEM at 1500 and reopened at ST LOUIS at the same hour. 105th Brigade H.Q. took over the command of the line from 106th Brigade H.Q. at 1630, the same battalions remaining in the line. Brigade H.Q. of 105th Brigade opened at P.10.a.9.7. 104th Brigade H.Q. moved to TANGE FARM (I.26.central) with battalions at ESSCHER and STACEGHEM. 106th Brigade H.Q. moved on relief to COURTRAI H.31.d.1.6 with one Company at INCOYGHEM.	
	8		Dull day with rain in afternoon. G.O.C. visited 105 and 106 Inf. Bdes. in morning. Corps Commander came to see G.O.C. in afternoon. G.S.O.2 went to officiate as Brigade Major 106th Infantry Brigade. 104th Infantry Brigade H.Q. moved to STACEGHEM 29/H.29.d.6.8. 35th Division Order No. 211 issued.	O.O.211.
	9		During night 8/9th news received that Germans were retiring from line of L'ESCAUT. 18th H.L.I., left front battalion, got first platoon across river at 0530 9th November. During day whole of 104 and 105th Inf. Bdes. with affiliated Companies of 35th Bn. M. G. C. and one platoon Corps Cyclists crossed L'ESCAUT by foot bridges. 105th Inf. Bde. less 4th N.Staffs. plus 18th H.L.I. reached line of NUKERKE - RENAIX as ordered by XIX Corps. Pontoon bridge over L'ESCAUT completed at 2230 and approaches completed at 0130 10th November. Army Commander visited H.Q. 35th Division. 35th Division order 212 issued.	O.O.212.

WAR DIARY

~~INTELLIGENCE SUMMARY.~~

(Erase heading not required.)

Sheet No. 3.
Headquarters, 35th Division
GENERAL STAFF.
November 1918.

Army Form C. 2118.

Place	Date	Hour	Summary of Events and Information	Remarks and references to Appendices
ST LOUIS.	10		104th Infantry Brigade passed through 105th Infantry Brigade and reached line BOEKOUTER 30/N.21.c. - N.27.d.2.0 - N.33.c.5.1 - T.3.a.5.0. (This was days objective ordered by Corps) without opposition. One prisoner deserter of 80th F.A.R. 39th Division, captured. 35th Division Artillery crossed L'ESCAUT. 106th Inf. Bde. crossed L'ESCAUT between 0600 and 1200. R.E. and Pioneers continued work on Pontoon Bridge and approaches and craters in BERCHEM RENAIX Road. Advanced H.Q. 35th Division moved from ST LOUIS to CHATEAU W.4.c.0.0. News received by telephone about 2000 that Germany had accepted our Armistice terms. H.Q. established as follows:- 104th Inf. Bde. LOUISE MARIE 30/S.2.a., 105th Inf. Bde. QUAREMONT 29/Q.34.c.5.9, 106th Inf. Bde. 29/R.31.b.1.9, 35th Div. Artillery 29/W.4.c.3.9. G.A.457 issued 1950 - Orders for 11th November. A fine bright day.	
CHATEAU W.4.c.0.0.	11		Wire received from Corps at 0830 to say that hostilities cease at 1100 hours 11th November, and every effort to be made to reach line of River DENDRE by that hour. Orders accordingly issued to 104 Bde.(G.A.470), G.210 (to other Units) who had previously been ordered to advance to the line EVERBECQ 30/U.9.a. and KALENBERGE 30/0.27.d. The Major-General set out from Div. H.Q. at about 0930 and reached GRAMMONT before 1100 being the first men from 35th Division to enter GRAMMONT. The 17th Lancashire Fus. 104th Inf. Bde. reached GRAMMONT before 1100 and established posts on bridges at V.2.b.1.9 and V.2.b.2.5 and on sluice at V.2.b.25.00. They observed small parties of Germans leaving. Eleven prisoners 6th I.R. 19th Res. Div. were captured in cellars in GRAMMONT West of the DENDRE at about 1200. 105 and 106th Inf.Bdes moved forward H.Qs. as follows:- 35th Division H.Q. 29/W.4.c.0.0., 35th Div. Artillery 29/W.4.c.3.9, 104th Inf. Bde. 30/T.5.b.9.6, 105th Inf. Bde. 30/S.4.b.2.5, 106th Inf. Bde. 30/N.26.c.2.0. Corps Commander visited Division H.Q. during the morning. A dull and misty day with a good deal of rain.	
	12		A fine bright day. G.O.G. and G.S.O.1 went round and visited Inf. Bdes. and battalions. Orders received from Corps about re-adjustment of areas. 41st Division to take over whole of Corps front and 35th Division to be concentrated in Northern portion of Corps Area behind 41st Division. Orders issued accordingly - G.A.554 and tracing. Notification received from XIX Corps of various Armies, Corps and Divisions who will proceed to Germany. 35th Division not included in this.	G.A.554

Sheet No. 4.
Headquarters 35th Division,
GENERAL STAFF,
November 1918.

Army Form C. 2118.

WAR DIARY

(Erase heading not required.)

Place	Date	Hour	Summary of Events and Information	Remarks and references to Appendices
CHATEAU W.4.c.0.0	13		Fine bright day. Troops moved in accordance with G.A.554 of 12th November. G.O.C. and G.S.O.1 went out in morning to see troops on march. Brigade H.Qs. as follows:- 104th Inf. Bde., M.11.c.5.9, 105th Inf. Bde. X.9.a.0.2, 106th Inf. Bde. R.15.d.5.3.	
	14		G.S.O.2 returned to H.Q. 35th Division after officiating as Brigade Major 106th Inf. Bde. G.O.C. visited 104th Inf. Bde. in morning and 105th and 106th Inf. Bdes. in afternoon. Fine bright day. Orders received to move to HARLEBEKE - HEULE and CUERNE Areas on 17th Nov.	
	15		Fine bright day.	
	16		Fine bright day. 35th Division Order No. 213 issued.	O.O.213.
	17		Church Parade of 105th Inf. Bde. at Division H.Q. and presentation of medal ribbons afterwards to 105th Inf. Bde., 19th N.F.(Pioneers), 204th Field Coy.R.E., and 106th Field Ambulance. Dull, fine and cold day. Pipers of 106th Inf. Bde. played at Division H.Q. during afternoon. 35th Division Artillery moved to CUERNE Area. Major A.E.SANDERSON, D.S.O., G.S.O.2 departed to assume duties of G.S.O.2 at H.Q. 74th Division.	
	18		Cold day with some snow and rain in morning. Fine later and warmer. Troops moved in accordance with 35th Division Order No. 213. Major Sir E.P.D.DUNCOMBE, Bart., D.S.O. returned to H.Q. 35th Division to act as G.S.O.2 pending arrival of Major MATTHEWS appointed to 35th Division but officiating at H.Q. III Corps. Rear Division H.Q. moved to HARLEBEKE.	
	19		Very misty day.	
	20		Very misty day. Major G. de C. GLOVER,D.S.O.,M.C. joined 35th Division to officiate as G.S.O.2 vice Major Sir E.P.D.DUNCOMBE, Bart., D.S.O.	
HARLEBEKE	21		Misty Day. Advanced Division H.Q. moved from CHATEAU CALMONT near BERCHEM to HARLEBEKE. Major Sir,E.P.D.DUNCOMBE, Bart.,D.S.O. rejoined 165th Inf. Bde. 55th Division.	
	22		Fine day. Order No. 208 received from XIX Corps re move of the Division to an area West of CASSEL, move to commence 27th November.	

Army Form C. 2118.

WAR DIARY

~~INTELLIGENCE SUMMARY~~

(Erase heading not required.)

Instructions regarding War Diaries and Intelligence Summaries are contained in F. S. Regs., Part II. and the Staff Manual respectively. Title pages will be prepared in manuscript.

Sheet No. 5.
Headquarters 35th Division
GENERAL STAFF,
November 1918.

Place	Date	Hour	Summary of Events and Information	Remarks and references to Appendices
HARLEBEKE	23		Fine day. G.O.C., G.S.O.1 and party of Officers preceeded to ZEEBRUGGE.	
	24		Fine day. Army Commander visited Division H.Q.	
	25		Dull day. G.O.C. visited 105th Inf. Bde.	
	26		Dull day. 35th Division Order No.214 issued.	O.O.214.
	27		Dull day. Division started move to EPERLECQUES area in accordance with Division Order 214.	
VOGELTJE	28		Very wet day. Division H.Q. moved from HARLEBEKE to VOGELTJE. H.R.H.Princess MARY took the salute of 17th Royal Scots as they marched through YPRES.	
	29		Fine day but dull. G.O.C. and G.S.O.1 visited 106th and 105th Inf. Bdes. on the march.	
	30		Misty cold day, but brighter later. Division H.Q. moved from VOGELTJE to EPERLECQUES. G.O.C. visited 104th Inf. Bde. on the march.	

H.Q. 35th Division,
30th November 1918.

Major-General,
Commanding 35th Division.

war diary

SECRET.

Copy No.

35th DIVISION ORDER No. 208.

Map 1/40,000 Sheet 29.   1st November 1918.

1.   Paragraphs 2 and 3 of 35th Division Order No. 206 dated 26th October (Partial relief of 35th Division by 30th Division) are cancelled.

2.   Paragraph 4(b) of 35th Division Order No. 207 dated 29th October (Relief of 106th Infantry Brigade on L'ESCAUT River front as far North as P.30.central by 122nd Infantry Brigade 41st Division on night 31st October/1st November) is confirmed.

3.   The 35th Division will be relieved by 41st Division in the line on night 1st/2nd November. P.30.central - U.10.central EEUWHOEK - Q.9.a.4.4.

4.   The 104th Infantry Brigade (H.Q. P.13.c.4.8) will be relieved by 124th Infantry Brigade and two companies 41st Bn. M.G.C. All arrangements to be made direct between Commanders concerned.

5. (a) 104th Infantry Brigade on relief will move to the area vacated by 105th Infantry Brigade.

   (b) 105th Infantry Brigade will move on afternoon 1st November to MARCKE Area

   (c) 106th Infantry Brigade will remain in the CHEVAL ROUGE Area.

   (d) Instructions for the billeting of 35th Division Artillery; 203, 204, 205 Field Companies R.E.; 19th N.F.(Pioneers); 35th Bn. M.G.C.; 105, 106, 107 Field Ambulances; 35th Div. Train A.S.C., and other Units will be issued by A.A.& Q.M.G.

6.   Completion of reliefs also new positions of Headquarters will be reported to 35th Division H.Q. SWEVEGHEM O.2.c.2.7.

7.   ACKNOWLEDGE.

                                        Lieutenant-Colonel,
Issued at 1300.   General Staff, 35th Division.

Copy No. 1. G.O.C.   14. "Q".
        2. C.R.A. 35th Division.   15. XIX Corps.
        3. C.R.E.   do.   16. XIX Corps.
        4. 104th Inf. Bde.   17. 10 Sqdn. R.A.F.
        5. 105th   do.   18. 30th Division.
        6. 106th   do.   19. 31st Division.
        7. 19th N.F.(Pnrs).   20. 41st Division.
        8. 35th Bn. M.G.C.   21. 35th Div. Reception Camp.
        9. 35th Div. Signal Coy. R.E.   22. Camp Commandant.
       10. A.D.M.S.   23. War Diary.
       11. 35th Div. Train, A.S.C.   24. War Diary.
       12. D.A.P.M.   25. File Copy.
       13. "A"   26-32. Spare.

SECRET.

Copy No. 23

35th DIVISION ORDER No. 208.

Map 1/40,000 Sheet 29.   1st November 1918.

1. Paragraphs 2 and 3 of 35th Division Order No. 206 dated 26th October (Partial relief of 35th Division by 30th Division) are cancelled.

2. Paragraph 4(b) of 35th Division Order No. 207 dated 29th October (Relief of 106th Infantry Brigade on L'ESCAUT River front as far North as P.30.central by 122nd Infantry Brigade 41st Division on night 31st October/1st November) is confirmed.

3. The 35th Division will be relieved by 41st Division in the line on night 1st/2nd November. P.30.central - Q.10.central EEUWHOEK - Q.9.a.4.4.

4. The 104th Infantry Brigade (H.Q. P.13.c.4.8) will be relieved by 124th Infantry Brigade and two companies 41st Bn. M.G.C. All arrangements to be made direct between Commanders concerned.

5. (a) 104th Infantry Brigade on relief will move to the area vacated by 105th Infantry Brigade.

   (b) 105th Infantry Brigade will move on afternoon 1st November to MARCKE Area

   (c) 106th Infantry Brigade will remain in the CHEVAL ROUGE Area.

   (d) Instructions for the billeting of 35th Division Artillery; 203, 204, 205 Field Companies R.E.; 19th N.F.(Pioneers); 35th Bn. M.G.C.; 105, 106, 107 Field Ambulances; 35th Div. Train A.S.C., and other Units will be issued by A.A.& QM.G.

6. Completion of reliefs also new positions of Headquarters will be reported to 35th Division H.Q. SWEVEGHEM O.2.c.2.7.

7. ACKNOWLEDGE.

                                        Lieutenant-Colonel,
Issued at 1300.   General Staff, 35th Division.

Copy No. 1. G.O.C.   14. "Q".
        2. C.R.A. 35th Division.   15. XIX Corps.
        3. C.R.E.   do.   16. XIX Corps.
        4. 104th Inf. Bde.   17. 10 Sqdn. R.A.F.
        5. 105th   do.   18. 30th Division.
        6. 106th   do.   19. 31st Division.
        7. 19th N.F.(Pnrs).   20. 41st Division.
        8. 35th Bn. M.G.C.   21. 35th Div. Reception Camp.
        9. 35th Div. Signal Coy.R.E. 22. Camp Commandant.
       10. A.D.M.S.   23. War Diary.
       11. 35th Div. Train, A.S.C.   24. War Diary.
       12. D.A.P.M.   25. File Copy.
       13. "A"   26-32. Spare.

SECRET.

35th Division No. G. 127.
2nd November 1918.
XIX Corps No. G. 813/15/27.

War Diary

XIX CORPS SPECIAL INSTRUCTIONS.

1. The next task devolving on the XIX Corps is the passage of L'ESCAUT on the front from P.30.d.0.0 to Q.10.central. Orders as regards this operation will be issued in due course; meanwhile the following preparatory work will be carried out by all concerned.

2. **ARTILLERY.**

   (a) Only sufficient Artillery will be kept in action to hold the River line and carry out counter-battery work, the remainder being kept outside the shelled area.

   (b) Vigorous counter-battery work will be carried out. Destructive counter-battery shoots are of even greater importance now than heretofore, on account of the difficulty the enemy has in replacing personnel and equipment.

   (c) Every preparation will be made for placing the whole of the Artillery, with the exception of the super-heavy guns and howitzers, in action, to support the crossing of the River L'ESCAUT and the Infantry advance on the East bank up to the limit of range of the guns.
   Positions for Field Artillery will be selected as close to the West bank of the River as possible, those for Heavy Artillery within about 2000 yards of the West bank.
   Positions will be resected and prepared so that they can be occupied at 24 hours' notice, but no guns or ammunition should be placed in them until definite instructions to this effect are issued.
   One Army Brigade R.F.A. will be attached to each Division on XIX Corps front.
   G.O.C.R.A., XIX Corps will co-ordinate all Artillery arrangements for the passage.

3. **MANNER OF EFFECTING PASSAGE.**

   (a) The passage of the river will be effected on a two Divisional front. 35th and 41st Divisions will at once commence the preparation of their plans and the preparation and dumping of equipment for crossing on the following fronts :-

   35th Division from P.30.d.0.0 to Q.20.a.8.8.
   41st Division from Q.20.a.8.8 to Q.10.central.

   (b) The passage will be effected under cover of :-

   (i) The utmost possible Artillery support including the use of smoke shell.
   (ii) The concentrated fire of Medium Trench Mortars, Stokes and Machine Guns.

   Two extra companies of Machine Guns will be allotted to each Division.

   (iii) Provided the wind is favourable a Smoke Screen from captured German Smoke Generators in position on the left bank of the River.

(c)/

(c) The actual means of passage may be divided into four phases:-

    (i) Infantry means, i.e., Foot bridges of the German type, cork floats, cylindrical floats, petrol tin rafts, etc., the policy being to develop all available means so that the passage may be effected simultaneously by the Infantry at the maximum number of points.

    (ii) Pontoon bridges to take Field Artillery and Horse Transport.
Pontoons will not be put into the water until the infantry have obtained a secure footing on the Right bank. The pontoon bridges will then be thrown across as rapidly as possible to admit of pushing forward Field Guns and Mobile Trench Mortars to give close support to the advancing infantry beyond the range of the artillery in action on the left bank of the river. (Divisions are responsible for (i) and (ii)).

    (iii) The replacement and supplementing of the pontoon bridges by Medium Bridges and Heavy Pontoon Bridges constructed by the Corps.

    (iv) The construction by the Army of semi-permanent bridges. In this connection Second Army G.329 of 31st October, copies of which have been sent to C.R.Es. of Divisions, will be studied. C.E., XIX Corps will be responsible for compilation of the report required so far as the XIX Corps front is concerned, co-ordinating the information obtained by Divisions and special reconnaissances carried out. He will deal direct with C.R.Es. of Divisions on this matter, the latter being responsible for keeping their General Staffs informed.

4.   To assist Divisions in studying the problem and in preparing their plans it may be stated that, subject to orders received from higher authority, the intention of the Corps Commander is, broadly speaking, to carry out the operation in two bounds. The first bound will be the passage of the River and the deployment of the Infantry along the railway on the East bank; the second bound, which will commence after the minimum time necessary to effect this deployment, will be the advance of the infantry under a barrage to a line approximating to that represented by the limit of range of the Field Artillery in position on the Left bank.

5.   The training now being carried out by 35th and 41st Divisions in effecting crossings will be continued. It is most important that the parties of Pioneers and R.E. to be employed on the approaches and means of crossing at each point selected should be detailed as soon as possible and that they should carry out practice at sites closely resembling those selected.

(Signed) C.N.MACMULLEN,
Brigadier-General,
General Staff, XIX Corps.

1st November 1918.

SECRET.

35th Division No. G. 127/2.
3rd November 1918.

C.R.A. 35th Division.
C.R.E.   do.
104th Infantry Brigade.
105th   do.
106th   do.
19th N.F.(Pioneers).
35th Bn. M.G.C.
35th Div. Signal Coy.R.E.

WARNING ORDER.

Map Reference 1/40,000 Sheet 29.

1.   At a date to be notified later the XIX Corps, in conjunction with troops on the flanks is to cross L'ESCAUT and occupy the high ground on the Eastern side including MONT DE LENCLUS.

2.   The front allotted to the XIX Corps is from P.30.d.0.0 East of RUGGE to Q.10.central EEUWHOEK; and is divided into two Divisional Sectors at Q.20.a.8.8.
     The Right Sector, P.30.d.0.0 to Q.20.a.8.8, has been allotted to 35th Division; and the Left Sector to 41st Division.

3.   The 35th Divisional Sector will be divided into two Sub-sectors at Q.19.d.4.0.
     The Right Subsector P.30.d.0.0 to Q.19.d.4.0 including road from VIERSCHAAT to WAERMAERDE CHURCH is allotted to 105th Infantry Brigade; and the Left Subsector from Q.19.d.4.0 to Q.20.a.8.8 including the South-west approach to River in TENHOVE to 106th Infantry Brigade.
     The 104th Infantry Brigade will be in Divisional Reserve.

4.   The three Field Companies R.E. and the 19th N.F.(Pioneers) will be employed to provide means of crossing L'ESCAUT and its branches within the 35th Division Sector.
     One Field Company and one Pioneer Company will work in each of the two Subsectors to effect crossings by means of improvised bridges e.g. cork floats, German Cylindrical floats, rafts, boats, light bridges etc. Further instructions as to sites for crossings and natures of bridges required will be issued later.
     The third Field Company and third Pioneer Company will be employed to make pontoon bridges to take Field Artillery and Horse Transport across L'ESCAUT and their work will not begin until the Infantry are established on the Eastern side.
     The Field Company will construct the pontoon bridges while the Pioneer Company makes the approaches.

5.   All available Artillery will support the crossing and smoke screens will be arranged.
     Medium and Light Trench Mortars will co-operate.
     Two Machine Gun Companies will be attached to 35th Bn. M.G.C. to assist in the attack.

(Page 2.)

6. The R.E. and Pioneers have received orders to practise various methods of crossing the River and the exercise is already in progress.
Infantry Brigade Commanders (105 and 106) will arrange direct with C.R.E. and O.C., 19th N.F.(Pioneers) for combined practices over the LYS while the 35th Division is out of the line.

7. Copies of XIX Corps Special Instruction No. G.813/15/27 dated 1st November 1918 has been issued to C.R.A., C.R.E., B.Gs.C. 105th and 106th Infantry Brigades, A.A.& Q.M.G.

8. In accordance with th verbal instructions issued by the Major-General on evening of 2nd November the C.R.A. and B.Gs.C. 105th and 106th Infantry Brigades will consider the methods and formations to be adopted for the crossing and attack and will prepare plans in outline.

9. Infantry Brigades will reconnoitre Light Trench Mortar positions and arrange to bring up Stokes Mortar ammunition into position at night; the outline arrangements to be reported to H.Q., 35th Division for communication to 41st Division.

10. Further orders will be issued later.

11. ACKNOWLEDGE.

H.Q. 35th Division,
3rd November 1918.

Lieutenant-Colonel,
General Staff, 35th Division.

Copy to :- A.A.& QM.G. 35th Division.
41st Division.

War Diary

SECRET.

35th Division No. G. 127/3.

3rd November 1918.

C.R.A. 35th Division.
C.R.E.   do.
104th Infantry Brigade.
105th   do.
106th   do.
19th N.F.(Pioneers).
35th Bn. M. G. C.
35th Div. Signal Coy. R.E.

PRELIMINARY INSTRUCTIONS.

1. With reference to 35th Division WARNING ORDER No. G.127/2 dated 3rd November 1918, Crossing of the L'ESCAUT within the 35th Division Sector on a date to be notified later, these PRELIMINARY INSTRUCTIONS for the crossing are issued for information and necessary action.

The following is an outline of th arrangements for crossing the SCHELDT. Details will be worked out on these lines and further orders issued later.

2. FIRST PHASE.   INFANTRY CROSSING.

(a) One R.E. Field Company and one Pioneer Company will work in each of the two Subsectors.

(b) There will be in each Subsector eight canvas boats, one cork bridge, one German float bridge and two bridges built on floats made of trench shelters filled with wood shavings; also strutted bridges as required for the subsidiary stream.

(c) The allotment of personnel in each of the two Subsectors is as follows:-

1 German Float Bridge   ) Carried into position and
1 Trench Shelter Bridge   ) constructed by R.E.
Strutted Bridges as required)

1 Cork Float Bridge   ) Carried into position and
1 Trench Shelter Bridge   ) constructed by Pioneers.
Strutted Bridges as required)

Eight (8) Trench Shelter Boats.   2 men for each boat to be found by Pioneers.
6 men for each boat to assist in carrying to be found by Infantry of the Subsector.

(d) Procedure.

At the fixed hour the boats will be carried down and launched, two on each Company front. One Pioneer will remain on the near bank, one Pioneer will paddle across with six Infantry taking rope, picket, and maul. Two of the Infantry will assist the Pioneer to establish the ferry and will then rejoin the other four who will have pushed on as scouts.

The Pioneer/

(Page 2).

(d) Procedure (Continued).

The Pioneer will then ferry Infantry across in batches of eight as fast as possible.

Meantime the bridging parties will construct one foot bridge on each Company front. As soon as constructed Infantry will be passed over as rapidly as possible both by bridge and boats.

3. **SECOND PHASE. ARTILLERY CROSSING.**

As soon as the crossing is secured the construction of the pontoon bridge at TENHOVE just West of the BERCHEM bridge will be begun by the third Field Company R.E.

The approaches will be improved by the third Pioneer Company.

4. In view of the above the following preparations must be made:-

(a) The points of crossing will be reconnoitred and selected under arrangements made between the Brigadier-General Commanding the Subsector and the R.E. and Pioneer Officers working in his Subsector.

(203rd Field Company is working in 105th Infantry Brigade or Right Subsector and 205th Field Company in 106th Infantry Brigade or Left Subsector).

The crossing immediately opposite the Western road in TENHOVE must be left clear for the pontoon bridge but a ferry boat may be put at this point temporarily.

(b) Places close to the points of crossing will be selected where the material can be hidden and material will be taken up by night as soon as definite orders are received for the attack.

(c) The Infantry parties detailed to carry the trench shelter boats down to the river for the first trip and to form the covering party as described in paragraph 2(d) will practise with the 19th Northumberland Fusiliers (Pioneers) beforehand under arrangements made direct between Brigadiers and O.C., 19th Northumberland Fusiliers.

5. The attached diagram shows the sequence and description of the bridges and ferries to be made across the main stream.

HWB Thorpe
Lieutenant-Colonel,
General Staff, 35th Division.

H.Q. 35th Division,
3rd November 1918.

Copy to:- A.A.& Q.M.G., 35th Division.
41st Division.

SECRET
35th Division G. 127/3
3rd November 1918

DIAGRAM to Accompany PRELIMINARY INSTRUCTIONS FOR BRIDGING

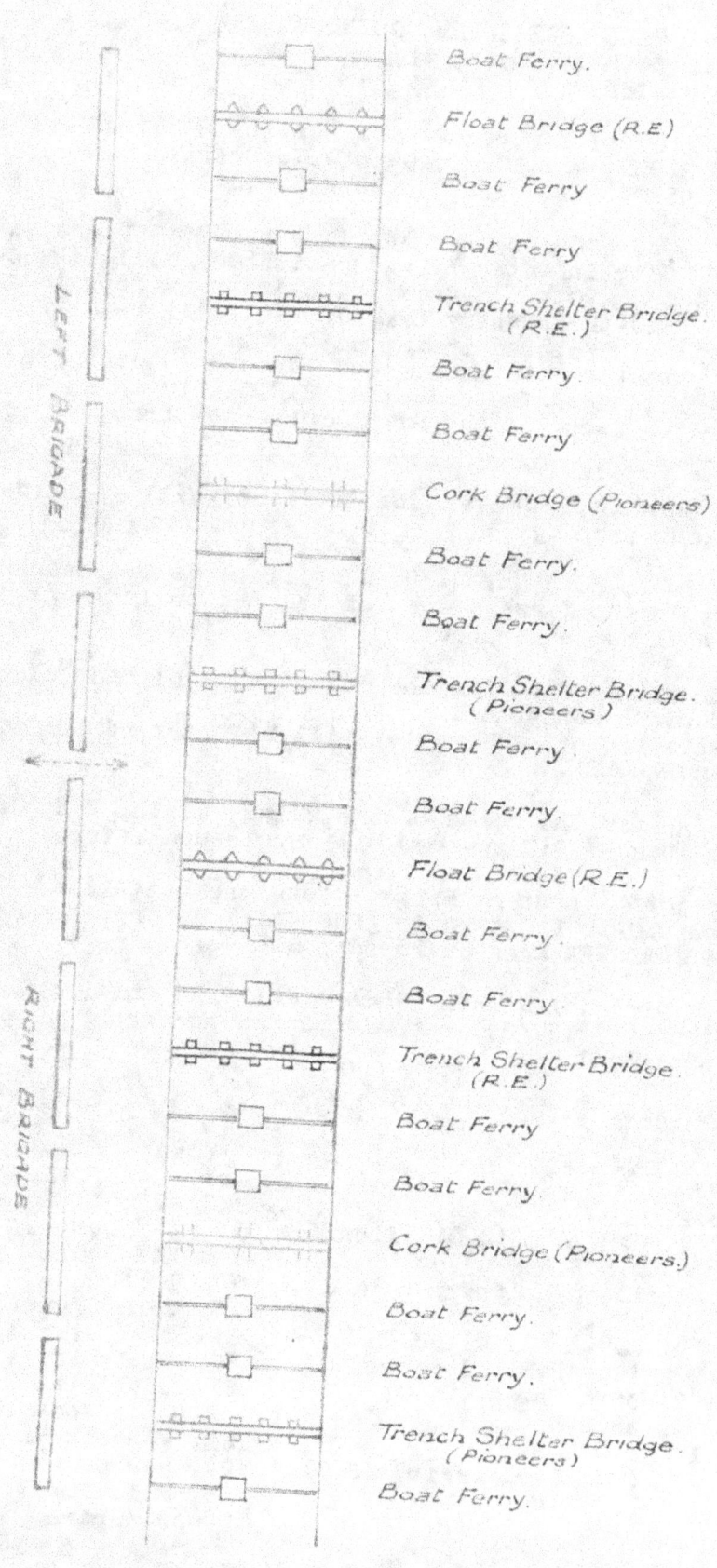

S E C R E T.

Copy No. 23

35th DIVISION ORDER No. 209.

Map 1/40,000 Sheet 29.   4th November 1918.

1. On night 4/5th November the 35th Division will relieve 41st Division from P.30.d.0.0 to Q.20.a.8.8.

2. (a) The MARCKE, SWEVEGHEM, OOTEGHEM and TIEGHEM Areas are allotted to 35th Division; the HARLEBEKE, VICHTE and CASTER Areas to 41st Division.

   (b) The provisional boundaries East of L'ESCAUT are :-
      RIGHT.   P.30.d.0.0 to W.7.central.
      LEFT.   Q.20.a.8.8 to W.5.c.0.0.

3. The 106th Infantry Brigade less two battalions, with one battalion 105th Infantry Brigade attached, will take over the front P.30.d.0.0 to Q.20.a.8.8 from 124th Infantry Brigade on night 4/5th November. 106th Infantry Brigade H.Q. will be at P.13.c.5.8. Troops will be disposed in depth.
   The battalion (15th Sherwood Foresters) of 105th Infantry Brigade will, under the orders of B.G.C., 106th Infantry Brigade, take over the front of the Right Subsector from P.30.d.0.0 to Q.19.d.4.0.

4. One Brigade 35th Division Artillery will go into action tonight to cover the front.

5. The O.C., 35th Bn. M. G. C. will place two Machine Gun Companies in the forward area of the Sector tonight; of these one Company will be in Support.

6. All arrangements for the relief will be made direct between the Commanders concerned.
   Completion of each relief will be reported to 35th Division H.Q. at SWEVEGHEM.

7. Orders for the moves of the 203rd, 204th, 205th Field Companies R.E. and 19th N.F.(Pioneers) will be issued later.

8. The 105th Infantry Brigade less one battalion, and two battalions 106th Infantry Brigade, will be prepared to move forward into the OOTEGHEM Area on Tuesday 5th November.

9. 35th Division Warning Order (G.127/2) and Preliminary Instructions (G.127/3), both dated 3rd November, have been issued to all concerned.

10. ACKNOWLEDGE.

Issued at 1630.

                              Lieutenant-Colonel,
                          General Staff, 35th Division.

Copy No. 1. G.O.C.
2. C.R.A. 35th Division.
3. C.R.E.   do.
4. 104th Infantry Brigade.
5. 105th   do.
6. 106th   do.
7. 19th N.F.(Pioneers)
8. 35th Bn. M. G. C.
9. 35th Div. Signal Coy.R.E.
10. A.D.M.S.
11. 35th Div. Train A.S.C.
12. D.A.P.M.
13. "A".
14. "C".
15. XIX Corps.
16. XIX Corps.
17. 10 Squadron R.A.F.
18. 30th Division.
19. 31st Division.
20. 41st Division.
21. 35th Div. Recep.Camp.
22. Camp Commandant.
23. War Diary.
24. War Diary.
25. File Copy.
26-32. Spare.

G/137

COPY OF TELEGRAM FROM 19 CORPS DATED 1125 4th NOVEMBER 1918.

To:- 35 DIVISION.

G.235   4/11.

35 Div. will relieve 41 Div tonight as far North as Q.20.a.8.8 AAA
MARCKE - SWEVEGHEM - OOTEGHEM and TIEGHEM Areas allotted to 35 Div.
and HARLEBEKE - VICHTE and CASTER Areas to 41 Div. AAA Command will
pass on completion of relief AAA Orders as to tactical boundaries
East of L'ESCAUT will be issued on receipt of Orders from Army but
should Divisions succeed in crossing the river unopposed meanwhile
they will advance to gain touch with the enemy the right of 35 Div.
being directed on W.7.central and the left of 41 Div. on Q.30.c. AAA
Inter-Divisional boundary Q.20.a.8.8 to W.5.c.0.0 AAA ACKNOWLEDGE AAA
Added 35 and 41 Divs. reptd List "A" plus 21, 25, 20, 29, 39 and 7
French Corps.

From:- 19 CORPS.

Time:- 1125.

See G/137/1

35th Division No. G. 137/1.

COPY OF TELEGRAM FROM XIX CORPS DATED 1125 4th NOVEMBER 1918.

To:- 35 DIVISION.

G.285.   4/11.

35 Div. will relieve 41 Div. tonight as far North as Q.20.a.8.8 AAA MARCKE - SWEVEGHEM - OOTEGHEM - and TIEGHEM Areas allotted to 35 Div. and HARLEBEKE - VICHTE and CASTER Areas to 41 Div. AAA Command will pass on completion of relief AAA Orders as to tactical boundaries East of L'ESCAUT will be issued on receipt of orders from Army but should Divisions succeed in crossing the river unopposed meanwhile they will advance to gain touch with the enemy the right of 35 Div. being directed on W.7.central and the left of 41 Div. on Q.30.c.AAA Inter-Divisional Boundary Q.20.a.8.8 to W.5.c.0.0 AAA ACKNOWLEDGE AAA Addsd 35 and 41 Divs. reptd List "A" plus 21, 25, 26, 29, 39 and 7 French Corps.

From :- 19 CORPS.

Time:- 1125.

(2)

C.R.A. 35th Division.
C.R.E.   do.
104th Inf. Bde.
105th   do.
106th   do.
35th Bn. M. G. C.
35th Div. Signal Coy.R.E.
A.D.M.S. 35th Division.
A.A.& Q.M.G., 35th Division.

    For information.

                            (Sd) H.W.B.Thorp.

H.Q. 35th Division,   Lieutenant-Colonel,
4th November 1918.   General Staff, 35th Division.

        Copy to:-   41st Division.

War Diary

S E C R E T.

Copy No. 22

35th DIVISION ORDER No. 210.

Map 1/40,000 Sheet 29.   6th November 1918.

1. The XIX Corps front from V.5.c.2.5 to Q.10.central is divided into three Divisional Sectors, of which the Centre Sector is allotted to 35th Division.
    The 35th Division boundaries on L'ESCAUT with effect from night 6/7th November are from P.30.d.0.0 to Q.21.a.8.6; the 31st Division will be on the right and 41st Division on the left of 35th Division.
    In the forward area the boundaries of 35th Division will be:-

    Southern:- P.30.d.0.0 - W.10.central - thence due East.

    Northern:- Q.21.a.8.6 - Q.30.d.0.0 - thence due East.

2. The extension Northward of the 35th Division left boundary from Q.20.a.8.8 to Q.21.a.8.6 will take place on night 6/7th November; the 106th Infantry Brigade will take over this additional front from 41st Division. Arrangements to be made direct between Commanders concerned.

3. The 35th Divisional Sector (P.30.d.0.0 to Q.21.a.8.6) will be subdivided into two Subsectors at Q.19.d.8.3 instead of at Q.19.d.4.0.

4. The amended boundaries of the 35th Divisional area West of L'ESCAUT are as follows :-

    Southern:- P.30.d.0.0 - P.8.central - P.1.a.0.0 - O.6.b.0.5 - I.31.c.0.3 - along railway exclusive to H.34.b.0.8.

    Northern:- Q.21.a.8.6 - cross roads at J.33.d.0.8 - H.11.d.0.0.

    Instructions for the movements into the amended area and for billeting will be issued by the A.A.& Q.M.G.

5. On a date to be notified later the 35th Division, in co-operation with troops on both flanks, will attack Eastwards across the river SCHELDT.
    The first objective of the 35th Division will be W.10.central - KRAAI (W.5.d.9.4) inclusive - KLEINHOOGVELD inclusive - LAMONT (Q.36.b.) inclusive - Q.30.d.5.0.

6. The attack of the 35th Division will be supported by five Field Artillery Brigades viz:-

    157th and 159th Brigades R.F.A.   35th Division Artillery.
    119th Army Brigade R.F.A.
    152nd and 160th Brigades R.F.A.   34th Division Artillery.

    The three Brigades R.F.A. last named will be attached to the 35th Division, but the 34th Division Artillery will not cross L'ESCAUT.

    The 4th Heavy Artillery Brigade will be affiliated to 35th Division.

7/

War Diary

SECRET.

Copy No. 22

<u>35th DIVISION No. 211.</u>

8th November 1918.

1. The remainder of 105th and 106th Infantry Brigades, 19th N.F. (Pioneers), 35th Bn. M.G.C., and two Companies 101st Bn. M.G.C. will move to the forward area on 9th November in accordance with attached table.

2. Units of above formations will be accommodated within the areas already allotted by 35th Division "Q".

3. (a) The distances laid down in S.S.724 paragraph 19 will be strictly adhered to.

(b) Troops moving East of the line OOTEGHEM - INGOYGHEM will not move East of this line as long as visibility is possible from the MONT L'ENCLUS RIDGE, South of L'ESCAUT River.

4. Completion of moves will be reported by wire to Headquarters 35th Division.

5. ACKNOWLEDGE.

H Elmhirst

Lieutenant-Colonel,
General Staff, 35th Division.

Issued at 1700.

Copy No. 1. G.O.C.	14. "Q".
2. C.R.A. 35th Division.	15. XIX Corps.
3. C.R.E. do.	16. XIX Corps.
4. 104th Infantry Brigade.	17. 10 Sqdn. R.A.F.
5. 105th do.	18. 30th Division.
6. 106th do.	19. 31st Division.
7. 19th N.F.(Pioneers).	20. 41st Division.
8. 35th Bn. M.G.C.	21. Camp Commandant.
9. 35th Div. Signal Coy.R.E.	22. War Diary.
10. A.D.M.S.	23. War Diary.
11. 35th Div. Train, A.S.C.	24. File Copy.
12. D.A.P.M.	25. 101st Bn. M.G.C.
13. "A"	26-33. Spare.

TURN OVER.

TABLE OF MOVES, 9.11.18.

To accompany 35th Division Order No. 211 dated 8th November 1918.

Serial No.	Unit.	From.	To.	Route.	Under Orders of.	Instructions.
1.	19th N.F. less 1 Coy.	COURTRAI.	Area P.2. & 3.	SWEVEGHEM – 0.3.a.0.4 – 0.1.c.4.5 – 0.1.b.0.4.	O.C., 19th N.F. (Pioneers).	To be clear of COURTRAI by 0030. 1130
2.(a)	35th Bn. M.G.C. less 2 Coys.	COURTRAI	Area P.8;9;15; within Divisional boundary.	SWEVEGHEM – 0.3.a.0.4 – OOTEGHEM.	O.C. 35th Bn.M.G.C.	To be clear of COURTRAI by 1030.
(b)	101st Bn. M.G.C.					
3.	4th Bn. N.Staffs	COURTRAI	Right forward area.		B.G.C. 105th Inf. Bde.	Not to leave COURTRAI before 1030
4.	2 Battalions 106 Inf. Bde.	COURTRAI	Left forward area.		B.G.C. 106th Inf. Bde.	1130

War Diary

S E C R E T.

Copy No. 22

35th DIVISION ORDER No. 212.

Map 1/40,000 Sheet 29.   9th November 1918.

1. **INFORMATION.**

    At a date to be notified later the 35th Division in conjunction with the 31st Division on the right and the 41st Division on the left are to force the passage of the SCHELDT and occupy the high ground on the Eastern side including MONT D'ENCLUS.

2. **BOUNDARIES AND OBJECTIVE.**

    The boundaries of the 35th Division are as follows:-

    Right Boundary.   P.30.d.0.0 - W.10.central - thence due East.

    Inter-Brigade Boundary.   Q.19.d.8.3 - QUAREMONT Church (Q.34.a.3.2) - road junction W.5.b.9.2.

    Left Boundary.   Q.21.a.8.6 - Q.30.d.0.0 - thence due East.

    Objective: W.10.central - KRAAI (W.5.d.) inclusive - KLEIN HOOGVELD (Q.36) inclusive - LAMONT (Q.36.) inclusive - Q.30.d.5.0.

3. **INTENTION.**

    The attack will be carried out by the 105th Infantry Brigade on the right, 106th Infantry Brigade on the left, 104th Infantry Brigade in Reserve.

    The actual attack on the Divisional front will be supported by five Brigades Field Artillery, one Brigade Heavy Artillery and eight Medium Trench Mortars.

    In addition the Corps is arranging for neutralization of hostile batteries and for masking the high ground by smoke.

4. **PHASES.**

    The operations will be divided into three phases - Preparatory Phase, Phase I, and Phase II, each of which is dealt with separately below.

5. **PREPARATORY PHASE.**

    In the preparatory phase the following arrangements will be carried out. These have been dealt with in separate orders.

    (a) Material for eight bridges and eight ferries will be in position by the night 8/9th November and for the remaining ferries by the night 9/10th November. One company R.E. and one company Pioneers with pontoon equipment will remain in INGOYGHEM. (Vide 35th Division Letters No. G.127/3 dated 3.11.18 and G.127/4 dated 8.11.18).

    (b) On evening of 9th November the six battalions of 105th and 106th Infantry Brigades will be distributed in depth within the

Divisional/

(Page 2).

Divisional boundaries between squares J.31., P.1. and the River (Vide 35th Division Order No.211 dated 8.11.18).

(c) By midnight 10/11th November the Artillery will be in position under arrangements made by C.R.A.

(d) By the evening of 9th November the 35th Bn. Machine Gun Corps and two Companies 101st Bn. Machine Gun Corps will be assembled in an area near INGOYGHEM assigned to them by "Q" and by midnight on 10/11th November they will be in position to cover the attack by barrage fire (Vide paragraph 6(c)).

6. PHASE I.

(a) <u>General Programme</u>. After dark on the night of 10/11th November boats for ferried and as much bridging equipment as possible will be moved forward as far as can be done without alarming the enemy so as to shorten the final carry. Most of this should be got across the RIJTGRACHT backwater and strutted bridges should be placed in position over the RIJTGRACHT during the night. If possible a footbridge will be placed over the main stream at BERCHEM.

At "G" hour the Artillery barrage will commence and at the same time the boats will be carried down and sixteen ferries established. Also work will be commenced on the 8 footbridges. One company from the Reserve Battalion of each Infantry Brigade will be detailed to assist in carrying down the heavier type bridge (2 platoons with the Field Company and 2 platoons with the Pioneer Company). This company will only carry forward the material to the river bank and will then be collected to rejoin its battalion.

The Infantry will cross by ferry and bridge and will attack and gain the line of the railway where it will be formed up ready for Phase II. The Artillery and Machine Guns will cover this advance as laid down in paragraphs 6(b) and (c).

As soon as the Infantry crossing is effected the Field Company and the Pioneer Company with the pontoon equipment will move forward from INGOYGHEM to TENHOVE and will commence construction of the pontoon bridge. The two Field Companies and two Pioneer Companies which had previously been working on the footbridges will in addition be at the C.R.E's disposal for constructing the approaches.

(b) <u>Artillery</u>. In the right Subsector the Artillery barrage will fall on the Canal Bank for 3 minutes and will then creep forward to a line 250 yards from the Canal where it will dwell for 15 minutes. It will then creep forward by lifts of 100 yards in 2 minutes to 250 yards beyond the railway where it will form a protective barrage parallel to the railway. In the initial stages Heavy Artillery and 2 6" T.Ms. will fire on the railway; Machine Guns at post (Q.32.a.70.90) will be picketed by 4.5" Howitzers.

In the Left Subsector the barrage will fall on a line 200 yards from the Canal Bank and dwell there 6 minutes and then creep forward till it forms a line of barrage along the MEULEBEKE and the front of BERCHEM Village where it will remain till "G" plus 30 minutes.

A box barrage will be formed during this time at each end of the village as shewn in the barrage Map. At "G" plus 30 the two sides of the box barrage will close towards the centre

of the village/

(Page 3).

of the village by short lifts, the frontal barrage shortening as the sides close in and the barrage along the MEULEBEKE on Southern side of the village moving towards the railway.

As soon as the sides of the barrage have closed to the centre of the village the barrage will jump to the line of the railway and then to a protective barrage 250 yards forward of the railway.

In the initial stages Heavy Artillery will fire on the railway.

4.5" Howitzers and 6" Howitzers will fire on the trench shown in air photos along the front of the village between the village and the Canal.

6" Stokes will fire on the houses at centre of the village which enfilade the road leading to TENHOVE and also on the MILL in Q.20.d.30.00.

(c) <u>Machine Guns.</u> Under arrangements made by O.C., 35th Bn. M.G.C. 4 companies machine guns will fire a barrage for the first 10 minutes on the line of the DORPBEKE - MEULEBEKE - front edge of BERCHEM, then on the line of the railway from "G" plus 10 to "G" plus 25 and then till "G" plus 50 on areas behind the line of protective barrage especially on roads leading towards the South-east up to the limit of range.

O.C., 35th Bn. M.G.C. will arrange direct with Brigadiers as to position of the last waves of Infantry and make the necessary arrangements for safety clearance.

After Phase I is complete two companies will be prepared to cross the river and go forward, one company being affiliated to each Infantry Brigade. These companies in moving forward must give precedence at the bridges and the roads to Artillery.

(d) <u>Infantry.</u> The 105th and 106th Infantry Brigades will capture BERCHEM and the line of the railway and re-organize for the second Phase under arrangements made by Brigadiers.

The 104th Infantry Brigade will stand by and as soon as the crossing is effected will move forward so that its leading battalion may reach the line of the TENHOVE - MOLENHOEK Road by the time the second Phase commences.

The Brigade will at once commence crossing and will establish itself on the far bank about the line of the railway ready to move forward in support if required or to take up the advance on the following day.

(e) <u>R.E. and Pioneers</u> will move forward from INGOYGHEM as soon as it is clear that the crossing has been made and will construct a pontoon bridge for Artillery at Q.20.a.7.7 leaving room opposite the road leading through BERCHEM for a heavy type bridge to be constructed by Corps.

7. PHASE II.

(a) <u>General Programme.</u> The further attack up to the objective given in the Map already issued and described in paragraph 2 will commence at "H" hour, under a creeping barrage arranged by XIX Corps. The objective line given does not terminate the operations but merely this Phase. Orders may be issued for an advance beyond this line either by the leading Brigades or by the Reserve Brigade. These orders will not be given till Artillery has crossed the river and is ready to support the further advance.

Infantry will therefore establish themselves on the given line pushing forward patrols as the Artillery barrage searches forward.

A Cavalry Regiment is being pushed forward under Corps

arrangements/

(Page 4).

arrangements as soon as the high ground is secured.

One Artillery Brigade, two mobile 6" T.Ms. and one Machine Gun Company will be affiliated to each Brigade as soon as they can cross the river. These will report to Infantry Brigadiers at their report centres at the Church at QUAREMONT.

(b) <u>Artillery.</u> The barrage will come down at "H"; the first lift will be at "H" plus 5 minutes and rate of advance will be 100 yards in three minutes with additional pauses of 10 minutes (i.e. 13 minutes) every 1000 yards. At 300 yards beyond the objective the barrage will pause for ten minutes and then search forward to limit of range.

4.5" Howitzer batteries and 6" Howitzer batteries will engage selected points in advance of the 18-pr barrage under arrangements made by C.R.A.

As soon as the barrage is completed and the pontoon bridge is ready for traffic 35th Divisional Artillery and 119th Army Brigade R.F.A. will cross the river, 159th Brigade R.F.A. being affiliated to 105th Infantry Brigade, 119th Army Brigade R.F.A. to 106th Infantry Brigade and 157th Brigade R.F.A. being in Divisional Reserve.

The two Brigades 34th Divisional Artillery (152nd and 160th Brigades R.F.A.) will stand fast covering the Divisional front till further orders.

(c) The Infantry advance will be carried out under arrangements made by Brigadiers.

Liaison Posts will be established on the flanks of Brigades with Brigades on right and left on the line of each pause of the barrage.

The leading Brigades will establish a post at the Church at QUAREMONT which will be able to direct Liaison Officers, runners etc. to the Headquarters selected by Brigadiers.

104th Infantry Brigade will establish Headquarters in or near TENHOVE with a post at the Cross Roads in TENHOVE (Q.14.c.4.2) for a similar purpose.

(d) <u>Machine Guns.</u> Two Companies will move forward as early as possible after the pontoon bridge is made (giving precedence to Artillery) and will report to the Brigadiers to whom affiliated at QUAREMONT.

Remainder will be in Divisional Reserve. They will not cross the River until orders are issued.

(e) <u>Front Line Transport.</u> In view of the congestion of traffic till further bridges are constructed the only First Line Transport that will in the first instance be allowed across the bridge at TENHOVE will be cookers and S.A.A. limbers of the two leading Brigades. These will be sent over after the Artillery Brigades and Machine Gun Companies have crossed.

8. <u>PRISONERS.</u>

The Divisional Prisoners of War Cage will be at P.10.d.8.5. Prisoners of War will be sent by Infantry Brigades to the Cage, where they will be taken over by escorts provided by D.A.P.M.

9. AEROPLANES/

(Page 5).

9. **AEROPLANES.**

(a) O.C. No.10.Squadron R.A.F. is arranging for a Contact Aeroplane (marked by one black flap projecting from each lower plane, also a streamer from the tail) to fly along the front at 0705, 0745, 0825 and 0900, and subsequently as ordered by XIX Corps. Troops will show their positions by lighting red flares, flashing tin discs, or by exposing strips when the aeroplane demands recognition signs by sounding an "A" in Morse on the KLAXON Horn or by firing a single WHITE light.
Headquarters of Infantry Brigades and Battalions will mark their position by means of ground signal sheets and strips. They will communicate by means of the POPHAM T PANEL.

(b) A Counter-attack Aeroplane will be in the air from daylight onwards on "J" Day. If hostile troops are observed massing apparently for counter-attack the pilot will drop a red parachute flare in the direction from which the counter attack is expected and will also fire his machine gun into the massed hostile troops.

(c) 10th Squadron R.A.F. can drop a limited quantity of S.A.A. Brigades will arrange to indicate the position where they wish the ammunition dropped by putting out strips making the letter "V".

10. **MEDICAL.**

The Advanced Dressing Station will be at P.7.b.3.7 and Main Dressing Station at H.30.a.1.1. Motor Ambulance Car Posts will be at P.15.a.1.0 and P.17.d.1.9.

11. **REPORTS.**

Situation and Progress Reports will be sent by telegram at every clock hour in addition to any special reports.

12. **ZERO HOUR.**

Zero Hour for Phase I will be known as "G" Hour and for Phase II as "H" Hour. Times will be notified later.

13. **SYNCHRONIZATION.**

A Staff Officer from Divisional Headquarters will synchronize watches at H.Q., 105th Infantry Brigade(P.10.a.9.8) at 1500 on "J" - 1 day, with representatives of 105th and 106th Infantry Brigades, C.R.E., and 35th Bn. M.G.C.

14. **HEADQUARTERS.**

Divisional Headquarters in the first instance will be at ST LOUIS with an Advanced Report Centre at WAEIJSHOEK FARM (P.10.a.9.8), where all written reports will be sent.
As soon as the objective in Phase II has been obtained an Advanced Report Centre will be established at TIEGHEM CHATEAU.

15./

(Page 6).

15. ACKNOWLEDGE.

H Sterbrooke

Lieutenant-Colonel,
General Staff, 35th Division.

Issued at 0600.

Copy No. 1. G.O.C.
2. C.R.A. 35th Division.
3. C.R.E   do.
4. 104th Infantry Brigade.
5. 105th   do.
6. 106th   do.
7. 19th N.F (Pioneers).
8. 35th Bn. M. G. C.
9. 35th Div. Signal Coy. R.E.
10. A.D.M.S.
11. 35th Div. Train A.S.C.
12. D.A.P.M.
13. "A".
14. "Q".
15. XIX Corps.
16. XIX Corps.
17. 10th Squadron R.A.F.
18.
19. 31st Division.
20. 41st Division.
21. Camp Commandant.
22. War Diary.
23. War Diary.
24. File Copy.
25. 101st Bn. M. G. C.
26-33. Spare.

G.A.554

URGENT OPERATIONS PRIORITY.

G.A.554.   12th.

41st Division is taking over outpost line on Corps front tomorrow AAA 35th Division will concentrate East of L'ESCAUT AAA Tracings showing new Brigade Areas are attached AAA 105th Infantry Brigade will be West of RENAIX - AUDENARDE Railway by 1200 on 13th November AAA 106th Infantry Brigade will be West of grid line T.1.c.0.0 - N.31.c.0.0 by 1200 on 13th November AAA 104th Infantry Brigade less one Company finding posts in GRAMMONT will not pass above grid line before 1200 13th November AAA Company and posts in GRAMMONT will be relieved by 41st Division at 1400 AAA C.R.E. will move one Field Company into each Infantry Brigade Area after 1600 13th November AAA Billets to be allotted by Brigade Staff Captains AAA 35th D.A., 35th Bn. M. G. C., and 19th N.F. will move on 14th November to areas which will be allotted by "Q" 35th Division AAA Field Ambulances will move under instructions from "Q" after 1400 on 13th or on 14th November AAA Brigades will wire locations of all detected mines not yet removed before leaving present areas for transmission to 41st Division AAA ACKNOWLEDGE AAA Addressed 104, 105, 106 Infantry Brigades, C.R.A., C.R.E., 19th N.F., 35th Bn. M. G. C., A.D.M.S., repeated 19th Corps, 35th Division "Q", D.A.P.M., Signals, 41st Division.

FROM:- 35th DIVISION.

TIME:- 1925

H Sherbrooke
Lt.-Col. G.S.

NOTE:- Completion of move and location of Brigade H.Q. will be reported by D.R. to 35th Division H.Q.

War Diary

S E C R E T.

Copy No. 20

35th DIVISION ORDER No.213.

16th November 1918.

1. The 35th Division will concentrate in HARLEBEKE – DEERLYCK – STACEGHEM – COURTRAI – HEULE – CUERNE Area between 17th and 20th November.

2. Formations and Units will move in accordance with Table attached.

3. The distances laid down in S.S.724 paragraph 19 will be strictly adhered to.

4. Billeting Areas will be allotted by "Q".

5. Completion of moves and locations of Brigade Headquarters will be wired to Divisional H.Q.

6. ACKNOWLEDGE.

Peter Brooke

Issued at 1245.

Lieutenant-Colonel,
General Staff, 35th Division.

Copy No. 1. G.O.C.
2. C.R.A. 35th Division.
3. C.R.E. do.
4. 104th Infantry Brigade.
5. 105th do.
6. 106th do.
7. 19th N.F.(Pioneers).
8. 35th Bn. M.G.C.
9. 35th Div. Signal Coy.R.E.
10. A.D.M.S.
11. 35th Div. Train A.S.C.
12. D.A.P.M.
13. "A".
14. "Q".
15. XIX Corps.
16. XIX Corps.
17. 10 Squadron R.A.F.
18. 31st Division.
19. Camp Commandant.
20. War Diary.
21. War Diary.
22. File Copy.
23-30 Spare.

MARCH TABLE TO ACCOMPANY 35th DIVISION ORDER No.213 dated 16th NOVEMBER 1918.

Serial No.	Date.	Formation.	From.	To.	Route.	Under orders of	Instructions.
1.	17	Divisional Arty. D.A.C. D.A.D.V.S. D.A.D.C.S. H.Q.Coy.Div.Train	BERCHEM Area	CUERNE Area	BERCHEM Eastern Pontoon Bridge - X Roads Q.7.b.8.6 - TIEGHEM-INCOYGHEM - DEERLYCK-HARLEBEKE	C.R.A.	Not to leave present billets before 0930.
2.	18	104 Inf. Bde. 203 Field Co.R.E.	SCHOORISSE Area	BERCHEM (Staging) Area.	MAERCKE - KERKHEM DRIESCH - R.10.a.4.3 - R.15.c.8.2 - R.14.b.3.6 - R.19.d.3.7 - BOOMGAANDRIES.	B.G.C. 104 Inf.Bde.	Not to pass R.19.d.3.7 before 1200.
3.	18	106 Inf. Bde. 205 Field Co.R.E.	BOYENBERG Area	INGOYGHEM (Staging) Area.	R.15.c.8.2 - R.14.b. 3.6 - R.19.d.3.7 - BOOMGAANDRIES BERCHEM Eastern Pontoon Bridge Q.7.b.8.6 - TIEGHEM.	B.G.C., 106 Inf. Bde.	Not to pass R.19.d.3.7 before 1030. To be clear of R.19.d.3.7 by 1200.
4.	18	19 N.F.(Pioneers)	SULSIQUE Area	DEERLYCK (Staging) Area.	BOOMGAANDRIES thence as for serial No.1.	O.C.,19th N.F.	Pass starting point R.19.d.3.7 at 0930.
5.	18	35th Bn.M.G.C.	SULSIQUE Area	TIEGHEM (Staging) Area.	-ditto-	O.C.,35th Bn. M.G.C.	Pass starting point R.19.d.3.7 at 0945 in rear of Serial No.4.
6.	18	H.Q.35th Div. (Q).	QUAREMONT	HARLEBEKE	As for Serial No.1.	Camp Commandant	Detailed instructions from "Q".
7.	19	104 Inf. Bde. 203 Field Co.R.E. 105 Field Amb.	BERCHEM (Staging) Area.	HARLEBEKE	As for Serial No.1.	B.G.C., 104 Inf. Bde.	Not to enter INGOYGHEM before 1100 to be clear of INGOYGHEM by 1230.

Serial No.	Date.	Formation.	From.	To.	Route	Under orders of	Instructions.
8.	19	105 Inf. Bde. 204 Field Coy.R.E. 106 Field Amb.	NUKERKE Area.	INGOYGHEM (Staging) Area.	SULSIQUE-BOOMGAARDRIES thence as for Serial No.1.	B.G.C., 105 Inf.Bde.	Not to enter INGOYGHEM before 1230.
9.	19	106 Inf. Bde. 205 Field Coy.R.E.	INGOYGHEM (Staging) Area.	COURTRAI STACEGHEM HARLEBEKE	VICHTE thence independently.	B.G.C., 106 Inf. Bde.	Not to enter DEERLYCK before 0945. To be clear of INGOYGHEM by 1030.
10.	19	19 N.F.(Pioneers)	DEERLYCK (Staging) Area.	GUERNE Area. HARLEBEKE.		O.C. 19th N.F.	To be clear of DEERLYCK by 0930.
11.	19	35th Bn.l.G.C.	TIEGHEM (Staging) Area.	DEERLYCK	INGOYGHEM	O.C. 35th Bn. M.G.C.	Not to enter INGOYGHEM before 1030. To be clear of INGOYGHEM by 1100.
12.	19	H.Q. 35 Div. (G).	GALLAIT CHATEAU.	HARLEBEKE	As for Serial No.1.	Camp Commandant.	Detailed instructions from "Q".
13.	20	105 Inf. Bde. 204 Field Coy.R.E. 106 Field Amb.	INGOYGHEM	HEULE	VICHTE - HARLEBEKE - GUERNE.	B.G.C., 105 Inf. Bde.	No restrictions.

Map Ref.:- 1/40,000 Sheets 5 & 5A. Copy No. 20

35th DIVISION ORDER No. 214.

26th November 1918.

1. The 35th Division will move to the ST OMER - EPERLECQUES - WATTEN Area in accordance with attached March Table and Map.

2. A Map showing the allotment of the final areas will be issued later.

3. (a) The following minimum distances will be maintained between units on the march :-

Between Artillery Brigades	500 yards.
,, Artillery Batteries or Sections	100 yards.
D.A.C.	500 yards.
,, Battalions	500 yards.
,, Companies	100 yards.
,, a unit and its transport	100 yards.

   (b) First Line Transport will march with units and will not be Brigaded.

4. Billets in Staging and final areas will be allotted by "Q".

5. (a) 35th Division H.Q. will move on 28th November to CONVENT just South of CHATEAU LOVIE, 1½ miles N.W. of POPERINGHE, and on 30th to final area to be notified later.

   (b) An Officer of the Divisional Staff will remain at HARLEBEKE until all troops of the Division are clear of the present areas.

6. ACKNOWLEDGE.

Lieutenant-Colonel,
General Staff, 35th Division.

Issued at 11.00.

Copy No. 1. G.O.C.
∅ 2. C.R.A. 35th Division.
∅ 3. C.R.E.   do.
∅ 4. 104th Infantry Brigade.
∅ 5. 105th   do.
∅ 6. 106th   do.
   7. 19th N.F.(Pioneers).
   8. 35th Bn. M. G. C.
   9. A.D.M.S. 35th Division.
∅ 10. 35th Div. Signal Coy. R.E.
∅ 11. D.A.P.M.
∅ 12. "A"
   13. "Q".
   14. D.A.D. Ordnance.
   15. D.A.D.V.S.
∅ 16. XIX Corps.
   17. XIX Corps.
∅ 18. 31st Division.
∅ 19. 35th Div. Reception Camp.
   20. War Diary.
   21. War Diary.
   22. File Copy.
   23-30. Spare.

∅ Map accompanies these copies only.

MARCH TABLE TO ACCOMPANY 35th DIVISION ORDER No. 214 dated 26th NOVEMBER 1918.

Unit.	From	To 27 Nov.	28 Nov.	29 Nov.	30 Nov.	1 Dec.	2 Dec.	3 Dec.	4 Dec.	Route and Instructions.
106 Inf. Bde. 35th Bn.M.G.C. 205 Fd.Coy.R.E. Under orders of B.G.C. 106 Inf. Bde.	COURTRAI - STACEGHEM - HARLEBEKE.	A Staging Area.	B Staging Area	C Staging Area	D Staging Area	Final Area.				VIA MENIN - Ypres - POPERINGHE - CASSEL - LEDERZEELE - thence independently. Areas to be cleared by outgoing troops by 1130 and not to be entered before 1130 by incoming troops.
105 Inf. Bde. 204 Fd.Coy.R.E. 105 Fd. Amb. Under orders of B.G.C. 105 Inf. Bde.	LAUWE		A Staging Area	B Staging Area	C Staging Area	D Staging Area	Final Area.			
104 Inf. Bde. 203 Fd.Coy.R.E. 106 Fd. Amb. Under orders of B.G.C. 104 Inf. Bde.	HARLEBEKE			A Staging Area	B Staging Area	C Staging Area	D Staging Area	Final Area		
R. A. 19th N.F. Under orders of C.R.A.	CUERNE.				A Staging Area	B Staging Area	C Staging Area	D Staging Area	Final Area	

35th DIVISION.

NARRATIVE of OPERATIONS - November 9th to 11th 1918.

1. On 8th November the 35th Division was holding the Right Sector of the XIX Corps Front, with the 105th Infantry Brigade in the front line. The 18th H.L.I. (106th Infantry Brigade) was attached to the 105th Infantry Brigade, and the 4th Bn. N.Staffordshire Regt. was attached to 106th Infantry Brigade. The front held was the line of the River SCHELDT from RUGGE to TENHOVE, the 15th Sherwood Foresters being on the Right, and the 18th H.L.I. on the Left. The 15th Cheshires were in support about INCOYGHEM.

    The 104th Infantry Brigade were about STACEGHEM, and remainder of 106th Infantry Brigade and 4th N. Staffords and 19th Northumberland Fusiliers, 35th Bn. M.G.C. (less 2 Companies in the line) and 2 Coys. 101st Bn. M.G.C. (attached) at COURTRAI.

    1 Coy. Pioneers and Divisional R.E. were about OOTEGHEM and INCOYGHEM. The 157th Brigade R.F.A. was supporting 105th Infantry Brigade holding the line. The 31st Division were on the Right and the 41st Division on the Left of 35th Division.

2. Preparations were being made and orders issued for an operation to force the crossing of the River SCHELDT on the whole of the Second Army Front at an early hour on the 11th November (vide. 35th Division Order No.212). In brief, this operation was to be carried out by 105th Infantry Brigade on the Right, and 106th Infantry Brigade on the Left, supported by five Brigades R.F.A. and 35th Bn. M.G.C., with two Companies 101st Bn. M.G.C. attached. The 104th Infantry Brigade were to be in Reserve.

    Each Infantry Brigade was to cross by means of eight improvised ferry boats and four improvised foot bridges, which were all to be collected near the points selected for the crossings by the night of 10/11th November.

    The first objective was the line of the AUDENARDE-AVELGHEM Railway, within the Divisional Boundaries, the attack on BERGHEM by 106th Infantry Brigade being supported by a squeezing barrage on the town from the North-East and South-West.

    The R.E. and Pioneers were to move forward from the INCOYGHEM area and start work on a pontoon bridge at TENHOVE as soon as the crossings were made good by the Infantry.

    After a certain pause on the first objective, a

further advance was to be made, under a creeping barrage, to the line of the RENAIX - NUKERKE Road.

3. About 0100 on 9th November information was received by telephone from 41st Division that patrols had crossed the river SCHELDT at various points and found the enemy posts unoccupied, pointing to the likelihood of a general withdrawal on the part of the enemy. This was not confirmed by 105th Infantry Brigade, on enquiry, who stated that there were enemy machine guns still in position along the 35th Division front. At 0500 the 105th Infantry Brigade reported that they were still unable to push any patrols over the river.

At 0500 the 31st Division, on Right of 35th Division, reported enemy machine guns still in position on South bank of the SCHELDT, but four posts established by 31st Division on the North bank.

At 0630 the 41st Division reported one Battalion across the river, and up to the line of the railway - and GRIJKOORT clear of the enemy. A prisoner captured by them stated that they had had orders to withdraw at 0500, and this was corroborated by civilians.

4. At 0700 the 105th Infantry Brigade reported one platoon of 18th H.L.I. across the river and pushing into BERCHEM, without opposition.

At the same time telephonic instructions (confirmed later by telegram) were received from XIX Corps, to make good the line of the AUDENARDE - AVELGHEM railway as soon as possible, and as soon as this line was secured an advance of the whole CORPS to the RENAIX - NUKERKE line would be ordered. Meanwhile one platoon of Corps Cyclists would be attached to 35th Division, and Cyclist Patrols were to be pushed beyond the railway as soon as possible.

5. On receipt of these instructions, orders were issued to 105th Infantry Brigade to push two Battalions across the river up to the line of the railway at once, using boats until R.E. and Pioneers arrived to construct bridges. One Brigade R.F.A. was placed at disposal of B.G.C. 105th Infantry Brigade in case of opposition. The remainder of 105 and 106 Infantry Brigade were ordered to stand by at short notice, 104 Infantry Brigade to move to TIEGHEM and OKKERWIJK. The Pioneers and remainder of R.E. were ordered to move forward to the river and start on footbridges and pontoon bridges at once.

6. By 0925 the 105th Infantry Brigade had two Companies of the 18th H.L.I. across the river and advancing through BERCHEM. One footbridge had been completed on this Battalion front and the rest of the Battalion were following across it, no opposition being met with. The 15th Sherwood Foresters were crossing one Company

over in boats, and one Company by the footbridge, on the 18th H.L.I. front, also meeting with no opposition.

7. At 1015 orders were received from XIX Corps to commence the advance from the railway line to the final objective (previously ordered for the attack on 11th November, viz:- the high ground from MONT de L'ENCLUS to KRAAI and thence Northward) at 1200. On attaining this objective the Corps was to pivot on its Left, and face due East, and then continue the advance Eastwards.

8. By 1225 the 105th Infantry Brigade was established with three Companies 15th Sherwood Foresters and the whole of the 18th H.L.I. along the railway with patrols pushed out beyond, and the advance to final objective commenced. At 1345 the 105th Infantry Brigade Headquarters moved forward to QUAREMONT, and the remaining Battalion (15th Cheshires) was across the river.

At 1420 the G.O.C. 35th Division visited BERCHEM. Inhabitants were returning there from RENAIX at that time and stated that there were 1,500 Germans in RENAIX on the 8th and that they had all withdrawn during the night 8/9 November.

9. By 1700 the 105th Infantry Brigade had reached the objective ordered, without any opposition, and by 1800 had swung forward its Right to the line HIJNSDAALE - KLEINHOOGVELD, and was establishing an outpost line along the line of the RENAIX - NUKERKE road. Touch was obtained in the course of the night, with 31st Division on Right and with 41st Division on Left.

10. By 2000 all the 104th Infantry Brigade were across the river and concentrated in BERCHEM, with H.Q. at TIEGHEM. The 106th Infantry Brigade (less 18th H.L.I) plus 4th N.Staffords) were concentrated about INCOYGHEM.

11. The night 9/10th November passed quietly. The pontoon bridge at TRNHOVE was completed for horse transport by 0200, and by 0700 on 10th November 159th Brigade R.F.A. had been passed across the river.

12. At 0200 on 10th November the advance was continued, the 104th Infantry Brigade with platoon of Corps Cyclists, 1 M.G. Coy., and 159th Brigade R.F.A. forming Tactical Advanced Guard, and passing through the outpost line at that hour.

by 1200 the Advanced Guard had cleared LOUISE MARIE.

13. At 1500 hrs Advanced Divisional Headquarters were established at Chateau 1 mile South of QUAREMONT. By 1600 the 104th Infantry Brigade was established on the line of the St. ANNE - NEDERBRAKEL road having encountered very slight opposition from mounted men, with no casualties.

14. The R.E. and Pioneers spent the day of the 10th in improving the Pontoon bridge and the approaches to it, and on repairing the BERCHEM - QUAREMONT road, which had been destroyed in many places.

15. By 2000 the whole Division was across the SCHELDT. The 106th Infantry Brigade passed through 105th Infantry Brigade to line of RENAIX - NUKERKE road.

16. At 0900 on 11th the advance was resumed without opposition, the 104th Infantry Brigade continuing to act as Advanced Guard.

17. At 0900 orders were received from XIX Corps that hostilities would cease at 1100, and every effort was to be made to reach the line of the DENDRE by that hour. G.O.C. Division went forward personally by car to endeavour to push cyclist patrols on to this line, and succeeded in reaching GRAMMONT by 1100 and established cyclist posts on the bridges over the DENDRE there. These posts were subsequently relieved by Infantry, and the main outpost line was established along the line EVERBECQ - KALENBERGE - OOSTALDRIES.

RESUMÉ.

18. On the 9th November the Division crossed the SCHELDT and gained the high ground 5,500 yards beyond.

The Pioneers and R.E. constructed a Pontoon bridge after a march of, in some cases, 15 miles.

On the 10th, 104th Infantry Brigade pushed on 11 miles, as the crow flies, from the river.

In actual distance by road, the Division advanced about 23 miles between 0600 on 9th and 1100 on 11th, and was able to lay claim to capturing the crossings over the DENDRE before hostilities ceased.

H.Q. 35th Division,
13th December 1918.

HSherbrooke
Lt Col GS
for Major-General,
Commanding 35th Division.

"A" Form.
MESSAGES AND SIGNALS.

Army Form C. 2121.
(In pads of 100.)

TO	106th Inf. Bde. A.D.M.S. Signal Coy.	D.A.D.O.S. Div. Train. D.A.P.M.	C.R.E. Q.

Sender's Number.	Day of Month.	In reply to Number.	AAA
G.A.726	10		

35th Div. G.A.718 of 18th is cancelled aaa Move of 17th Royal Scots to POPERINGHE area will be carried out as follows aaa Transport will move in two portions first portion on 19th second on 20th staging at WINDMILL CAMP 27/E.13.d.4.3. on the nights 19/20 and 20/21 respectively aaa Personnel entrain WATTEN as follows 5 Officers 150 O.R. at 10.30 on 20th aaa 5 Officers 150 O.R. at 10.30 on 21st. aaa On arrival at POPERINGHE Battalion will come under command of Labour Commandant ST\ENVOORDE and will march to final

"A" Form.
MESSAGES AND SIGNALS.

Army Form C. 2121.
(In pads of 100.)

Prefix ...... Code ...... m.	Words. Charge.	This message is on a/c of:	Recd. at ...... m.
Office of Origin and Service Instructions.	Sent		Date ......
	At ...... m.	...... Service.	From ......
	To		
	By	(Signature of "Franking Officer.")	By ......

TO — 2

| Sender's Number. | Day of Month. | In reply to Number. | AAA |

billets as follows a a a On 21st one Coy. to H.Q. 32nd Labour Group 28/B.26.c.6.4. One Coy. to H.Q. 65th Labour Group 28/J.13.central On 22nd one Coy.to H.Q 66th Labour Group 28/S.14.c.central Battalion H.Q. will remain at POPERINGHE a a a A car will report at H.Q. 17th Royal Scots at 10.00 on 19th to convey O.C. Battalion to arrange details with Labour Commandant, STEENVOORDE Car will return to MERCKEGHEM on completion of journey.

From: 35th Division.
Place:
Time:

The above may be forwarded as now corrected. (Z)

(Sd)G. de C. GLOVER
Censor. Signature of Addresser or person authorised to telegraph in his name.
Major, G.S.

* This line, except **AAA**, should be erased if not required.
Wt. W 3253/P511. 500,000 Pads. 1/18. B. & S. Ltd. (E2389.)

Army Form C. 2118.

WAR DIARY
or
INTELLIGENCE SUMMARY.   General Staff, 35th DIVISION.
(Erase heading not required.)

Place	Date	Hour	Summary of Events and Information	Remarks and references to Appendices
EPERLECQUES	Dec.1st.		G.O.C. visited 106th Infantry Brigade in their final area HOULLE and SERQUES with Brigade H.Q. at HOULLE.	
"	2nd.		105th Infantry Brigade reached their final area BAYENGHEM, MONNECOVE, with Brigade H.Q.BAYENGHEM. G.O.C. visited 104th Infantry Brigade on the march, who reached their final area, MERCKEGHEM - MILLAIN with Brigade H.Q.at BOLLEZEELE in the evening.	
"	3rd		Lieut.Rev.A.MOFFAT, 18th H.L.I. took on duty as Educational Officer.	
"	4th.		G.O.C. visited 105th Infantry Brigade, Divisional R.A., and 19th N.F.(Pioneers)	
"	5th.		G.O.C. visited XIX Corps H.Q. 35th Division telegram No.G.A.150 issued.	
"	6th		106th Infantry Brigade moved from MOULLE to MILLAIN area in accordance with 35th Div.G.A.150.	
"	7th.		G.O.C. visited 106th Infantry Brigade in new area.	
"	8th.		Dull wet day.	
"	9th.		" " " .	
"	10th.		G.O.C. visited prospective new R.A. billets and 19th N.F.(Pioneers).	
"	11th.		G.O.C. visited 105th Infantry Brigade training grounds and 106th Infantry Brigade H.Q. 1st.Round of Divisional Football Competition (18th Lancs.Fus3 - 35th D.A.C. 2) played off.	
"	12th.		G.O.C. presented medal ribbons to 35th D.A.	
"	13th.		G.O.C. presented medal ribbons to 104th Infantry Brigade Group.	

Army Form C. 2118.

WAR DIARY
or
INTELLIGENCE SUMMARY.
(Erase heading not required.)

Instructions regarding War Diaries and Intelligence Summaries are contained in F. S. Regs., Part II. and the Staff Manual respectively. Title pages will be prepared in manuscript.

Place	Date	Hour	Summary of Events and Information	Remarks and references to Appendices
EPERLECQUES.	Dec.14th.		159th Bde.R.F.A. beat 4th North Staffs in First Round of Div.Football Competition.	
"	15th.		G.O.C. presented medal ribbons to 106th Infantry Brigade. Mr.H.T.M.STUTFIELD lectured 105th Infantry Brigade on "Exploration in the Alps".	
"	16th.		D.A.C.Transport Competition - No.3 Section Winners.	
"	17th.		Rev.G.A.STUDDART KENNEDY lectured to 106th Infantry Brigade on "Demobilization".	
"	18th.		Div.Train Transport Competition - No.4 Coy.Winners.	
"	19th.		R.A.M.C. and 35th Bn.M.G.C. Transport Competition - 107th Field Amb. and "D" Coy.Winners.	
"	20th.		Infantry Transport Competition - Winners 19th N.F.(Pioneers).	
"	21st.		R.A. and R.E. Transport Competition - Winners 35th Div.Signal Coy.and "B" 159 Bde.R.F.A. Lectures by Dr.VAUGHAN CORNISH and Lord ROBERT Hall.. at	
"	22nd		35th Bn.M.G.C. less 2 Coys.moved to Gas School, MERCKEGHEM. Dull wet day.	
"	23rd.		Mr.G.W.PRIOR lectured on "Educational Systems of Nations" at MERCKEGHEM.	
"	24th		Mr.BRENNAN lectured 105th Infantry Brigde. on "Russia" at MONNECOVE.	
"	25th		Christmas Day.G.O.C. visited all units in the Division.	
"	26th.		Fine Day.	
"	27th.		G.O.C. visited 15th Cheshires, Brigadier-General SANDILANDS Commanding 104th Infantry Brigade and Brigadier-General MADOCKS C.R.A. 35th Division attended a conference with Major General at Div.H.Q.	

Army Form C. 2118.

WAR DIARY
or
INTELLIGENCE SUMMARY.
(Erase heading not required.)

Instructions regarding War Diaries and Intelligence Summaries are contained in F. S. Regs., Part II. and the Staff Manual respectively. Title pages will be prepared in manuscript.

Place	Date	Hour	Summary of Events and Information	Remarks and references to Appendices
EPERLECQUES.	Dec.28th.		G.O.C. visited Corps H.Q.	
"	29th.		G.O.C. proceeded on leave.	
"	30th.		Wet Day. Mounted Paperchase in TOURNEHEM WOOD.	
"	31st.		Brigadier-General POLLARD took over the Command of the Division in the absence of Major-General MARINDIN on leave.	

Holbrooke Lt.Col.
for
Br.Genl Commanding 38 Division

5.1.19

Army Form C. 2118.

WAR DIARY
or
INTELLIGENCE SUMMARY.

GENERAL STAFF, 35th DIVISION.

(Erase heading not required.)

January 1919.

Place	Date	Hour	Summary of Events and Information	Remarks and references to Appendices
EPERLECQUES	Jan.1		Dull wet day.	
	" 2		Mounted Paperchase held by 106th Inf.Bde. near WATTEN. Weather fine.	
	" 3		Captain J.HUME,R.E. proceeded on leave and his duties as Hon.Sec.Rugby and Association Football competitions were taken over by Lieut.G.A.MURRAY, 17th Royal Scots.	
	" 4		Fine day. 35th Division took over care of Ranges in EPERLECQUES and WATTEN areas from Second Army Musketry School, LUMBRES.	
	" 5		Lieut-Colonel BLACKER Commanding 35th Bn.M.G.C. and Major VIGGARS D.A.Q.M.G. returned from leave to B.E.F. Wettest day yet experienced.	
	" 6		Wet dull day.	
	" 7		Mounted Paperchase by R.A., BOIS DE HAM.	
	" 8		Captain R.P.HARRISON, G.S.O.3 returned from leave. Fine day.	
	" 9		Fine day.	
	" 10		Colonel SUERBROOKE G.S.O.1 and Colonel JONES A.A.& Q.M.G. proceeded on leave to U.K. Major GLOVER took over duties of G.S.O.1 and Major VIGGARS duties of A.A.& Q.M.G.	
	" 11		Fine day. B.G.,G.S., XIX Corps visited the Division.	
	" 12		Dull misty day.	

Army Form C. 2118.

WAR DIARY
or
INTELLIGENCE SUMMARY.
(Erase heading not required.)

GENERAL STAFF, 35th DIVISION

January 1919.

Place	Date	Hour	Summary of Events and Information	Remarks and references to Appendices
BOERLECQUES	Jan.13		Dull raw day; heavy mist.	
"	14		35th Division Mounted Paperchase, FORET D'EPERLECQUES.	
"	15		Dull and wet day.	
"	16		Dull and wet day.	
"	17		Fine day. Corps Commander visited 106th Inf.Bde. Paperchase at MERCKEGHEM.	
"	18		Fine day.	
"	19		Fine day.	
"	20		Fine day; frost.	
"	21		Fine day. R.A.Paperchase at MOULLE CHATEAU.	
"	22		Fine day; frost.	
"	23		Fine day; frost.	
"	24		Frost. G.O.C., G.S.O.1 and A.A.& Q.M.G. returned from leave.	
"	25		Fine cold day.	
"	26		Thaw and rain; froze again at night.	
"	27		Bright day with sleet in morning. Cold.	
"	28		105th Inf.Bde. ordered to CALAIS to quell riots. Div.Rifle Meeting which was to have	

WAR DIARY
or
INTELLIGENCE SUMMARY.
(Erase heading not required.)

Army Form C. 2118:

GENERAL STAFF, 35th DIVISION.

January 1919.

Instructions regarding War Diaries and Intelligence Summaries are contained in F. S. Regs., Part II. and the Staff Manual respectively. Title pages will be prepared in manuscript.

Place	Date	Hour	Summary of Events and Information	Remarks and references to Appendices
EPERLECQUES	Jan.28		commenced this day was cancelled (35th Div.G.A.584) Major-General visited 105th Inf.Bde.	G.A.584
			105th Inf.Bde. moved to CALAIS by lorry. At 2300 (about), all Division ordred to move to CALAIS.	
	29	0900	105th Inf.Bde. and 35th Bn.M.G.C. moved by train from WATTEN. Train was taken to DUNQUERKE	
			in error. Train arrived CALAIS at about 1700 and Brigade was billeted in No.6 Leave Camp West.	
		1000	104th Inf.Bde. moved by train from WATTEN to CALAIS arriving there about 1400. Billeted in No.5 Leave Camp.	
			Div.H.Q. opened at No.4 Officers Rest Camp, BEAUMARIS, at 1200 (35th Div.G.A.594)	G.A.594.
			105th Inf.Bde. had posted pickets along the moat to the West of the Mutineers' Camp, No.6 Leave Camp East from evening of 28/29th January onwards, to prevent the mutineers entering the town and attempting to rush the English leave boats	
			1st Life Guards and 2nd Life Guards M.G.Bns. arrived at MONNECOVE CAMP and were administered by 35th Division Rear H.Q.	
		1400	G.O.C. visited General BYNG, G.O.C. Troops, CALAIS.	
	30	0030	G.O.C.Troops Order B/1 received.	
		0145	35th Division G.A.615 issued.	G.A.615

Army Form C. 2118.

WAR DIARY
or
INTELLIGENCE SUMMARY.

GENERAL STAFF, 35th DIVISION.

(Erase heading not required.)

Instructions regarding War Diaries and Intelligence Summaries are contained in F.S. Regs., Part II. and the Staff Manual respectively. Title pages will be prepared in manuscript.

January 1919

Place	Date	Hour	Summary of Events and Information	Remarks and references to Appendices
EPERLECQUES	Jan.30	0730	Conference of Brigadiers at Div.H.Q. Gen! Byng's	
		0930	G.O.C. attended Conference at H.Q. Advd.Div.H.Q. formed at H.Q. 105th Inf.Bde., No.6 Camp West about 1030.	
		1100	104th Inf.Bde.advanced against Mutineers' Camp, whilst 105th Infantry Brigade blocked approaches to the West and North, and 106th Infantry Brigade stood by in Reserve, and blocked approaches to the East. Operations completely successful; four ringleaders were arrested, and remainder of mutineers, who were returning leave men, proceeded up country by train to join their units. The Calais Ordnance personnel, who had also mutinied, returned to work.(For full report see Appendix).	
	31		Quiet day. Troops remained in Camp.	
			G.O.C. visited 104th, 105th, and 106th Inf.Bdes.	
			Complimentary Order G.A.617 issued.	G.A.617
			R.H.Guards M.G.Bn. arrived at MOULLE and was administered by 35th Division Rear H.Q.	

H.S.......
for
Major-General,
Commanding 35th Division.

"A" Form
MESSAGES AND SIGNALS.

Army Form C. 2121
(In pads of 100.)

TO: 105th Infantry Brigade.

Sender's Number.	Day of Month.	In reply to Number.	
GA584.	28		AAA

105th Infantry Brigade will proceed to CALAIS by lorry AAA Lorries are rendezvousing at MOULLE 1600 hours to-day where they will be met by Staff Officer of 105th Infantry Brigade AAA Staff Officer from 105th Infantry Brigade will report forthwith by box car to Base Commandant CALAIS for orders. AAA Acknowledge

From 35th Division.
Place
Time 1340.

(Sgd.) R.P.Harrison, Capt.

CALAIS OPERATIONS.

28th Jan.1919.

1130. 'Phone message from XIX Corps to be prepared to send one Brigade less 1 Battalion to CALAIS to-day - 140 lorries would be at MOULLE at 1600 and 105th Inf. Brigade suggested - Staff Officer to meet lorries - Staff Officer of 105th Brigade to go at once to report to Base Commandant CALAIS to learn situation - 105th Inf. Brigade warned by 'phone Corps informed that Battalions are very weak, and suggest sending whole Brigade.

1230. 'Phone message from XIX Corps - send whole Brigade - Brigade on arrival will come under orders of Base Commandant CALAIS.

1300. G.O.C. Division visited 105th Inf. Brigade and arranged with B.G.C:-

(a) Brigade Transport to remain in Camp until ordered forward by Brigade.
(b) Capt. LYLE and one Officer per Battalion to proceed to CALAIS in Signal Box Car.
(c) 105th Inf. Brigade to establish Report Centre at EMMERY (Road and Railway Crossing) where Capt. LYLE will report to B.G.C. 105th Inf. Brigade
(d) Signals to establish a wireless Station at EMMERY or other suitable spot, and to arrange for communication between this spot and Div. H.Q. A Trench Wireless Set to accompany 105th Inf. Brigade.
(e) Two extra D.Rs to be placed at the disposal of 105th Inf. Brigade.
(f) A.D.M.S. to place one Motor Ambulance at the disposal of B.G.C. 105th Inf. Brigade at 1530, and also to make necessary medical arrangements for first aid, sending such bearer personnel and ambulances as necessary - these to report to 105th Bde at 1600.
(2 M.Os 39 O.R. & 3 Cars detailed).

1311. G.336 from XIX Corps received confirming telephonic instructions already issued.

1335. GA.583 sent acknowledging G.336.

1340. GA.584 sent to 105th Inf. Brigade confirming telephonic orders already issued.

1440. 291 QA1 from G.H.Q. received re 140 lorries at MOULLE.

1520. A868 received from XIX Corps, stating B.G.C. 105th Inf Brigade will act under orders Base Commandant CALAIS to whom he will report.
GA.585 sent to 105th Inf. Brigade repeating above.

1615. 105th Inf. Brigade Order No. 1 received.

1623. A869 received from XIX Corps explaining nature of duty of 105th Bde at CALAIS :- Ordnance strike.

1800. GA.583 sent to 105th Bde repeating above.
1845. GA.591 to 19 Cps - 1118 all ranks 105 I.B. left for CALAIS.
2215. Rang up XIX Corps and told them O.C. Signals had been to CALAIS and found things quiet and that 105 Inf. Brigade were going to No 3 Leave Camp BEAUMARIS.
Corps said they had spoken to Base Commandant CALAIS who said most of 105 Inf. Brigade had arrived.

2220.	T.1 from Gen. Turner 105th Inf. Brigade arrived.
2300.	Telephone message from XIX Corps warning that 35th Division would move to CALAIS on 29th January.
2345.	Division to move less Artillery and Divisional Troops. Entrain WATTEN 0900 and 1000. Transport by road.
2351.	Q.400 from XIX Corps. Orders for move to CALAIS.

29th Jan.1919.

0010	Q.401 from XIX Corps. Train arrangements for move.
0025.	G.348 from XIX Corps. Precautions to be taken on approaching destination.
0230.	G.350 from XIX Corps. 31st and 35th Divisions will come under Gen. BYNG when he arrives at CALAIS. Divisional Commanders to act as circumstances demand till then.
0300.	GA.594. Circulated to all units.
0410.	OO.65 from A.D.M.S.
0523.	BM.196 from 105th Inf. Brigade, reporting Brigade Headquarters at No. 6 Rest Camp and in telephonic communication. One Battalion finding piquets. Remaining two in Camp.
0900.	106th Inf. Brigade and 35th Battalion M.G.C. entrained at WATTEN.
1000.	104th Inf. Bde. entrained at WATTEN.
1200.	Advanced Headquarters 35th Division established at Officers' Rest Camp BEAUMARIS.
1500.	104th Inf. Brigade & M.G.Bn. concentrated in No. 5 Camp CALAIS.
2038.	106th Inf. Brigade concentrated in No 6 Camp West, CALAIS.
2130.	105th Inf. Brigade. reported Car, stolen from O.C. Train this morning, recovered by a picquet of Sherwoods with 5 mutineers in it.
2230.	After much telephonic conversation, No.GA.614 was sent to 105th Inf. Brigade, under instructions of Gen. BYNG, ordering two mutineers -- if answering certain descriptions -- to be released, remainder to be detained.
2359½	Telephone message from G.O.C. Troops, CALAIS, asking for G.S.O.I. to go to Headquarters Troops, CALAIS, and receive orders for 30th. G.S.O.I. received G.O.C. Troops Order No, B/1.

30th Jany.

0145.	G.S.O. II conveyed order G.A. 615 to Headquarters 104, 105, and 106th Infantry Brigades.
0730.	G.O.C. held a conference at Divisional Headquarters with B.Gs.C. 104, 105, 106 Infantry Brigades, and G.S.O.1 attended.
0900.	G.O.C. attended a conference at Headquarters of G.O.C. Troops, CALAIS.
1030.	Advanced Divisional Headquarters established at 105 Infantry Brigade Headquarters. No. 6 Leave Camp West.

Summary from Advanced Divisional Headquarters at 105 Inf. Bde.

1112. 105th Infantry Brigade report by telephone that 104th Infantry Brigade have surrounded southern part of mutineers' camp. The mutineers crowded round apparently quite peaceably.

1135. 105th Infantry Brigade report by telephone that 104th Infantry Brigade are in the mutineers' camp, No. 6 Camp East, and that the mutineers are being divided into two parties.

1150. 104th Infantry Brigade report that "sheep" are coming in quickly, about 1000 already. Sergeant of Scottish Rifles taken and under escort. He and other delegates attempted to prevent "sheep" coming in, so he and the other three were placed under arrest.

1155. 105th Infantry Brigade report that about 2000 in already. Delegates under arrest.

1200. Message G.A.1 sent to 106th Infantry Brigade and stating that 2 Battalions of 31st Division no longer required.

1205. Digest of situation sent to Base Commandant by an Officer.

1330. G.A.2 sent by D.R. to Base Commandant stating all mutineers have given themselves up except four ringleaders who have been arrested.

1340. Advanced Divisional Headquarters closed and returned to Divisional Headquarters. BEAUMARAIS.

1005. Base Headquarters telephoned to ask for present whereabouts of G.O.C. as they had an urgent message for him and he had already left General BYNG.
Told that Major General would probably be found at 105th Infy. Brigade Headquarters, No. 6 Leave Camp West.

1125. 92nd Infantry Brigade rang up and asked location of 106th Infantry Brigade as they were told to route march there and "liase." Told them G.S.O.ii would visit them. Explained situation to G.S.O.ii, 31st Division, who immediately went to 92nd Infantry Brigade.

1330. All "sheep" from No. 6 Leave Camp East moved with equipment to No.5 Camp, where they were fed.

1500. Men for 2nd Army fell in about this hour and proceeded to SANDUNES Station to entrain. Train left about 1600.

1620. Men for 4th Army moved off to SANDUNES Station to entrain. Train left about 1710. Remaining men from No. 5 Camp moved with their equipment to No. 6 Camp East to await orders re entraining.

1710. Men for 3rd Army moved to SANDUNES Station to entrain. Train left about 1800.

1800. Men for 1st Army moved to FONTINETTES to entrain. Train left about 1945.

1900. Men for 5th Army moved to FONTINETTES to entrain, and men for N. area left shortly afterwards. Train left about 2115.

2215. G.A.616 sent to G.O.C. Troops CALAIS stating that all troops from No. 6 Camp East had moved up country, last train 2115 except Canadians and L. of C. Troops, who were leaving 31st January.

"A" Form.
Messages and Signals.

URGENT OPERATIONS.   Priority.
    Sd. H. Smerbrooke,
              Lieut. Colonel.

104th Inf. Bde.	35th Divl. Train.	A and Q.	C.R.A.
106th Inf. Bde.	19th N.F. (Pnrs.)	19th Corps.	C.R.E.
35th Bn. M.G.C.	A.D.M.S.	Base Comdt. Calais.	

G.A.594. 29th.
35th Divl. H.Q., 35th Divl. Signal Co.,R.E., 104th and 106th Inf. Bdes. and 35th Bn. M.G.C. with proportion of R.A.M.C. will move to CALAIS to-day 29th personnel by train entraining WATTEN AAA All wheeled transport by road AAA Extra regimentally employed personnel will not be taken AAA Only essential stores and fighting troops to be taken AAA Troops will probably return in a few days AAA Non-essential stores will be left and supply arrangements made for troops left behind AAA rations for 29th to be taken on Train AAA Rations for 30th to be sent on supply waggons AAA Divl. Train will move by road less No. 1 Company and any other supply waggons needed for details left behind AAA Trucks for baggage and stores will be on trains AAA Train for 106th Infantry Brigade and 35th Bn. M.G.C. leaves WATTEN 0910 (0910) hours AAA Train for 104th Inf. Bde. Signals and R.A.M.C. 1000 1000 hours AAA Leading troops to be at station 1 hours before departure of train AAA Above units of 35th Division will encamp on arrival at No. 5 Leave Camp north of CALAIS--MARCK road about 2 miles west of MARCK AAA Trains on arrival will be met by a Staff Officer Divisional Headquarters 1st Line Transport will accompany units to Railway station and after departure will continue its march under Brigade Transport Officers to No. 2 Overflow Camp CALAIS near BEAUMARIS on south side of CALAIS-MARCK road AAA Route NORDASQUES--ARDRES--EMMERY station to level crossing on south-east entrance to CALAIS AAA After passing level crossing turn sharp to right past Cemetery on to CALAIS-MARCK main road thence to Camp AAA Divisional Train will move independently starting as early as possible under orders of O.C. Train AAA Due precautions should be taken by all Units whilst approaching destinations and if circumstances require positions outside town must be taken up AAA Advanced Divisional Headquarters will open at No. 5 Leave Camp at 1200 hours AAA All units and details left in present Divisional area will come under orders of C.R.A. AAA ACKNOWLEDGE AAA Addressed 104 and 106 Inf. Bdes 35th Bn. M.G.C. 35th Divl. Train, repeated A.D.M.S. A. and Q., 19th N.F. (Pioneers), C.R.A., C.R.E., Signals, and 19th Corps Base Commandant CALAIS.

From 35th Division.   Sd.   H. Smerbrooke,
0250 hours   Lieut. Colonel,
                                 General Staff, 35th Division.

No. 1 Copy.   B/1.

G.O.C. 35th Division.
----

1.   It is reported that O.C. No. 4 and 6 Leave Camp East
has been evicted from his office by men in the Leave Camps.

2.   The G.O.C. Troops CALAIS has decided that the O.C.
is to be reinstated to-morrow. You will therefore arrange for
this to be done with such force as you consider necessary.

3.   The above camps will be occupied by you. It is under-
stood that there are about 3/500 men in the Camps of which a
certain proportion are quite ready to rejoin their units.
All such men will be given the opportunity of doing so. Leave
trains will start leaving at 2 p.m. 30th. ※

4.   You will explain to all ranks under your command that
the camps are being taken over to allow those men who wish
to return to their units to do so. At present they are being
intimidated by men who have just completed their fortnight's
leave in England and who are now demanding to be sent back to
England for an additional ten days in order to be demobilized
out of their firm. Those men who do not wish to return to
their units will be confined to their camp until the G.O.C.
Troops CALAIS has decided as to their disposal.

5.   The G.O.C. 35th Division will report to the G.O.C.
Troops CALAIS at 9 a.m. at the Grand Hotel on January 30th,
1919.

                                Sd.   J.D. Logan, B.G.,
2355.   S.O. to G.O.C. Troops, CALAIS
29.1.19.

No. 1 Copy to G.O.C. 35th Division.
    2   "   Base Commandant,
    3   "   G.O.C. 31st Division.
    4.   Retained.

※ Trains will leave FONTINETTES and CALAIS DUNES Station Siding.
Details will be given later.

35th Division No. G.A.615.

SECRET.

104th Infantry Brigade.
105th Infantry Brigade.
106th Infantry Brigade.

1.	Herewith copy of instructions received from G.O.C. Troops, CALAIS.

2.	The operation will probably be carried out between 1000 and 1100, 30th January, by 104th Infantry Brigade moving round the East of No. 4 and 6 East Camps, and driving towards the Canal, which will be blocked by 105th Infantry Brigade. 105th Infantry Brigade will find a suitable force to make a stop between the Chinese Camp and No. 6 East Camp.

3.	Details will be discussed at a conference at Divisional Headquarters at 0730 on 30th January.

4.	A car will be at the South East entrance of No. 6 West Camp near the Canal at 0700 hours on 30th January to fetch B.Gs.C 104, 105, and 106 Infantry Brigades.

5.	The telephone is not to be used on the subject of this operation.

6.	Acknowledge verbally.

					Sd.	G. de C. Glover, for
							Major, G.S.,
						Lieut. Colonel, Gen.Staff.
							35th Division.

Issued personally by Staff Officer
at 0145 hours 30th January, 1919.

35th Division No. G.A. 617.

104th Infantry Brigade.
105th Infantry Brigade.
106th Infantry Brigade.
35th Bn. M.G.Corps.
19th N.F. (Pioneers).
C.R.A.
C.R.E.
A.D.M.S.
35th Divl. Signal Company.
O.C. Divl. Train.

        The Major General wishes to express his appreciation of the smart and soldierly manner in which all ranks of 104, 105, and 106 Infantry Brigades, Machine Gun Battalion, R.A.M.C., R.A.S.C., and Signals have carried out their duties during the past few days. Officers and men have showed tact and zeal and the good discipline of the Division has been particularly noted.

        General Sir Julian BYNG, K.C.B., K.C.M.G., M.V.O., Commanding 3rd Army, and temporarily Commanding Troops CALAIS, has told the Divisional Commander that he has reported to the C. in C. in the highest terms on the Division and wishes all ranks to be informed of his satisfaction with what they have done.

        The Major General hopes the Division will maintain this same reputation for smartness and good discipline during the rest of its stay in the CALAIS area.

H. SHERBROOKE,

A.D.H.Q.,
31st January, 1919.
                    Lieut. Colonel,
                    General Staff, 35th Division.

Copy to A.A. and Q.M.G.

Army Form C. 2118.

WAR DIARY
or
INTELLIGENCE SUMMARY.

GENERAL STAFF, 35th DIVISION.

(Erase heading not required.)

Instructions regarding War Diaries and Intelligence Summaries are contained in F. S. Regs., Part II. and the Staff Manual respectively. Title pages will be prepared in manuscript.

Place	Date	Hour	Summary of Events and Information	Remarks and references to Appendices
EPERLECQUES	Feb.1		G.O.C. visited H.Q. XIX Corps. L.of C. wire W.A.14120 of 1.2.19 received appointing Major-General G.O.C. Troops, CALAIS. Orders received for two Infantry Brigades to remain at CALAIS and for remainder of Division to return to Divisional area EPERLECQUES.	
			35th Division Order No.1 issued.	D.O.1
	2.		106th Infantry Brigade and 35th Bn.M.G.C. proceeded by train to WATTEN to return to their former billets. Transport proceeded by road.	
			104th Infantry Brigade moved to COULOGNE Camp CALAIS.	
			105th Infantry Brigade moved to No.3 Leave Camp, CALAIS.	
			Advanced Divisional Headquarters returned to EPERLECQUES.	
			1st Life Guards and 2nd Life Guards Machine Gun Battalions left Divisional area.	
	3		Quiet day. G.O.C. visited 106th Infantry Brigade. Freezing hard.	
	4.		Fine day; freezing hard. G.O.C. visited R.A.	
	5.		G.O.C. visited 104th and 105th Infantry Brigades at CALAIS. Freezing. Heavy fall of snow in afternoon and evening.	
	6		Freezing. Country covered in snow.	
	7.		Freezing. Country covered in snow.	

Army Form C. 2118.

WAR DIARY
or
INTELLIGENCE SUMMARY.

GENERAL STAFF, 35th DIVISION.

(Erase heading not required.)

Instructions regarding War Diaries and Intelligence Summaries are contained in F. S. Regs., Part II. and the Staff Manual respectively. Title pages will be prepared in manuscript.

Place	Date	Hour	Summary of Events and Information	Remarks and references to Appendices
EPERLECQUES	Feb.8		Freezing. Country covered in snow. Divisional Boxing Competition.	
	9		Freezing. Country covered in snow. 106th Infantry Brigade moved to CALAIS.	
	10.		15th Cheshire Regt.moved from AUDRICQ to BEAUMARIS Camp, CALAIS. Still freezing.	
			G.O.C. and G.S.O.1 visited Infantry Brigades at CALAIS.	
	11.		G.O.C. visited ZENEGHEM to see 4th North Staffs.	
			106th Infantry Brigade returned from CALAIS to MILLAIN.	
	12th		G.O.C. visited BERGUES to visit 18th Highland L.I. G.S.O.1 visited 104th and 105th Inf.Bdes.	
	13.		G.O.S. and Staff attended funeral of Major TAYLOR late D.A.D.V.S. of Division, at LONGNESSE Cemetery. G.O.C. visited C.R.A. G.S.O.1 visited 106th Inf.Bde. and 35th Bn.M.G.C.	
	14.		Thaw set in.	
	15		G.O.C. attended Lecture at 106th Infantry Brigade.	
			Final of Divisional Association Football Competition(won by 159th Bde.R.F.A., runners-up 157th Bde.R.F.A.) at WATTEN, Corps Commander presented Cups and Medals.	
	16		The Major-General and Brigadier-General POLLARD met Army Commander at XIX Corps Commander's house, CASSEL.	
			Wire received stating that Staffs of 35th Division would be kept intact. All retainable men	

Army Form C. 2118.

WAR DIARY
or
INTELLIGENCE SUMMARY.
(Erase heading not required.)

GENERAL STAFF, 35th DIVISION.

Instructions regarding War Diaries and Intelligence Summaries are contained in F. S. Regs., Part II. and the Staff Manual respectively. Title pages will be prepared in manuscript.

Place	Date	Hour	Summary of Events and Information	Remarks and references to Appendices
EPERLECQUES	Feb.16		would be left in the Division, but Division would not be made up to strength;	
	17		Lord DENBIGH lectured to the Division at MERCKEGHEM.	
	18		G.O.C. and A.A.& Q.M.G. visited G.H.Q.	
			Telephonic orders received for 17th Royal Scots to proceed to YPRES area by train from WATTEN on 20th inst. Transport by road starting on 19th.	
	,19		G.O.C. attended a Lecture by Mr.CALDERWOOD at the Royal Scots' Theatre, MERCKEGHEM.	
			Transport of 17th Royal Scots commenced march to POPERINGHE in accordance with order G.A.718	G.A.718
	20		½-Battalion Royal Scots proceeded to POPERINGHE by train from WATTEN. Train should have started at 10.30 hours, but was very late and did not leave WATTEN until 15.30.	
			G.O.C. visited 104th and 105th Infantry Brigades at CALAIS.	
	21.		Two companies 17th Royal Scots proceeded by lorry to BAILLEUL and YPRES area, and rejoined the remainder of the Battalion, which was split up by Companies guarding Chinese Labour Camps in the YPRES - BAILLEUL Area, Battalion H.Q. being at STEENVOORDE. Dull day, some rain.	
	22		Gusty and wet day. Band of Royal Artillery played in Hangar at TILQUES from 10.00 to 11.45; G.O.C. was present.	
			159th Bde.R.F.A. played 101st M.G.Bn. at TILQUES and won 2 - nil., and 157th Bde.R.F.A. played	

Army Form C. 2118.

WAR DIARY
or
INTELLIGENCE SUMMARY.   GENERAL STAFF, 35th DIVISION.

(Erase heading not required.)

Instructions regarding War Diaries and Intelligence Summaries are contained in F. S. Regs., Part II. and the Staff Manual respectively. Title pages will be prepared in manuscript.

Place	Date	Hour	Summary of Events and Information	Remarks and references to Appendices
EPERLECQUES	Feb.22		1st M.M.G.Brigade at NOORDPEENE and lost 3 - nil. Both matches were in the first Round of the Fifth Army Association Football Competition. G.O.C. watched the match at TILQUES.	
	23		Dull mild day. G.O.C. presented colours to 19th N.F. and 12th Highland L.I. Official photograph of Staff taken at GANSPETTE at 14.00.	
	24.		Bright day, mild. G.O.C. went with B.G.C.106th Infantry Brigade to visit 17th Royal Scots in devastated area.	
	25		Dull day.	
	26		Dull showery day. G.O.C. went to LILLE to witness Football match between 159th Bde.R.F.A. and No.4 A.A.Defence Team(Second Round of Fifth Army Compeitition.) 159th Bde.R.F.A. won 4 - 1.	
	27		Dull showery day. G.O.G. returned from LILLE.	
	28		Bright day.	

Alerbrooke Lt Col GS
for Major-General,
Commanding 35th Division.

Spare

35th DIVISION ORDER NO. 1.

1. 106th Infantry Brigade and 35th Battn. M.G. Corps will return to their camps at MILLAIN and MERCKEGHEM by rail on 2nd February, 1919.

2. 104th Infantry Brigade will move to COULOGNE CAMP and LADY CARPENTERS CAMP and 105th Infantry Brigade to No. 2 and 3 Leave Camps on 2nd February, 1919.

3. 106th Infantry Brigade and 35th Battn. M.G. Corps and detachments of 105th and 107th Field Ambulances, all under orders of B.G.C., 106th Infantry Brigade, will entrain at CALAIS DUNES STATION at 09.00 hours. Train leaves at 10.00 hours.

4. 104th Infantry Brigade will be clear of its present camp by 09.00 hours.
105th Infantry Brigade will not leave its present camp before 09.00 hours and will be clear before 10.00 hours.

5. 106th Infantry Brigade, 35th Battn. M.G. Corps Transport and No. 4 Coy. Div. Train will move independently by road to MILLAIN and MERCKEGHEM.

6. Advanced Divisional Headquarters will close at BEAUMARAIS at 09.00 hours and rejoin Rear Headquarters at EPERLECQUES.

7. Six lorries will report to Headquarters, 106th Infantry Brigade at 08.00 hours 2nd February to convey blankets to SAND DUNES Station and a further six lorries will meet the train on arrival at WATTEN.
106th Infantry Brigade will allot the lorries for use of all troops travelling by the train.

8. ACKNOWLEDGE.

1st February, 1919.
PH.

Lieut-Colonel.
General Staff, 35th Division.

```
Copy No. 1.   104th Inf. Bde.
 "   "   2.   105th Inf. Bde.
 "   "   3.   106th Inf. Bde.
 "   "   4.   35th Bn. M.G. Corps.
 "   "   5.   35th Div. Train.
 "   "   6.   "A" and "Q".
 "   "   7.   A.D.M.S.
 "   "   8.   35th Div. Signal Co. R.E.
 "   "   9.   File.
```

Army Form C. 2118.

WAR DIARY
or
INTELLIGENCE SUMMARY.

General Staff, 35th Division.

(Erase heading not required.)

Instructions regarding War Diaries and Intelligence Summaries are contained in F.S. Regs., Part II. and the Staff Manual respectively. Title pages will be prepared in manuscript.

WW 39

Place	Date	Hour	Summary of Events and Information	Remarks and references to Appendices
EPERLECQUES.	1st March.		Fine day.	
	2nd March.		Fine day.	
	3rd March.		159th Brigade R.F.A beat 1st M.M.G. Brigade in 3rd round of Fifth Army Association Football Competition.	
	4th March.		Wet day.	
	5th March.		Fine.	
	6th March.		Wet morning. Fine afternoon.	
	7th March.		Dull., wet day. G.O.C. presented colours to 104th Infantry Brigade at BOLLEZEELE. 159th Brigade R.F.A. beat 10th Liverpool (Scottish) Battalion in semi-final of Fifth Army Competition at BRUSSELS.	
	8th March.		Fine morning. G.O.C. went to YPRES to present colours to 17th Royal Scots and from thence proceeded to BRUSSELS to witness final of Fifth Army Association Football Competition.	
	9th March.		Dull day. Paper chase EPERLECQUES forest. 35th Division Rugby Football team beaten 22--12 by XV. Corps team in semi-final of Fifth Army Competition at BRUSSELS.	
	10th March.		Mild, windy day. 159th Brigade R.F.A. played 8th Bn. M.G.C. in final of Fifth Army Association Football Competition and drew 1--1.	

Army Form C. 2118.

WAR DIARY
or
INTELLIGENCE SUMMARY. General Staff, 35th Division.
(Erase heading not required.)

Place	Date	Hour	Summary of Events and Information	Remarks and references to Appendices
EPERLECQUES.				
	11th March.		Warm fine day. Brig. General A.F. TURNER, C.M.G., D.S.O., R.A., Commanding 105th Infantry Brigade, proceeded to England to report to War Office before going to ARCHANGEL.	
	12th March.		Fine, windy day. 159th Brigade R.F.A. beat 8th Bn. M.M.G. Corps in final of Fifth Army Association Football Competition. Paper Chase arranged by Machine Gun Battalion near MILLAIN.	
	13th March.		Fine, windy day. G.O.C. returned from BRUSSELS. Orders received for Major General A.H. MARINDIN, D.S.O., Commanding 35th Division, to proceed to take over command of a Brigade in the 62nd Highland Division, Army of the Rhine, to arrive by the 18th March.	
	14th March.		G.O.C. presented colours to 15th Cheshires and 15th Sherwood Foresters at CALAIS. Dull, wet day.	
	15th March.		Dull, but fine day. G.O.C. visited Units to say 'Good-bye.' Mounted Paper Chase WATTEN and MILLAIN.	
	16th March.		Dull day. Some rain. Major General A.H. MARINDIN, D.S.O., departed to take command of a Brigade in the 62nd Highland Division in the Rhine Army. Major G. de C. GLOVER, D.S.O., M.C., G.S.O.2, accompanied him to be a Brigade major in the Rhine Army. Brigadier General J.W. SANDILANDS, C.M.G., D.S.O., assumed command of 35th Division.	

Army Form C. 2118.

WAR DIARY
or
INTELLIGENCE SUMMARY.

General Staff, 35th Division.

(Erase heading not required.)

Instructions regarding War Diaries and Intelligence Summaries are contained in F. S. Regs., Part II. and the Staff Manual respectively. Title pages will be prepared in manuscript.

Place	Date	Hour	Summary of Events and Information	Remarks and references to Appendices
	17th March.		Dull day. Lieut. Colonel SHERBROOKE, D.S.O., R.A., G.S.O.1., admitted hospital, sick.	
	18th March.		Fair day. Headquarters, 35th Division, moved from EPERLECQUES Village to EPERLECQUES Chateau.	
	19th March.		Fine, bright day.	
	20th March.		Dull, wet day. B.G.G. visited 105th Infantry Brigade at CALAIS.	
	21st March.		Fair day.	
	22nd March.		Fine day.	
	23rd March.		Fine day. Officers' Mounted Paper chase MENTQUE.	
	24th March.		Dull day, cold wind.	
	25th March.		Dull day, cold wind.	
	26th March.		Dull day, cold wind.	
	27th March.		Fair day.	
	28th March.		Fair day. Mounted Paper chase at TOURNEHEM FOREST.	
	29th March.		Snow in morning. Later fair day. Brig. General W. MADDOCKS, C.B., C.M.G., D.S.O., C.R.A. 35th Division, proceeded to England to report to War Office.	
	30th March.		Fair day. Some snow in afternoon.	
	31st March.		Fair day.	

[signature] Capt

for Brigadier General,
Commanding 35th Division.

31st March, 1919.